EXCEL FOR WINDOWS MADE EASY, FOURTH EDITION

EXCEL FOR WINDOWS MADE EASY, FOURTH EDITION

Martin S. Matthews

Osborne **McGraw-Hill**

Berkeley New York St. Louis San Francisco
Auckland Bogotá Hamburg London Madrid
Mexico City Milan Montreal New Delhi Panama City
Paris São Paulo Singapore Sydney
Tokyo Toronto

Osborne **McGraw-Hill**
2600 Tenth Street
Berkeley, California 94710
U.S.A.

For information on translations or book distributors outside of the U.S.A.,
please write to Osborne **McGraw-Hill** at the above address.

Excel for Windows Made Easy, Fourth Edition

1234567890 DOC 9987654

ISBN 0-07-881973-3

CONTENTS AT A GLANCE

CONTENTS

ACKNOWLEDGMENTS

Behind the author on the cover of most books are many talented people who put in not only numerous hours and much skill but also more than a little of themselves. That is true with this book and I would like to recognize a few of the ones who truly stand out and without whom the book could not have been done:

Wendy Rinaldi, Project Editor at Osborne, whose editorial talents are matched only by her kind and gentle nature that makes her a constant joy to work with.

Sherith Pankratz, Editorial Assistant at Osborne, whose enthusiasm for life and dedication to getting a job done made every phone call enjoyable and played a significant part in getting the book out.

Bob Myren, Associate Editor at Osborne, whose hard labors are greatly appreciated.

Carl Wikander, free-lance copy editor, whose soft touch and considerable insight let the author be the author while significantly improving the readability of the book.

Bob Kermish, free-lance technical editor, added a number of tips and techniques that I overlooked as well as materially improved the technical accuracy of the book.

Bruce Dobson, author, consultant, and programmer, not only gave of his considerable talents to write Chapters 12 and 13 on Visual Basic, but he also agreed to work under and meet a very tight schedule.

Carol Boggs Matthews, author, mother, and life partner, not only ably worked on several of the chapters, but also provided the understanding and support that allowed me to dedicate the attention and time necessary to producing a quality book on a demanding schedule.

Martin Matthews

INTRODUCTION

Microsoft Excel, at version 5, has matured into one of the most capable and easy to use of all software products. By adding full three-dimensional spreadsheets, many new Wizards, tools, and toolbars, as well as significantly improved data handling, charting, and macro building capabilities, Excel 5 provides substantially enhanced ease of use together with greatly improved functionality. *Excel for Windows Made Easy* brings you the full capability of Excel 5 in an easy to use, hands-on approach that shows you how to make the most of this power.

About This Book

Excel for Windows Made Easy supplements Microsoft's own documentation by continuing where that documentation leaves off. Whereas the Microsoft documentation presents you with short and simple explanations, *Excel for Windows Made Easy* provides more substantial examples designed not only to get you started, but also to guide you in building your skills so that you can perform more advanced business tasks—all with clear, step-by-step instructions.

How This Book Is Organized

Excel for Windows Made Easy was written the way most people learn Excel. The book starts by reviewing the basic concepts. It then uses a learn-by-doing method to demonstrate the major features of the product.

Next, the book provides examples and clear explanations of many advanced features.

Introducing Windows and Excel

The book begins by introducing Windows and Excel and providing the basic concepts needed to use them. This section includes four chapters. The first chapter explains the features and functions of Windows and the mouse that are needed to use Excel. Included are all parts of the screen, windowing, menus, the mouse buttons and moves, and using the keyboard.

The second chapter describes each of the three components of Excel—spreadsheets, databases, and charts, with particular attention to spreadsheets. It quickly introduces rows, columns, sheets, and workbooks as well as cells, references, ranges, formulas, functions, commands, and macros. Also introduced are shortcut menus, tools, toolbars, and Wizards.

The third chapter looks at how Excel uses the Windows graphical environment and the mouse to build and maintain spreadsheets. Each of the menus is described, as are the keystrokes and mouse moves necessary to utilize them. This chapter introduces the Standard and Formatting toolbars and all of their tools, and tells you how to display the other 11 toolbars.

Chapter 4 focuses on how to create and modify a workbook, including using the menus, mouse, and keyboard to enter, edit, and align text and numbers. Excel's shortcut menus and Zoom feature are demonstrated in this chapter as are saving a workbook and leaving Excel.

This first part of the book provides the foundation for the rest of the book. This section is slower paced due to the importance of building a firm foundation. If you are a new user of Excel, the first four chapters are vital to your success. If you have some experience with Excel, you need them to a lesser extent. At the very least, you should skim these chapters to assure that you have an understanding of the terms and concepts.

The Fundamentals of Excel

Next, the book covers the fundamentals of Excel—creating and manipulating spreadsheets, producing charts, and using a database. This section includes four chapters.

Chapters 5 and 6 are companions. Chapter 5 shows you how to create a three-dimensional spreadsheet. Included are planning, placing text and headings, entering numbers and formulas, copying formulas, inserting and deleting rows—all on multiple sheets—as well as summing across several sheets. The spelling checker, centering text across columns, and using drag and drop to copy formulas are all demonstrated. In Chapter 6 you format, change, and print the workbook. Included are loading the workbook, formatting numbers and headings, moving, deleting, erasing, and setting the parameters for and printing the workbook. You also learn about the AutoFormat and note capabilities of Excel.

Chapter 7 looks at producing charts, including three-dimensional charts. It describes the chart types and includes selecting the type of chart, determining the workbook ranges to plot, adding legends and titles, viewing, and printing. Both the ChartWizard and manual chart creation methods are used.

In Chapter 8 you learn how to build and use databases. The chapter includes sorting a database and selecting and analyzing information from a database. In analyzing information, you are shown how, almost automatically, you can add subtotals and totals to a database as well as how the PivotTable Wizard is used to build a pivot table that summarizes the database and then allows you to interactively manipulate that summary. The chapter also demonstrates how statistical functions and data tables are used.

These chapters should be read by all levels of users. For new users it provides the experience with which you can create your own spreadsheets, charts, and databases. For intermediate and advanced users, Chapters 5 through 8 provide a refresher course that also offers considerable insight into Excel.

Advanced Uses of Excel
The last five chapters discuss the advanced features of Excel. The pace of presentation quickens here; the focus is almost entirely on advanced topics, with little or no time spent on building the spreadsheets used to demonstrate the topics. You are still encouraged, though, to continue to follow along on your computer.

Chapter 9 describes linking spreadsheets and using external files. Included are setting up links and transferring information among spreadsheets as well as combining spreadsheets, exporting and importing text files, dividing or parsing a text file, and saving related documents in a workbook.

Chapter 10 looks at dates and times, functions, and macros. Under dates and times, you look at entering, formatting, and handling them as well as the functions that relate to them. The section on functions ties together the work already done on functions in previous chapters. It provides a general discussion on using them as well as discussion and examples of the types of functions not previously examined. The macro section looks at macro functions in general, discusses how they are built, used, and debugged using the Excel 4 macro language, and provides a number of examples.

Chapter 11 demonstrates how to use the very powerful analysis tools included in Excel: Goal Seek, the Scenario Manager, and Solver. The tools are used both independently and in various combinations. They provide the means of finding optimal solutions as well as keeping track of solutions as you generate them.

Chapter 12 introduces Visual Basic. It discusses all of the elements of the language and how they are combined to make a program. Included are explanations and examples of procedures, functions, objects, methods, properties, variables, and constants.

Chapter 13 brings together what was presented in Chapter 12 and guides you through all of the steps needed to create an automated spreadsheet using Visual Basic. Included are automatic loading, custom menus, and updating of a database from a custom data entry dialog box, all operated by a set of macro commands. Chapter 13 shows you the full power of Excel.

Rather than reading these last five chapters immediately, new users may want to wait until they have completed several spreadsheets of their own and know they want more out of the capability of the product. Intermediate users probably will want to continue on immediately; it is the next logical step in their Excel education. If you are an advanced user—this is what you've been waiting for!

All readers are encouraged to go through these chapters at some point. The "booster rockets" of Excel are discussed here. Such things as linking spreadsheets, functions, and macros are not as hard to use as you might think, and they significantly increase the power of Excel.

Installing Windows and Excel

Appendix A provides both the background and detailed steps to install Windows and Excel. It describes what equipment you need and how to start and use both the Windows and Excel Setup programs. In addition, it discusses how you prepare to store the data you will create with Excel and how to leave Windows and Excel.

Toolbars

Appendix B describes each of the 13 toolbars and their tools. Additionally, the appendix discusses how to customize an existing toolbar by adding and removing tools, how to create a new toolbar, and how to customize a tool.

Conventions Used in This Book

Excel for Windows Made Easy uses several conventions designed to make the book easier for you to use. These are as follows:

✦ **Bold** type is used for text you are instructed to input from the keyboard.

✦ Keys on the keyboard are presented in key-shaped boxes; for example, ⏎ and ⌜Enter⌟.

✦ When you are expected to enter a command, you are told to *press* the key(s). If you enter text or numbers, you are told to *type* them.

CHAPTER

1

THE WINDOWS ENVIRONMENT

Excel is a Windows application. This means that Excel requires Microsoft Windows for it to run. Windows provides the interface *between you and Excel—the way Excel tells you on the screen what it is doing, and the way you tell Excel what to do. This chapter introduces you to some of the essentials of Microsoft Windows 3.1 (Excel 5 requires Windows 3.0 at a minimum). You may never use all of the capabilities and tools available in*

Windows 3.1, but when you become acquainted with them, you will appreciate the potential power of using Excel in the Windows environment.

This chapter is more of a tutorial than the rest of the book. It proceeds more slowly in order to establish a common ground for using this book and Excel. If you are already familiar with Windows and using a mouse, simply scan the chapter to verify that you know the vocabulary used here and the basic operating procedures used in Windows 3.1.

Introducing Windows

Excel is designed to run "under" Microsoft Windows, an extension of the MS-DOS operating system. This is desirable for several reasons, but primarily because Windows offers a standard environment for all of the programs, or *applications*, that run under it. This environment consists chiefly of a standard screen display, or *visual interface*, that you use in communicating with Windows applications. Once you learn to use Windows, you will find that the ways of working with the various applications, including Excel, that run under Windows are very similar.

Windows also provides a way to transfer information among applications, such as from Excel to Word for Windows or to PageMaker. With this feature, called the Clipboard, you can easily move a portion of an Excel spreadsheet or an Excel chart to a word processing document.

Windows allows you to load multiple applications into memory simultaneously and to switch among them with a minimum of effort. You can work with a word processor, a graphics application, and Excel all at the same time. Of course, the degree to which this can be done depends on the amount of memory in your computer.

Finally, Windows provides a set of applications that are handy accessories. Table 1-1 lists these accessories and their functions.

Because it operates under Windows, Excel has all these accessories available to it on demand.

The quickest way to learn about Windows is to start using it. If you have not already done so, turn on your computer and start Windows. (If you have not already installed Windows and Excel, refer to Appendix A. When you complete the installation and your mouse is connected, return here.)

The Windows Screen

When Windows 3.1 is started, you first see a screen similar to the one shown in Figure 1-1, if you installed Windows and Excel according to the instructions in Appendix A. (Your screen may look different depending on how you

Accessory	Function
Calculator	A calculator program for adding, subtracting, dividing, and multiplying numbers
Calendar	A scheduling program for jotting down your appointments and commitments
Cardfile	A list-management program
Character Map	A table of available characters not found on most keyboards
Clock	A clock that can be displayed on the screen at all times
Notepad	A program that lets you keep notes, reminders, and other memos handy
Media Player	A program to control media hardware and software such as CD ROMs
Object Packager	A program that lets you embed or link a full or partial document (in the form of an icon) into another document
Paintbrush	A graphics program
Recorder	A means of recording and playing back sets of keystrokes to produce macros
Sound Recorder	A program that lets you play, edit, and record sound files when applicable hardware and software are installed
Terminal	A communications program that lets you connect via a modem and telephone lines to another computer
Write	A word processing program

Windows
Accessories
Table 1-1.

installed Windows and whether you have non-Windows applications or other Windows applications.) The screen in Figure 1-1 shows two windows, both with several standard features that appear in most windows of Windows 3.1. The top line, or *Title bar*, of a window contains its title. The two windows in the figure are titled Program Manager and Microsoft Excel 5.0. On the left end of the Title bar is the *Control-menu box*. You use this box to access the *Control menu*, which contains window options that allow you to perform such operations as moving, sizing, or closing a window.

On the right end of the Title bar are the *Minimize* and *Maximize* buttons, which are used for changing the size of the window.

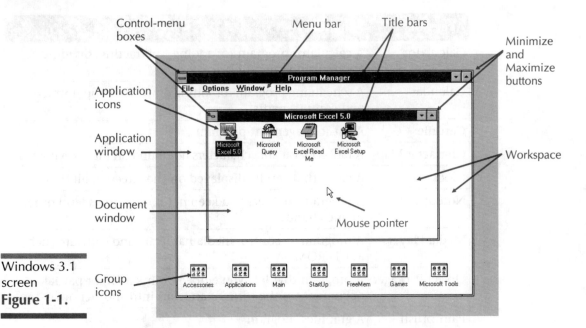

Control-menu boxes

Menu bar

Title bars

Minimize and Maximize buttons

Application icons

Application window

Workspace

Document window

Mouse pointer

Windows 3.1 screen
Figure 1-1.

Group icons

Below the Title bar in the Program Manager window is the *Menu bar*. The menus available (File, Options, Window, and Help) apply only to the Program Manager. The menus displayed in the Menu bar change as the window changes.

Below the Menu bar is the *workspace*, which contains, at the top, the Excel group document window. At the bottom of the workspace, as shown in Figure 1-1, are graphic symbols, called *group icons*, that represent the groups of programs you can use. Inside the Excel group window are three *application icons* that represent three Excel-related programs and one *document icon* that represents an information file that you can open. As you saw if you went through the installation in Appendix A, double-clicking on an application icon starts that program. When you start an application such as Excel, and then temporarily set it aside while you do something else, the application becomes an icon again, but now it is at the bottom of the screen in the icon area. An application icon in the icon area can be reactivated, moved around the screen, or deactivated. Whatever you were doing in the application remains frozen just as you left it, until it is reactivated or the application is closed. Double-clicking on a document icon starts a program (the Notepad accessory, for example) that in turn displays that document.

Several indicators show where you are on the screen. First, the *active window*—the one you are currently working in—is indicated by a Title bar and border that are normally composed of a dark-colored background and light letters. Both the Program Manager and Excel group windows are active in Figure 1-1. Second, the *selected object* or *objects*—what your next action will effect—are highlighted. In Figure 1-1 the Microsoft Excel program icon is the selected object, and the program name is reversed with white or light-colored letters on a black or dark-colored background. The third indicator is the *mouse pointer,* which tells you where the mouse is pointing. In Figure 1-1 the mouse pointer is an arrow in the Excel group window. All three indicators change as you work. The varying symbols tell you something about the task being done, as you'll see in examples given later.

Using the Mouse

Although Windows allows you to use either the mouse or the keyboard to enter commands, using a mouse will greatly increase the power of Windows for you. Most instructions in this book assume that you'll use a mouse. The keyboard occasionally does offer shortcuts, so these shortcuts and some general rules for using the keyboard are also covered later in this chapter.

The mouse is used to move the pointer on the screen. You can *select* an object by moving the mouse until the pointer is on top of it (pointing *on* it) and then pressing the mouse button. Using the mouse in this way allows you to choose, for example, an option on a menu. A mouse can have one, two, or three buttons. Normally, Windows and Excel use only one button, called the *mouse button* in this book. By default the left button is used, but you can change the default to another button, which you may want to do if you are left-handed. (You'll see how later in this chapter.)

Mousing Around

If you move the mouse across a flat surface such as a table or desk, the mouse pointer (the arrow on the screen) also moves. Practice moving the mouse as follows:

1. Place your hand on the mouse. The button(s) should be under your fingers with the cord leading away from you.

2. Move the mouse now, without pressing the mouse button, and watch the pointer move on the screen.

   If you run out of room while moving the mouse, simply pick it up and place it where there is more room. Try experimenting with this now.

3. Move the mouse to the edge of your work surface, then pick it up and place it in the middle of your work surface, and then move it again.

Watch how the pointer continues from where the mouse was picked up. When you point on the border of the window, the arrow changes to a double-headed arrow. This tells you that the pointer is on the border. If you press the mouse button here, you can change the size of the window, as you will see shortly.

This book uses the following standard Windows terminology to describe your actions with the mouse:

Term	Action
Click	Quickly press and release the mouse button once
Point on	Move the mouse until the tip of the pointer is on top of the item you want
Click on	Point on an item and click
Double-click	Press and release the mouse button twice in rapid succession
Drag	Press and hold the mouse button while you move the mouse (to move an object in the work area or to highlight contiguous text that you want to delete, move, or copy)
Select	Point on an item and click the mouse button (same as "click on")
Choose	Click on a menu option

After the upcoming demonstrations of these terms, this book will assume that you know them. For example, the instruction "Select the File menu and choose the Run option" indicates that you should point on the word "File" in the Menu bar and press and release the mouse button to open the File menu. Then point on the Run option in the File menu and click to choose that option. Practice using the mouse to perform some of these actions:

1. *Point on* the Microsoft Query icon by moving the mouse (and the corresponding pointer) until the pointer is resting on it.

2. *Select* the Microsoft Query icon by *clicking*—quickly pressing and releasing the mouse button while pointing—on it. The Title bar beneath the icon is highlighted, indicating it is selected.

3. *Drag* the Microsoft Query icon to the lower-left corner of the Excel group window. First point on the icon, and then press and hold the mouse button while you move the mouse until the pointer and the icon move to the lower-left corner of the window, as shown in Figure 1-2.

4. *Drag* the Microsoft Query icon back to its original position.

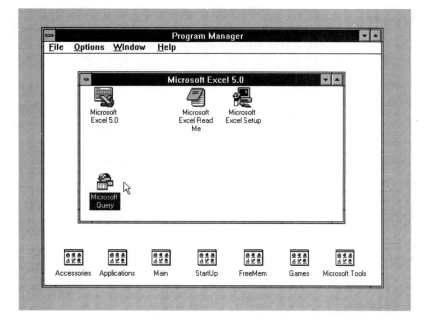

Microsoft
Query icon
moved to the
lower-left
corner of the
window
Figure 1-2.

5. *Click* on the Minimize button—the downward pointing arrow in the upper-right corner of the Excel group window. The window closes and becomes another group icon, as shown in Figure 1-3.

6. *Double-click* on the Accessories group icon in the lower part of the Program Manager window. The Accessories window opens, as shown in Figure 1-4.

7. *Double-click* on the Control-menu box in the upper-left corner of the Accessories window. The Accessories window closes.

8. *Double-click* on the Accessories icon again to reopen the Accessories window.

It sometimes takes a couple of tries to get the rhythm of double-clicking. A frequent problem is double-clicking too slowly. You will see later in this chapter how to adjust the speed of double-clicking.

Using Windows

A window is an area of the screen that is assigned a specific purpose. There are two types of windows: *application windows*, which contain running programs or applications such as Excel, and *document windows*, which contain documents used with applications, such as an Excel spreadsheet. An application window may contain one or more document windows. The

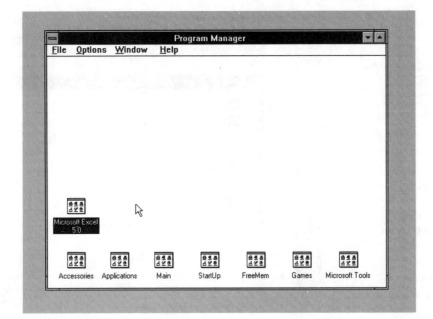

Excel group
window
closed to a
group icon
Figure 1-3.

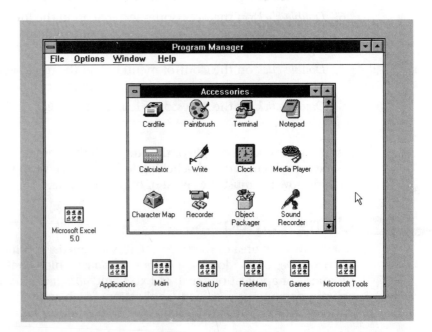

Accessories
window open
Figure 1-4.

1

Accessories and Excel group windows that you have been looking at on your screen (and in figures shown in this chapter) are document windows, whereas the Program Manager window is an application window. An application window has a Menu bar while a document window does not. Both types of window have a Title bar with the window title in the middle, the Control-menu box on the left, and the Minimize and Maximize buttons on the right.

Windows can be quite small (about 1×1/4-inch minimum), can fill the screen, or can be any size in between. By clicking on the Maximize button, you can make a window fill the screen. When you maximize a window, a new button—the *Restore button*—appears in place of the Maximize button. If you click on the Restore button, the window is returned to the size it was just before you clicked the Maximize button. As you have already seen, if you click on the Minimize button, the window shrinks to an icon at the bottom of the screen. By double-clicking on that icon you can return it to an open window that is the size it was when you minimized it.

You can make an open window that is not maximized any size by dragging on the border of the window. When you place the mouse pointer on top of the border around the window, the mouse pointer becomes a double-headed arrow. By holding down the mouse button while the pointer is a double-headed arrow and dragging the border, you can change the window size. By dragging on any side, you can change the size of the window in one dimension. By dragging on a corner, you can change the size in two dimensions—for example, you can enlarge a window upward and to the right by dragging the top-right corner.

Finally, both an open application window and an application icon can be dragged anywhere on the screen. A document window can be dragged only within its application window. To drag an open window, point on the Title bar of the window (anywhere except on the Control-menu box or the Minimize or Maximize buttons) and drag it where you want. To drag an icon, point anywhere on the icon and drag it.

Practice using some of the window-sizing features by following these instructions:

1. Click on the Maximize button in the upper-right corner of the Accessories window. The Accessories window expands to fill the Program Manager window.

   Notice that the Title bar has changed. The title is now "Program Manager - [Accessories]," which tells you that the Accessories window has filled the Program Manager window. Also note that the Control-menu box in the Title bar is for the Program Manager, while the Control-menu box in the Menu bar is for the Accessories window.

2. Click on the Restore button that now appears just under the Program Manager's Maximize button. The Accessories window returns to its former size.

3. Click on the Maximize button of the Program Manager window, and the window expands to fill the screen.

4. Click on the Restore button of the Program Manager window, and the window shrinks to its former size.

5. Point on the lower-right corner border of the Accessories window. A double-headed arrow appears precisely when you are on the border.

6. Drag the lower-right corner toward the bottom right as far as you can. Notice that you cannot drag it outside of the Program Manager's window.

7. Drag the lower-right corner toward the upper left until the Accessories window is about one-quarter of the size it was before you enlarged it, as shown in Figure 1-5.

8. Point on the Title bar of the Accessories menu, anywhere but the Control-menu box and the Minimize and Maximize buttons. Drag the Accessories window to the lower-right corner of the Program Manager window. Notice again that you cannot get out of the Program Manager window.

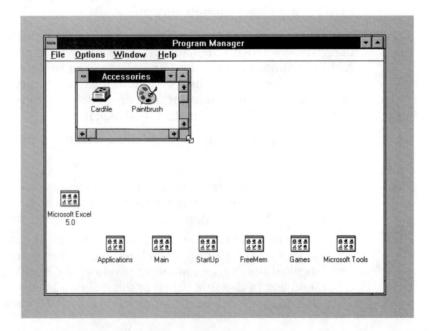

Shrunken
Accessories
window
Figure 1-5.

9. By pointing on the Program Manager's Title bar, drag it around the screen.

10. Click on the Minimize button of the Program Manager window. It closes to an icon at the bottom of the screen.

11. Double-click on the Program Manager icon. Notice how the Program Manager and Accessories windows open in the same location in which they closed.

12. Drag both the Accessories window and the Program Manager window back to their original positions, as shown in Figure 1-5.

Using Scroll Bars

A window on the screen is just that—an opening through which you can see something displayed. If what is displayed is very small, a small window can adequately display it all. If what is displayed is very large, the largest window you can create (one that covers the entire screen) may not be large enough to display it all. In that case, you can horizontally or vertically move, or *scroll*, through the contents of the window.

Imagine that you are looking through a microscope looking at a specimen on a glass slide. You must move the slide left and right (horizontally) and up and down (vertically) to see all of the specimen. The *scroll bars* perform the same function for a window. The scroll bars move the *area being displayed* (not the window itself) up or down or left or right.

Each of the two scroll bars has three mechanisms for moving the area being displayed. First, there are four *scroll arrows,* one at each end of each scroll bar. By clicking on one of the scroll arrows, you can move the display area in the direction of the arrow by a small increment—one line vertically. Second, there are the two square *scroll boxes* in the scroll bars. By dragging a scroll box, you can move the display area by a corresponding proportional amount. Third, there are the scroll bars themselves. By clicking on the scroll bars (in areas other than the scroll arrows and scroll boxes), you can move the display area by the height or width of one window in the direction corresponding to where you clicked.

Use the reduced Accessories window in the following instructions for practicing with the scroll bars:

1. Click on the down scroll arrow at the bottom of the vertical scroll bar on the right of the window. Notice that the display area moved up to display the information below what was previously shown. Notice also that the scroll box has moved down in the scroll bar.

The position of the scroll box in the scroll bar represents the approximate position of the portion of the file displayed within the total file. When the vertical scroll box is at the top of its scroll bar, you are looking at the top of the file. Similarly, when the horizontal scroll box is at the left end of its scroll bar, you are looking at the left edge of the file. When both scroll boxes are in the middle of their scroll bars, you are looking at the middle of the file.

2. Click on the right scroll arrow several times until the scroll box is at the far right of the horizontal scroll bar. Your screen should look like Figure 1-6.

3. Click on the horizontal scroll bar, on the left of the scroll box, until the scroll box is at the far left of the scroll bar. Notice how it takes fewer clicks to move over the length of the scroll bar.

4. Drag the vertical scroll box a small amount toward the middle of the scroll bar. Note how this allows you to move the display area in very precise increments.

The three scrolling mechanisms give you three levels of control. Clicking on the scroll bar moves the display area the farthest; dragging the scroll box can move the display area in the smallest and most precise increments; and clicking on the scroll arrows moves the display area a small to intermediate amount.

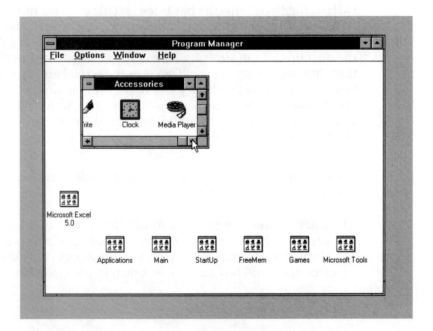

Accessories
window
scrolled to
the right
Figure 1-6.

Now that you can scroll the Accessories window, your next step is to use the window to select an application.

Starting Applications

The Accessories window contains the icons for the various accessories available in Windows. Each of these accessories is an application that runs under Windows, just like Excel. To start an application you simply double-click on its icon. Do that now to work with several application windows.

1. Scroll the Accessories window until you can see the Clock icon.

2. Double-click on the Clock icon. The Clock application starts and opens a window entitled Clock, as shown in Figure 1-7.

   Notice how the Clock window's Title bar and border are dark with light letters while the Program Manager's Title bar and border have become light with dark letters. This means that the Clock is now the active application while the Program Manager is inactive. (There may be some differences between your screen and the screens shown in the figures and illustrations shown in this book because of differences in displays and display adapters and in the options you selected during Windows installation. Also, the clock can be analog as shown here or digital.)

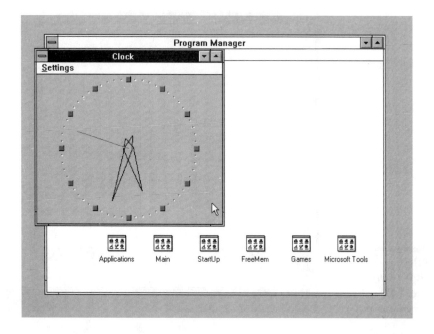

Clock window
open
Figure 1-7.

3. Click on the Clock's Maximize button, and the Clock window expands to fill the screen.

4. Click on the Restore button, and the Clock window returns to its original size.

5. Drag the Clock window (by dragging on the Clock window's Title bar anywhere except the buttons or the Control-menu box) to the lower-right corner of the screen.

6. Click on the Accessories window to activate the Program Manager, scroll the Accessories window until you can see the Notepad icon, and then double-click on it. The Notepad application starts; its window opens and becomes the active window, as shown in Figure 1-8.

7. Drag the Notepad window until it overlaps but does not completely cover the Clock (unless it was that way originally).

8. Click on the Clock to activate it. Notice how it now overlaps the Notepad.

9. Click on the Notepad window to reactivate it. Then drag on the upper-left corner to reduce the size of the Notepad to about half its original size so you can see the Accessories window.

10. Click on the Accessories window to activate the Program Manager, scroll the Accessories window until you can see the Paintbrush icon,

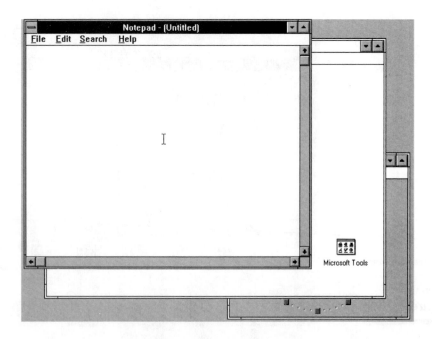

Notepad
window open
Figure 1-8.

1

and then double-click on it. The Paintbrush application starts; its window opens and becomes the active window.

11. Size the Paintbrush window so you can see parts of the Clock, the Notepad, and the Program Manager windows, as shown in Figure 1-9.

You now have four applications running in Windows: the Program Manager, the Clock, the Notepad, and Paintbrush. Move them around, size them in various ways, and activate first one and then another. Continue this until you are comfortable working with these windows.

Notice that as you move the mouse among these windows the mouse pointer changes. In the Paintbrush window the mouse pointer can be a paint roller, a dot, a crosshair, or several other shapes; in the Notepad window the pointer is an I-beam; and in the Clock and Program Manager windows the pointer is the familiar arrow. The pointer is telling you what can be done when it is in the various windows. With the dot in Paintbrush you can draw, while the crosshairs are for cutting away a part of a drawing. The I-beam is used with text; its skinny shape allows you to insert it between characters. When you click an I-beam you are establishing an *insertion point*, which determines where text you type is placed.

12. Click on the Minimize button of the Notepad, Clock, Paintbrush, and Accessories windows. The first three become application icons at the

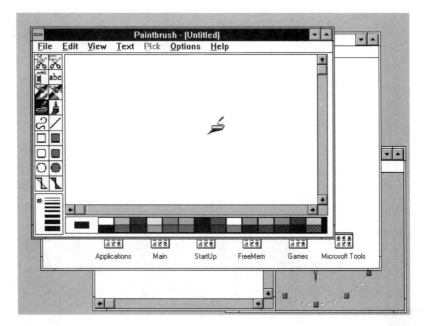

Paintbrush window added
Figure 1-9.

bottom of the screen while the Accessories window becomes the now familiar group icon at the bottom of the Program Manager window, as shown in Figure 1-10.

Notice how the clock still tells time even though it has turned into an icon. This is generally true about application icons—they are running programs that are just temporarily inactive on the screen. An inactive window and an application icon differ only in the amount of the screen they use and in their method of application: double-click on an icon to activate it, single-click on a window.

13. Drag the three application icons to reorder them, and place them in other locations on the screen just to see how it's done. When you are finished, drag them back to their original location and order, as shown in Figure 1-10.

Manipulating windows and their icons—by selecting, dragging, maximizing, minimizing, sizing, and scrolling—is one of the primary functions of the Windows environment. Practice these techniques until they are second nature. You will use them often. Another primary function of the Windows environment is the use of menus.

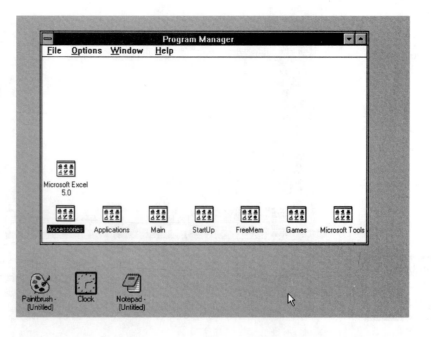

Applications turned into icons

Figure 1-10.

Using Menus

A menu is the primary device you use to give instructions to Windows and its applications. MS-DOS, by itself, is command oriented—you type commands at a system prompt. Within Windows, you give a command by making a choice in a menu. The menus available to you at any given time are shown in the Menu bar. By clicking on a menu name—*selecting* a menu—you open the menu. By clicking on a menu option—*choosing* an option—you make the option perform its function.

Menu options can represent several different functions. Often when you choose a menu option you are telling the application to carry out a command, such as saving a file or copying something. Other menu options allow you to set parameters or defaults for the items you are working on, such as selecting the size of a page to be printed or the color of an object. Still other menu options are themselves menus—in other words, selecting a menu option opens another menu. This is called *cascading menus.*

Look at several menus now and get a feel for how they operate.

1. Click on the Program Manager's File menu. It opens as shown here:

The Program Manager's File menu has eight options. Notice that some of the options (Move and Copy, for example) are dimmed while others are not. Dimmed options are not available in the context in which you are working. For example, if you do not have a selected object in the current window's workspace, you cannot move an object in that window; therefore, the Move option is dim. Many of the options, such as New, Copy, and Run, have an ellipsis (...) after them. When you select such an option, a dialog box opens. A *dialog box* is a place for you to provide further information or answer questions about the option you selected. For example, if you ask to save a file but have not provided the application with a filename, a dialog box opens asking you for the filename.

2. Click on New in the File menu.

A dialog box opens asking if you want to add a new group or a new application to a group and what to name the group or application.

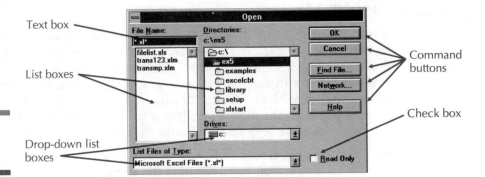

Text box

List boxes

Command buttons

Check box

File Open
dialog box
Figure 1-11.

Drop-down list
boxes

3. Click on Cancel to close the dialog box.

4. Click on the File menu again. Then click on Properties and then on Run so that you can look at their dialog boxes. Click on Cancel in each case to close the dialog boxes.

5. Click on the Options, Window, and Help menus in succession to look at each of them.

Notice in the Window menu that one of the listed windows has a check mark to the left of it. This means that window is currently active. One of the options of the Window menu allows you to choose the active window. When you click on your choice, a check mark is placed beside it so that the next time you open the menu you can tell which is active.

Notice also that a menu option may have a series of keystrokes to the right of the option name. These are *shortcut keys*. By pressing these keys you can choose the menu option directly without first opening the menu.

Using Dialog Boxes

As you have seen, dialog boxes are a means of providing information about an option you have chosen. The dialog boxes you just looked at are rather simple, with only a couple of items. Dialog boxes can be very complex, with many different components. Windows uses several types of components to gather different types of information. These components are shown in the dialog boxes displayed in Figures 1-11 and 1-12. These Excel dialog boxes are used for opening files and setting up a sheet to be printed.

The various dialog box components and their uses are shown in Table 1-2.

Dialog boxes provide a very powerful and fast means of communicating with Windows and its applications. It is important that you know the terms described above and are comfortable using dialog boxes.

Component	Usage
Check box	To select several items from among a series of options. Click on as many check boxes as desired to select those options. When selected, a check box contains an "X"; otherwise, the box is empty.
Command button	To take immediate action; for example, to close a dialog box, to cancel a command, to open another dialog box, or to expand the current dialog box. Clicking on a command button activates it. OK, the most common command button, is used to complete the dialog box and close it. An ellipsis (...) indicates that a command button opens another dialog box, and two greater-than symbols (>>) indicate that a command button expands the current dialog box.
Drop-down list box	To select usually one item from a list in a constrained space. The current selection is shown. Clicking on the arrow to the right opens the drop-down list box. Click on the option desired, possibly using the scroll bar first.
List box	To select usually one item from a list. The current selection is highlighted. Click on the option desired, possibly using the scroll bar first.
Option button	To select one item from a set of mutually exclusive options. A selection is changed by clicking on another option.
Text box	To enter text, such as a filename. The mouse pointer turns into an I-beam in a text box. Clicking the mouse in a text box places an insertion point, and any text typed will follow the insertion point. Without clicking an insertion point, any existing text in a selected text box is replaced by anything typed. The [Del] key removes existing selected text in a text box.

Dialog Box
Components
Table 1-2.

Using the Keyboard

You can do almost everything (except enter text) with a mouse, but in several instances the keyboard provides a useful shortcut. You have seen how several of the menu options have direct shortcut keys. You can also choose any of the other menu options with a general keyboard procedure. You can open any menu by pressing [Alt] (you do not have to hold it down) followed by the underlined letter in the menu name. After pressing [Alt] you can also use [←] and [→] to highlight a menu name, and then [↓] to open the

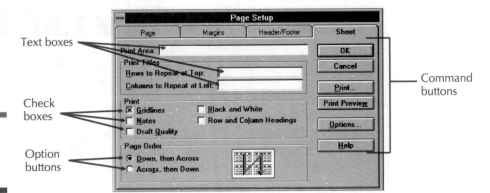

Text boxes

Check boxes

Option buttons

Command buttons

Page Setup dialog box for a sheet
Figure 1-12.

menu and highlight an option. After a menu is open you can choose an option by typing the underlined letter in the option name or highlighting the option with the direction keys and pressing ⟨Enter⟩. ⟨Enter⟩ can also be used to open a menu once you have highlighted the menu name, and the ⟨F10⟩ function key can be used in place of ⟨Alt⟩ to initiate the process. To cancel a menu selection and return to the workspace, press ⟨Alt⟩ or ⟨F10⟩ a second time. To cancel a menu selection but stay in the Menu bar so that another menu selection can be made, press ⟨Esc⟩.

Give the mouse a rest for a moment and access several Menu options using the keyboard.

1. Press ⟨Alt⟩-⟨F⟩ to open the Program Manager's File menu.

2. Press ⟨R⟩ to select the Run option. The Run dialog box opens.

3. Press ⟨Tab⟩ to move among the various fields in the dialog box, and then press ⟨Esc⟩ to cancel the dialog box, close the File menu, and deactivate the Menu bar.

    In general, to move around in a dialog box you first press ⟨Tab⟩ to move through the major groups of options, normally from left to right and top to bottom, or use ⟨Shift⟩-⟨Tab⟩ to reverse the direction. Alternatively, press and hold ⟨Alt⟩ while typing the underlined letter in the option or group name to move directly to that option or group. Then use the direction keys to highlight an option within a group, and use ⟨Spacebar⟩ to make the final selection of the option. Finally, press ⟨Enter⟩ to complete and close the dialog box.

4. Press ⟨F10⟩ to reactivate the Menu bar.

5. Press ⟨→⟩ twice to move to the Window menu.

6. Press ⟨Enter⟩ to open the Window menu, and then press ⟨↓⟩ four times to highlight the second group of applications.

7. Press [Enter] to select the highlighted menu item and open the selected group window.

8. Press [Alt]-[-] (hyphen) to open the Control menu of the open group window and then press [N] to minimize it once again to an icon.

1

Using the Control Menu

The Control menu, located in the upper-left corner of most windows and icons and some dialog boxes, allows you to use the keyboard to perform many other of the Windows functions that you have previously learned to perform with the mouse. There is some difference among Control menus but, for the most part, the options are the same.

Click on the Control-menu box or press [Alt]-[Spacebar] to open the Program Manager's Control menu shown here:

The options available in this Control menu and their functions are as follows:

Option	Function
Restore	Restores the window to the size it was prior to being minimized or maximized
Move	Allows moving the window with the keyboard
Size	Allows sizing the window with the keyboard
Minimize	Minimizes the window size to an icon
Maximize	Maximizes the window size, usually to fill the screen
Close	Closes the window
Switch To	Switches among the currently running applications and allows rearrangement of their icons and windows

The following additional options are available on other Control menus:

Option	Function
Edit	Opens an Edit menu with four options (non-Windows applications in 386 enhanced mode only):
Mark	Allows selection of text to be copied to the Clipboard
Copy	Copies text to the Clipboard
Paste	Copies the contents of the Clipboard to the insertion point in the active document window
Scroll	Scrolls the active document window
Next	Switches to the next open document window or document icon (on document windows only)
Paste	Copies the contents of the Clipboard to the insertion point in the active document window (real and standard mode only)
Settings	Allows entering settings for multitasking (non-Windows applications in 386 enhanced mode only)

Now try several of the Control menu options using the keyboard.

1. Press ⬇ to highlight Move and press [Enter] to choose it. The pointer becomes a four-headed arrow.

2. Press one or more of the direction keys to move the window in the direction you choose. An outline shows you where you are going.

3. When the outline of the window is where you want it, press [Enter]. If you want to cancel the move, press [Esc] before pressing [Enter].

4. Press [Alt]-[Spacebar] to reopen the Program Manager's (the active window) Control menu.

5. Press ⬇ twice to highlight Size and press [Enter] to choose it. The pointer again becomes a four-headed arrow.

6. Press one arrow key to select one side whose size you want to change, or press two arrow keys simultaneously to select two sides whose sizes you want to change. (Pressing two arrow keys simultaneously is the same as selecting a corner with the mouse.)

7. Press one or two arrows until the window is the size you want it. Then press [Enter]. If you want to cancel the sizing, press [Esc] before pressing [Enter].

8. Press [Alt]-[Spacebar] to reopen the Program Manager's Control menu.

9. Press [X] to choose Maximize. The Program Manager window expands to fill the screen.

10. Press Alt-Spacebar to open the Program Manager's Control menu, and press Enter to choose Restore. The Program Manager window returns to its original size.

11. Press Alt-Spacebar again, and press N to choose Minimize. The Program Manager window shrinks to an icon.

12. Press Alt-Esc to cycle through the various application icons (or windows if any were opened). When you have reached the Program Manager again, press Alt-Spacebar to open the Control menu.

13. Press Enter to choose Restore. The Program Manager window reopens at its last size and location.

14. Press Ctrl-F6 or Ctrl-Tab to cycle through the various document (group) icons (or windows if any were opened).

15. When you reach Main, press Alt-- (hyphen) to open the Main group's Control menu.

16. Choose Restore by pressing Enter (Restore is already highlighted). Your screen should look like that shown in Figure 1-13.

Notice that for application windows and document windows you use different key combinations to open their Control menus and to cycle through windows and icons. Use Alt-Spacebar to open an application window Control menu, and use Alt-Esc to cycle through the application windows and icons that are running (on the screen). Use Alt-- (hyphen) to open a document window Control menu, and use Ctrl-F6 or Ctrl-Tab to cycle through the document windows and icons in the active application window.

One important Control menu option you have not tried yet is Close. In most windows, Close simply closes the window. With the Program Manager, Close closes Windows and returns you to DOS. You will do that later in the chapter. Once the Control menu is open, you can choose Close in the normal ways: by clicking on it, by highlighting it and pressing Enter, or by pressing C. You can choose Close with the Control menu closed by double-clicking on the Control-menu box or by pressing Alt-F4. The other Control menu commands (Switch To, Edit, Next, Paste, and Settings) are not relevant to Excel and thus are beyond the scope of this book.

The keyboard and the Control menu are important adjuncts to the mouse. But they should be viewed as that and not the other way around. With Windows and Excel the mouse is by far the most effective and expeditious way to do most things. For that reason, this book usually has instructions for the mouse. Keyboard instructions normally are given only for shortcut keys when you are already typing on the keyboard.

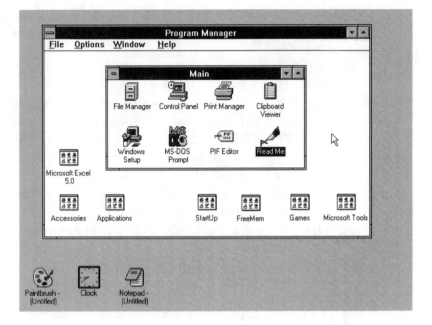

Main group
displayed in
the Program
Manager
window
Figure 1-13.

Using the Main Group Applications

The Main application group, which should currently be displayed on your
screen, includes eight applications with the following functions:

Application	Function
File Manager	Viewing and manipulating files
Control Panel	Setting defaults such as color, double-click speed, and date and time
Print Manager	Managing the queuing and printing of files
Clipboard Viewer	Displaying the contents of the Clipboard
DOS Prompt	Providing a DOS command-line prompt at which any DOS command can be entered. Type **exit** to return to Windows
Windows Setup	Making changes to the hardware and software configuration you are using with Windows
PIF Editor	Editing PIF files
Read Me	Displaying notes on Windows 3.1. Supplements written documentation

Take a brief look at two of these applications: the Control Panel and the File Manager, which are discussed next.

Setting Defaults with the Control Panel

The Control Panel is the primary place in Windows where you set the parameters or defaults that tell Windows how you want a number of different functions handled. Open the Control Panel now and look at the options.

Double-click on the Control Panel icon. The Control Panel opens as shown here:

Table 1-3 lists the functions available within the Control Panel, each with its own icon, for which you can set defaults.

You can set any of the functions by selecting the appropriate icon (by clicking on it) and then entering the necessary parameters in the dialog box that opens. Try that now by setting the double-click rate of the mouse.

1. Double-click on the Mouse icon in the Control Panel. The Mouse dialog box opens as shown here:

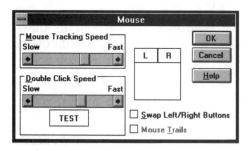

Icon	Function Set
Color	Colors associated with the various parts of the screen
Fonts	Fonts available for both screen and printer(s)
Ports	Communications parameters used with serial ports
Mouse	Behavior of the mouse, including the double-click rate, the speed the pointer moves across the screen, and whether the left or right mouse button is primary
Desktop	Characteristics of the screen or "desktop," including the cursor blink rate, the presence or absence of a "magnetic" grid to better align objects, and the patterns used for various areas
Keyboard	Keyboard repeat rate and delay before repeating
Printers	Parameters applicable to your printer(s), including ports assigned, paper size and orientation, graphics resolution, and the identification of the default printer
International	Formats for numbers, currency, dates, and times
Date/Time	System date and time
Network	Parameters applicable to your network (available only if you are using a network)
ODBC	Data sources based on Microsoft's Open Database Connectivity standard
386 Enhanced	Sharing of resources in multitasking environment, size of virtual memory, and use of 32-bit disk access (available only if you are using 386 enhanced mode)
Drivers	Addition, removal, and configuration of drivers for audio and video equipment
Sound	Enabling of system sounds and the assigning of sounds to events

Control Panel
Icons
Table 1-3.

2. If you are left-handed and want to make the right mouse button the primary mouse button, click on the Swap Left/Right Buttons check box at the bottom middle of the screen.

3. Double-click on the Test command button. If the button darkens, the double-click speed is set correctly.

4. If the Test button does not darken, you need to change the speed. Click on the Slow or Fast scroll arrow, whichever is correct for you, and try double-clicking again.

5. Repeat steps 3 and 4 until the double-clicking speed is set correctly.

6. When you are done with the mouse settings, click OK to close the dialog box and return to the Control Panel window.

7. On your own, look at the other Control Panel functions. You'll find you can do a lot to tailor Windows to your tastes. Unless you want to change something, click on Cancel in each dialog box so you won't change anything inadvertently.

8. When you are done with the Control Panel, double-click on the Control Panel's Control-menu box in the upper-left corner. This closes the Control Panel and returns you to the Main group window of the Program Manager.

Creating a Directory with the File Manager

The File Manager provides all of the customary DOS file-handling commands, such as COPY, DELETE, and RENAME, as well as a number of file-manipulation tools that have been available only with such packages as XTree and PC Tools. Open the File Manager now and create a new directory named SHEET to store your Excel documents.

Double-click on the File Manager icon in the Main group window of the Program Manager. The File Manager window opens, and a directory tree window also opens, as shown in Figure 1-14.

The directory tree provides a very powerful way of viewing and working with your directories and their files. The initial view shows you an alphabetical list of all the subdirectories under your root directory in a Tree window on the left, and a directory of all contents (both subdirectories and files) within the root directory on the right. Each subdirectory is represented by a file folder. Files are displayed either by a single sheet (data files) or by an index card (.COM, .EXE, and other executable files). The directory tree by itself looks like this:

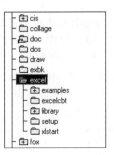

You can choose to display the directory tree, the detailed directory, or both. Within the directory tree, indicators in the file folders show if it contains a subdirectory or not. If that indicator is a plus sign, subdirectories are not displayed. If it's a minus sign, they are displayed.

You may open and list the files and subdirectories in any directory by clicking on the folder icon. If you were to click on the Excel directory folder (c:\excel) with Excel 5.0 installed, you would get this directory window:

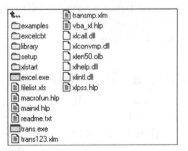

In the Directory window you can select or highlight files you want to move, copy, rename, or delete. To move a file, drag its icon from the current directory on the right to a new directory or subdirectory in the Tree window on the left. To copy a file, press and hold (Ctrl) while you drag the file icon. If you wish to move, copy, rename, or delete several files at one time and the files are listed sequentially, click on the first filename, and then press and hold (Shift) while you click on the last filename in the sequence. If you want to select several files that are not in sequence, press and hold (Ctrl) while you click on each of the items. To cancel a selected item, press and hold (Ctrl) while you click on the item. To delete or rename files, select the files and then choose the appropriate command from the File menu.

The File menu provides access to several other file functions, which include creating directories. Use that command now to complete creating the

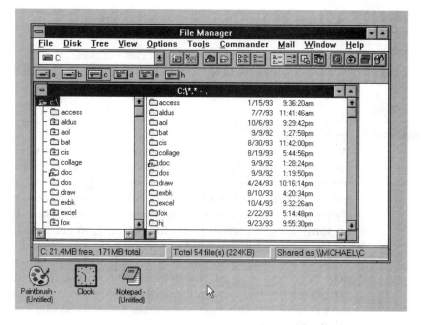

File Manager
and directory
tree
Figure 1-14.

SHEET directory to store your Excel spreadsheets (if you did not do this in Appendix A).

1. Click on the File Manager's File menu to open it.
2. Click on Create Directory to choose that option. The Create Directory dialog box opens, as shown here:

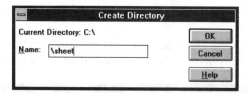

If you had correctly selected the directory under which you wish to create a new subdirectory, all you would need to enter is the new directory's name. Otherwise you need to type the full pathname of the new directory. (If you already did this in Appendix A, you won't be able to do it here.)

3. Type **sheet** or, if necessary, precede it with the pathname you want to use, for example typing **\sheet**, as shown in the preceding illustration.

4. Press (Enter) to close the dialog box, create the directory, and return to the File Manager window.

5. When you are done with the File Manager, double-click on its Control-menu box to close it and return to the Main group window of the Program Manager.

Getting Help

Windows online help is very extensive and context sensitive—it tries to provide specific help about what you are doing. You can get help by several methods. The fastest method is to press (F1). You'll get an index of help topics. In Excel and most other Windows applications, you can also press (Shift)-(F1). The mouse pointer will become a question mark that you can click on something, a menu option for example, to get specific help about that option. The second method of getting help is to click on the Help button available in most dialog boxes. The final and most general-purpose method of getting help is to use the Help menu on most application windows. You can access the Help menu by either clicking on it or pressing (Alt)-(H). Do that next and look at the Program Manager's Help facility by going through the following steps:

1. Click on Help in the Menu bar. The Program Manager's Help menu opens, as shown here:

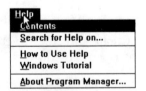

Most Help menus within Windows have the same set of options. These options, with the information they provide, are as follows:

Option	Information Provided
Contents	Topic summary
Search for Help on	Quick access to Help contents
How to Use Help	Tutorial on how to use Help
Windows Tutorial	Starts the Windows tutorial
About	Information about the application and your system resources

If you want information about the File menu commands proceed with these steps:

2. Click on Contents. A window appears, as shown in Figure 1-15. In the Help window you make a choice by clicking on an underlined topic. When the pointer is pointing on a topic that can be chosen, it becomes a grabber hand, as shown here:

> **Commands**
> File Menu Commands
> Options Menu Commands
> Window Menu Commands

3. Click on File Menu Commands. The File Menu Commands Help window opens, as shown in Figure 1-16.

   The command buttons at the top of a Help window return you to the Contents screen, allow you to search for a topic, retrace the path you have taken to get to the current Help window, see a listing ("History") of your previous Help choices, or see topics covered in alphabetical order.

4. Use the Help command buttons on your own to review the Windows Help facility.

5. When you are done reviewing Help, double-click on the Control-menu box to close Help. You will be returned to the Main group window of the Program Manager.

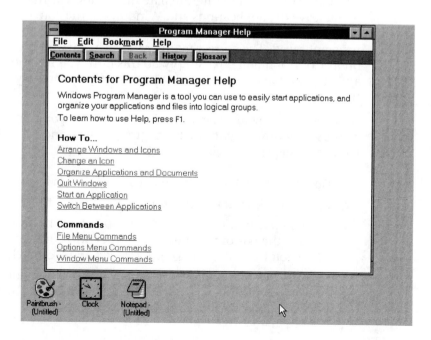

Contents for
Program
Manager Help
Figure 1-15.

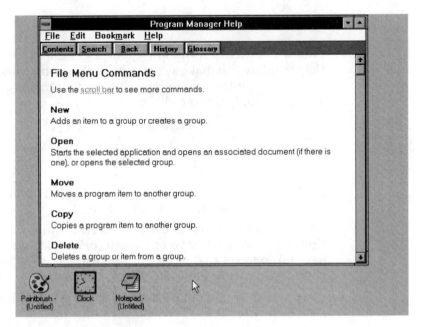

File Menu
Commands
Help window
Figure 1-16.

Leaving Windows

Windows and many of the applications that run under it, like Excel, use temporary files to store intermediate information as the program is running. If you leave the applications and Windows in the correct manner, not only are these temporary files erased, but you are reminded to save any files you have not saved. The correct manner to leave any window is to double-click on its Control-menu box. Simply do this until you reach the DOS prompt and you will have correctly left Windows. Then, and only then, can you safely turn off your computer.

Arrange your Program Manager window the way you want it to be when you next use Windows—with the Excel group open—and then leave Windows with these steps:

1. Double-click on the Control-menu box of the Main group window to close it.

2. Double-click on the Excel group icon to open it.

3. Size and position the two windows and icons in those windows (not the icons at the bottom of the screen—they will automatically be closed when you leave Windows) so they look approximately like Figure 1-17.

4. Double-click on the Program Manager's Control-menu box. You are asked to confirm that you want to leave Windows. Click on OK to leave Windows. You are returned to the DOS prompt.

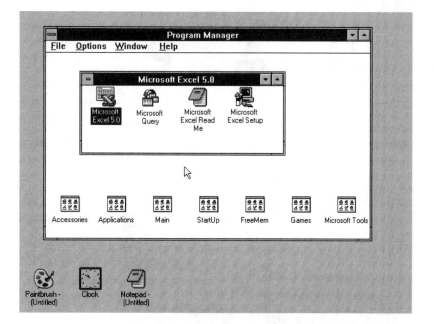

Program
Manager's
windows in
final position
Figure 1-17.

This chapter has laid a foundation on which you can now begin to add
specific knowledge of Excel. Windows is not a simple subject, but it provides
a very powerful framework that is fully utilized by Excel. You now have
enough knowledge of that framework to use it in Excel, which you will begin
doing in Chapter 2.

CHAPTER

2

THE COMPONENTS OF EXCEL

This chapter explains the three components of Excel—spreadsheets, databases, and charts—paying particular attention to spreadsheets. It also quickly introduces references, ranges, cells, commands, formulas, functions, and macros.

Excel is considered a spreadsheet program, yet it really has three components that perform three different tasks: the spreadsheet component displays and analyzes text and numbers in rows and columns, the *database* component manipulates lists of information, and the *chart* component produces charts.

Each component is really just a different way of looking at and interacting with data that has a common structure based on *rows* and *columns*. This common structure is the spreadsheet. It may contain data from the other components, but underlying the different components is the same row and column structure that contains all of the data. This common data structure makes Excel *integrated*—able to transfer and manipulate data easily among the three components.

Spreadsheets

The easiest way to think of a spreadsheet is to consider an accountant's multicolumn paper spreadsheet—a piece of paper that is divided into rows and columns. Generally there is a wide column on the left for text labels that describe what is in each row. To the right of the label column are several columns for entering numbers. Paper spreadsheets are used for manually listing sales or expenses, for preparing budgets or financial plans, or for any other similar task.

The spreadsheet component of Excel, shown in Figure 2-1, is an electronic multicolumn spreadsheet far more flexible than its paper namesake. Excel provides up to 255 sheets each containing 256 columns and 16,384 rows. Each column can be between 0 and 255 characters wide, and words and numbers can be intermixed as needed. Excel allows many types of calculations over rows, columns, and sheets; and copying or moving information from one sheet, column, or row to another is easy with Excel.

Spreadsheets and Files

Both the paper spreadsheet and Excel's spreadsheet are a means of analyzing data by organizing it into rows and columns. Excel's spreadsheets, however, are stored on your computer's hard disk in *files* called *workbooks* (*books* for short). Think of a workbook as a file of spreadsheets (*sheets* for short), although it can also contain charts and module pages. When you build a workbook, you do so in your computer's *RAM* (random access memory). When you load another program, or turn off your computer, what is in RAM is lost. You must save your workbook in a file on disk for it to be permanent. A file that has been stored on disk can be read back into Excel, reviewed, altered, and saved again. Also, because a file on disk can be run on another computer running Excel, work can be shared. The only outwardly distinguishing feature of an Excel file is the name you give it. Like a manila file folder, an Excel file is just a collection of information with a name.

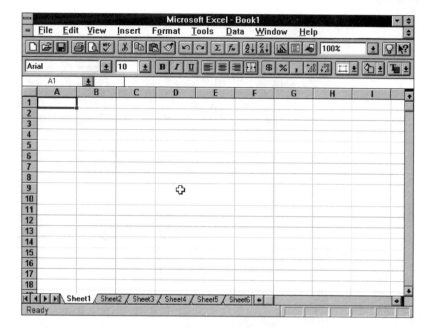

Excel's
Spreadsheet
window
Figure 2-1.

Rows, Columns, and Sheets

The row and column structure of a traditional spreadsheet has been
expanded in Excel 5 to a three-dimensional structure of rows, columns, and
sheets. This structure provides a powerful framework for financial analysis.
Consider a company's financial plan or budget, as shown in Figure 2-2. Each
row is an account—an element of revenue or expense. Each column is a
period of time—months, quarters, or years. Each sheet is a unit of the
company—stores, plants, offices, or divisions. Summing across columns you
get the total for an account, summing down rows you get the total for a time
period, and summing through the sheets you get the total for the company.

The horizontal rows and vertical columns make a two-dimensional grid and
the sheets gives it a third dimension of depth. The rows are numbered 1
through 16,384, while the 256 possible columns are labeled A through IV (A
through Z, then AA through AZ, BA through BZ, and so on through IV).
Sheets start out labeled Sheet1 through Sheet255, but you can rename them
anything you want. With this grid, you could build a formula that, for
example, adds column C from row 24 through row 32 or sums sheet1
through sheet4, or you can create a graph from the data in row 15 from
column AC through column AH.

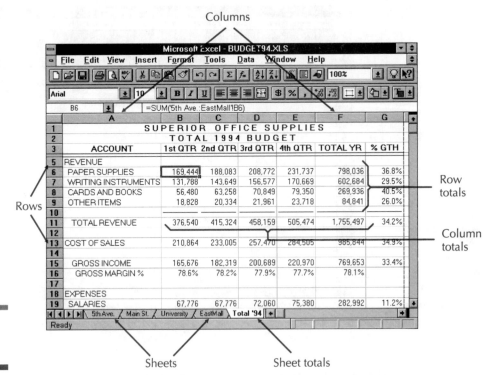

Columns

A company's
financial plan
Figure 2-2.

Sheets   Sheet totals

Addresses, Cells, and References

When information is entered on a sheet, it is stored in a specific location.
You know what that location is by the row and column in which the
information is located. Using Excel's row and column grid, you can give the
information you stored an *address*; for example, column D, row 7. Excel
addresses are written with the column reference first, followed by the row.
Using this convention, you can write the example address as D7. To add a
sheet reference to this, you place the sheet name and an exclamation point
(!) in front of the column and row—for example: Sheet1!D7.

A single address, the intersection of a row and a column on a single sheet, is
called a *cell*. You can think of a sheet as a collection of over four million
cells. These are addressed from A1 for the cell in the upper-left corner to
IV16384 for the cell in the lower-right corner. Of course, the amount of
memory you have in your computer limits the number of these you can use
at a time.

Numbers and Text

A cell may contain either numbers or text. Numbers, which include formulas that evaluate to numbers, can be formatted in many ways, including dollars, percentages, dates, or time. Text can include numbers and can be used as titles, row and column labels, and notes on a sheet.

The primary difference between numbers and text is that you can perform arithmetic functions on numbers but not on text. Think of numbers as arithmetic values and text as everything else.

Based on what you type, Excel determines whether your entry is a number or text. If you type only numbers (0 through 9) or these numeric symbols,

$$+ \; - \; (\;) \; . \; , \; : \; \$ \; \% \; / \; E \; e \; (\text{in scientific notation})$$

Excel considers your entry a number. If you enter a date or time value in one of Excel's built-in formats, it is considered a number. Finally, a recognizable formula that results in a number is treated as a number. Everything else is text.

You can enter numbers that range from $-1E-307$ to $9.99999999999999E307$ and format them in several ways. For example, you can enter **3.25**, **3.25%**, **$3.25**, **3 2/5**, **32.5E–1**, or **3,250,325.25**. In other words, you can include commas, dollar signs, fractions, and percent signs in numbers and Excel will interpret them correctly. Methods for entering formulas, which are also numbers, are discussed below, as are procedures for entering, formatting, and aligning text and numbers.

References, Ranges, and Names

A *reference* identifies one or more cells for use in a formula or in an instruction. A reference can be a single cell address like D14; a group of cells identified by multiple cell addresses and a *reference operator*, such as C5:E12; or a name or names that refer to one or more cells, like "Salaries." The reference operators, their name, and their meaning are as follows:

Operator	Name and meaning
: (colon)	*Range*, a rectangular group of adjacent cells
, (comma)	*Union*, the combination of two references
(space)	*Intersection*, the cells common to two references

Other than an individual cell address, the next most common reference is a *range*. Figure 2-3 shows the four kinds of ranges that can exist on a sheet: a row of cells, a column of cells, a rectangular block of cells, or a single cell.

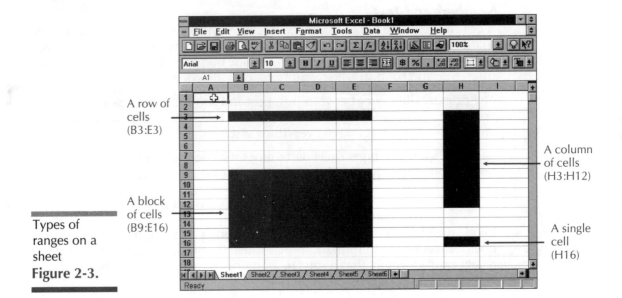

A row of cells (B3:E3)

A column of cells (H3:H12)

A block of cells (B9:E16)

A single cell (H16)

Types of ranges on a sheet
Figure 2-3.

A range cannot be an L-shaped or otherwise nonrectangular arrangement of cells; it must be a complete rectangle. A range can also extend over multiple sheets.

Ranges are used in many Excel commands to specify a group of cells you want Excel to work on. To specify a range in a command, you may use the pair of addresses representing the first and last cells in the range (the upper-left and lower-right corners, respectively) separated by a colon, as in B11:G18. Or, you may highlight the range on the screen or use a name that you have previously given to that particular cell reference. If you want to reference an entire row or column or sequence of rows or columns, you may do so without identifying the second element. For example, to identify all of row 6 you might enter A6:IV6, but you can abbreviate it 6:6. Similarly if you want to reference all of columns C through E, you can enter C:E.

Unions and intersections are used to describe groups of cells that cannot be described by a range, like those shown in Figure 2-4. *Unions* can describe L-shaped references such as E3:H3,I3:I12 as well as disjoint references like I3:I12,I16. *Intersections* describe the group of cells that are in both of two other references. For example, the intersection C6:C14 B10:E17 produces the range C10:C14. Unions and intersections are referred to using two other references separated by a comma or a space, respectively. Alternatively, you can highlight a union or an intersection by holding down Ctrl while you

2

Union of E3:H3,I3:I12

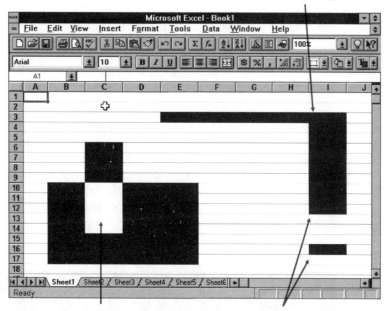

Unions and
intersections
on a sheet
Figure 2-4.

Intersection of C6:C14 B10:E17   Union of I3:II2,I16

highlight the cells on the screen, or you can use a reference name you have previously defined.

A *reference name* is a text string that begins with a letter and can be as long as 255 characters and cannot contain a space. A reference name such as "Salaries" is often used because it is easier to remember and more meaningful than an address reference such as G16:T16. Many of Excel's arithmetic functions use references as arguments and, when a name is substituted for the address, they become very descriptive. For example, to total a group of cells that contain salaries you can use the Excel function =SUM(Salaries) if you have previously defined the name Salaries.

Formulas and Functions

The ability to enter text and numbers is not very useful unless you can do something with them. You need to be able to total columns of numbers, calculate percentages, and perform numerous other mathematical operations. Formulas are the means of doing this. Formulas may operate on numbers, other formulas, or text. When a formula uses text it is called a *text formula* and may contain the text operator (&) for *concatenation* (combining two text strings). Formulas that contain the arithmetic operators

    + – * / ^ %

are *numeric formulas*, and formulas that contain the comparison operators

    < > <= >= <>

are *logical formulas* that produce the logical values True or False.

Formulas use standard algebraic notation with nested parentheses, if necessary, and they typically begin with an equal sign (=). You may also enter a formula beginning with a plus sign (+) or a minus sign (–) and Excel will automatically add an equal sign in front of the plus or minus. Formulas may be up to 255 characters long but may not contain spaces, except within a *literal*—a set of letters, numbers, or symbols enclosed in quotation marks. Formulas usually use data in other locations on a sheet by referencing either a cell, a group of cells, or a reference name.

Examples of formulas are shown here:

If the Formula Is	Contents of the Cell Containing the Formula Will Be
=B5	The contents of B5.
=C6–C7	The result of subtracting the contents of C7 from the contents of C6.
=.45*1590	The product of 0.45 times 1590.
=subtotal*tax	The product of the references named Subtotal and Tax.
="Dear "&D5	The combination of the literal string "Dear " with the contents of D5. (Quotation marks define a literal string, character for character.)
=date<=today()	The logical value True if a reference named Date is less than or equal to a function named TODAY() that produces the current date; otherwise, the logical value False.

Order of Calculation

Excel calculates or evaluates a formula in a particular order determined by the *precedence number* of the operators being used and the parentheses placed in the formula. Table 2-1 describes each operator and gives its precedence number. Operators with a lower precedence number are performed earlier in the calculation. When two operators in a formula have the same precedence number, Excel evaluates them sequentially from left to right.

2

Operator	Description	Precedence
:	Range of cells	1
(a space)	Intersection of cells	2
,	Union of cells	3
–	Negation	4
%	Percentage (/100)	5
^	Exponentiation	6
*	Multiplication	7
/	Division	7
+	Addition	8
–	Subtraction	8
&	Concatenation	9
=	Equal to	10
<	Less than	10
>	Greater than	10
<=	Less than or equal to	10
>=	Greater than or equal to	10
<>	Not equal to	10

Excel
Operators
Table 2-1.

Parentheses in a formula change the order of calculation. For example, to add two amounts before multiplying them by a third, you cannot use the formula =A+B*C because the multiplication is performed before the addition, in accordance with the order of calculation. When you put parentheses around the addition operation, the formula becomes =(A+B)*C, and the addition is performed first. Excel performs the calculation within the innermost parentheses first. Parentheses must always be added in pairs and may be nested more than 25 levels deep. Excel has a very handy feature that shows the matching left parenthesis as you enter the right parenthesis. That way you know your parentheses match without having to count them.

Functions

Excel has a number of built-in formulas, called *functions*, that can be used within other formulas or can be used alone. Functions always begin with an equal sign and include calculations of the following types: mathematical, informational, date and time, lookup, logical, database, text, financial, and statistical. A function can be either text or a number, depending on whether it is operating on text or numbers. Table 2-2 lists some examples of functions and their uses.

Functions are discussed throughout this book and are given in-depth treatment in Chapter 10.

Commands

You can give Excel commands in six ways:

+ Choose an option from a regular menu at the top of the screen.
+ Choose an option from a shortcut menu.
+ Select a tool in a toolbar.
+ Use the mouse directly on a sheet.
+ Press particular keys on the keyboard.
+ Activate a set of commands you have stored in a workbook.

In this book, *command* refers to one of the first five methods: those implemented directly with the mouse, a toolbar, either type of menu, or with keys on your keyboard. Commands stored in a workbook are called *macros*.

Commands from a Menu

The primary means of giving Excel a command is by choosing an option from a menu presented to you on the screen. When you use menus to choose an option, you sometimes are asked for more information with a dialog box, or you may be presented with a secondary menu. As you saw in Chapter 1, you can begin a menu selection in several ways: by clicking with

Function	Purpose
=SUM(A4:A7,A9)	Adds A4, A5, A6, A7, and A9
=NOW ( )	Produces the current date and time
PI()*G3^2	Calculates the area of a circle whose radius is in G3
=PV(C4,F6,B1)	Calculates the present value of a series of equal payments at an interest rate contained in c4, for the number of periods in F6, and with the payment amount contained in B1
=RIGHT(T22,5)	Displays the rightmost five characters of a text string contained in T22

Some Excel Functions
Table 2-2.

the mouse on the name of the menu you want to use or by pressing (Alt), (F10), or (/) (slash). This book assumes that you usually use the mouse, but you should become familiar with all of the menu selection techniques. For the most part, the instructions in this book state "Select the File menu" or "From the File menu." Whether you use the mouse or the keyboard is up to you.

If you use the keyboard, the (Alt), (F10), or (/) key gets you only to the Menu bar; you must still select the menu you want to use (which is one of many good reasons why using the mouse is preferable). Once the Menu bar is activated there are two methods to select a menu with the keyboard: you can type the underlined letter in the menu name you want, or you can use the direction keys to highlight the menu name and then press either (↓) or (Enter) to open the menu.

Once a menu is open, you can choose a menu option in one of three ways: click on the menu option with the mouse, type the underlined letter in the option name, or use the direction keys to highlight the option and press (Enter) to choose it. Examples of the three methods follow, in which you select the Edit menu and choose the Copy option, as shown in Figure 2-5. The message area on the left side of the Status bar at the bottom of the Excel window displays an explanation of the highlighted menu or menu option. No other change appears on the screen as a result of these steps.

Mouse Method

1. Click on the Edit menu.
2. Click on the Copy option.

Keyboard Method 1

1. Press (Alt), (F10), or (/).
2. Press (E), (you can use uppercase or lowercase), the underlined letter in Edit.
3. Press (C), the underlined letter in Copy.

Keyboard Method 2

1. Press (Alt), or (F10), or (/).
2. Press (→) one time (twice if sheet is maximized).
3. Press (↓) four times.
4. Press (Enter).

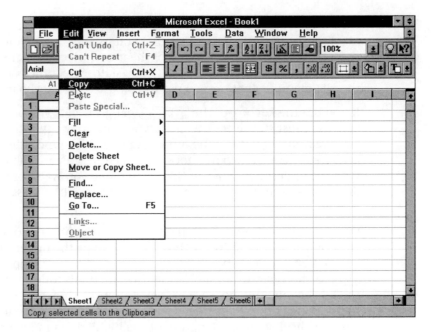

Choosing
Copy from the
Edit menu
Figure 2-5.

Because you will be using the menu system extensively as you work with Excel, menu commands are a primary subject of this book. Chapter 3 introduces each Excel menu.

Commands from the Shortcut Menu

By using your *right* mouse button, Excel will open a Shortcut menu that gives you direct access to the most commonly used commands for whatever you clicked on. For example, clicking your right mouse button on the active cell will give you a shortcut menu of editing and formatting options, as shown here:

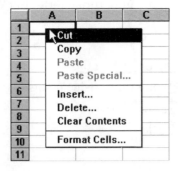

Shortcut menus are also available for manipulating toolbars, rows, columns, and sheets, which are described in Chapter 3, and for editing and formatting charts and databases, which you will read about in Chapters 7 and 8.

Direct Mouse Commands

In addition to its use in choosing commands from menus, the mouse can also be used directly on the sheet. Most importantly, you can use the mouse to highlight a group of cells on which you want to operate—copy, move, or format, for example. You do this by pointing on a cell in one corner of the group of cells, pressing the mouse button, and dragging the mouse (pressing and holding the mouse button while moving the mouse) to the opposite corner. For example, the highlighted range in Figure 2-6 was created by pointing the mouse on C7 and dragging the mouse to E13.

If you want to highlight or select a union or an intersection on a sheet, hold down Ctrl while dragging across the two or more ranges. For example, if you want to select the L-shaped group of cells shown in Figure 2-7, you would first drag down the column from C4 to C17, then press and hold Ctrl while dragging from D12 through H17. This technique can also be used to

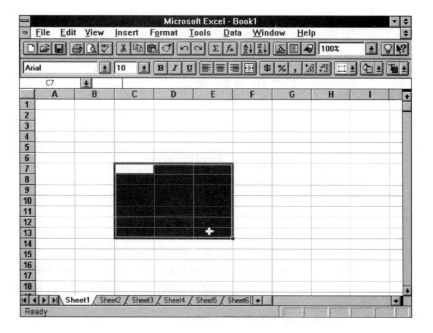

Highlighting a
range

Figure 2-6.

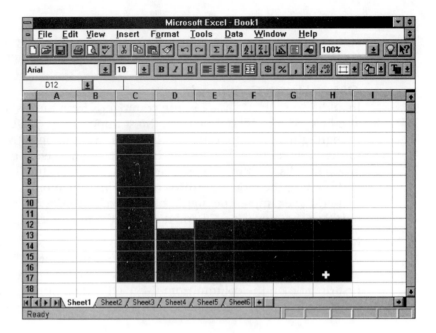

Highlighting
several ranges
or a union
Figure 2-7.

highlight several ranges on different sheets—just hold down Ctrl as you are dragging across each new range and clicking on each new sheet. If you want to highlight the same range on several sheets in a row, click on the first sheet tab, press and hold Shift while clicking on the last sheet tab, and then drag across the range on the first sheet (you don't have to keep holding down Shift while you drag across the range).

Other direct mouse commands in Excel include placing an insertion point in a formula or text string, selecting an entire row or column by clicking on the row or column headings, widening a column or heightening a row by dragging on the intersection of two columns or two row headings, and dividing the window into panes by dragging the horizontal or vertical split bar. (The parts of the Excel window are discussed in Chapter 3.) Of course, you can also use the mouse with the scroll bars to change what is being displayed and to size and move the window, as you learned in Chapter 1.

A large part of this book focuses on using the mouse. Therefore, you will see many examples of using the mouse directly on the sheet and throughout a workbook and you will have ample opportunity to practice such maneuvers.

Commands from a Toolbar
By default, Excel has a pair of *toolbars* as the third and fourth bars on the screen. These toolbars have a series of buttons that you can simply click on

2

to accomplish a task that would otherwise take several steps with a menu or the keyboard. For example, to make a title bold with the toolbar, you select the title and click on the B button in the Formatting toolbar (two steps). With the menu, you would select the title, select the Format menu, choose the Cells option, click on the Font tab, click on Bold as the Font Style, and then click on OK (six steps).

You can tell what the tools in the toolbars do by pointing on the tool for a second (don't click); a short description will appear below the tool, like this:

There are many handy tools described in Chapter 3 and other chapters. One of the handiest, located in the top or Standard toolbar, allows you to enter the most used function—the =SUM function—by clicking on the AutoSum tool, as shown in Figure 2-8. Otherwise, you would have to type it on the keyboard or select it from the menu. Additionally, a toolbar is the only means for selecting a drawing tool.

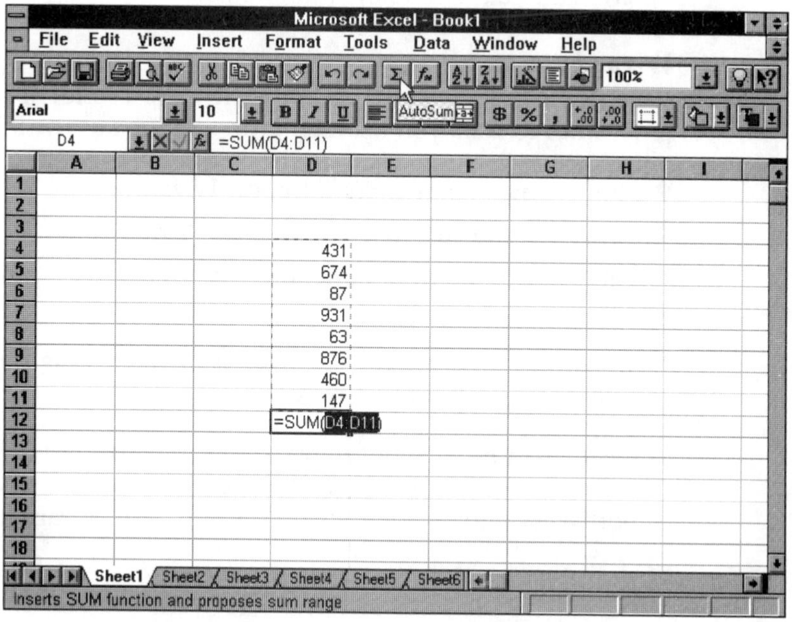

Entering a =SUM formula using the AutoSum tool in the Standard toolbar
Figure 2-8.

There are actually 13 toolbars in Excel 5. Each toolbar contains special tools for various activities. The Standard and Formatting toolbars, shown on the screens in this chapter, are displayed unless you turn them off or replace one or both of them with one of the other toolbars. Additional toolbars can be displayed on the screen at the same time and you can customize each toolbar by adding and deleting tools and selecting the order in which the tools appear. Also, you can create a totally new toolbar, which you can name and add tools to of your choosing. Finally, you can position and change the shape and orientation of one or more toolbars. Chapter 3 describes each of the tools in the Standard and Formatting toolbars, and Appendix B describes all 13 toolbars and their tools as well as how to customize both tools and toolbars.

Commands from the Keyboard

Most of the keys on the keyboard that are not standard typewriter keys can be used to give Excel commands. Many of the keyboard commands are implemented with the *function keys* F1 through F10 or F12 on the top or left of most keyboards. On the right of most keyboards are the *direction keys*—the keys marked with the four arrows and Home, End, Pg Up, and Pg Dn. Use these keys to move around the screen, from cell to cell, or through a menu.

Some Excel commands are implemented through the use of two or more keys. Just as the Shift key is used with the normal typewriter keyboard to produce alternate characters, the Ctrl and Alt keys are used with other keys to produce alternate commands. Chapter 3 describes these keys as well as the function and direction keys in more detail.

Wizards

Wizards provide guidance and in some cases a series of step-by-step procedures to walk you through processes such as the following:

✦ Importing a text file (Text Import Wizard)

✦ Creating and editing a chart (ChartWizard)

✦ Inserting a function (Function Wizard)

✦ Suggesting easier ways of doing something (TipWizard)

✦ Building a interactive table from data on existing sheets or in an external database (PivotTable Wizard)

You will learn more about how to use the TipWizard in Chapter 3, the ChartWizard in Chapter 7, the PivotTable Wizard in Chapter 8, the Text Import Wizard in Chapter 9, and the Function Wizard in Chapter 10.

Macros

A *macro* is either a set of Visual Basic statements or a set of Excel 4 macro commands that behave like automatic menu, mouse, and keyboard commands when they are executed. Macros, which are stored in a workbook on either Visual Basic module pages or macro sheets, are used to automate or speed up repetitive Excel procedures. You can have Excel record a macro for you by starting the recording, carrying out the steps you want to record, and then stopping the recording. When you are done, you can have Excel execute the macro by pressing two keys such as Ctrl-A. For example, you can format a table with a macro that accomplishes many keystrokes with just two.

Almost all commands that you can perform with a menu, the mouse, the toolbar, or the keyboard can be stored in a macro and activated as you choose. In addition, macros, especially Visual Basic procedures, can perform programming functions such as repeating a sequence, testing a condition, or accepting input from the keyboard. With this additional capability you can build custom menus and automate a workbook. Chapter 10 discusses recording and using command macros, Chapter 12 introduces you to Visual Basic, and Chapter 13 demonstrates workbook automation with a set of Visual Basic macros.

Workbook Windows

The Excel workbook window, as it appears in Figure 2-8, displays a single portion of one sheet. With the scroll bars or direction keys you can change the rows and columns being displayed, and with the sheet tabs you can change which sheet you are looking at. In every case, however, the view is similar. In addition to this basic view, Excel provides several other views that give you a different look at one or more sheets.

By splitting the window into *panes,* vertically or horizontally or both, you can look at two or four parts of the same sheet at the same time, as shown in Figure 2-9. By doing this, you can scroll each pane separately and look at different parts of the same sheet at the same time. You can also freeze the panes so they move together. To split a window into panes, you can choose split from the Window menu, or you can drag either the horizontal *split-bar* that is in the upper-right corner of a window or the vertical split-bar that is in the lower-right corner as shown in the following:

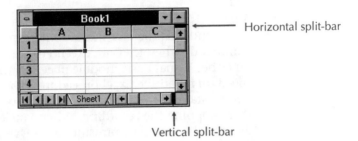

By displaying multiple document windows on the screen simultaneously, you can look at several sections of the same sheet, or you can look at several sheets either from the same workbook or from different workbooks. To display several windows, you can either open several workbooks with the Open option in the File menu or create one or more new windows for an existing workbook with the New Window option in the Window menu. Using the Arrange option in the Window menu, several windows on the screen can be *tiled* (as shown in Figure 2-10), arranged horizontally or vertically, or arranged in a *cascade* (as shown in Figure 2-11).

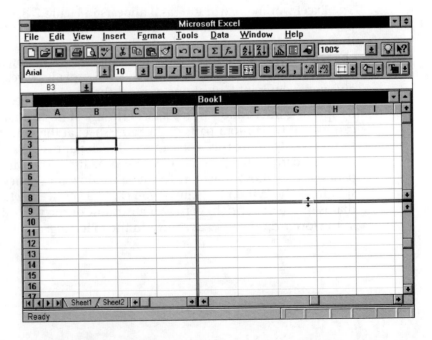

A single sheet window split into four panes

Figure 2-9.

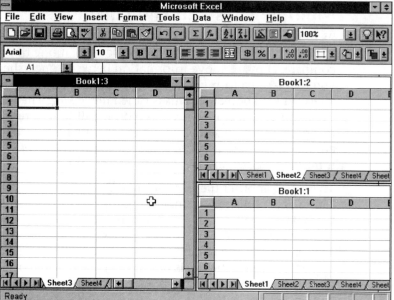

Three
windows tiled
Figure 2-10.

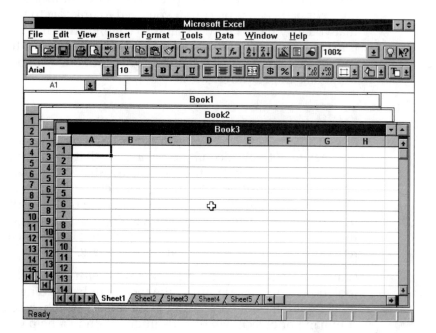

Three-window
cascade
Figure 2-11.

Multiple Files and File Linking

As implied by the last paragraph and as shown in Figure 2-11, Excel allows you to have more than one workbook open at one time. That means you can compare, copy, or move information between open sheets. Excel also allows you to refer in a formula in one workbook file to cells or ranges contained in a second workbook file. This is called *file linking*. The files may both be open in memory, or one may be closed on the disk. As a result, you can easily combine information contained in separate files. A change in one linked file automatically is reflected in the second file. If the second file is on the disk, it must be loaded and recalculated before the change is apparent.

To refer to another file in a formula, the formula must contain the filename. This is accomplished by appending the filename, enclosed in square brackets, to the front of an address or reference name. For example, [QTR3BUD.XLS]TOTAL!SALARIES refers to a reference named Salaries on the Total sheet in a file named QTR3BUD.XLS. If you need to add a path to the filename because the file is not in the current directory, do so to the left of the left bracket (outside the brackets), like this:

C:\BUDGET\[QTR3BUD.XLS]TOTAL!SALARIES

Since you can have multiple sheets in a single workbook, you might ask why one would want to link multiple workbooks. The most common reason is that you have several people, perhaps in different locations, preparing different parts of a project that you need to link together. A second reason is that you may have a model that is so complex that it is easier to handle if it is in separate files. Another reason is that you may want to look at the same data in a different way so you link portions of one workbook into another workbook and rearrange it.

Help

As you are learning Excel, and possibly even after you know it fairly well, you may forget how a command works or what the arguments are for a function. To assist you in these instances, Microsoft provides three types of help: context-sensitive help, dialog box help, and a help table of contents. There are, additionally, a quick preview of the product online, a detailed set of examples and demonstrations including a detailed set of *How To* steps that you can leave on your screen after closing Help, and a TipWizard to remind you of other ways of performing a task.

Context-sensitive help in Excel is activated either by clicking on the Help tool located on the far right of the toolbar or by pressing [Shift]-[F1]. The mouse pointer then becomes a question mark which, when clicked on any command or object, will provide information in a help window describing that command or object. For example, if you have a question on the Edit Cut option, click on the Help tool or press Shift-F1 to get the question mark, and then click on the Cut option located on the Edit menu. You will get information in a help window describing the Edit Cut option, as shown in Figure 2-12. Additionally, when you get an alert or error message, you can press Shift-F1 and get a help window describing the message.

Help is also available by clicking on the Help button in any Excel dialog box. Information on the function of that particular dialog box will appear in a help window. You can accomplish the same thing by pressing Shift-F1 while a dialog box is open.

The Help menu on the far right of the Menu bar provides a number of Help options, as shown here:

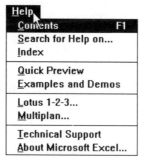

Included on the menu are a table of contents that provides a listing of help topics, a topic-sensitive searching procedure, an index of help topics, a quick overview of Excel that you can run through in 25 minutes, a set of examples and demonstrations of using Excel and its features, and help for Lotus 1-2-3 and Multiplan users. Finally, there are instructions on how to reach and use Microsoft Technical Support.

Most help topics have cross-references, or *jump terms,* leading to other help topics that cover related areas. You can easily identify the jump terms because they are colored green and underlined. If you place the mouse pointer on them, the pointer turns into a grabber hand. To look at a jump term, click on it. If you follow many subjects to their conclusion, you will get a How To window that lists the steps that are needed to perform a given task. Each help window has a series of command buttons that allow you to go to the help contents list, conduct a topic-sensitive search, see a history of your most recently selected help topics, or open the help index.

The final way that Excel provides help is with the TipWizard, which watches what you are doing and gives you tips on how to do it faster or in different ways. You can turn on the TipWizard by clicking on the light bulb on the right end of the Standard toolbar. When you do that, another bar appears on

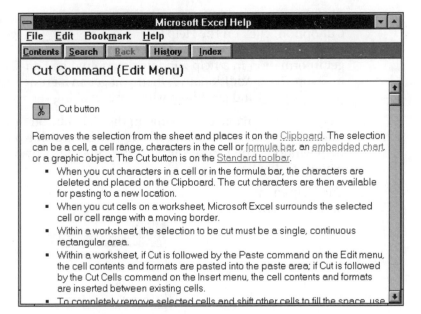

Help window
for the Edit
Cut command
Figure 2-12.

the screen with a tip about the last thing you did. As you work, you will see tips appear that relate to what you are doing.

Databases

The row and column structure of Excel is excellent for storing lists of information. Consider the phone list shown in Figure 2-13. Each entry in the list is called a record and is stored in a single row of the sheet. Each part of an entry—the name, company, or phone number in Figure 2-13—is called a *field* and is stored in a column. You therefore have a natural and common relationship between records and fields in a list and rows and columns in a sheet.

A list of related information organized in a consistent, logical manner is called a *database*. A database must be completely contained on a single sheet, but a single sheet can contain more than one database.

Rows and Records

Each row of a database, other than the first row, is a record representing a single entry. The first row of a database must contain the names of each field, one per column. These *field names* are used to identify the fields in commands and functions. All rows after the first in a database are data records. They can be blank or contain a divider line (a line across the

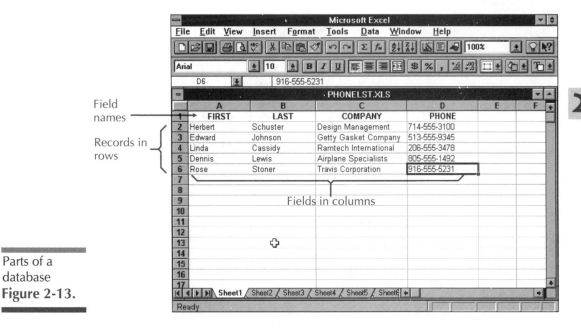

Field names

Records in rows

Fields in columns

Parts of a database
Figure 2-13.

database), for example, but they are still considered data records. A database can contain a maximum of 16,383 records (one less than the number of rows in a sheet).

Columns and Fields

Each column of a database is a field representing a common data element in all records. For example, the company name in Figure 2-13 is a field. Each field can contain a number, text, or a formula. A database can contain a maximum of 256 fields, one for every column in a sheet, but you cannot have two fields with the same field name in one database.

Using Databases

You can use a database any time you need a list of items. Examples of databases, in addition to the phone list, are stocks in a portfolio with dates and prices, parts of a machine with the part number and supplier, salespeople with their quotas and commissions, and products with their prices and margins.

Within Excel there are specific commands that let you manipulate databases. These commands are called *data commands* because they are all accessed through the Data menu shown in the following:

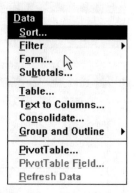

The options in the Data menu provide for sorting databases, selecting information from them based on a filtering criteria, entering data into a database using a form, applying functions to a database such as summing, and rearranging a database in several ways. For example, you can sort the phone list by company, select stocks that are performing below your expectations, find the machine parts from a given supplier, and analyze the change in sales commissions that would result from changes in quotas. Database-related commands and functions are explored in Chapter 8.

Charts

If a picture is worth a thousand words, a chart is worth at least a thousand numbers. A chart allows you to give visual meaning to a set of numbers, to show the differences or similarities between them, and to show the patterns produced. Many people find that they absorb information faster and easier from charts and even that they see things in charts they do not see in the numbers that produce the charts.

An Excel chart is a pictorial representation of one or more groups of cells in a workbook. If you have a reference on a sheet that contains company sales by month, you can produce a line chart that would make it easy to show fluctuations in monthly sales. Given references for expenses and earnings by month, you can produce additional lines on the same chart and determine not only if they are going up or down, but also show how any trends relate to each other. Figure 2-14 shows such a line chart.

The Pie chart in Figure 2-15 shows the proportion each product line contributes to total company sales by charting a reference containing the sales by product. Given references containing sales by quarter for each of four regions, the chart shown in Figure 2-16 can be produced.

Excel provides eight two-dimensional types of charts: Area, Bar, Column, Line, Pie, Radar, Scatter, and Doughnut; and six three-dimensional types of

2

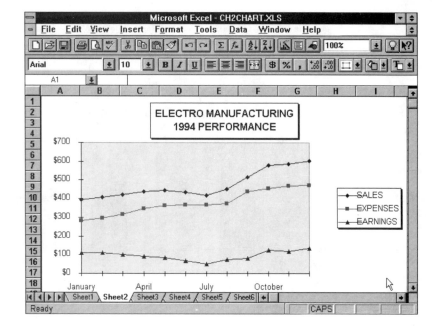

A Line chart
showing
financial
performance
Figure 2-14.

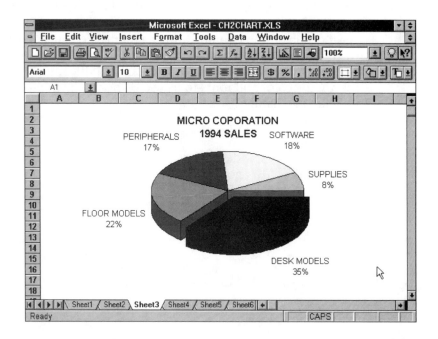

Pie chart
showing
proportional
contribution
of each
product line
Figure 2-15.

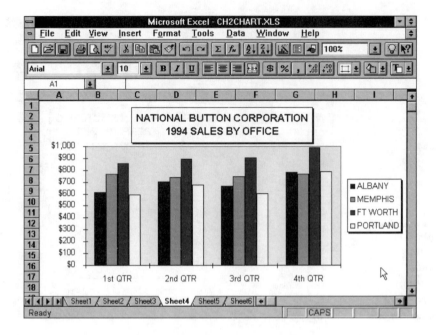

Chart
produced
from
references
containing
quarterly
regional sales
Figure 2-16.

charts: Area, Bar, Column, Line, Pie, and Surface. There are also several alternatives for each type and several ways to combine two types. As a result you have many ways to chart information on a sheet.

To produce these charts, Excel provides the ChartWizard to lead you step-by-step through the process and a unique set of menus and a chart sheet or the option of embedding a chart on a regular sheet. You can select the type of chart you want to produce and identify the references in the workbook that will generate it. You can add titles and annotations, as well as specify the color and fonts to be used. The production of charts is discussed in detail in Chapter 7.

CHAPTER

3

THE EXCEL ENVIRONMENT

This chapter and the remainder of the book are written based on the assumption that you will follow along on your computer as you read. This process allows you to see for yourself what a keystroke does and how the screen looks as a result. Most people find that they learn much faster by doing while reading than by reading alone.

To use Excel on your computer, you must first install Windows and then Excel. This process is discussed in Appendix A.

If you have not installed Windows or Excel yet, turn to Appendix A and complete the installation, including the startup procedure. When you are done, you can return to this chapter.

If you have already installed Windows and Excel, start them now, following the procedure described in Appendix A.

Excel's Screen and Menus

When you first start Excel, after a brief display of the Microsoft copyright message, you'll see a blank sheet on your screen like the one shown in Figure 3-1. This screen contains two windows. On the outer perimeter of the screen is the Excel application window. This contains Excel's menus, the toolbars, the address of the currently active cell, the Formula bar, and the Status bar. Within the Excel window is a single workbook document window. The workbook window is the primary working area in Excel. The Excel application window may contain several document windows, as you saw in Chapter 2. The two primary windows, Excel and workbook, are discussed in the following sections.

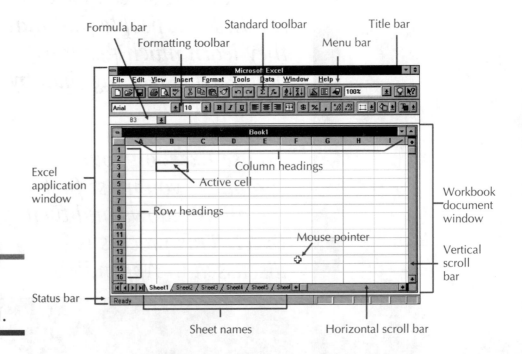

Blank
workbook
screen
Figure 3-1.

The Workbook Window

Initially, Excel opens a single workbook window. As you saw in Chapter 2, you can open additional workbook windows as well, but you generally use only a single workbook window and open other windows only for special purposes.

The workbook window in which you are currently working is called the *active window.* If you have other windows open, they are not active until you click the mouse on them or choose a different window from the Window menu. You can tell which workbook is active because its Title bar and an active cell are highlighted. In Figure 3-2, Book1:3 is the active window.

A workbook window provides the area in which to enter numbers, text, and formulas in order to build what you want. The workbook's inherent structure—its rows, columns, and sheets—allows you to enter and organize your work easily.

Rows, Columns, and Sheets

The blank workbooks in Figures 3-1 and 3-2 show the row, column, and sheet nature of the workbook: the row and column headings are across the top and down the left side and the sheet names are across the bottom. This three-dimensional grid forms individual *cells*: the intersection of one row and one column on one sheet. A cell is where you enter numbers, text, or a formula. Only one cell at a time is active and available for entry or editing.

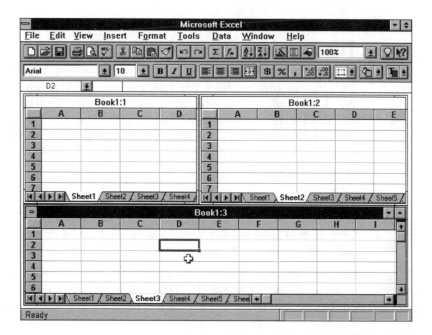

Book1:3 is the active window
Figure 3-2.

You know which cell is active because it has a heavy border around it. In Figure 3-1, cell B3 on sheet 1 is active. This is the cell formed by the intersection of column B and row 3 on Sheet1. Cell D2 on Sheet3 in windows Book1:3 is active in Figure 3-2. The address of the active cell can be seen in the upper-left corner of the spreadsheet, just under the toolbar, in the reference area.

You can make a different cell active either by clicking on it with the mouse (moving the mouse pointer to the new cell and pressing the mouse button) or by using the direction keys on the right side of your keyboard to move the active cell border to the new cell.

You can make a different sheet active by clicking on the *sheet tab* at the bottom of the window. Once on a different sheet, you can independently move the active cell where you want it. Often you will work independently on each sheet, but you can make several sheets active at one time and have entries that you make on one sheet appear on all the active sheets, as you will see in Chapters 4 and 5.

By clicking on the scroll bars on the right and bottom of the workbook window, or by using the direction keys, you can look at and work on other areas of the active sheet. Compared to Excel's total potential area, the area actually displayed on your screen is quite small—17 or 18 out of 16,384 rows and 9 out of 256 columns (the number of rows and columns depends on your monitor and graphics card). Of course most applications in Excel also use only a small amount of the total area but often are larger than what you initially see on the screen.

The Excel Window

The default Excel window contains six bars—five at the top and one at the bottom. The top two bars, the Title bar and the Menu bar, are common to all Windows applications. The other four bars—two toolbars, the Formula bar, and the Status bar—are used by Excel and some other applications. The Title bar is standard throughout Windows applications, with only the name it contains ever changing. The Menu bar, while consistent in layout with other Windows applications, has a unique set of menus.

The Menu Bar

The Excel Menu bar includes eight Excel menus and the standard Windows Control and Help menus. Since you looked at Control and Help in Chapter 1 and Help again in Chapter 2, only the eight Excel menus are reviewed here.

Remember that to open a menu you can click on the menu name with the mouse. Also, you can press ⒶⓁⓣ, Ⓕ10, or ⑦ to activate the Menu bar and then either type the underlined letter in the menu name or move the highlight to the menu name with the direction keys and press [Enter]. With a menu open you can look at another menu either by clicking on the menu name or by using the direction keys to move to the other menu. If you want to close a menu without choosing an option, press [Esc].

File Menu   The File menu provides the means of creating new workbooks, opening existing workbooks and other files stored on disk, and closing and saving workbooks or saving all open files. You can search for a file based on either its name and location or on information you place in the summary information area. The File menu also allows you to set up the page you will print, look at a preview of what you are going to print, print some or all of a workbook, and exit Excel. If you are connected to a network and have a mail system, you can access it through the File menu Send option or add a routing slip to a workbook that distributes it to mail boxes on the network. Near the bottom, the File menu provides a list of the last four files you have used. If you want to open one of these files, simply click on the one you want or press its number on the keyboard. Lastly, the File menu provides a way to exit Excel.

Edit Menu   You use the Edit menu to undo or repeat the last thing you did and to copy, move, clear (delete), or fill the contents of a cell or a group of cells. With this menu you can also delete the cells themselves as well as rows, columns, and sheets. You can move and copy sheets, search and replace cell contents, and go to a named cell or reference. Finally, if you bring objects into Excel, such as graphics or text that you have created in other applications, the Edit menu allows you to display and update the links between the objects and their original applications and to activate the original application from within Excel by selecting the object and choosing the Object option.

View Menu   The View menu is a means for controlling how your screen looks. It allows you to turn on or off the Formula and Status bars, and to select the toolbars you want to display. It provides access to the View Manager add-in program that allows you to save a particular screen setup including print settings and hidden rows and columns. Also, the View menu allows you to display only the Excel menu and

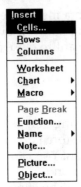

the workbook document window, getting rid of all other bars and giving you the maximum display area for a sheet. Finally, the View menu allows you to change the magnification of the workbook window, from very small cells to very large ones.

Insert Menu   The Insert menu is used to add (insert) cells, rows, columns, sheets, and chart and macro pages to a workbook. You can also insert a page break; add functions through the Function Wizard; create, use, and delete reference names; add notes to cells; and insert pictures and other objects created outside of Excel.

Format Menu   Through the Format menu you determine how a cell entry looks. If it contains a number, you can format it as dollars or percentages, with or without commas, and set the number of decimal places. You can align both text and numbers to the left, right, or center in a cell; determine the font and style; place a border around or shade them; and protect a cell from being overwritten. Also, you can determine the size, fit, and hidden status of rows and columns and the name of a sheet and whether it is hidden.

The Format menu's AutoFormat option provides automatic formatting for a selected range. The AutoFormat option provides 16 formatting styles within 7 categories: simple, classic, financial, accounting, colorful, list, and 3-D effects. Each style has an example of how it will look. Autoformatting is discussed further in Chapter 6. With the Format menu, you can define your own style including number format, font, alignment, type of border and patterns, and the cell protection status. Finally, the format menu allows you to determine the relative placement of objects on a sheet.

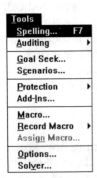

Tools Menu   The Tools menu provides access to the many add-ins that come with Excel. These include a spelling checker; auditing package; the Goal Seek, Scenarios, and Solver analysis packages; and means of accessing other add-ins. The Tools menu also allows you to turn on or off protection for either a workbook or a single sheet and to record and run macros or assign a macro to a tool. (Macros, you remember, are Excel commands that have been stored in a workbook.) Finally, the Tools menu Options option lets you customize Excel as you wish. Among the settings you can make are the standard font, the number of sheets in a new workbook, the kind of menus, the type of calculation, whether or not to allow cell drag and drop, and how you want the screen to look.

Drag and drop allows you to copy and move the active cell contents with a mouse and without using a menu. When drag and drop is activated, the

3

lower-right corner of the active cell will contain a small box. Point on the small box with the mouse pointer and the pointer will change like this:

As you drag the small box, the contents of the cell are *copied* to adjacent rows or columns, in what is knows as a *fill* operation. If you drag the active cell border instead of the small box while drag and drop is activated, you *move* the contents of the active cell to any other cell. Finally, if you press and hold Ctrl while dragging the active cell border, you *copy* the contents of the active cell to any other cell.

Data Menu   The Data menu is used to sort a list on a sheet, to select information from a list based on filtering criteria, to enter data into a database using a form, and to apply functions such as summing to a database. Also, for existing lists, you can create a table, consolidate and group data ranges on one or multiple sheets, and interactively transform the layout of data with PivotTables.

Window Menu   The Window menu allows you to open another window for the active workbook, to arrange all open windows so they can be seen on the screen, and to hide or unhide a window. Additionally, you can split a sheet into different size horizontal and vertical panes and freeze a pane so that, for example, column headings remain in place while the rest of the sheet is scrolled. Finally, you can select among open windows.

Dialog Boxes   Menu options with an ellipsis (...) after them require that, after choosing the option, you enter additional information or choose from additional options. For example, you may have to enter the name of a file to save or choose the type of cell alignment you want. In these situations, a dialog box opens and asks you for more information or to make a further choice. As you saw in Chapter 1, a dialog box employs one or more devices for collecting information. Many of the devices are illustrated in the Options dialog box shown in Figure 3-3. The Options dialog box also shows two devices you may not have seen before: across the top of the dialog box is a set of *tabs* that, when you click on them, allow you to select different options, and in the middle of the dialog box is a *spinner* that allows you to increase or decrease a number by clicking on either the up or down arrow.

You will have many opportunities in the chapters that follow to become more familiar with Excel's menus and their related dialog boxes.

Toolbars

The third and fourth bars from the top, just under the Menu bar, are toolbars. The Standard toolbar is on top and the Formatting toolbar is below, as shown here:

A toolbar provides a number of tools and buttons to quickly do tasks that would take several steps with the menus, or could not be done at all. Table 3-1 lists the tools on the Standard toolbar. Table 3-2 lists the tools on the Formatting toolbar. A toolbar is used only with a mouse, so if you don't have a mouse, you can turn off (Hide) the two default toolbars with the View Toolbars option.

There are 13 possible toolbars in Excel 5 when first installed, but you can add your own. These and their purposes are summarized in Table 3-3.

You can display one, none, or multiple toolbars, as you choose. To select a toolbar other than one of the two initial ones, choose Toolbars from the

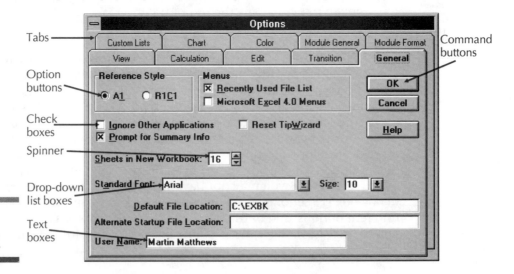

Options
dialog box
Figure 3-3.

Standard Toolbar		
Tool	**Description**	**Purpose**
	New Workbook	Creates a new workbook
	Open File	Displays the Open File dialog box
	Save File	Saves the active workbook
	Print	Prints selected sheets from the active workbook
	Print Preview	Displays the Print Preview window, which shows how each page will look when printed
	Spelling	Checks the spelling in documents
	Cut	Removes a selected range or object and places it on the Clipboard
	Copy	Copies a selected range or object and places it to the Clipboard
	Paste	Pastes the contents of the Clipboard to a selected location
	Format Painter	Pastes only the format of a selected range
	Undo	Reverses the last action
	Repeat	Repeats the last action
	AutoSum	Creates a SUM function in the active cell with a reference to the contiguous range of numbers (either in the column above or in the row to the left)

Tools on the
Standard
Toolbar
Table 3-1.

Standard Toolbar		
Tool	**Description**	**Purpose**
 f_∞	Function Wizard	Assists you in using functions
 A/Z↓	Sort Ascending	Sorts a list from lowest to highest value (A to Z) in the column with the active cell
 Z/A↓	Sort Descending	Sorts a list from highest to lowest value (Z to A) in the column with the active cell
	ChartWizard	Assists you in creating charts
	Text Box	Allows you to position a text box in which you can enter text and place it anywhere on the sheet
	Drawing	Displays the Drawing toolbar
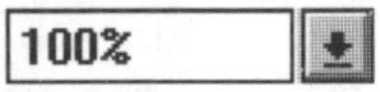 100% ↓	Zoom Control	Changes the scale so you can see smaller or larger areas of the sheet
	TipWizard	Assists you with tips for using Excel more efficiently
 \?	Help	Changes the mouse pointer to a question mark. Clicking with the question mark on a command or screen area displays context-sensitive help

Tools on the
Standard
Toolbar
(*continued*)
Table 3-1.

View menu; the Toolbars dialog box will appear. Alternatively, you can open the Toolbars Shortcut menu by clicking on a toolbar with your right mouse button. The dialog box lists the available toolbars and provides a button to create customized toolbars.

Formatting Toolbar		
Tool	**Description**	**Purpose**
Arial	Font	Applies a font to selected cells
10	Size	Selects the size for the selected font
B *I* <u>U</u>	Bold, Italic, and Underline	Applies and removes their respective type styles
Alignment buttons	Alignment	Applies left, center, and right alignment, respectively, to selected cells
Center button	Center Across Columns	Horizontally centers text in the leftmost cell across selected columns
$	Currency Style	Applies the current currency style to the selected cells
%	Percent Style	Applies the current percent style to the selected cells
,	Comma Style	Applies the current comma style to the selected cells
+.0 .00	Increase Decimal	Increases the number of decimal places in the selected cells by one when clicked on
.00 +.0	Decrease Decimal	Decreases the number of decimal places in the selected cells by one when clicked on
Borders button	Borders	Applies a border style to the selected cells
Color button	Color	Applies a color to selected cells or objects
Font Color button	Font Color	Applies a color to the characters in the selected cells

Tools on the Formatting Toolbar
Table 3-2.

3

Toolbar	Purpose
Auditing	Find errors, track cell relationships, and attach notes to cells
Chart	Create and format charts
Drawing	Create lines, rectangles, ellipses, arcs, and arrows, and add text
Formatting	Format cells, cell contents, and other objects
Forms	Add controls to sheets and charts to allow interaction with user
Full Screen	Expand the document window to take up all of the screen except for the Menu bar
Microsoft	Switch between Excel and other Microsoft applications such as Word
Query and Pivot	Retrieve and analyze both Excel data and external data
Standard	Access the most frequently used commands, like new, open, save, and print
Stop Recording	Stop macro recording
TipWizard	Display tips on current operations
Visual Basic	Insert a new Visual Basic module, create menus, and record and debug macros
Workgroup	Find Excel files, share them within a workgroup, and work with Scenarios

The Default
Toolbars for
Excel 5
Table 3-3.

The Customize dialog box provides a list of tool categories and displays the tools that are associated with each category. You can drag individual tools to an existing toolbar to add to it or to almost anywhere on the screen to create a new toolbar. Microsoft Excel provides over 210 predefined tools and 28 that you can define. All of these tools are displayed in the Customize dialog box.

Toolbars can be moved, sized, and arranged to suit your individual needs. They provide a fast and flexible means to make working in Excel as efficient as possible. A complete listing of tools by toolbar can be found in Appendix B.

The Formula Bar

Beneath the toolbars is the Formula bar, which is shown in Figure 3-4. On the left side of the Formula bar is the *reference area,* which contains the address of the currently active cell on the sheet. For example, when the cell address C10 is displayed, this tells you that the currently active cell is in the third column (column C) and the tenth row. If you give cell C10 the name Sales_Qtr1, then Sales_Qtr1 will appear in the reference area while cell C10 is the active cell.

If cell C10 is currently the active cell and you want to name it, you simply click in the reference area and type the name. This is much simpler than using the Name option of the Insert menu. You can also use the reference area to move the active cell to a particular location by typing the cell address in the reference area and pressing Enter. On the right of the reference area is a drop-down arrow that, when you click on it, opens a list of reference names in the current workbook like this:

By opening the list of names and clicking on a name, you will move the active cell to the cell referenced by the name.

While you are in the process of selecting a range of cells—C3:E4, for example—the reference area tells you the number of rows and columns being selected—2RX3C in the example, for 2 rows by 3 columns. The reference area also has some specialized uses with charts and during several operations. These are discussed later in this book with the related topics.

On the right side of the Formula bar is the *edit area,* where you enter and edit text, numbers, and formulas for the active cell. If you are entering or editing a cell's contents, three boxes appear to the right of the reference area: the Cancel box with an "X" in it, the Enter box with a check mark in it, and the Function Wizard tool. Clicking on the Cancel box cancels any changes you made in the edit area and returns a cell's original contents. The Cancel box is similar to pressing Esc. Clicking on the Enter box is like pressing Enter. Doing so transfers the edited contents of the edit area to the active cell. The Function Wizard tool is used to place a function in the edit area.

When you begin typing in an empty cell, the letters or numbers that you type go into both the cell itself and the edit area of the Formula bar. In many instances the cell is not wide enough to display all of what you type, but the edit area expands to the maximum 255 characters a cell can hold. After you complete the entry and press Enter, the edit area still displays the cell's contents. If you move to another cell and then come back, the edit area again displays the cell's contents.

If you want to change or edit the contents of a cell, you do so in the edit area of the Formula bar. First make the cell you want to edit active by clicking on it or by using the direction keys. You then click on the Formula bar, or you can press the F2 function key to activate the edit area. While you are entering or editing a cell's contents, a vertical line appears in the edit area, as shown in Figure 3-4. You'll remember from Chapter 1 that this line is called the insertion point. Characters you type, or a function if you add one, are added to the immediate left of the insertion point. When the mouse pointer is in the edit area, it becomes an I-beam. The I-beam is thin enough to be inserted between characters in the edit area. By placing the I-beam between two characters and clicking, you move the insertion point to where you clicked. You can then insert new characters between existing characters.

While you are making an entry, what you see in the edit area and what you see in the cell are the same. Once you complete a formula entry, the formula is displayed in the edit area, while the cell displays the value resulting from the formula. If the entry is a number or text, it is displayed in both the Formula bar and the cell. Figure 3-4 shows a formula in the edit area.

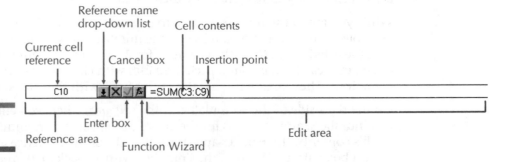

Figure 3-4.

The Status Bar

The Status bar, at the bottom of the Excel window, displays messages on the left and up to six keyboard indicators on the right, as shown here:

Edit		EXT	CAPS	NUM	SCRL	OVR	FIX

Message Area   The message area has several uses that are determined by what you are doing. If you highlight a menu name or a menu option, the message area displays a brief description of the menu or option. If you point on a tool in a toolbar, the message displays an explanation of what the tool does. When you are using a dialog box or have an alert message on the screen, the message area tells you how to get help. At other times the message area serves as a mode indicator that tells you what Excel is doing. The most common mode is Ready, meaning that Excel is ready for you to make an entry or use a menu. The other modes are shown with their meanings in the following table:

Mode	Meaning
Calculate	With manual calculation, this indicates that a change has been made to the workbook and it needs to be recalculated.
Circular	A circular reference has been detected where, through whatever route, a cell is referencing itself. One of the cells in the circular path will be identified.
Edit	An entry is being edited in the Formula bar.
Enter	Data is being entered into the active cell.
Filter	A database is being filtered.
Point	You are being asked to highlight a cell or group of cells for use in a formula.
Ready	Excel is ready for a command or entry.
Recording	The macro recorder is recording what you are doing with Excel.

Keyboard Indicators   The keyboard indicators on the right of the Status bar tell you that a certain key has been pressed or that a certain condition exists. The status indicators and their meanings are as follows:

Indicator	Meaning
ADD	The Add key, Shift-F8, has been pressed to make multiple selections.
CAPS	Caps Lock has been pressed for uppercase letters.
END	The End key has been pressed. When an arrow key is pressed, the active cell will go to the last occupied cell in the direction of the arrow.
EXT	The Extend key, F8, has been pressed to extend a selection.
FIX	The Fixed Decimal option has been chosen from Tools Options Edit. This adds a fixed number of decimal places on all numeric entries, similar to an adding machine.
NUM	The Num Lock key has been pressed, enabling the numeric keypad to be used for the entry of numbers.
OVR	The Ins key has been pressed while a cell is being edited, turning on overtype mode instead of the normal insert mode.
SCRL	The Scroll Lock key has been pressed, causing the direction keys to move the entire sheet instead of just the active cell.

Excel's Use of the Keyboard

Between the mouse and the screen, you can accomplish a lot in Excel. Eventually, though, you will need to use the keyboard, if for no other reason than to enter the text and numbers that represent the body of your work. As you are typing on the keyboard, you may find it easier to also use the keyboard to accomplish other tasks that you could also accomplish with the mouse. Also, there are some keyboard shortcuts that are just plain faster than the alternatives. This section covers how you can use the keyboard for uses other than typing text and numbers.

Most keyboards can be divided into three areas. On the left or along the top are a set of function keys, F1 through F10 or F12. You use these keys to give Excel commands, such as to recalculate the workbook or display a help screen. In the center of all keyboards are the normal typewriter keys, and on the far right of most keyboards is a set of direction keys, either superimposed on or separate from the numerical keypad. The direction keys can move the active cell around the sheet and the highlight bar down a menu. These three regions of the keyboard are discussed in the following sections.

Direction Keys

Eight keys comprise the direction keys: the four arrow keys ⬇, ⬅, ➡, and ⬆ plus (Home), (End), (Pg Up), and (Pg Dn). These keys, either alone or in combination with (Ctrl) and (Shift) on the typewriter keyboard, can move you quickly and easily anywhere on the sheet. Also, the same keys can move you within the menus and dialog boxes and within the Formula bar for cell editing. With mouse capability, the use of the direction keys is not as important as it would otherwise be. Nevertheless it is important to understand how the direction keys can be used.

The direction keys have the three-dimensional task of moving the active cell up or down a column, left or right along a row, and back and forth through the sheets. Excel has ways to do this one cell at a time, one screen at a time, to the beginning or end of contiguously occupied cells, or to the first or last cell in the active sheet.

Using Direction Keys in a Workbook

The easiest way to learn about the direction keys is to use them. Try them now with the following instructions. Your computer should be turned on, Excel should be loaded (see Appendix A for loading procedures), and you should be looking at the blank workbook screen shown in Figure 3-1, with cell A1 selected as the active cell. If your Scroll Lock light is on, press (Scroll Lock) to turn it off.

Moving One Cell at a Time   The simplest way to move about a single sheet is to go from cell to cell. The four arrow keys perform this task, as shown with the following instructions:

1. Press ➡. The active cell moves one cell to the right, to cell B1.
2. Press ⬇. The active cell moves down one cell, to cell B2.
3. Press ⬅. The active cell moves one cell to the left, to cell A2.
4. Press ⬆. The active cell moves up one cell, to cell A1—where you started from.

The four arrow keys are the most frequently used of the direction keys. Their function is to move you one cell in any direction, as you saw in the one-cell square you just made.

Moving One Screen at a Time   Moving one cell at a time can be slow if you have very far to go. The next set of direction keys moves you a screen at a time. (Depending on the type of display and display adapter you have and the mode you are running them in, one "screen" may be different than that described here—it may be larger or smaller.) Make a larger square now with these keys.

1. Press (Pg Dn). The active cell and the portion of the sheet shown in the window move down one window-height to the first cell in column A beyond that originally shown—cell A17 (depending on the type of monitor you have and how your screen is set up, you may go to a different row).

2. Press (Alt)-(Pg Dn) (press and hold (Alt) while pressing (Pg Dn)). The active cell and the portion of the sheet shown in the window move to the right one window-width to the first cell in row 17—cell J17 (again, yours may be different).

3. Press (Pg Up). The active cell and the portion of the sheet shown in the window move up one window-height to cell J1.

4. Press (Alt)-(Pg Up) (press and hold (Alt) while pressing (Pg Up)). The active cell and the portion of the workbook shown in the window move to the left one window-width to cell A1.

You have completed another square, one window high and one window wide. (Pg Dn) and (Pg Up) are used frequently, but (Alt)-(Pg Dn) and (Alt)-(Pg Up) are often forgotten.

Moving Around the Periphery of the Active Sheet   The set of keystrokes used to move around the periphery of the active sheet requires that you first enter some information on the sheet to establish what is "active." Simply type the information in one cell using the typewriter keyboard, and then press one of the arrow keys to go to the next cell. You can then use a set of direction keys to move around the periphery of the sheet. Try that now.

1. Type **a** and press (→). The letter "a" is placed in cell A1, and the active cell moves to B1.

2. Do the *combination* of typing **a** and pressing (→) six more times. The final active cell is H1.

3. Type **a** and press (↓). The letter "a" is placed in cell H1, and the active cell moves to H2.

4. Do the *combination* of typing **a** and pressing ⬇ nine more times. The final active cell is H11. Your screen should look like Figure 3-5. Now use the direction keys to jump around the information you just entered.

5. Press ⟨Home⟩. The active cell jumps to cell A11—the cell on the far left of the current active area.

6. Press ⟨↑⟩, ⟨Ctrl⟩, and ⟨→⟩. The active cell jumps to H10—the cell on the far right of the current active area.

7. Press ⟨Ctrl⟩-⟨↑⟩. The active cell jumps to cell H1—the cell at the top of the active area.

8. Press ⟨Ctrl⟩-⟨←⟩. The active cell jumps to cell A1—the far left again.

9. Press ⟨Ctrl⟩-⟨→⟩. The active cell jumps to cell H1—the far right again.

10. Press ⟨Ctrl⟩-⟨⬇⟩. The active cell jumps to cell H10—the bottom again.

11. Press ⟨Ctrl⟩-⟨Home⟩. The active cell jumps to cell A1.

12. Press ⟨Ctrl⟩-⟨End⟩. The active cell jumps to cell H10.

The ⟨Ctrl⟩ plus direction key combinations are very powerful and extremely useful. You will use them often if you do not have a mouse. You can

3

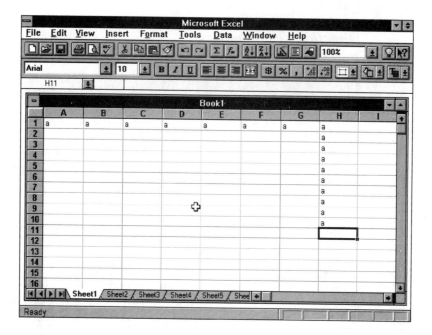

Screen after entries
Figure 3-5.

accomplish the same movement around the periphery of the active area with the [End] key. Try that next.

1. Press [End]-[↑]. The active cell jumps to cell H1.
2. Press [End]-[←]. The active cell jumps to cell A1.
3. Press [End]-[→]. The active cell jumps to cell H1.
4. Press [End]-[↓]. The active cell jumps to cell H10.
5. Press [Ctrl]-[Home]. The active cell jumps to cell A1.
6. Press [End]-[Home]. The active cell jumps to cell H10.
7. Press [Ctrl]-[Home] to return to cell A1.

You can see that the functions performed with [End] and a direction key almost duplicate those performed with [Ctrl] and a direction key. The two exceptions are [End]-[Home], which has the opposite effect from [Ctrl]-[Home], and [End]-[End] which doesn't exist.

Moving One Sheet at a Time   Excel provides only two keys to move you across sheets. These are [Ctrl]-[Pg Dn] and [Ctrl]-[Pg Up] to move you *down* through the stack of sheets (from Sheet1 to Sheet2) and back up again. Try these on your own.

Direction Key Summary
The following table summarizes the direction keys:

Key	Moves the Active Cell
[→] or [←]	Right or left one column.
[↑] or [↓]	Up or down one row.
[Pg Up] or [Pg Dn]	Up or down one window height.
[Alt]-[Pg Dn] or [Alt]-[Pg Up]	Right or left one window width.
[Ctrl]-[↑] or [Ctrl]-[↓]	Up or down to the first intersection of blank and nonblank cells.
[Ctrl]-[→] or [Ctrl]-[←]	Right or left to the first intersection of blank and nonblank cells.
[Home]	Left to column A in the row with the active cell.
[End]	Turns on end mode. When a direction key is next pressed, the active cell moves to the last occupied cell in the direction of the arrow.
[Ctrl]-[Home]	Up and/or to the left to cell A1.

Key	Moves the Active Cell
Ctrl-End	Down and/or to the right to the lowest and rightmost occupied cell.
End-Home	Down and/or to the right to the lowest and rightmost occupied cell.
Ctrl-Pg Dn	Down one sheet (from Sheet1 to Sheet2).
Ctrl-Pg Up	Up one sheet (from Sheet2 to Sheet1).

3

Function Keys

The function keys F1 through F10 or F12 are located on the top or left of most keyboards. With function keys you can give Excel special commands using one or several keystrokes (when you press the key itself or in combination with Shift, Ctrl, or Alt while pressing a function key). Many of the commands performed by the function keys are used only in certain circumstances and could not be easily demonstrated here. Try several that can be easily demonstrated now with the instructions that follow. You will use many of the others later in the book. Following the instructions is a table that summarizes each function key.

Using Function Keys

The following instructions assume that you are picking up where you left off in the previous section. The active cell is A1, and the sheet is the one in which you entered the "a"s. Excel should be in Ready mode. Also, from your previous work, cell A1 should contain the letter "a." If you do not have an "a" in A1, type it now and press Enter.

1. Press F1 (Help). A help window opens with the Help Contents screen shown in Figure 3-6. From this window you can select subjects on which to get help.

2. Double-click on the help window Control-menu box or press Alt-Spacebar and press C to return to the sheet. A1 is still the active cell.

3. Press F2 (Edit). The edit area of the Formula bar becomes activated to edit cell A1. Also, an insertion point appears just to the right of the letter "a" in the cell.

4. Press Backspace. The "a" is removed.

5. Type **b** and press Enter. Excel is returned to ready mode, and "b" replaces "a" in cell A1.

6. Press Alt-Backspace (Undo). The contents of cell A1 are again "a."

7. Press F5 (Goto). A dialog box appears, asking for the address to jump to.

8. Type **e14** and press Enter. The active cell jumps to cell E14.

9. Press Ctrl-Home. The active cell returns to cell A1.

10. Press F12 (Save As) or Alt-F2 if you have only ten function keys. The File Save As dialog box opens.

11. Type **ch3** (for Chapter 3) and press Enter to save the active workbook with the filename CH3.XLS (the .XLS extension is automatically added by Excel).

12. Press Shift-F11 (New Sheet) or Alt-Shift-F1 if you have only ten function keys. A new sheet appears (probably Sheet17).

Both F2 (Edit) and F5 (Goto) will get increasingly heavy use as you learn Excel. Also useful, although not a function key, is Alt-Backspace (Undo). The Undo command reverses many commands if they were the last thing you did. You can even undo an Undo command. Note that Undo *cannot* undo File commands, such as saving a file on top of another.

Several function keys are shortcut keys for menu options. For example, F3 is the Insert menu's Name option Paste command and F12 is the File menu's Save As option.

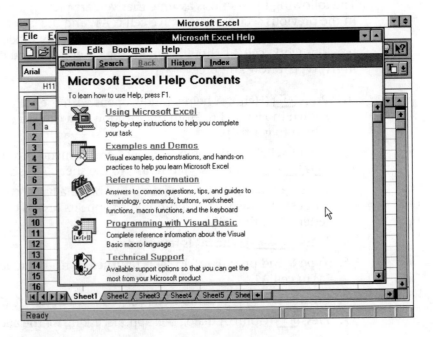

Excel Help
Contents
screen
Figure 3-6.

Function Key Summary

Table 3-4 provides a summary of the function performed by each function key. The keys are discussed further in later sections of this book dealing with the particular subject to which they apply. For example, `F11` (New Chart) is covered in the discussion on charting in Chapter 7.

Key	Name	Function
`F1`	Help	Opens a help window
`Shift`-`F1`		Displays context-sensitive help
`Alt`-`F1`	New	Creates a new chart sheet
`Alt`-`Shift`-`F1`		Inserts a new sheet
`Alt`-`Ctrl`-`F1`		Creates a new Excel 4 macro sheet
`F2`	Edit	Activates the Formula bar for editing
`Shift`-`F2`	Note	Allows entering, editing, or deleting a note that is to be attached to the active cell
`Ctrl`-`F2`	Info	Displays a window containing information about the active cell
`Alt`-`F2`	Save	Opens the File Save As dialog box
`Alt`-`Shift`-`F2`		Saves the active document
`Alt`-`Ctrl`-`F2`		Opens the File Open dialog box
`Alt`-`Ctrl`-`Shift`-`F2`		Opens the File Print dialog box
`F3`	Name	Opens the Paste Name dialog box
`Shift`-`F3`		Opens the Function Wizard dialog box
`Ctrl`-`F3`		Opens the Define Name dialog box
`Ctrl`-`Shift`-`F3`		Opens the Create Name dialog box
`F4`	Absolute	While editing, makes a cell address or reference name absolute, mixed, or relative
`F4`		When not editing, repeats the last action taken
`Ctrl`-`F4`	Close	Closes the active document window
`Alt`-`F4`		Closes the application window (Excel)

A Summary of Function Keys and the Functions They Perform
Table 3-4.

Key	Name	Function
F5	Goto	Moves the active cell to the cell address, reference name, or file entered
Shift-F5	Find	Opens the Edit Find dialog box
Ctrl-F5	Restore	Restores the size of the active document window
F6	Pane	Moves the active cell clockwise to the next pane
Shift-F6		Moves the active cell counter-clockwise to the previous pane
Ctrl-F6	Window	Moves the active cell to the next document window
Ctrl-Shift-F6		Moves the active cell to the previous document window
F7		Checks spelling
Ctrl-F7	Move	Sets up the active document window to be moved with the direction keys
F8	Extend	Toggles the extension of the current selection
Shift-F8	Add	Allows adding a second selection to the current selection
Ctrl-F8	Size	Sets up the active document window to be sized with the direction keys
F9	Calculate	Recalculates all open documents
Shift-F9		Recalculates the active sheet
Ctrl-F9	Minimize	Minimizes the active workbook
F10	Menu	Activates the menu bar
Shift-F10		Displays the shortcut menu for the active cell
Ctrl-F10	Maximize	Maximizes the active workbook
F11	New	Creates a new chart sheet
Shift-F11		Creates a new sheet

A Summary of
Function Keys
and the
Functions
They Perform
(*continued*)
Table 3-4.

Key	Name	Function
Ctrl-F11		Creates a new Excel 4 macro sheet
F12	Save	Opens the File Save As dialog box
Shift-F12		Saves the active document
Ctrl-F12	Open	Opens the File Open dialog box
Ctrl-Shift-F12	Print	Opens the File Print dialog box

A Summary of Function Keys and the Functions They Perform (*continued*) **Table 3-4.**

3

Quitting Excel

You are done with Excel for this chapter. Use the following instructions to leave it:

1. Double-click (click twice in rapid succession) on the Excel Control-menu box in the upper-left corner of the Excel application window. (From the keyboard, press Alt-Spacebar-C.)

2. Click on No (or press N) to not save the workbook again. You will return to the Windows Program Manager window.

3. If your Program Manager is an icon, restore it and double-click on the Program Manager's Control-menu box, and click on OK to end the Windows session. You will return to DOS.

4. If you desire, you can now shut off your computer following your normal shutdown procedure.

CHAPTER

4

ENTERING AND EDITING INFORMATION

In several examples in Chapter 3, you practiced entering and editing information. Entering text and numbers is a simple matter of typing what you want in each cell. You can edit as you type or, after you have completed the entry, you can come back and edit it. These operations are more subtle than they first appear, however, and their considerable power demands further study.

Typing on a Sheet

All information that you type on a sheet is stored in cells. While there are a lot of cells, each cell can hold only 255 characters. The normal practice is to place only a single number or a short text string (usually much smaller than 255 characters) in a cell and to spread most of the information over many cells, using the row and column structure to organize it.

A cell on a sheet can hold either a number or text (which can be both numbers and letters), but not both. You therefore must decide what a cell will contain before you make an entry. If you decide an entry is text, you can then decide if it will be aligned to the left, right, or center in the cell. If an entry is a number, you can determine not only the method of alignment but also the type of format, such as numbers as dollars, percentages, or dates. You can also determine the font, size, and style of type and whether an entry has a border around it. Finally, when you complete an entry and determine what you want to do next, you can move the active cell in order to accomplish your purpose.

Entering Text Versus Numbers

Whether your entry is considered a number entry (including dates, times, and formulas) or a text entry (letters as well as numbers) depends on the characters you type and the context in which they appear. If your entry contains only numbers or these numeric symbols

. , ( ) % $ E e / :

then the entry is a number. If the entry contains anything other than a number or numeric symbol, or the symbols are not in the proper context, the entry is text. For example, if you start an entry with the letter "E," Excel will interpret the entry as text, whereas "1.25E + 2" will be considered a number since the letter "E," in this context, is a numeric scientific notation symbol.

General Alignment

When Excel recognizes that text is being typed, it automatically left-aligns the text in the cell (meaning that it pushes text up against the left side of the cell). When you enter a number, Excel automatically right-aligns it in the cell (pushes it up against the right side). This default alignment—left-aligned text and right-aligned numbers—is called *general alignment*. General alignment also aligns logical values (TRUE or FALSE) and error values (#NUM!, for example) in the center of a cell. With the Format menu's Cells option, or the shortcut menu Format Cells option, or the Formatting toolbar, you can align text, numbers, and logical or error values to the left, in the center, or to the right, as you choose. You can also change the horizontal or vertical alignment of your cell contents or even change the orientation of how your data is displayed.

Figure 4-1 shows some of the various types of alignment.

Typing Text

Try entering some text now, following these instructions:

1. Load Windows and Excel as discussed in Appendix A. A blank workbook should appear on the screen. (If you still have the work you did in Chapter 3 on your screen, double-click on the workbook's Control-menu box to close the workbook. Then, from the File menu choose New and click on OK to create a new workbook.)

2. As shown in Figure 4-1, you'll want to have the Standard and Formatting toolbars displayed on the screen as well as the Status bar.

   If your screen looks different from Figure 4-1, click on the View menu and make sure that there are check marks beside Formula bar and Status bar. If not, click on these options to place a check mark beside them. Then choose Toolbars (also on the View menu) to open the dialog box and, if they are not already checked, click on both the Standard and Formatting options to display both of these toolbars. Then click on OK.

4

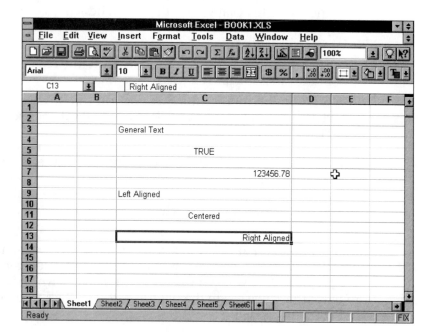

Types of
alignment
Figure 4-1.

3. In cell A1, type **This is some text**. As you type you will see the letters go into the edit area of the Formula bar as well as into cell A1. If you make a mistake, press ⌷Backspace⌷ to correct it. The top-left corner of your screen should look like this:

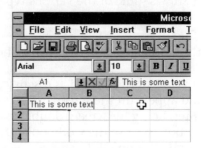

You will notice that the text in A1 spills over into cell B1. Also notice whether the blinking line, which is the insertion point where new text will be entered, is in the cell or the edit area. The default is for it to be in the cell, so that is probably where you'll see it. If not, you will see in the following step how to change the position of the insertion point.

4. Press ⌷Enter⌷ or click on the Enter box (the check mark) in the Formula bar. The edit area is deactivated (the insertion point, Cancel box, Enter box and Function Wizard disappear). Also, the text in A1 adjusts itself so you can see it all, although it does not fit completely in a single cell and seems to occupy cell B1 as well. The active cell remains in A1. (If your pointer moves to A2, you'll see why in the following step as well as how to change it.)

   The choice of whether you type text into the cell or the edit area is set in the Tools menu. You will set that next.

5. Click on the Tools menu, then click on Options near the bottom of the menu, and again on the Edit tab. You will see the dialog box in Figure 4-2.

The first option, Edit directly in Cell, controls whether your editing changes will be entered into the active cell or into the edit area located in the Formula Bar. The default is to edit directly into the cell and that option should be checked. If it is not, click on it to place a check mark next to the option.

Another option that you will be using is the Move Selection After Enter. This controls whether the active cell moves to the cell below the current cell after ⌷Enter⌷ is pressed, or whether the active cell remains where it is. The default is to move the active cell to the cell below it. You'll want to turn that option

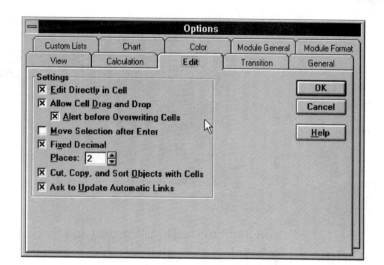

The Edit tab in
the Options
dialog box
Figure 4-2.

4

off so that the active cell will stay where it is. (There are other ways to immediately move to another cell with one keystroke, as you will see in a moment, and Enter is the only way to complete an entry and stay in the cell.) If the Move Selection after Enter option contains a check mark next to it, click on it to remove it.

6. After you have verified that the Edit directly in Cell option is checked and that the Move Selection After Enter option is not checked, click on OK to return to the sheet.

    You may also have observed that the text in A1 is left aligned, unless your alignment default has been changed. You did not align it; it is left-aligned because of Excel's general alignment default. Look at the various types of alignment next and see how you can change them.

7. Press ↓ on the right side of your keyboard. The active cell moves to A2.

8. Type **left** and press →. The word "left" is left-aligned in cell A2, and the active cell moves to B2. Notice how you completed the entry and moved to the next cell in one keystroke as promised. Arrow keys are used as movement keys, and ← is a preferred alternative to Enter.

9. Type **right** and press Enter. The word "right" also is left-aligned in B2.

10. To experiment with aligning text, click on Format in the Menu bar and then on the Cells option.

11. Click on the Alignment tab and the Alignment dialog box opens, as shown in Figure 4-3.

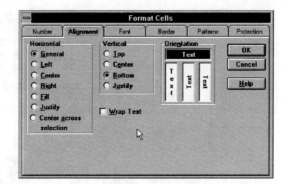

The Alignment
tab in the
Format Cells
dialog box
Figure 4-3.

12. Click on Right in the Horizontal list and then click on OK to close the dialog box. The word "right" in cell B2 is right aligned. Press → to move to C2.

13. Type **center** and click on the Enter (check mark) box in the edit area. Then click on the Center tool in the toolbar, as shown here:

The word "center" is centered in C2. You can see that both Left align and Right align are also available from the toolbar. Press → to move the active cell to D2.

14. Type = and press Enter. With the mouse pointer in cell D2, click the right mouse button to get the shortcut menu. Click on Format Cells, then on the Alignment tab and Fill option, and finally OK. The = is repeated to fill D2, less one space. Press →.

15. Type **555-1234** and press →. Cell E2 contains a left-aligned text string in the format of a phone number.

16. Type **=555-1234** and press Enter. The equal sign turns this into a formula, and the cell contains the right-aligned number –679 (the results of 555 minus 1234). From this example, you can see that to make this entry a number that can be used in calculations, you must tell Excel it is a formula.

Your screen should now look like Figure 4-4. The contents of F2 look different in the edit area and in the cell.

You may have noticed that use of the Format menu, Cells option, and Alignment tab combination to align a cell is cumbersome. The shortcut

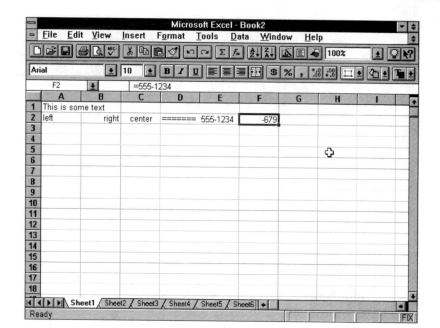

Text and
numbers on
the sheet
Figure 4-4.

menu is only a little better. The alignment tools in the Formatting toolbar
are by far the fastest way to change the alignment of one or more cell's
contents. You can align the contents of a group of cells by highlighting the
group before selecting the alignment from the shortcut or Format menus, or
by clicking on an alignment tool.

Column Width Versus Contents Width

The first entry you typed in the previous exercise, shown in cell A1 in Figure
4-4, is wider than the cell—it hangs over into cell B1. Because there is
nothing in B1, the full text from A1 is displayed. If you enter something in
B1, the text in A1 would appear truncated, limited by the width of column
A. Try that now:

1. Press Ctrl-Home and then → to move the active cell to B1.

2. Type **new text** and press Enter. The words "new text" fill B1 and, on the
   screen, truncate the text from A1. The full original entry is still in A1;
   you just can't see it all in the cell.

The top portion of your screen should look like the following:

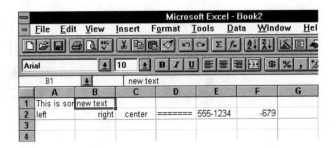

The width of a sheet area is considered in terms of column width, not cell width. You cannot adjust the width of an individual cell, only the width of the column that contains the cell. In Chapter 6 you will see how to change the width of both individual columns and a range of columns.

Entering Numbers

Excel gives you a lot of flexibility in entering numbers. You can enter numbers with commas, dollar signs, percent signs, and scientific notation. Excel converts your entry into a number with up to 15 significant places. You can then format the cell to display the number in any way you choose, no matter how you entered it.

Try entering several numbers now:

1. Press ⟨Home⟩ and then press ⊕ four times. The active cell moves to A5.
2. Type **1,234,567** including the commas. The number appears in the edit area.
3. Press ⊕. The number disappears from the edit area, and 1,234,567 appears in A5. If you entered the same number with an added digit—1,234,567.8, for example (you must do this on a new entry; editing the entry just made will round the decimal to 1,234,568)—it would be too wide to fit in the standard column width. The cell would fill with a series of number signs (#). The edit area would display the full number, with the exception of the commas. Unlike text, numbers do not hang over the adjacent cell when they are too big for the column they are in. The column must be widened for the number to show.
4. Type **3.25** and press ⊕. The number 3.25 appears in A6 as entered.
5. Type **$3.25** and press ⊕. The number $3.25 appears in B6.
6. Type **3.25%** and press ⊕. The number 3.25% appears in C6.
7. Type **3 1/4** and press ⊕. The number 3 1/4 appears in D6.
8. Type **32.5E–1** and press ⊕. The number 3.25E+00 appears in E6.

9. Type **=e6** and press (Enter). The number 3.25E+00 appears in F6. You entered a formula by placing = in front of a cell reference, and you used it to put up the contents of cell E6 in cell F6.

Figure 4-5 shows how your screen should look when you have completed these entries.

Being able to enter commas, dollar signs, percent sign, and fractions is an important capability, even if you must change them later. When you enter numbers that you are copying from a source that has dollar signs, commas, and so on, you might naturally type the symbols as well as the numbers. In some spreadsheet packages you would get an error with such an entry. Excel gives you the flexibility to enter numbers with or without symbols.

Some formatting symbols can be entered by clicking on the Formatting tools in the toolbar. For example, if you type **325**, press (Enter), and then click on Currency Style (the $) in the Formatting toolbar, Excel will format the cell as $325.00. Convenient toolbar formatting is also available to apply the Percent and Comma styles and to increase or decrease the number of decimal places.

Using the Numeric Keypad

Although you were not told to do so, it is likely that you entered the numbers in the previous exercise using the numeric keys at the top of the

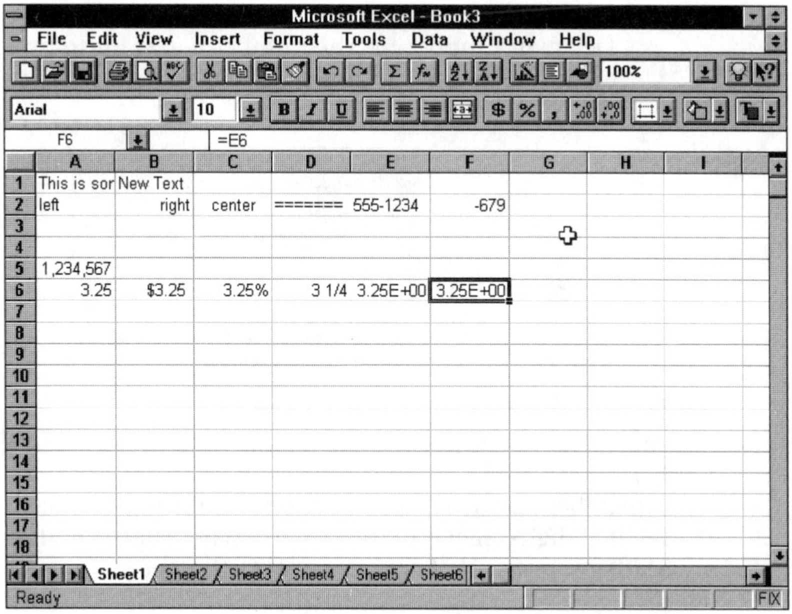

4

Text entries

Figure 4-5.

typewriter keyboard. Unless you are using a laptop or notebook computer, you also have a numeric keypad on the right of your keyboard. The numeric keypad performs two functions: movement of the active cell when [Num Lock] is off and numeric entry when [Num Lock] is on. The [Num Lock] key is at the top of the numeric keypad. Most keyboards have a light to tell you if it is on or off, and Excel has a status indicator, NUM, that appears at the bottom of the window to tell you when [Num Lock] is on.

When [Num Lock] is on, the numeric keypad can be used for numeric entry like a 10-key adding machine. The direction keys on the numeric keypad are no longer available when [Num Lock] is on, unless you press and hold down [Shift] while pressing a direction key. Enhanced keyboards have a set of direction keys, separate from the numeric keypad, that can be used at any time. Throughout your work with Excel, you may use either set of keys for numeric entry without affecting the results.

Fixing the Number of Decimal Digits

If you are experienced using a 10-key adding machine or calculator and like the ability to enter numbers with a fixed number of decimal digits without typing the decimal point, you can do that with Excel. To set up a fixed number of decimal digits, follow these steps:

1. Select the Tools menu, choose Options, and then click on the Edit tab.

2. If there is no "X" next to the Fixed Decimal option, click on the check box. An "X" appears in the box.

3. To change the number of decimal digits after clicking on the Fixed Decimal, simply type the number you want to use. The applicable part or your Options Edit dialog box should look like this:

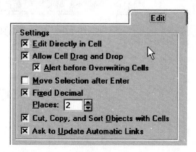

4. Click on OK to close the dialog box and return to the sheet.

Remember that when you turn on this setting you have a fixed number of decimal digits in every number you type. Typing **6** gives you .06, and typing **3500** gives you 35. Excel remembers this the next time you start it up—it is a permanent setting until you turn it off. There is a status indicator, FIX, that appears in the Status bar to remind you that you have fixed the number of decimal digits.

Try it out now. Type a number like **3675** in a blank cell and press (Enter). If you left 2 as the number of decimal places, you will get 36.75 without having to type the decimal point. For the sake of the work you do with this book, you need to turn the Fixed Decimal option *off.* Use the instructions above to do so now.

Completing an Entry and Moving to the Next Cell

As you saw in the previous examples, you can complete an entry either by pressing (Enter) or by pressing one of the direction keys, depending on where you want to go next. If you use (Enter), the active cell remains the cell in which you made the entry (unless you did not turn off the Move Selection after Enter option described above). After using (Enter) you can then use one of the direction keys to move where you wish. If you want to go directly to another cell, you can save one keystroke by pressing a direction key to complete the entry.

You are not limited to the arrow keys. You can complete an entry using (Home), (End) plus arrow keys, or even (Pg Up), (Pg Dn), (Ctrl)-(Pg Up), or (Ctrl)-(Pg Dn)—it just depends on where you want to go next.

Making Changes

Making changes to the information you are entering or have entered into Excel is a task at least equal in importance to making the initial entry. One of the beauties of an electronic spreadsheet is that changes can be made easily and often. You can make changes in four ways. First, you can replace a completed entry in a cell by typing over the original entry. The original entry disappears and the new entry takes its place. Second, you can edit an entry as you are entering it. Third, immediately after completing an entry you can remove it and restore the previous contents of the cell by pressing one of the Undo keys ((Alt)-(Backspace) or (Ctrl)-(Z)), clicking on the Undo tool in the Standard toolbar, or choosing Undo from the Edit menu. Fourth, with the cell you want to change selected as the active cell, you can edit a completed entry by pressing (F2) or clicking in the edit area of the formula bar. The next several sections explore the last three of these methods.

Editing During Entry

Editing during entry has a Simple mode that uses the (Backspace) or (Esc) key and an Edit mode using the (F2) (Edit) key. In the Simple mode, while you are entering data, press (Backspace) to erase one or more characters to the left of the insertion point, or press (Esc) to erase the entire entry. After pressing one of these keys, you can continue to type the corrected or new entry. When you press (F2) (Edit), the mode indicator in the Status bar changes from Enter to Edit, and you have full use of the edit keys. (The Edit mode of editing is the same during and after entry, and is explained in the "Editing After Entry" section coming up shortly.) Now try simple mode editing:

1. Select the File menu, choose New, and click on OK to create a new workbook.

2. Type **Spring 92**. "Spring 92" appears in the edit area.

3. Press (Backspace) and type **4**. "Spring 92" changes to "Spring 94" in the edit area.

4. Press (Esc) and type **Fall 94**. "Spring 94" changes to "Fall 94" in the edit area.

5. Press (Enter). The edit area closes and "Fall 94" is the final contents of cell A1.

Simple mode editing is just that, simple. You will use it frequently to correct the many small errors made during data entry.

Using Undo

The Undo option, which is available from the Edit menu, the Undo tool, and from its shortcut keys (Alt)-(Backspace) or (Ctrl)-(Z), is a great lifesaver. It lets you remove the last thing you did and restore the sheet to the way it was before you did it. The definition of "the last thing you did" is usually whatever happened between two Ready modes, but there are exceptions. One important thing you *cannot* undo is the effect of recalculating the sheet. You can undo an Undo. When you are editing, you can use Undo to reverse the last change you made to a cell. Try that now:

1. Make sure the active cell is still the cell in which you last entered "Fall 94."

2. Type **Spring 95** and press (Enter). "Spring 95" replaces "Fall 94" in cell A1.

3. Click on the Undo tool in the Standard toolbar (or press (Alt)-(Backspace) or (Ctrl)-(Z)). "Fall 94" is restored in A1.

When you make a mistake that requires retyping, immediately choose Undo from the Edit menu, click on the Undo tool, or press (Alt)-(Backspace) or (Ctrl)-(Z) and see if it restores the sheet to its condition before the mistake. It cannot make the situation worse.

Editing After Entry

To edit a cell entry after it is completed, highlight the cell and press ⟨F2⟩ (Edit). The Edit mode indicator is displayed, and in the cell the insertion point is blinking on the right of the entry. The ⟨←⟩, ⟨→⟩, ⟨Home⟩, and ⟨End⟩ keys all move the pointer within the entry so that individual characters can be changed. Pressing ⟨Backspace⟩ removes the character to the left of the insertion point, and pressing ⟨Del⟩ removes the character to the right of the insertion point. Also, you can press ⟨Ins⟩ to switch from *Insert mode,* which pushes existing characters to the right of new characters, to *Overtype mode,* which replaces existing characters with new ones at the insertion point. Try editing now:

1. Make sure the active cell still contains "Fall 94."

2. Press ⟨F2⟩ (Edit). The edit area is activated (the Cancel box, Enter box, and Function Wizard appear in the Formula Bar) and the insertion point appears to the right of 94 in the cell.

3. Press ⟨Home⟩. The insertion point moves to the left of Fall.

4. Type **Summer/**. The entry becomes "Summer/Fall 94."

5. Press ⟨←⟩ four times. The insertion point moves so it is between the two "m"s in Summer.

6. Press ⟨Ins⟩. The OVR mode indicator is displayed in the Status bar and the insertion point covers the second "m."

7. Type a period (**.**). The period replaces the second "m" in "Summer."

8. Press ⟨Del⟩ twice. The "e" and "r" are removed from "Summer."

9. Press ⟨End⟩ and then ⟨←⟩ three times. The insertion point moves to the right of the second "l" in "Fall."

10. Press ⟨Ins⟩. The OVR mode indicator is removed, and Excel returns to Insert mode.

11. Type **/Win.**. The entry now reads "Sum./Fall/Win. 94."

12. Press ⟨End⟩. The insertion point moves to the right end of the entry.

13. Type **/95**. The entry now has "/95" at the right end. The top part of your screen should look like this:

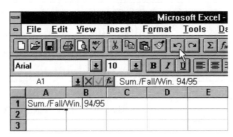

14. Press (Enter). The edit area closes and A1 reflects the final entry. Unlike in Enter mode, where you can press a direction key to finish editing a cell and move to a new cell, Edit mode requires you to press (Enter) and then press a direction key to move to another cell.

Edit Keys

The functions of the keys you can use while editing are summarized here:

Key	Function
(Alt)	Activates Menu bar
(Alt)-(Enter)	Inserts carriage return into cell
(Alt)-(Backspace), (Ctrl)-(Z)	Undo previous action
(Backspace)	Deletes the character to the left of the insertion point
(Ctrl)-(Alt)-(Tab)	Inserts tab into cell
(Ctrl)-(←) or (Ctrl)-(→)	Moves the insertion point one word to the left or right in the entry
(Ctrl)-(Del)	Deletes text from the insertion point to the end of the current line
(Ctrl)-(')	Inserts the formula in the cell above the active cell at the insertion point
(Ctrl)-(`)	Switches between displaying formulas and values in the active cell
(Ctrl)-(")	Inserts the value in the cell above the active cell at the insertion point
(Ctrl)-(;)	Inserts the current date in your computer at the insertion point
(Ctrl)-(:)	Inserts the current time in your computer at the insertion point
(Del)	Deletes the character to the right of the insertion point
(End), (Ctrl)-(End)	Moves the insertion point to the right end of the current line of the entry
(Enter)	Completes editing, closing the edit area, and leaving the active cell where it was originally

Key	Function
Esc	Cancels any changes made during editing, closes the edit area, and returns the original contents to the active cell
F2	Activates the cell and edit area so you can do a character-by-character edit on the active cell
Home, Ctrl-Home	Moves the insertion point to the left end of the current line of the entry
Ins	Switches between Insert mode, in which newly typed characters push existing characters to the right, and Overtype mode, in which newly typed characters replace existing characters
← or →	Moves the insertion point one character to the left or right in the entry
↑ or ↓	Moves the insertion point between lines in the edit area if the entry occupies more than one line; otherwise does nothing
Shift-← or Shift-→	Selects the previous character or the next character
Shift-Ctrl-→ or Shift-Ctrl-←	Selects the next or previous word
Shift-Tab	Completes cell entry and moves to previous cell
Tab	Completes cell entry and moves to next cell

4

Editing with the Mouse

Editing with the keyboard is effective and often preferred if you are doing a lot of typing. However, the mouse has two benefits: you can jump immediately to the characters you want to change by clicking on the spot, and you can easily highlight characters to be deleted or otherwise changed by dragging across them. These benefits often make it worthwhile to take your hands off the keyboard to use the mouse. Try it now:

1. The workbook that you have on your screen should have "Sum./Fall/Win. 94/95" in cell A1.

2. Click on E12. The active cell moves to E12.

Assume that you want to edit cell A1. If it were not in the home position, it would take at least two keystrokes to get there. With the mouse, it only takes one movement.

3. Click on A1. The active cell moves to A1.

4. Drag across "Sum./" in the edit area, *not* in the active cell. (Place the mouse pointer on the "S" in "Sum" in the edit area, not in cell A1. Press and hold the mouse button while dragging the mouse pointer across "Sum./," then release the mouse button.) "Sum./" in the edit area is highlighted.

   Notice that the mouse pointer becomes an I-beam when you move it into the edit area. This allows you to click between characters in placing the insertion point. Notice, also, that you activated the edit area as soon as you pressed the mouse button while pointing anywhere in the edit area.

5. Press ⌈Del⌉. The edit area contains "Fall/Win. 94/95."

6. Drag across the period following Win. Type **ter**. The edit area now reads "Fall/Winter 94/95," as shown here:

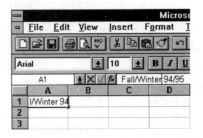

7. Click on E12 to carry on where you started.

The ability to jump quickly to a cell, make a change by clicking and dragging in the edit area, and then jump back to where you started is powerful. Use it for awhile and you will agree.

Using Menus

Menus are the primary means of having Excel perform tasks such as opening a file, copying a group of cells, printing a workbook, or creating a chart. All menu operations begin in one of three ways:

✦ Clicking on a menu name.

✦ Clicking the right mouse button or pressing ⌈Shift⌉-⌈F10⌉ to access the shortcut menu.

✦ Pressing ⌨Alt, ⌨F10, or ⌨/ to activate the Menu bar and then either typing the underlined letter in the menu name or pressing the direction keys to move to the correct menu name and pressing ⌨Enter.

Any of these methods causes the selected menu to be displayed. Once a menu is displayed, you have three ways to choose an option:

✦ Clicking on an option name.

✦ Typing the underlined letter in the option name (this does not work in the shortcut menu, but you can type the first letter of the option, possibly several times if more than one option starts with the same letter, to highlight it and then press ⌨Enter).

✦ Using the direction keys to highlight an option and pressing ⌨Enter.

4

Once you have selected a menu and chosen an option, either the option immediately executes (as does Save in the File menu or Copy in the Edit menu, for example) or a dialog box opens. When you choose a menu option with an ellipsis (...) after it, a dialog box opens. Excel (and all Windows applications) uses a dialog box to get further information. Dialog boxes give you additional choices and provide the means for you to type in a name or some other information.

Take a look now at how the menu system works. In the following instructions the keyboard and mouse methods are intermixed to give you experience with both.

1. Press ⌨Alt. The File menu name in the Menu bar is highlighted if your document is not maximized. If it is, the document Control menu is highlighted. Notice that the Status bar at the bottom of the window gives you a brief description of the File (or Control) menu.

2. Press ⌨Enter. The File menu opens.

3. Press ⌨↓, and then press it several more times. Notice that the Status bar provides a description of each option as you highlight it.

4. Press ⌨→. The File menu closes and the Edit menu opens.

   Some of the options in the Edit menu are light gray or dimmer than the other options. These options are not available because they are not applicable to the current situation. For example, some of the light gray options in the current Edit menu deal with pasting (copying something from the Clipboard to the sheet). To paste you must *first* cut or copy, both of which place something from the sheet onto the Clipboard.

5. Press ⌨→ slowly several more times. Look at each of the menus in succession. Use ⌨↓ to explore some of the options that interest you. Look at the Status bar to see the description of the option.

6. Press ➡ until the Help menu is selected. Then press it once more. If your document window is maximized, the Restore button will be highlighted and you need to press ➡ once more. The highlight wraps around and opens first the Excel Control menu; then, if you keep pressing ➡, it opens the workbook Control menu and finally returns to the File menu where you started.

    If you continue to press ➡, you continue to move around the set of menus. If you press ⬅ you move the other way. If you press ⬆ or ⬇, you move up or down through the options in the menu that is currently selected. The direction keys provide a sure way to move through the menu system.

7. Press Esc twice. The Menu bar is deactivated and you return to the sheet.

8. Click on A1, and it becomes the active cell. A1 should still contain Fall/Winter 94/95. If it doesn't, type anything in it (your first name, for example) so you have something to work with in the next set of instructions.

9. Click on Edit in the Menu bar. The Edit menu opens.

10. Click on Copy in the Edit menu. The Edit menu closes, and a blinking *marquee* appears around the active cell, A1, telling you that a copy of the contents of A1 is ready to be placed in some other cell on the sheet.

11. Click on C5 to select it as the destination of the copy. Press Enter to complete the copy. C5 now contains a copy of A1's contents.

12. Press Alt to activate the Menu bar.

13. Press E to open the Edit menu.

14. Press T to choose the Cut option. The Edit menu closes and again a blinking marquee forms around the active cell, in this case C5. The contents of C5 are placed on the Clipboard.

15. Click on E9 and press Enter. The contents of C5 are moved to E9. In other words, the contents of C5 are removed (cut) and placed (pasted) in E9.

16. Drag on the Edit menu until Undo Paste is highlighted (point on the Edit menu name in the Menu bar, press and hold the mouse button while dragging the highlight bar down to the Undo Paste option, and then release the mouse button). The contents of E9 are restored to C5 and a blinking marquee reappears. With Edit Undo Paste you have completely undone step 15 and you are back where you were when you completed step 14, except that E9 is the active cell.

17. Drag to highlight cells C5, C6, C7, and C8 (place the mouse pointer on C5, press and hold the mouse button while dragging the mouse pointer over C6, C7, and C8, and then release the mouse button). Cells C5 through C8 are highlighted.

18. Click on the Edit menu to select it, and then click on Fill. A submenu is displayed. Choose Down by pressing (Enter). The contents of C5 are replicated in cells C6 through C8, as shown in Figure 4-6.

19. With the mouse pointer in the C5 through C8 highlighted range, click the right mouse button to display the shortcut menu. Click on Clear Contents. The contents of C5 through C8 are cleared from the screen. (If you find the highlight disappearing from the screen when you bring up the shortcut menu, you have not placed the cursor in cells C5 through C8 before pressing the right mouse button.)

20. Click on the Edit menu to select it, and then click on Undo (the word Clear is added to the Undo option to let you know which command you are restoring). The screen returns to its original look, as in Figure 4-6.

4

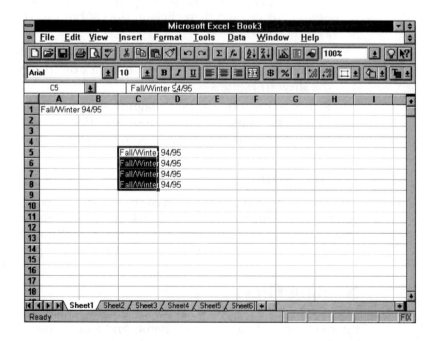

Results of choosing Fill Down from the Edit menu

Figure 4-6.

Cut, Paste, Copy, and Undo all have tools in the Standard toolbar which can easily and quickly be used instead of the Edit or shortcut menu.

The majority of menu options are discussed in later chapters of this book. The same procedures are used throughout the book to open a menu and choose an option. The ease and flexibility with which you can make a menu selection and choose an option constitute one of Excel's and Windows' greatest strengths. Most instructions in this book do not tell you to use one method or the other when using the menus; you can choose the method you prefer.

Using Zoom

Another feature is Zoom. Much like a camera lens, Zoom allows you to increase or decrease the magnification of the sheet. You can choose from five magnifications provided by Excel or create your own, anywhere from 10 to 400 percent of normal (normal being 100 percent). Zoom changes only the size of the sheet; the window that contains the sheet stays the same.

The Zoom option is available both from the View menu and with the Zoom Control tool on the Standard toolbar. Try some zooming exercises now.

1. Click on the View menu, and then click on the Zoom option. The Zoom dialog box appears. Choose 200 percent magnification by clicking on its option button, and then click on the OK button. The sheet is enlarged as shown in Figure 4-7.

2. Again, click on the View menu, choose Zoom, but this time choose the Custom option button. Type **40** and click on the OK button to display the sheet in Figure 4-8.

3. Return to the original sheet magnification by clicking on the Zoom Control tool on the Standard toolbar. Click on 100% to return the sheet to its normal magnification as seen earlier in Figure 4-6.

Using Files

Files provide a permanent record of the workbooks you build. To create a file you must save the workbook on a disk. If a workbook is not saved, it is lost when you leave Excel or turn off the computer (although you will receive a warning if you try to leave Excel without saving an open workbook).

Naming Files

When you save a file you must give it a name. The full name of a file has three components: a path, a filename, and an extension. The *path* is made up of the drive letter (for example, C: or A:) and one or more directory

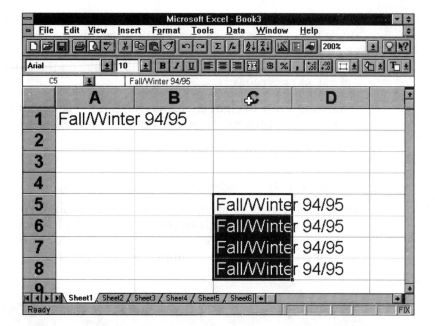

Sheet enlarged
in size
Figure 4-7.

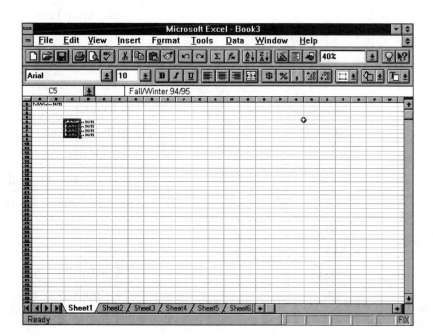

Sheet reduced
in size
Figure 4-8.

names—for example, \WINDOWS\ or \EXCEL\PLAN\. The drive letter is a single letter followed by a colon, and a directory name is one to eight characters enclosed in backslashes. In a tree structure set of directories, several directory (or subdirectory) names make up the path, as in \PLAN\SALES\1994\.

A *filename* is one to eight characters long. A filename can consist of any combination of letters, numbers, and the following special characters:

~ ` ! @ # $ % ^ & ( ) - _ { } '

A filename may not include blanks.

The filename *extension* is optional but highly recommended. It begins with a period and can be up to three characters long. Unless you override it, Excel automatically adds an extension to all files. The extensions and the types of files they are applied to are summarized in Table 4-1.

Extension	File Type
.CSV	Comma-separated values
.DBF	dBASE II/III/IV
.DIF	Data Interchange Format (VisiCalc)
.SLK	Symbolic Line (SYLK) (MultiPlan)
.TXT	Text
.WKS, .WK1, .WK3, .FMT, or .FM3	Lotus 1-2-3
.XLA	Macro Add-ins
.XLB	Toolbar
.XLC	Chart (Excel 4)
.XLL	Commercial Add-ins
.XLM	Macro sheet (Excel 4)
.XLS	Workbook or Excel 4 Worksheet
.XLT	Templates
.XLW	Workbook (Excel 4)
.WQ1	QuattroPro/DOS
.PRN	Formatted Text (space-delimited Lotus print format)

Default Filename Extensions Created by Excel

Table 4-1.

Saving Files

You already saved a file when you worked through some steps in Chapter 3. That example required only a minimum of explanation, so use the following instructions to save another file now (even though there is not much in the workbook to save):

1. Click on File. The File menu opens, as shown here:

2. Click on Save As. The Save As dialog box opens, asking for the name of the file you want to save, as shown here:

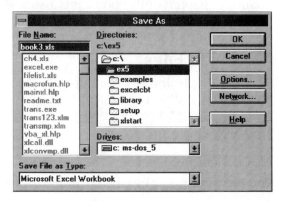

3. Type **ch4**. The name CH4 goes into the filename text box of the Save As dialog box. Excel automatically adds the workbook extension .XLS (the

current drive and directory are used if no others are specified, as described in the next section, "Using Directories").

4. Click on OK. A second dialog box is displayed which allows Summary Information to be entered. Type **Test Sheet** for the Title and click on OK. The sheet is saved in a file named CH4.XLS, and Excel returns to Ready mode.

Using Directories

In the previous example, you saved a file without specifying a drive or directory. When you do that, Excel uses the current drive and directory. Unless you have changed your default drive and directory, the current drive and directory on your computer are the ones in which you installed Excel. In other words, you store your workbook files in the same directory as your programs are stored.

While there is nothing inherently wrong with using the program directory to store data files, it is not a good idea for files that are important. You should not keep data and program files together because you can end up erasing the data files that you want to save along with all the program files that you want to erase when you install a new release of the program. Also, the number of Excel program files in the directory makes it hard to find your data files.

It is recommended that you create one or more separate directories to hold your data files. You can then specify one of these directories when saving files. Appendix A describes creating a directory named SHEET in which you can store the sample files created in this book. If you have not done that, it is recommended that you turn to Appendix A now and do it. In the remaining chapters of this book, it is assumed that you are using a path of \SHEET\ for your files.

Retrieving Files

Retrieving files is similar to saving files. You select the File menu and then choose Open. A dialog box opens that asks you for the filename, and a list of files in the current directory is displayed. Try that now with the following instructions:

1. Click on the File menu. The File menu opens.
2. Click on Open. The Open dialog box opens, as shown here:

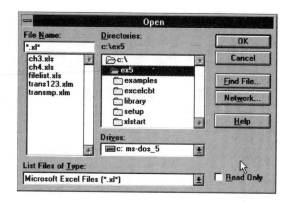

3. Double-click on ch3.xls in the files list box. The file CH3.XLS opens.

If you don't know a filename, you can use the two *wildcard characters*, ? and *. To replace a single character, use ?; to replace any number of consecutive characters, use *. For example, ?QTRPLAN.XLS refers to 1QTRPLAN.XLS, 2QTRPLAN.XLS, 3QTRPLAN.XLS, and so on, while *.XLS refers to all files with an .XLS extension.

It is important to note that when Excel opens a file, it creates a new workbook window that is added to the other workbook or document windows you have open. You can find out what document windows are open by opening the Window menu.

You can see that you currently have three windows open. If you want to go to another window, choose that window from the Window menu or click on the window if you can see it on the screen. To display all windows currently open, choose Arrange from the Window menu, click on the Tiled option button, and then click on the OK button. With the current windows available, this will produce a screen that looks like Figure 4-9.

Quitting Excel

When you are done using Excel you should formally leave it—rather than just turn off your computer—either by choosing Exit from the File menu or Close from Excel's Control menu, or by double-clicking on Excel's Control-menu box. The main reason for this is that if you have forgotten to

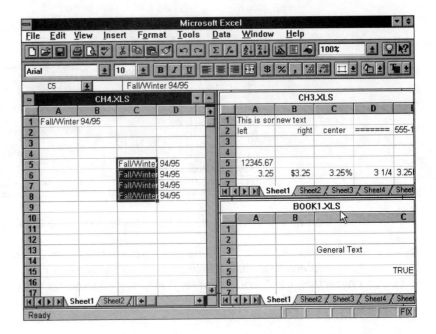

Effect of
choosing Tiled
from the
Window
Arrange dialog
box
Figure 4-9.

save a file, using one of the formal exiting options reminds you as part of the quitting process. Also, with the formal options, Excel erases any temporary files it has written, thus keeping your hard disk from getting filled with them. Use the following steps to leave Excel:

1. Double-click on Excel's Control-menu box. A Save Changes dialog box opens, as shown here:

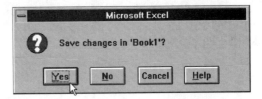

The dialog box asks if you want to save changes in Book1 and gives you four command buttons to choose from: Yes, No, Cancel, and Help. Choosing Yes saves Book1 in a file named BOOK1.XLS in the current directory. Choosing No exits Excel without saving Book1—in essence throwing away Book1. Choosing Cancel interrupts the quitting process and puts you back in Ready mode. Choosing Help provides a Help menu that explains the features of the command buttons. You can then look at Book1 and determine if you want to save it. Since you want to throw away Book1, choose No.

2. Click on No to leave Excel without saving Book1.

3. Double-click on the Program Manager's Control-menu box to leave Windows and return to DOS.

4. Click on OK to end your Windows session.

Excel and Windows shut themselves down, erasing any temporary files and returning you to the DOS prompt.

4

CHAPTER

5

CREATING A SPREADSHEET

Creating a spreadsheet is a primary function in Excel and it is the one thing every user of Excel does. The importance of learning how to do this well, and becoming familiar with as many spreadsheet tricks and shortcuts as possible, cannot be overemphasized. This chapter provides the foundation for that learning process by taking you through the actual construction of a spreadsheet to demonstrate how it is done. Chapter 6 builds upon this foundation to demonstrate additional spreadsheet capabilities in Excel.

You will benefit from following along on your computer as you read this chapter. It is not absolutely necessary to do this—there are plenty of figures and illustrations to show you what is going on—but you will learn far more by actually seeing for yourself what is happening as the spreadsheet progresses. More importantly, you will learn how to untangle yourself from the many small mistakes that everyone makes but are impossible to predict in a book.

Creating a spreadsheet has a number of steps. This chapter covers planning the spreadsheet, placing headings and titles, entering numbers and formulas, copying formulas, and completing and saving the workbook that contains the spreadsheet.

Planning a Spreadsheet

You *could* start building a spreadsheet by simply entering the necessary headings, labels, and numbers or formulas. If you need an extra row or column, you could just insert it and delete those you do not need. A great number of spreadsheets—probably the majority—are built that way. As with most things, however, a little planning up front saves considerable time as you go along. Planning involves simply visualizing what the spreadsheet will look like and making a note of it so you have something to follow as you build the spreadsheet. This takes only a few minutes and can save more time later.

Figure 5-1 shows a layout for a third-quarter budget spreadsheet that you will build in this chapter. This layout was done using Excel, but most are simply sketched on a piece of paper. To construct this layout you first need to answer four questions: How many revenue, cost of sales, and expense accounts are to be included? How many time periods are covered? What assumptions are involved? How many organizational units are to be separately included?

The answers to these questions allow you to make the following determinations regarding the layout in Figure 5-1:

+ A title will appear at the top of each sheet with a blank line under it.

+ There will be three assumptions, one each for the growth of revenue, cost of sales, and expenses. Each requires a row, and there will be a blank line following the third assumption.

+ Each column heading will take two rows and have a blank line below it.

+ The row headings will be in columns A and B and take 17 rows, 10 through 26 (five for revenue, four for cost of sales and gross income, six for expense, and two for net income).

+ The data area will occupy six columns: C through H (two for quarters, three for months, and one for the percent growth).

+ Three stores will each have their own budget, each taking a sheet, plus a total company budget sheet, so that there will be four sheets altogether.

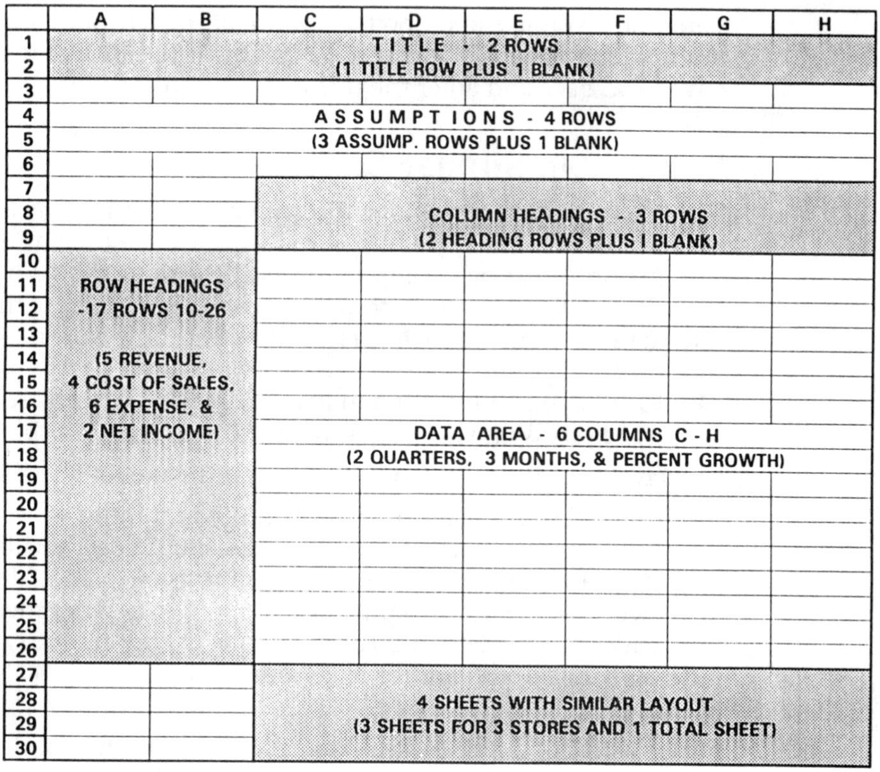

	A	B	C	D	E	F	G	H
1				TITLE · 2 ROWS				
2				(1 TITLE ROW PLUS 1 BLANK)				
3								
4				A S S U M P T I O N S · 4 ROWS				
5				(3 ASSUMP. ROWS PLUS 1 BLANK)				
6								
7								
8				COLUMN HEADINGS · 3 ROWS				
9				(2 HEADING ROWS PLUS I BLANK)				
10								
11	ROW HEADINGS							
12	-17 ROWS 10-26							
13								
14	(5 REVENUE,							
15	4 COST OF SALES,							
16	6 EXPENSE, &							
17	2 NET INCOME)			DATA AREA · 6 COLUMNS C - H				
18				(2 QUARTERS, 3 MONTHS, & PERCENT GROWTH)				
19								
20								
21								
22								
23								
24								
25								
26								
27								
28				4 SHEETS WITH SIMILAR LAYOUT				
29				(3 SHEETS FOR 3 STORES AND 1 TOTAL SHEET)				
30								

Layout for a
third quarter
budget
Figure 5-1.

5

If you cannot visualize the spreadsheet from the layout in Figure 5-1 and these decisions, don't feel bad. Sneak a look at the finished product in Figure 5-19 at the end of the chapter. As you build more spreadsheets, you will be able to visualize them more easily before you start them.

That's all there is to the planning process: constructing a rough layout of what will go where in the workbook after making a series of decisions about what is to be included and how much room it will take. Use the plan to begin building the spreadsheet by placing headings and other elements where you have decided they belong.

Placing Labels, Headings, and Titles

Where you begin a spreadsheet probably has as much to do with how you visualize or create it in your mind as with anything else. It is important to minimize the number of keystrokes and therefore the traveling you must do around the spreadsheet, but trying to reach the absolute minimum path is more trouble than it's worth and does not allow for possible errors. Therefore, start where you like and don't worry about it. Here, after preparing to use multiple sheets, you will start with the row labels, knowing that you will have to go back and enter the title and assumptions.

Setting Up Similar Sheets

Since you will be creating four sheets that will be the same except for the numbers they contain, you can save yourself some time by entering the common information on all the sheets at the same time. You do that by initially selecting the sheets to work on and then entering the common information on one of them. Select the sheets now with these steps:

1. Turn or your computer and load Windows and Excel so that a blank workbook is on your screen with Sheet1 selected as the active sheet.

2. Press and hold (Shift) while clicking on the tab for Sheet4.

   This will select sheets 1 through 4. If you want to select a set of sheets that are not next to each other, press and hold (Ctrl) while clicking on the sheet tabs. As you are working on this chapter, make sure these four sheets remain selected until you are told to deselect them and to begin work on just one sheet. This is especially important to remember if you leave this project and/or Excel and then return.

When you have multiple sheets selected, if you want to work on just one of them you need to first click on another sheet and then back on the sheet you want to work on. For now, though, leave all four sheets selected.

Entering a Column of Labels

You are now ready to begin entering information that will be placed on all four sheets. Begin that by using the following instructions to enter a column of labels (you should be on Sheet1):

1. Click on A10 to move the active cell to A10.

2. Type **REVENUE** and press ⬇. All capital letters are used to set off an account title. If you make a mistake in typing before pressing ⬇, use (Backspace) or (Esc) or to correct it. If you notice a mistake after pressing ⬇, ignore it. You will come back later and edit the labels.

3. Press (Spacebar) four times. This indents a detail account.

4. Type **Forms** and press ⬇.

5. Indent (press (Spacebar) four times), type **Supplies**, and press ⬇.

6. Type **Total Revenue** and press ⬇ twice. When you complete this instruction you should be in A15.

Using this process, type the remaining row labels as shown in Figure 5-2. Use Backspace to correct any errors you notice prior to completing an entry, but ignore errors you notice after completion. Leave the space between P/R Taxes and Other Expenses to allow for its use later. Press Enter when you complete Net Income since it is the last account.

Editing Completed Entries

Look over the row labels carefully for any typing errors. Then read through the following steps that show you how to correct any errors that you have made or might make in the future. (As an example, assume that the second "a" in "Salaries" has been left out.)

1. Click on the entry to be corrected (A20 for Salaries).

2. Move the mouse pointer to the edit area, place the I-beam at or to the right of the error (between the "l" and "r" if the second "a" is missing in "Salaries"), and click to place the insertion point. Excel enters Edit mode.

3. Correct the error. If you need to delete an incorrect character, press Del to delete a character to the right of the insertion point, or use Backspace to delete a character to the left. Then type the correction. In the case of Salaries, type the missing **a**.

4. Press Enter. Excel returns to Ready mode.

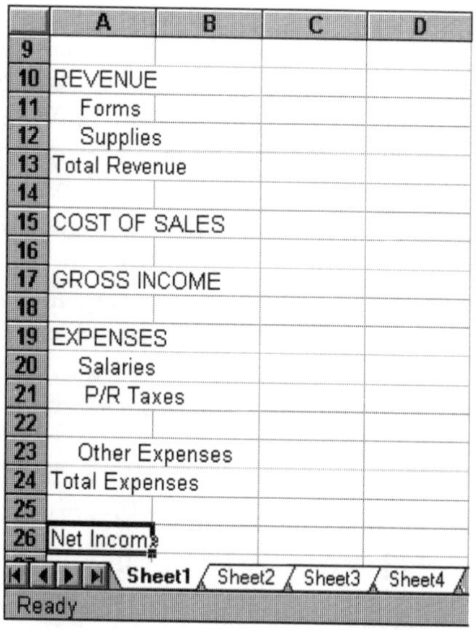

5

Completed
row labels

Figure 5-2.

Correct all of the errors you see in the row labels this same way: move the active cell to the incorrect label, go into Edit mode (you can press F2 as well as click in the edit area), get to the incorrect character using the mouse or the arrow keys, use Backspace or Del to remove characters you do not want, type characters that need to be added, and press Enter to complete the editing.

Spelling   The Spelling tool on the Standard toolbar or the option on the Tools menu provides an easier (and often more accurate!) way to edit misspelled words than the method just described. Your entire workbook is checked by default unless you select a range, a word, or an embedded chart, in which case only the smaller object is spell-checked. The Spelling dialog box, shown here, offers suggested alternative spellings to words it does not find in the standard dictionary.

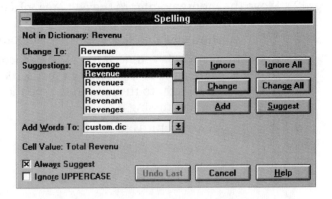

Spelling starts spell-checking the workbook from your selected cell. You can replace a misspelled word in your workbook with the suggested word in the Change To box by clicking on the Change All button (Change All changes all occurrences of the misspelled word). If you prefer one of the words in the Suggestions box, click on the word, and then click on the Change button. You can change the present use of the word or choose to change all instances throughout the workbook. Additionally, you can add to the custom dictionary commonly used words, acronyms, or abbreviations unique to your work. Finally, after you have made your selections, Excel will ask you if you want to continue spell-checking the workbook from its beginning, or stop and return to the workbook. Try the following exercise to get a feeling for the use of Spelling:

1. Click on cell A10 to move the active cell to A10.
2. Press F2 to change to Edit mode.
3. Press Backspace once to delete the "E" and change "REVENUE" to "REVENU."

4. Click on the Enter box in the editing area.

5. Press ⬇ three times. Repeat steps 2 through 4 to change "Total Revenue" to "Total Revenu."

6. Click on Spelling tool in the Standard toolbar or click on the Tools menu and then choose the Spelling option.

7. Click on "Revenue" in the Suggestions box. "Revenue" becomes highlighted.

8. Click on the Change All button. Excel substitutes the proper spelling of Revenue for the misspelled contents of cell A13; then it asks if you want to continue checking from the beginning of the workbook.

9. Click on the Yes button since "REVENU" in cell A10 is still misspelled.

10. Excel automatically corrects the spelling of "REVENU" in A10 and on the other sheets. Excel lets you know spell-checking is finished. Click on OK. Since the Spelling dialog box did not reappear, there are no additional misspelled words.

5

Long Labels

As you look at the row labels, notice that many are longer than the width of column A. They hang over into the next column. This works fine while there is nothing in the next column. As you saw in Chapter 4, if you place a label or number in the cell to the right of the long label, the label will appear to be truncated. This workbook was laid out with that in mind, providing a blank column B. In Chapter 6 you will see how columns can be widened to accommodate long labels and numbers, eliminating the need for a blank column beside them.

Centering a Title

The second step is to add a title to the sheet: Third Quarter Budget. You want to center it across the width of the sheet. Excel has the capability to center text across several columns. In this example, the title will fill columns D and E and part of F, leaving G and H on the right balanced against A and B on the left.

Follow these steps to add the title:

1. Press ⟨Ctrl⟩-⟨Home⟩ to move the active cell to A1.

2. Press ⟨Caps Lock⟩ for uppercase letters.

3. Type **THIRD QUARTER BUDGET**. Check your entry for mistakes. If you made any, either press ⟨Backspace⟩ or click in the edit area to correct them. When you are satisfied, press ⟨Enter⟩ to complete the title.

4. Drag across row 1, from column A through column H. (Move the mouse pointer to A1, press and hold the mouse button while moving the mouse

to H9, and then release the mouse button.) Row 1 from cell A through cell H is highlighted.

5. Click on the Format menu and the Cells option.

6. The Format Cells dialog box opens. Click on the Alignment tab and then on the Center Across Selection option button, and then on OK. (Alternatively, you can click on the Center Across Columns tool in the Formatting toolbar.)

7. Click on cell A1 and then press (Caps Lock) to turn off uppercase letters.

8. The top of your screen should look like this:

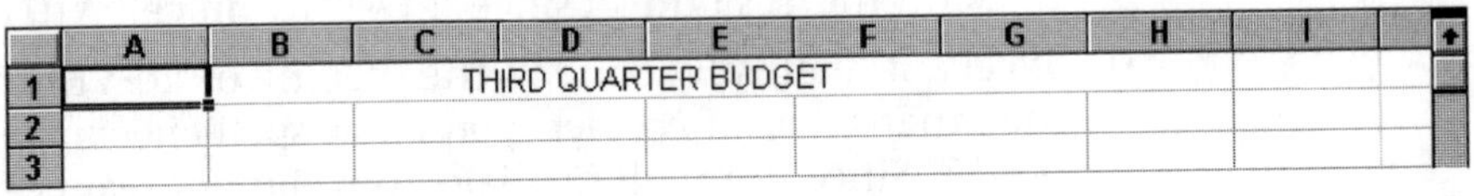

	A	B	C	D	E	F	G	H	I	
1				THIRD QUARTER BUDGET						
2										
3										

Entering a Row of Headings

Each column of data on this sheet needs a heading. Two rows have been left for this purpose, plus one row for a double line under the headings. Enter these now.

1. Click on C7 to make that the active cell.

2. Type **Second** and press ⊡.

3. Type **Quarter** and press ⊡.

4. Type **July** and press ⊡.

5. Type **August** and press ⊡.

Use Figure 5-3 as a guide to finish the remaining column headings.

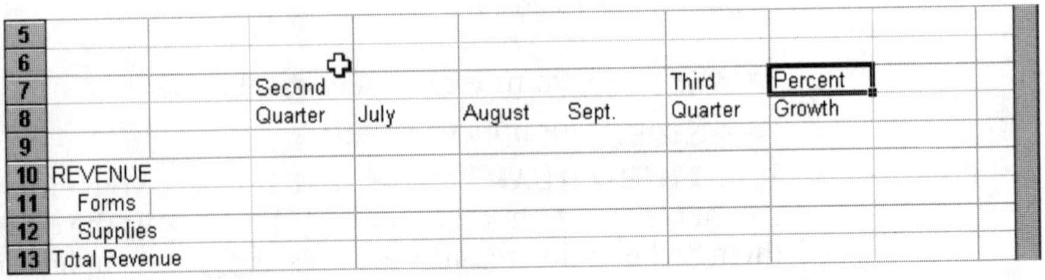

Completed
column
headings
Figure 5-3.

5								
6								
7			Second				Third	Percent
8			Quarter	July	August	Sept.	Quarter	Growth
9								
10	REVENUE							
11	Forms							
12	Supplies							
13	Total Revenue							

Placing a Border

In this exercise you'll separate your row labels and column headings with a border. With Excel you can format a cell or range of cells to have a border on any or all of its four sides. This is different from using a string of hyphens, equal signs, or vertical lines to produce a border. It is actual formatting of a cell to include a line on one or more of its sides while keeping its text or number intact. The border is placed on the grid lines, so adjoining cells share a border.

To create a double line, it's easiest to make one of the borders on a cell a double line. The line will be on the edge of the cell, not centered within it. To center a double line, you need to place a top and bottom border on a row and then reduce the height of the row to the space you want between the lines. You cannot read anything else contained in that row.

Add a double-line border across row 9 using the second method and a single-line border between columns B and C with the following instructions:

1. Drag across row 9 from column A through column H. (Move the mouse pointer to A9, press and hold the mouse button while moving the mouse to H9, and then release the mouse button.) In row 9, columns A through H are highlighted.

2. Click on the Format menu, the Cells option, and the Border tab. The Border dialog box opens.

3. Click on Top and Bottom in the Border dialog box. The thin solid line should already be selected, as shown in Figure 5-4.

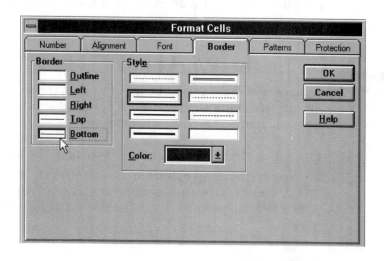

Creating a
double-line
border
Figure 5-4.

4. Click OK. The dialog box closes and a top and bottom border is placed across row 9.

5. Point on the row numbers on the left of the window at the intersection of rows 9 and 10. The mouse pointer becomes a vertical two-headed arrow with a bar in the middle. This allows you to change the height of a row.

6. Press and hold the mouse button while dragging the mouse upward to reduce the height of row 9 to roughly 1/16 inch, as shown here:

		Second				Third	Percent	
6								
7		Second				Third	Percent	
8		Quarter	July	August	Sept.	Quarter	Growth	
10	REVENUE							
11	Forms							
12	Supplies							

7. Drag down column B from row 10 through row 26. B10 through B26 are highlighted.

8. Click on the drop-down arrow of the Borders palette, which is the second tool from the right in the Formatting toolbar. The Borders palette will open.

9. Click on the right-hand vertical line, which is the fourth line style in the top row, to add a single-line border down the right side of B10 through B26. Figure 5-5 shows the results.

You can also add shading to groups of cells with the Format Cell Patterns dialog box. Figure 5-1 is an example of how such shading can be used.

Saving the Workbook

You have now done a fair amount of work in the workbook that you probably would not want to redo. It is a good idea to save your workbooks early and often, so save this workbook now.

1. Click on the File menu and Save As option. The Save As dialog box opens.

2. Type **c:\sheet\qtr3bud** in the File Name text box. (The path C:\SHEET\ is the path example discussed in Appendix A. If your path is different, use your path.) The Save As dialog box looks like this:

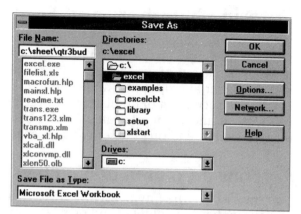

3. Click on OK. The workbook is saved on your hard disk, and Excel returns to Ready mode.

Saving a file is simple and should be done often to prevent losing your work from a power failure or human error. As you will see later in this chapter, once you have saved a file, you can resave it with the File Save command without reentering the filename.

5

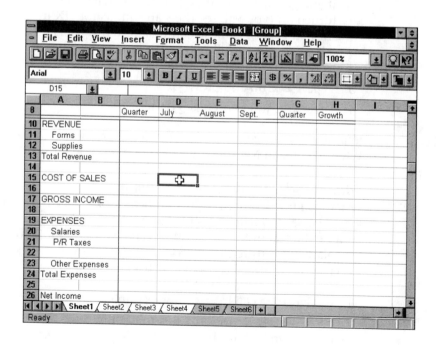

Horizontal
and vertical
borders in
place
Figure 5-5.

Entering Numbers and Formulas

Your next task is to enter the body of the spreadsheet—the numbers and formulas that make up the budget proper. Most budgets are projections based on actual sets of numbers. In this example you'll start with an actual second quarter to project the third quarter. In other words, the second quarter is an actual set of numbers, while each month of the third quarter contains a formula that calculates its value based on values from the second quarter. Start by entering the second quarter actuals.

Entering a Column of Numbers

You enter a column of numbers just as you entered the column of labels earlier: you type one number and press ⊕ to move to the next one. If you enter the numbers with commas, you will get automatic comma formatting. Follow these steps to enter the column of numbers:

1. Click on C11. The active cell moves to C11.

2. Type **87,000** and press ⊕. If you make a mistake while typing, use (Backspace) or (Esc) to correct it. If you see a mistake after completing an entry, wait until you finish the column to correct it.

   If you got 870 instead of 87,000, you have the fixed decimal feature turned on (you will see the status indicator FIX in the right corner of the Status bar). Choose Options from the Tools menu, click on the Edit tab, and then click on Fixed Decimal to turn it off. Finally click on OK to close the Options dialog box.

3. Type **147,300** and press ⊕.

4. Type **234,300** and press ⊕ twice.

In a similar manner, complete the column of numbers shown in Figure 5-6. When you reach Net Income, cell C26, press (Enter) instead of ⊕.

Editing and Completing the Column

When you finish entering the numbers, look back over them and compare what you see to Figure 5-6. It is important that the numbers be accurate because the rest of the spreadsheet is based on them. If you see an error, use the following instructions to correct it. (As an example, assume that Other Expenses was entered as 14,660 instead of 14,760.)

1. Click on the cell in error (for example, C23 for Other Expenses).

2. Click or drag on the edit area to highlight the error. The mode indicator changes to Edit. In this example you would drag across the left 6 in 14,660.

3. After dragging over any number(s) to be replaced, type the replacement number(s). For this example, type **7**. You can also use (Backspace) or (Del) to remove unwanted characters and type correct ones.

4. Press (Enter). The correct number is placed on the sheet, and Excel returns to Ready mode.

Use this procedure to correct as many errors as you have, moving up the list as you go. For the next section, you must be near the top of the list.

Building Formulas

The next three columns (D, E, and F) represent the projected amounts for July, August, and September. The amounts for each month are totally derived, using formulas based on the actual second quarter. There are 11 figures per month (including one for the blank after P/R Taxes) and three months. This means you have 33 formulas, which is a lot if you had to enter them all. Thankfully, the copying facility for formulas is very powerful in Excel, so most of the work will be done for you.

If you look ahead a month and think about the formulas there, you will notice that four of the formulas are based on other numbers in the same column—the summation formulas for Total Revenue, Gross Income, Total

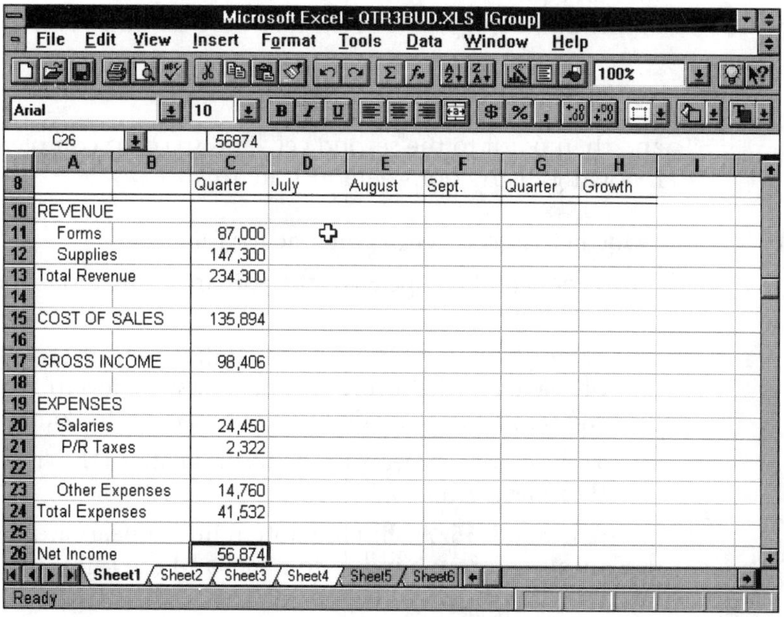

5

Completed
column of
numbers
Figure 5-6.

Expense, and Net Income. They are the same formula for all three months. It would be worthwhile doing them first in July so they can be copied to the other months.

In building the formulas, you can use + and – either from above the typewriter keyboard or on the right of the numerical keypad, and you can use either uppercase or lowercase letters. As you are building the formulas, check them carefully. It is easier to catch an error and correct it as formulas are being built rather than after the fact. The following steps build the first formula:

1. Click on D13, Total Revenue for July.

2. Type **=d11+d12** and the formula appears in the edit area and in D13. The formula adds Forms (D11) to Supplies (D12) to get Total Revenue.

3. Press [Enter]. Excel returns to Ready mode.

On the sheet you'll see only a 0 in D13, but in the edit area you'll see the formula. When numbers are available in D11 and D12, D13 will reflect them.

Pointing Versus Typing

When entering the first formula, you directly typed it as you would text or a number. This works fine when you can see on the screen the cell addresses that you want to use in the formula. Excel has another method of entering formulas that works even if the cell is not on the screen. The process is to start a formula with an equal sign (=), use the mouse or direction keys to point to the first cell in the formula, type one of the following arithmetic symbols

$$+ \ - \ * \ / \ \wedge \ \% \ \& \ : \ , \ (\ )$$

and then point to the second cell, and so on to complete the formula. The following instructions demonstrate this.

1. Click on D17, Gross Income for July.

2. Type = and = appears in the edit area. The mode indicator changes to Enter.

3. Click on D13. A blinking dotted line appears around D13. D13 is displayed in the formula under construction in the edit area and in the cell, and the mode indicator changes to Point.

4. Type – and – appears in the formula after D13. The blinking dotted line disappears from D13.

5. Click on D15. A blinking dotted line appears around D15, and D15 goes into the formula in the edit area and the cell. Your screen should look like that shown in Figure 5-7.

6. Press [Enter]. The formula is completed, and Excel returns to Ready mode.

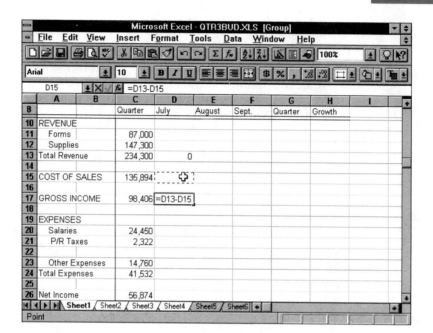

Formula under
construction
Figure 5-7.

5

Again you see only a 0 on the sheet, but the formula appears in the edit area.
The process of entering an arithmetic symbol and pointing at a cell can go
on as long as you want up to a maximum of 255 characters in a formula.
Also, there are shortcuts for formulas, as you are about to see.

Functions Versus Formulas

The next formula is for total expenses in D24. This is the sum: D20+D21+
D22+D23. You *can* type in such a formula; with an = in front, it is 16
keystrokes. You also can point to the four cells and type + four times.
Alternatively, you can use the SUM function that Excel uses for summing.
Instead of identifying each cell, you identify (type or point to) the range
encompassing the cells to be summed. Here is how it is done.

1. Click on D24. The active cell moves to D24, Total Expenses for July.

2. Type **=sum(** which will appear in the edit area and the cell. The ENTER
   indicator comes on.

3. Click on D20. The blinking dotted line appears around D20. D20 is
   displayed in the formula under construction and the mode indicator
   changes to Point.

4. Type **:** to indicate a range and the starting address of a range is
   anchored at D20. The EXT keyboard indicator comes on.

5. Click on D23. The blinking dotted line appears around the range D20:D23, and the formula includes that range, as shown in Figure 5-8.

6. Type **)** and press Enter. The completed formula is placed in D24, and you can see it in the edit area. (For future reference, you don't need to type the ending parenthesis in simple SUM formulas, just press Enter and Excel will add it automatically.)

The SUM function is the most heavily used Excel function. You will find it very useful. A rule of thumb is to use SUM if you are summing three or more cells, and to individually add if you are summing two cells. Depending on how big the cell addresses are, you may not save keystrokes with SUM on three cells, but it provides another benefit—it is expandable.

When you insert a row or column between cells that are being summed, the summation adjusts so you are still summing the same cells you originally identified, but you do not add the new cell in between. For example, if your original formula is =C4+C5+C6 and you insert a new row between rows 4 and 5, the formula adjusts to become =C4+C6+C7. The formula is still the way you specified it—the old C5 has become C6 and is so recognized in the formula. The problem is that the new C5 is not included, and usually when you insert a new cell in a range, you want that cell included in the summation.

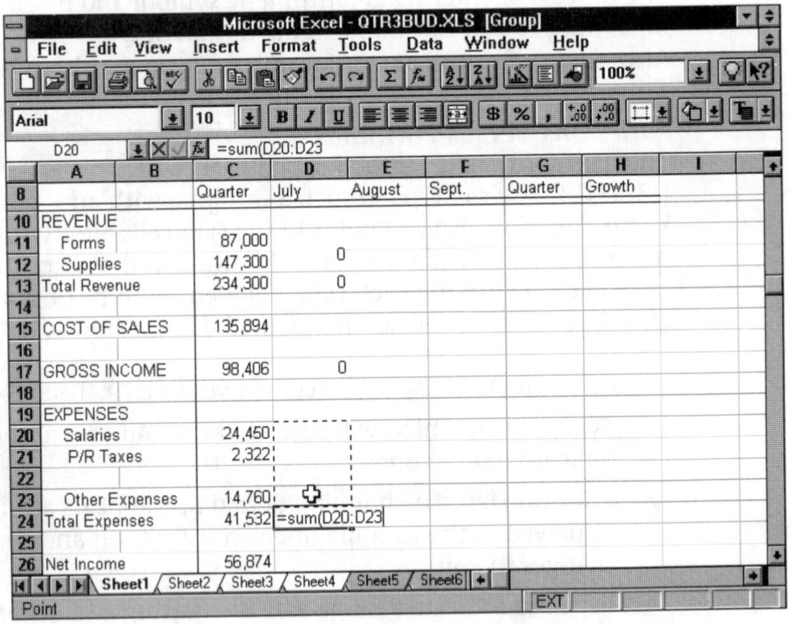

SUM formula
under
construction
Figure 5-8.

If you use SUM, the new cell *is* included. In the previous example, the original formula is =SUM(C4:C6). After inserting the new row, the formula becomes =SUM(C4:C7) and includes the new C5.

Finishing the Columnar Formulas

One columnar formula is left—Net Income in D26. Use these instructions to enter it:

1. Click on D26. The active cell moves to D26.

2. Type = and the mode indicator changes to Enter. The = goes into the cell and the edit area.

3. Click on D17. The blinking dotted line appears around D17, Gross Income. D17 is reflected in the formula, and the mode indicator changes to Point.

4. Type – and the blinking dotted line disappears from D17.

5. Click on D24. The blinking dotted line appears around D24, Total Expense, and D24 is reflected in the formula.

6. Press (Enter). The formula is completed, and Excel returns to Ready mode.

Copying Formulas

You have now completed the four columnar formulas and are ready to copy them to the columns for the other two months. You could copy the same formulas to the Third Quarter total in column G, but you will handle that differently. Also, you will be copying other formulas from August to September and you can include the totals in that copy. Therefore, the copying you do here is just from July to August, columns D to E.

You might wonder how you can copy a formula from column D—for example, =D11+D12—to column E and have it work. It would need to be changed to =E11+E12. Excel knows that and, unless you tell it otherwise, it automatically changes the formula *relative* to the location to which it is copied. Follow these steps to copy one formula, and look at it for yourself (the active cell should be D26):

1. Click on the Edit menu and the Copy option. A blinking marquee appears around D26, indicating that it is the source of the copy.

2. Click on E26. The active cell moves to E26, indicating that E26 is the destination of the copy.

3. Press (Enter). The copy finishes by placing the copied formula in E26.

5

Look now at the formula from E26 in the edit area. It is =E17–E24, as you can see here:

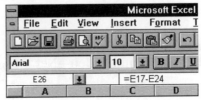

In the process of copying from D26 to E26, the formula automatically changed from =D17–D24 to =E17–E24.

Relative Addressing

This ability to adjust a formula from one location to another, as you just did, is called *relative addressing*. The formula is always adjusted relative to its location. This means that the net income formula within Excel is

="the cell 9 cells up"-"the cell 2 cells up"

Such a formula will work anywhere in the workbook. Of course, sometimes you want to fix one or more parts of an address. If the entire address is fixed—locked on to a particular cell no matter where you copy it—the addressing scheme is called *absolute addressing.* If some parts of the address are fixed and some are not, the addressing scheme is called *mixed addressing.* Mixed and absolute addressing will be discussed shortly.

Copying the Rest of the Columnar Formulas

You have seen how to copy formulas using the Edit Copy option. Now you can use the drag and drop feature to copy the rest of the columnar formulas with the mouse, following these instructions (E26 should still be the active cell):

1. First, you may have to activate Cell Drag and Drop if it isn't already activated. Click on Tools, Options, and Edit; then click on the Allow Cell Drag and Drop check box if an "X" does not already fill the check box. Click on OK. The active cell, E26, will now contain a small box in its lower-right corner, called the *fill handle.*

2. Drag on D13 through D24 (point on D13, and then press and hold the mouse button while dragging down to D24). The range D13:D24 is highlighted.

3. Position the mouse pointer on the right border of the highlighted range. Ensure the mouse pointer becomes an arrow.

4. Press and hold Ctrl while you drag (by holding down the mouse button) the range D13:D24 to range E13:E24. When you have the shaded border

in position over the range E13:E24, release first the mouse button and then [Ctrl]. The contents of range D13:D24 are copied to E13:E24, as shown in Figure 5-9.

The three remaining columnar formulas are thus copied from column D to E and adjusted relative to their new location. You can now calculate all of the totals for July and August.

When you pressed [Ctrl], you probably noticed the mouse pointer changed, as shown here:

	A	B	C	D	E	F
8			Quarter	July	August	Sept.
10	REVENUE					
11	Forms		87,000			
12	Supplies		147,300			
13	Total Revenue		234,300	0	0	
14						
15	COST OF SALES		135,894			
16						
17	GROSS INCOME		98,406	0	0	
18						

Pressing [Ctrl] while using drag and drop *copies* the contents of a cell or range to a new location. Using drag and drop without pressing [Ctrl] *moves* the contents to a new location and the original cell or range contents are cleared. Copy and move indicators are displayed in the message area of the Status bar.

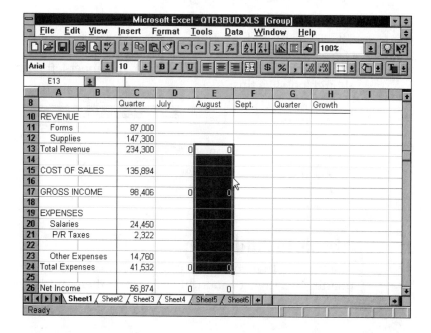

Copying a column of formulas

Figure 5-9.

Drag and drop is a powerful Excel feature. In the remaining chapters of this book, it is assumed you are using drag and drop.

Using Assumptions

The formulas used for projection in this model are simple growth formulas that use an assumption for the rate of growth. This assumption can be built into the formula, but if you want to change it, you must edit each formula that uses the assumption. Even in this small budget, that is a lot of formulas. Also, when an assumption is buried in a formula, you cannot see it without moving the active cell to the formula. A better technique is to have all assumptions in a separate table that you can see and easily change. Then the formulas that use these assumptions can reference the table.

The next step, then, is to build a table of assumptions. It consists of three growth factors, one each for revenue, cost of sales, and expenses. Enter these assumptions now with the following instructions:

1. Press Ctrl-Home and ↓ twice. The active cell moves to A3.
2. Type **Revenue Growth/Mo.** and press ↓.
3. Type **C O S Growth/Mo.** and press ↓.
4. Type **Expense Growth/Mo.** and press Enter.
5. Click on C3. The active cell moves to C3.
6. Type **.012** and press ↓.
7. Type **.013** and press ↓.
8. Type **.01** and press Enter.

When you finish the last assumption, the upper-left corner of your screen should look like this:

	A	B	C	D
1				THIRD QUAR
2				
3	Revenue Growth/Mo.		0.012	⊹
4	C O S Growth/Mo.		0.013	
5	Expense Growth/Mo.		0.01	
6				

Absolute Addressing

The formula that you use to project July from the second quarter divides the quarter by 3 (to get a monthly value) and then multiplies by 1 plus the growth rate. It is the same formula for all accounts: revenue, cost of sales, and expense. The only difference is in the growth rate you use. For the two revenue accounts, the growth rate is the same. Therefore, when you copy the formula from D11 to D12, if you do not use absolute addressing (which you'll learn more about in a moment) for the growth rate, it is changed by the copy and points to the growth rate for cost of sales. The growth rate in the formula, then, must use an absolute address. Use the following instructions to build a formula for projecting July forms revenue with an absolute address for the growth rate and then copy it for use in projecting July supplies revenue.

1. Click on D11, Forms revenue for July.

2. Type **=** and press ⏴. The mode indicator changes to Point, and =C11 is placed in the formula.

3. Type **/3*(1+** which is added to the formula under construction.

4. Click on C3. The blinking dotted line appears around C3, the revenue growth rate, and C3 is added to the formula.

5. Press F4 (Absolute). The address C3 in the edit area is changed to $C$3, an absolute address. The upper-left section of your screen should look like this:

C3		⬍ ✕ ✓ *fx*	=C11/3*(1+$C$3		
	A	**B**	**C**	**D**	**E**	**F**
1			THIRD QUARTER BUDGET			
2						
3	Revenue Growth/Mo.		0.012			
4	C O S Growth/Mo.		0.013			
5	Expense Growth/Mo.		0.01			
6						
7			Second			
8			Quarter	July	August	Sept.
10	REVENUE					
11	Forms		87,000	=C11/3*(1+$C$3		
12	Supplies		147,300			

6. Type **)** (you need to type the parenthesis here) and press Enter. The formula is completed and placed in D11, which becomes the active cell. Note that the totals immediately reflect the number.

7. Press Ctrl to start drag and drop and place the mouse pointer on the lower border of D11.

8. While holding down Ctrl, drag D11 to D12.

9. Release first the mouse button and then Ctrl to complete drag and drop. The copy operation is completed; the formula in D11 is copied to D12

and the active cell moves to D12 so you can see the resulting formula in the edit area. It should look like this:

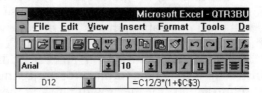

In the formula in D12, the reference to the second quarter has changed from C11 to C12, but the reference to the growth rate has remained C3. The $ in front of each part of the growth rate address means that it is an absolute reference and remains the same no matter where it is copied.

Types of Mixed Addresses

When you make an address absolute, each part of the address—the column and the row—is fixed. You also can have various combinations of fixed and relative. These are called mixed addresses. To get a mixed address, press F4 repeatedly to cycle through all four possible combinations, as follows:

If you have	Pressing F4 will give you	Type of address
C3	$C$3	Absolute address
$C$3	C$3	Mixed (fixed row)
C$3	$C3	Mixed (fixed column)
$C3	C3	Relative

F4 (Absolute) always cycles through the alternatives in the same order independent of where you start.

Editing Formulas

The formulas for projecting cost of sales and expenses are relatively the same as the formulas for projecting revenue, except for the growth rate. You can easily copy the revenue formula to cost of sales and expense and then edit the formula. Once the first expense account is corrected, it can be copied to the other expense accounts. Use these steps to do the copying and editing of July's formulas. Your active cell should be D12.

1. Press Ctrl and drag and drop D12 to D15. The active cell moves to D15 along with a copy of the contents of D12.

2. Press ⌈Ctrl⌉ and drag and drop D15 to D20. D15 is copied to D20 and the active cell moves to D20.

3. Drag across the rightmost 3 in the formula in the edit area. Excel goes into Edit mode, and the row reference to the growth rate is highlighted.

4. Type **5**. The formula reference, previously referring to the growth rate in C3, is changed to C5, as shown here:

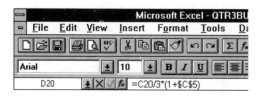

5. Press ⌈Enter⌉. The correct formula is placed in D20, and Excel returns to Ready mode.

6. Drag D20 through D23. The range D20:D23 is highlighted.

7. Click on the Edit menu, then on Fill, and finally on Down. The formula in D20 is copied to D21, D22, and D23, as shown in Figure 5-10.

   As you can see, Fill is fast way to copy when you have a range immediately next to the area to which you want to copy.

8. Click on D15 and drag across the rightmost 3 in the formula in the edit area.

9. Type **4** and the formula reference to the growth rate in C3 is changed to C4.

10. Press ⌈Enter⌉. The correct formula is placed in D15, and Excel returns to Ready mode.

A similar situation exists in the formulas that project July and those that project August. In the formulas used in July, the second quarter amounts (in the cell to the left) were divided by 3 to a monthly amount and then multiplied by the growth factor. In the formulas for August, you will multiply the July amounts (in the cell to the left) by the same growth factor. The only difference is that for July you divide the cell to the left by 3 and for August you do not. You can copy the July formulas to August and edit out the /3. Follow these steps to build the projection formulas for August:

1. Click on D11.

2. Press ⌈Ctrl⌉ and drag and drop D11 to E11. D11 is copied to E11.

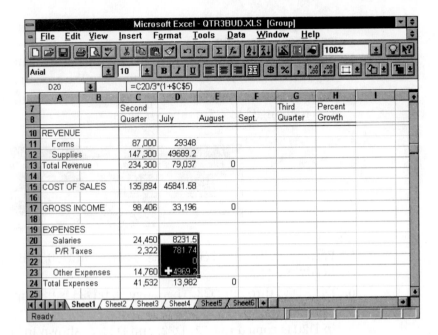

Copying
expense
formulas
Figure 5-10.

3. Drag across /3 in the formula in the edit area, press Del and then press Enter. The formula for projecting August Forms revenue in E11 is modified to remove the division by 3, as shown here:

| | E11 | | =D11*(1+$C$3) | | |
	A	B	C	D	E	F
7			Second			
8			Quarter	July	August	Sept.
10	REVENUE					
11	Forms		87,000	29348	29700.18	
12	Supplies		147,300	49689.2		

4. Press Ctrl and drag and drop E11 to E12. E11 is copied to E12.

5. Click on D15.

6. Press Ctrl and drag and drop D15 to E15. D15 is copied to E15.

7. Drag across /3 in the formula in the edit area, press Del, and press Enter. August Cost of Sales in E15 is modified to remove the division by 3.

8. Click on D20.

9. Press Ctrl and drag and drop D20 to E20. D20 is copied to E20.

10. Drag across/3 in the formula in the edit area, press Del, and press Enter. E20 is modified to remove the division by 3.

Next use drag and drop to fill a contiguous range. This feature is called *AutoFill* and uses the little square in the lower-right corner of the active cell border.

11. Point on the lower-right corner of the active cell border on E20. The mouse pointer will become a plus sign.

12. With mouse in the lower-right corner of E20, drag down through E23. The range E20:E23 is highlighted and the formula in E20 is copied to E21 through E23.

Your screen should look like the one shown in Figure 5-11. AutoFill accomplished by dragging the lower-right corner is very handy, as you can see.

Copying a Column of Formulas

Once the August projection is completed, you can copy the entire month to September. There are no differences between the relative formulas as they are now constructed in August and what is needed for September. Use the following instructions to produce September's projection.

1. Drag from E11 through E26. The entire range of Revenue, Cost of Sales, and Expense (E11:E26) is highlighted.

2. Press Ctrl and drag and drop E11:E26 to F11:F26. E11:E26 is copied to F11:F26, as shown in Figure 5-12.

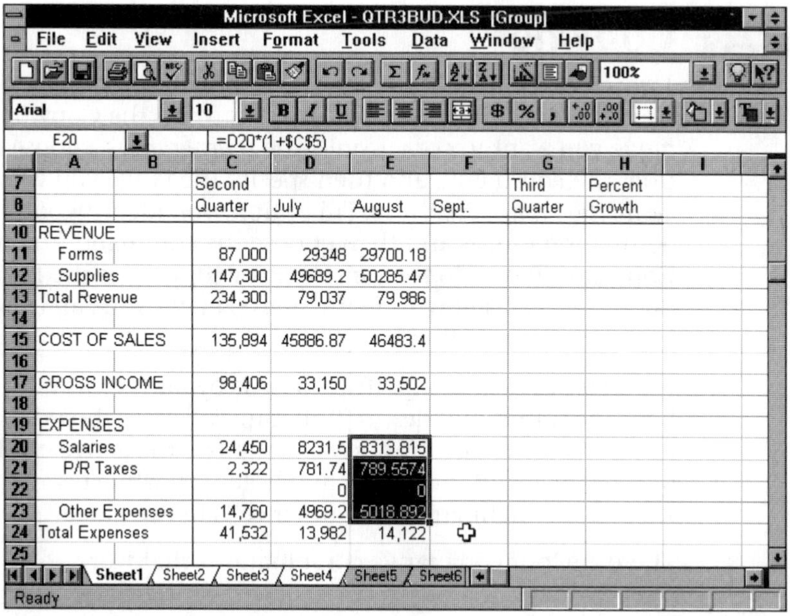

Completed
August
projection
Figure 5-11.

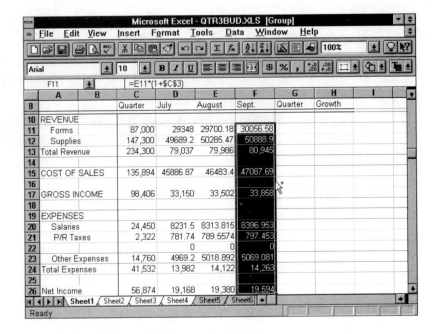

Copying
August
formulas to
September
Figure 5-12.

Here again you see the power of the Copy command. If you want to build an annual budget by month, all you have to do is build one month and copy it to the other eleven.

Copying

The copying capability is extremely valuable and quite simple. As you have seen, there are three types of copying. With the Copy option, you identify a range you want to copy from—the *source range*—choose the Copy option from the Edit menu, and then specify the range you want to copy to—the *destination range*. With the Fill option, you identify both the source and destination ranges and then choose the command from the Edit menu. The Copy option can do the same type of copying as the Fill options, but the Fill options do it faster with fewer steps. Finally you can use drag and drop for both copying and filling.

For all types of copying, the mouse is by far the easiest means of identifying both the source and destination ranges. The keyboard can, however, also be used. Using the direction keys, first move the active cell to one of the corners of the range, and then press and hold (Shift) while using the direction keys to expand the highlight to the other cells in the range.

There are four copy range combinations that work:

✦ Copying a single column to a range spanning several columns. The destination is a single row—the top row of the receiving columns.

✦ Copying a single row to a range spanning several rows. The destination is a single column—the left column of the receiving rows.

✦ Copying a single cell to another single cell, to a row of cells, to a column of cells, or to a block of cells. The destination is another cell, a row, a column, or a block.

✦ Copying a block to a second block. The destination is a single cell—the upper-left corner of the receiving range.

Figure 5-13 shows these four copy range combinations.

5

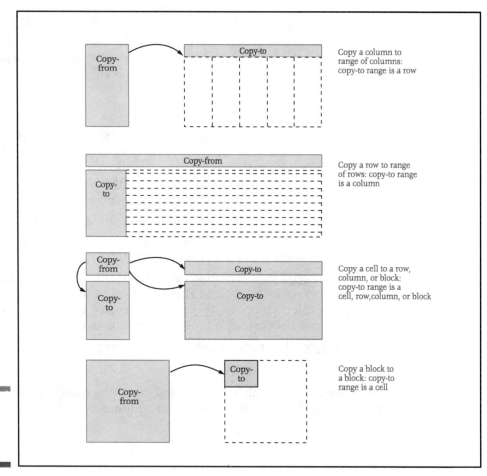

Four copy range combinations
Figure 5-13.

Completing the Spreadsheet

The basic three-month projection is now complete. Still to be added, however, are the quarterly total and percentage growth columns. Also, you will customize the individual stores, do the total company sheet, and spruce up the spreadsheet a bit before finishing this chapter.

Producing a Total

The quarterly total is just the sum of the three months. Use the SUM function again to produce a quarterly total:

1. Click on G11. The active cell moves to G11.

2. Click on the AutoSum tool in the toolbar. The edit area contains =SUM(C11:F11), as shown here:

	C11	↓X√ƒ	=SUM(C11:F11)					
	A	B	C	D	E	F	G	H
8			Quarter	July	August	Sept.	Quarter	Growth
10	REVENUE							
11	Forms		87,000	29348	29700.18	30056.58	=SUM(C11:F11)	
12	Supplies		147,300	49689.2	50285.47	50888.9		
13	Total Revenue		234,300	79,037	79,986	80,945		
14								

The AutoSum tool automatically builds a SUM formula in the active cell based on a contiguous range of numbers, either above or to the left of the active cell. In this case, the contiguous range of numbers is to the left and includes the second quarter, which you don't want. You therefore need to revise the range to be summed.

3. Press →. The range in the SUM formula changes to just D11.

4. Press Shift-→ twice. The range in the SUM formula becomes D11:F11, which is what you want to sum in the third quarter.

   Pressing Shift and any arrow key extends the selection of cells in the direction of the arrow key. This is also true with Home, End, Pg Dn, and Pg Up. Unless you press Shift, you will replace D11 with the new active cell instead of creating a range as you intended.

5. Press Enter. The summation formula is completed, and Excel returns to Ready mode.

The summation formula will be copied down the third-quarter summary column with the percentage growth in a moment.

Calculating a Percentage

The percentage growth formula is the difference between the second and third quarters divided by the second quarter. Build that formula by following these instructions:

1. Click on H11.

2. Type **=(** and click on G11. The mode indicator changes to Enter and then to Point, and =(G11 is placed into the cell and the edit area.

3. Type **–** and click on C11. –C11 is added to the formula.

4. Type **)/** and click on C11 again. The edit area now looks like this:

	C11			=(G11-C11)/C11					
	A	**B**	**C**	**D**	**E**	**F**	**G**	**H**	**I**
8			Quarter	July	August	Sept.	Quarter	Growth	
10	REVENUE								
11	Forms		87,000	29348	29700.18	30056.58	89104.75	=(G11-C11)/C11	
12	Supplies		147,300	49689.2	50285.47	50888.9			
13	Total Revenue		234,300	79,037	79,986	80,945			

5. Press (Enter) to complete the percentage growth formula.

Copying a Row of Formulas

The quarterly summation and percentage growth formulas now must be copied down their columns. There are three ways to do this. One way is to copy the formulas in five operations to the five segments that need it (Revenue, Cost of Sales, Gross Income, Expenses, and Net Income). The second method is to copy the formulas to the entire column at one time and then erase the four blank lines that divide the segments. Finally, you can use AutoFill to copy the quarterly summation and percentage growth formulas to the entire column. As you have seen, AutoFill allows you to create a filled range of fixed values (as in this case) or extend a *series* by incrementing numbers or dates. (Series will be discussed in Chapter 7.) In this example, you will still need to erase the four blank lines that divide the segments, but now the copy operation can be done in a single mouse operation. Use AutoFill in the following exercise:

1. Drag across G11 and H11 and point on the fill handle in the lower-right corner of the highlighted range G11:H11. The mouse pointer will again become a plus sign as you can see in the following:

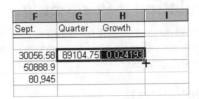

2. Keeping the mouse a plus sign, drag the mouse pointer down the right border of the range G11:H26. Release the mouse button when the highlighted area covers the range. Columns G and H are filled with figures, as shown in Figure 5-14.

On the unused rows, like 14, you get the message #DIV/0!. This is an error message stating you are dividing by zero. Don't let it bother you. You are going to erase or clear these next.

Clearing a Range of Cells

Clearing a range (which, you remember, can be a cell, a column, a row, or a block) is very easy: highlight the range, and press Del. Do that next for row 14:

1. Drag across G14 and H14. The range G14:H14 is highlighted.

Completed
totals and
percentages
Figure 5-14.

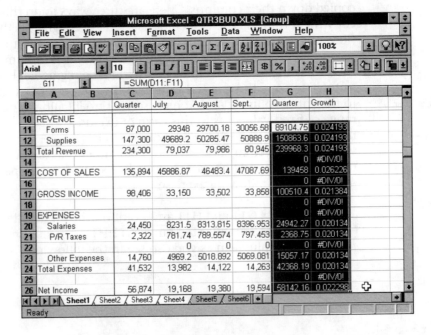

2. Press ⌐Del⌐. G14 and H14 are cleared as shown here:

	A	B	C	D	E	F	G	H	I	
8			Quarter	July	August	Sept.	Quarter	Growth		
10	REVENUE									
11	Forms		87,000	29348	29700.18	30056.58	89104.75	0.024193		
12	Supplies		147,300	49689.2	50285.47	50888.9	150863.6	0.024193		
13	Total Revenue		234,300	79,037	79,986	80,945	239968.3	0.024193		
14										
15	COST OF SALES		135,894	45886.87	46483.4	47087.69	139458	0.026226		
16								0	#DIV/0!		

If you want a little more control over what you are deleting, you can use the Clear option in the Edit menu. When you do that, you get a chance to clear everything in the cell, or clear just the formats, contents, or notes. Try that next.

3. Drag across G16 and H16. Then click on the Edit menu and on the Clear option. A submenu opens up, like this:

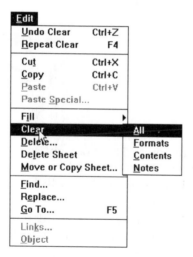

The options that are available on the Clear submenu and their results are as follows:

✦ *All*   Erases everything (contents, formats, and notes) from the cell and returns it to the General format.

✦ *Formats*   Erases only the formats, leaving the contents and notes. The cell is returned to the General format.

5

✦ *Contents* Erases only the contents, leaving the formats and notes.

✦ *Notes* Erases only the notes, leaving the contents and formats.

4. Click on All to clear everything in G16 and H16.

5. Use either the ⌷Del⌷ key or Edit Clear option to erase rows 18, 19 (which can be done together), and 25. Leave row 22 for the moment.

Inserting a Row

To make the sheet easier to read, you will now insert a line between the expense and revenue totals and the detail accounts above them. To do this, you insert a blank row and then copy a line across it.

1. Drag across A13 through H13.
2. Click on the Insert menu and on the Cells option. The Insert dialog box opens, as shown here:

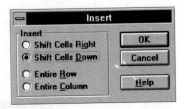

The Insert dialog box gives you four options: Shift Cells Right, Shift Cells Down—which is what you want here—Entire Row, or Entire Column. Since Shift Cells Down is the default, you need only click on OK.

3. Click on OK. A new, blank row 13 is inserted, and all the cells below A13:H13 are shifted down.
4. Click on C13, type -, and press ⌷Enter⌷. C13 contains a single hyphen.
5. Click on the Format menu, the Cells option, and the Alignment tab. The Alignment dialog box opens.
6. Click on Fill and OK. The dialog box closes, and C13 fills with hyphens.
7. Drag C13 through H13. Click on the Edit menu and the Fill Right option. The line in C13 is copied across the range D13:H13, as shown here:

	A	B	C	D	E	F	G	H	I
10	REVENUE								
11	Forms		87,000	29348	29700.18	30056.58	89104.75	0.024193	
12	Supplies		147,300	49689.2	50285.47	50888.9	150863.6	0.024193	
13									
14	Total Revenue		234,300	79,037	79,986	80,945	239968.3	0.024193	
15									

Go down to A25 and, following the previous instructions, insert a new row and copy a line across columns C through H. Note that in both cases the total formulas remain unaffected by the new rows.

Deleting a Row

You have been hanging on to what is now row 23 with the idea that you will do something with it. You will, you'll delete it. Row 23 was added to demonstrate deleting a row in a SUM range. Do that now by following these instructions:

1. Drag across A23 through H23.

2. Click the right mouse button (shortcut menu) and the Delete option. The Delete dialog box opens with the options Shift Cells Left (to delete columns) or Shift Cells Up (to delete rows), as shown in Figure 5-15. The default, Shift Cells Up, is what you want. Therefore, you need only click on OK.

3. Click on OK. The range A23:H23 is deleted and all the cells below that row shift up. Note that the row deletion did not change the Total Expenses or Net Income amounts.

Inserting and Deleting

Inserting and deleting rows and columns are simultaneously very powerful and potentially dangerous operations. They are powerful because they allow you to easily change the structure of a spreadsheet after it is built by, for example, adding new or forgotten accounts or deleting unwanted elements. Inserting and especially deleting can also be dangerous because, under certain circumstances, you can cause a formula to become incorrect.

Excel has many safeguards against causing a formula error with an insertion or a deletion. You have seen how both cell-by-cell addition and SUM formulas are not affected by inserting rows. Even an absolute range is

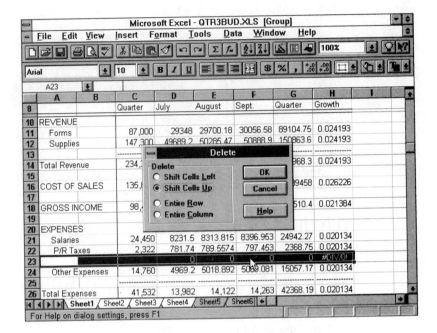

Row deletion
in progress
Figure 5-15.

correctly adjusted if an inserted row changes its position. For example, if a row is inserted between rows 2 and 3, pushing the assumptions in C3 through C5 down a row, the absolute references to those cells are corrected automatically.

One safeguard is that both inserts and deletes can be undone if you choose Undo from the Edit menu or press Ctrl-Z or Alt-Backspace before you carry out another operation that takes Excel out of Ready mode. You can look at a formula, but do not try to edit it, which will take it out of Ready mode. Get into the habit of pausing after doing an insert or delete and looking around the sheet. Highlight several formulas to see if they have been correctly changed, thereby giving yourself a chance to use Undo if necessary.

Excel's formulas are extremely flexible, especially SUM. Not only can you insert or delete cells in the middle of a summation range, but you can also delete the named first and last cells in a summation and the formula will be correctly adjusted.

When you do an insert or delete, it is handy to think of it as inserting or deleting rows or columns. However, there is good reason for Excel's not using this terminology in its dialog boxes: you insert or delete only the specific cells you previously highlighted. You do not insert or delete a row or column across or down the entire sheet.

While it may be obvious that to delete three rows, you need to highlight three rows, it is not so obvious that to insert three rows, you need to highlight three rows. The number of rows highlighted are inserted immediately above the top row highlighted. For columns, the number of columns highlighted are inserted immediately to the left of the leftmost column highlighted.

Making Corrections

This completes the work you will do on the spreadsheet in this chapter. Your screen should now look like the one shown in Figure 5-16. If your numbers are different, you may have an error in one of your formulas. Although it is a bit of a pain, you might want to look for it just to see how a search is done. Go down columns D and E, highlighting each cell. Also, look at cells G11 and H11. Compare the cell contents in the edit area with various figures and descriptions in this chapter. It should not take long to find it. A good rule is to thoroughly check formulas as you are building them to avoid having to go back and correct them later.

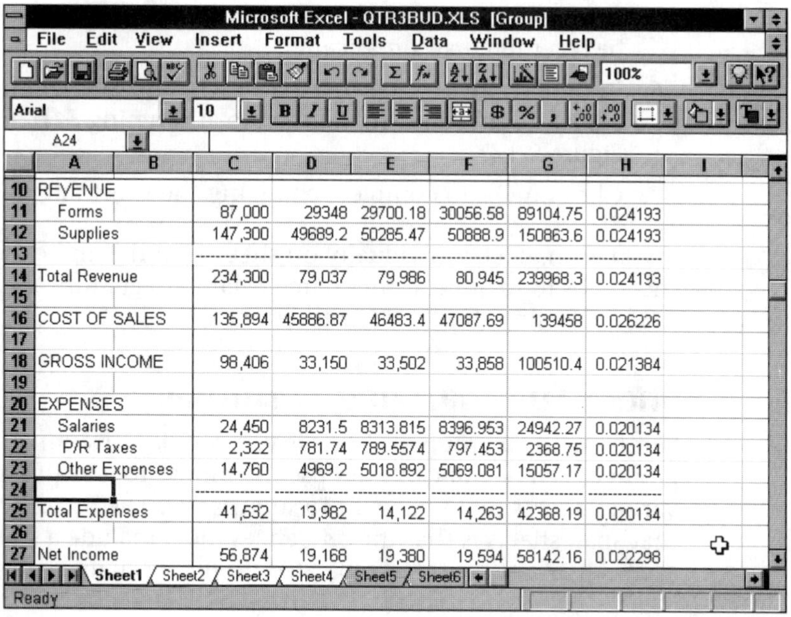

5

Finished sheet
Figure 5-16.

Customizing Individual Sheets

All of the work you have done so far in this chapter has been entered onto four sheets. All the titles and headings and all of the numbers and formulas that you have entered or created on Sheet1 have been automatically duplicated on sheets 2 through 4. It is now time to unlink the four sheets and customize each sheet. In a real-world situation, this would entail, at a minimum, putting an identifying title on each sheet and customizing the assumptions and the starting numbers. In addition, you need to change Sheet4 so that it sums the other sheets. For this exercise, you will customize only two of the sheet titles and change Sheet4 so that it is a summary. You have already changed enough numbers that you do not need further practice in that.

Begin the customization with these instructions for unlinking the sheets and changing the titles :

1. Click on Sheet5 to select that sheet and in the process unlink the other four sheets.

2. Click on Sheet1 to select just that sheet. Note after you select Sheet1 that sheets 2 through 4 are no longer selected.

3. Press Ctrl-Home to go to cell A1 which contains the title.

4. Click in the edit area of the Formula bar to the left of the "T" in "THIRD."

5. Type **5TH AVENUE STORE** - and press Enter. The title will change and be recentered automatically.

6. In order to tell which sheet is which, also change the name on the sheet tab by double-clicking on the tab and typing **5th Ave**, as shown in Figure 5-17.

7. Click on OK to complete changing the sheet tab.

If you wish, click individually on sheets 2 and 3 and change their titles and sheet tabs to include a store name (Main Street Store and University Store for example) using the above instructions.

Sheet Summarizing Formulas

Summarizing a group of sheets is very similar to summarizing any other group of cells—you can even use the mouse to identify the cells on the various sheets that you want to summarize. The major difference in formulas that span sheets is that the references must include a sheet name prior to each cell reference and be separated from the cell reference by an exclamation

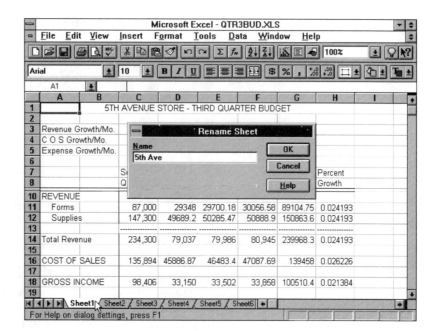

point. For example, if you want to refer to the range C4:D8 on Sheet2, you would write it Sheet2!C4:D8. Also, the Excel functions work as well across sheets as they do across any other range.

See how sheet summarization works by entering formulas to summarize sheets 1 through 3 on sheet 4. Enter the title for Sheet4, change the sheet tab, and use the AutoSum tool to build the formulas, following these instructions:

1. Double-click on the sheet tab for Sheet4 to select that sheet and open the renaming dialog box.

2. Type **Total** and press (Enter) to create a new tab name.

3. Press (Ctrl)-(Home), click to the left of "Third" in the edit area, type **TOTAL COMPANY -** , and press (Enter) to change the title.

4. Click on C11, which will contain the first formula summarizing the other sheets.

5. Click on the AutoSum tool in the Standard toolbar to create a SUM formula.

6. Click on Sheet1 (5th Ave) and press and hold (Shift) while clicking on Sheet3 (Univer.) to select the range of sheets.

7. Click on C11 to select that as the cell to summarize on all three sheets as shown here:

		C11	↓ X ✓ ƒ×	=SUM(5th Ave:Univer.!C11)		
	A	B	C	D	E	F
1			5TH AVENUE STORE - THIRD QUARTER BUD(			
2						
3	Revenue Growth/Mo.		0.012			
4	C O S Growth/Mo.		0.013			
5	Expense Growth/Mo.		0.01			
6						
7			Second			
8			Quarter	July	August	Sept.
10	REVENUE					
11	Forms		87,000	29348	29700.18	30056.58
12	Supplies		147,300	49689.2	50285.47	50888.9

8. Press (Enter) to complete the formula building process.

9. Use drag and drop with (Ctrl) to copy C11 to C12, C14, C16, C18, C21:23, C25, and C27. Make sure you are firmly holding down (Ctrl) before dragging or you will move the formula instead of copy it. If you do that, you will change the percentage formula in column H, and you will need to correct it before completing the sheet.

10. Drag down C11:C27 and use AutoFill with (Ctrl) (drag on the lower-right corner of the range) to copy the formulas in that range to columns D, E, F and G. (Column H, the percentages, needs to use its original formulas to calculate the percent growth.) When you are done, your screen should look like Figure 5-18.

As you can see, summing over sheets is both easy and very powerful. With Excel 5 you truly have a full three-dimensional work area.

Saving and Quitting Excel

The only task remaining is to save the workbook and leave Excel. Use the following instructions for that purpose.

1. Click on the Save tool (the third tool from the left in the Standard toolbar). The file is saved under the name you originally gave it: QTR3BUD.

As a default, when Excel saves a file it simply copies over the last copy of the same file on disk. The save you just completed copied over the file that you created by saving the workbook early in the chapter. You can also have Excel make a new file each time you save a file. Since you can have only one file with a given name, Excel automatically renames

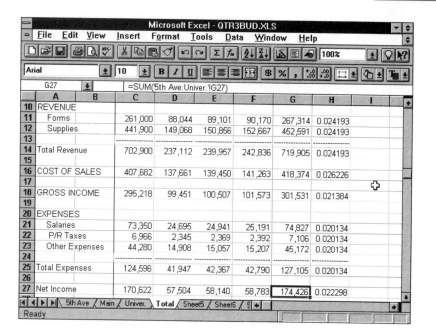

Completed
total company
sheet
Figure 5-18.

5

the old file by changing its extension to .BAK (for backup). The third
time you save a file, the first copy is deleted and the second copy is
given the .BAK extension.

To have Excel make a backup, use the Options button in the File Save
As dialog box, as shown in the following steps:

2. Click on the File menu and click on Save As. The File Save As dialog
    box opens.

3. Click on the Options button in the File Save As dialog box. A new
    dialog box opens, as shown here:

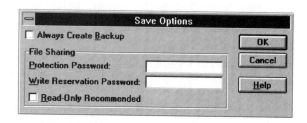

4. Click on the Always Create Backup check box, and then click on OK
    twice. The Options and the File Save As dialog boxes close, and another

```
                    TOTAL COMPANY - THIRD QUARTER BUDGET

   Revenue Growth/Mo.       0.012
   C O S Growth/Mo.         0.013
   Expense Growth/Mo.        0.01
```

	Second Quarter	July	August	Sept.	Third Quarter	Percent Growth
REVENUE						
Forms	261,000	88,044	89,101	90,170	267,314	0.024193
Supplies	441,900	149,068	150,856	152,667	452,591	0.024193
	--------	--------	--------	--------	--------	--------
Total Revenue	702,900	237,112	239,957	242,836	719,905	0.024193
COST OF SALES	407,682	137,661	139,450	141,263	418,374	0.026226
GROSS INCOME	295,218	99,451	100,507	101,573	301,531	0.021384
EXPENSES						
Salaries	73,350	24,695	24,941	25,191	74,827	0.020134
P/R Taxes	6,966	2,345	2,369	2,392	7,106	0.020134
Other Expenses	44,280	14,908	15,057	15,207	45,172	0.020134
	--------	--------	--------	--------	--------	--------
Total Expenses	124,596	41,947	42,367	42,790	127,105	0.020134
Net Income	170,622	57,504	58,140	58,783	174,426	0.022298

Printed
spreadsheet
Figure 5-19.

dialog box opens asking if you want to replace the existing
QTR3BUD.XLS file.

5. Click on Yes.

The previous file, which was called QTR3BUD.XLS, is now renamed
QTR3BUD.BAK, and a new file named QTR3BUD.XLS will be created.
You now have two files on disk. The file backup capability is handy if
you need to reuse the earlier file for any reason.

You are done with Excel and Windows for this chapter. Therefore shut
them both down now.

6. Double-click on Excel's Control-menu box and then on Windows'
Control-menu box. Click on OK to end your Windows session.

At this point, the spreadsheet in printed form is not particularly pretty
without the grid, as shown in Figure 5-19. The formatting of the numbers is
messy and the columns seem to run together. Making it look better in a
number of ways, as well as printing it, will be covered in Chapter 6.

CHAPTER

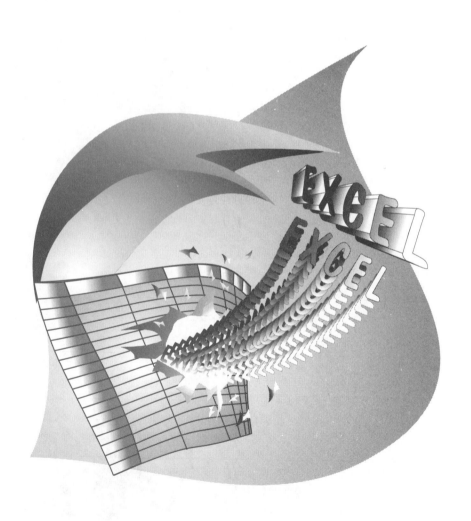

ENHANCING A WORKBOOK

In Chapter 5 you created a workbook for preparing a third quarter budget. The results were usable, but they were difficult to read and not particularly attractive. In this chapter you'll use a number of techniques to make the budget easier to read and more attractive. The techniques include changing the formatting of numbers and headings, and moving, deleting, and erasing sections of the workbook. You will also set the parameters for and print the workbook. Finally, you'll change the

Third Quarter Budget workbook into a template that can be used to set up any quarterly budget.

Loading a Workbook

To begin working on the budget workbook, you must load the file that holds it on the disk. Remember that the last thing you did in Chapter 5 before leaving Excel was to save the file. You must now load that file back into memory so you can work on it. Load Windows and Excel, if necessary, and use the following instructions:

1. Click on the File menu and the Open option. The File menu opens, followed by the Open dialog box, which asks for the name of the file to open. A list of files is shown in the File Name list box, similar to what is seen here:

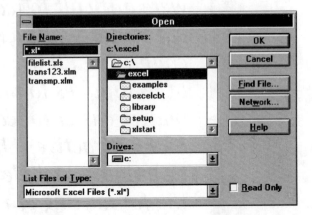

If you continued here directly from Chapter 5 without leaving Excel, you are probably looking at the correct directory and can skip the next two steps. However, if you closed Excel and Windows as suggested in Chapter 5 and restarted both here, the directory you are looking at in the Open dialog box is probably the \EXCEL program directory, not the \SHEET directory where you stored QTR3BUD. Your first task, then, is to change directories. Make the necessary changes with the following steps.

2. Double-click on c:\ in the Directories list box. A new Directories list box is shown. (If you need to use the keyboard, press [Alt]-[D] and, if necessary, an arrow key to highlight c:\, and then press [Enter].)

3. Double-click on "sheet" in the Directories list box. If you do not see "sheet," use the vertical scroll bar (click on the down arrow scroll box) to find it. In the list of files, QTR3BUD.XLS should appear, as shown here:

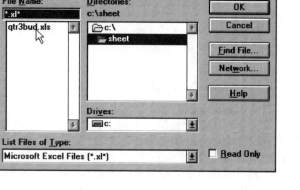

4. Double-click on QTR3BUD.XLS in the File Name list box.

The third quarter budget opens on your screen, as shown in Figure 6-1. You can now begin working on it.

6

Formatting

Excel lets you *format* (change the appearance of) individual characters and cells as well as groups of cells, an entire sheet, or even an entire workbook.

Third quarter
budget as
initially loaded
Figure 6-1.

After formatting a group of cells with the most common format in that group of cells, you can come back and change specific cells that you want to be different from the overall format. You can also set overall formats for several aspects of the workbook, but here you will set the overall format just for numbers and for the width of columns.

Overall Number Format

The overall number format determines how numbers appear on a sheet, both on the screen and when printed. Most of the numbers in the workbook are formatted with the General format, which is the format Excel starts with. It is the most versatile format in terms of the variety of numbers it can display, but it looks the least appealing. Let's first see how to change the number format and then look at some of the formatting alternatives. Start out by reselecting the four sheets and then highlighting the area to be formatted.

1. Click on the sheet tab for the 5th Avenue store (old Sheet1).

2. Press and hold Shift while clicking on the sheet tab for the Total Company (Sheet4) to reselect all four sheets together.

3. On the 5th Avenue sheet (Sheet1), drag the mouse from C10 through H27 to highlight that area, as shown in Figure 6-2.

4. Click on the Format menu, the Cells option, and the Number tab. The Number Format Cells dialog box opens, as shown here:

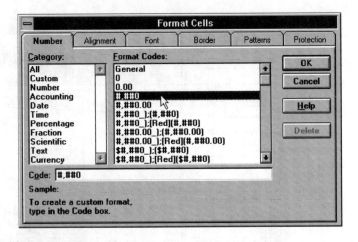

5. Double-click on the fourth alternative (#,##0) in the Format Codes list box. The Format command finishes, and the workbook is redisplayed in the new format.

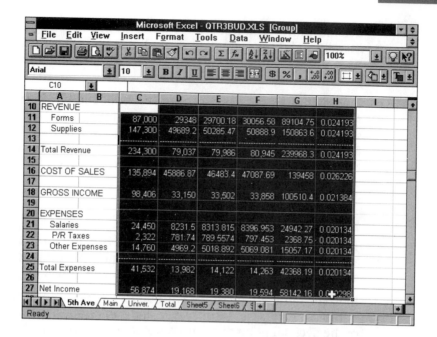

Highlighting
the range to
be formatted
Figure 6-2.

Your screen should now look like the one in Figure 6-3. Don't be concerned that all of the percentages disappeared. When you selected #,##0 from the Number Format dialog box, you told Excel to format the numbers without

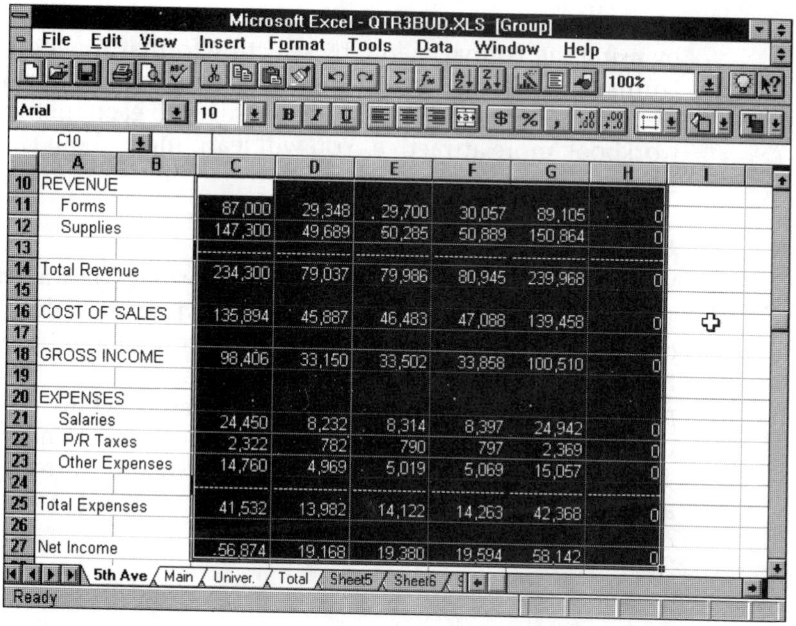

Third quarter
budget after
setting the
overall format
Figure 6-3.

6

decimal places (you'll see how this works in a moment). Excel took this literally and displayed no decimal places even when decimals were all you had. You will come back soon to override the overall format with a specific percentage format for column H.

You might wonder why you use the format chosen, when the majority of numbers in the workbook are currency. If you use a currency format, the sheets become cluttered with dollar signs. Later in this chapter you will format just the total lines at the bottom of each sheet as currency. That sets the totals off from the rest of the numbers and doesn't clutter the entire page with dollar signs.

Formatting Alternatives

The Number Format Cells dialog box offers many formatting alternatives, and you can also construct your own format. This chapter discusses both the built-in formats and how you can construct a format of your own.

In Excel, numbers are stored with up to 15 significant digits. All 15 significant digits can be displayed and can be all to the left or all to the right of the decimal point or some combination. Of course, the column must be wide enough. For all formats except the General format, the column must be wide enough to display all of the whole digits to the left of the decimal point, the number of decimal digits specified, and any other characters such as dollar signs, commas, or periods that are part of the format. If the column is not wide enough, it is filled with # symbols.

There are three ways Excel allows you to add formatting to your workbook: by using the Format menu, by selecting formatting tools from the Formatting toolbar, and by choosing the automatic formats provided by Excel (AutoFormat). There are advantages to each method in making your workbook more attractive. You will learn more about each of these in the exercises in this chapter.

Format Symbols

You communicate to Excel the type of format you want to use with symbols. The symbols describe such things as the number of decimal places; whether or not a dollar sign, percent sign, or comma should be used; and how to handle negative numbers, zero values, and text. Excel provides 36 built-in *format codes,* including the General format. Excel divides these 36 format codes into 11 *categories,* as follows: All, Custom, Number, Accounting, Date, Time, Percentage, Fraction, Scientific, Text, and Currency. Each category has a certain number of the 36 total format codes. For example, the Date category has five codes, as shown here:

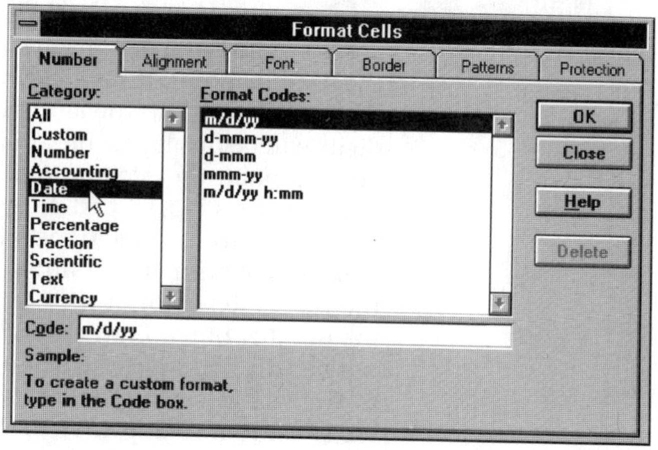

Each of these built-in format codes, plus any that you build, use the formatting symbols shown in Table 6-1 to communicate their formats. Note that the first three symbols in Table 6-1, 0, #, and ?, are placeholders that may be filled with numbers if there are numbers available for that place. If there is no number to fill 0, a 0 will take the place; if there is no number to fill #, nothing takes its place and no space is left; if there is no number to fill ?, a blank space takes its place.

When you have a fixed number of decimal places, the decimal digits are rounded to fit the format. Also, if you have blank format sections (semicolons with nothing between them), that type of number is not

Symbol	Usage
0	Specifies the number of *fixed* decimal places to the right of the decimal point and the minimum digits to the left of the decimal point. For example, with the built-in format 0.00, you always have two decimal places to the right of the decimal point and at least one digit to the left of the decimal point. With the 0.00 format, the following numbers are formatted as shown:

	Entry	**Display**
	.456	0.46
	45	45.00

Formatting
Symbols
Table 6-1.

Symbol	Usage

#	Specifies the number of *optional* digits on either side of the decimal point. If there are more digits in the number than there are #'s to the left of the decimal point, the digits will be displayed, but on the right side of the decimal point the decimal digits will be rounded to the number of #'s in that part of the format. For example, in the built-in format #,##0 the # provides the optional digits surrounding the comma, which is used as a thousands separator. If there are not enough digits to fill the number of places, these will be blank and space will not be left. You want the first place to be a 0 and not a #, so you will get at least a 0 printed if you have a decimal too small to round to 1. With the #,##0 format, the following entries are formatted as shown:
	
	    Entry **Display**
	    46.67 47
	    12345 12,345

?	Specifies the number of spaces to leave on either side of the decimal point in order to align the decimal point with fewer digits. For example, the built-in format # ??/?? provides space for six characters to the right of the decimal place (one to separate the whole number from the fraction, two for the denominator, two for the numerator, and one for /). Space is always left for each ?. With the # ??/?? format, the following entries are formatted as shown:
	
	    Entry **Display**
	    5.8125 5 13/16
	    5.25 5 1/4

. (period)	Specifies where a decimal point is to be placed.

Formatting
Symbols
(*continued*)
Table 6-1.

Symbol	Usage
, (comma)	Specifies that the thousands separator is a comma if a comma is surrounded by zeros or # symbols, for example, #,##0. One or more commas on the right of a format will scale the resulting number by a thousand for each comma. For example, formatting 5,650,000 by typing **0.00,,** in the Code text box would produce the number 5.65.
;	Separates sections of a format. You can have up to four sections. The first, or leftmost, specifies how to format positive numbers, the second section specifies how to format negative numbers, the third specifies how to format zero, and the fourth section specifies how to handle text. All numbers are handled the same way if there is only one section. With two sections, positive and zero values are formatted with the first, and negative numbers are formatted with the second. Text is not given special treatment with only three sections. An example of using a semicolon is shown with the next set of symbols.
_ (underline)	Specifies that a space be left that is equal in width to the character immediately following the underline. For example, in the built-in format $#,##0_);($#,##0), the "_)" shifts positive numbers to the left an amount equal to the width of a ")". This aligns positive and negative numbers by leaving room for the ")".
$ + − ( ) / : space	Specifies a literal character to be displayed. For example, the built-in format $#,##0_);($#,##0) places a $ to the left of the leftmost number and ( ) around negative numbers. With the $#,##0_);($#,##0) format, the following numbers are formatted as shown:

6

Entry	**Display**
−45.67	($46)
1234	$1,234

Formatting
Symbols
(*continued*)
Table 6-1.

Symbol	Usage
	If you want to enter a literal character other than $ + – ( ) / : or space, precede the character with a backslash (\) or enclose one or more of the characters in double quotation marks (" "). These are explained shortly.
"text"	Specifies that whatever is between the " " is displayed. As an example, $#,##0"DB" ;$#,##0"CR";0 places DB after positive numberrrs, CR after negative numbers, and 0 for zero values.
\	Specifies that the character following the \ is displayed. This is the same as enclosing a single character in " ". For some characters, you do not have to enter the \ because Excel will automatically do it for you. These characters are

~ ! ^ & ` ' = { } < >.   +

For example, you can enter the format `#,##0'! and Excel will in effect (but not on the screen) change it to \`#,##0\'\!. If you format the number 45 with this format you will get `45'!. |
| @ | Specifies where any text in a cell is placed in a format. For example, 0.00 ;@ formats all numbers with 0.00 and displays any text appearing in the cell. (0.00 by itself does the same thing.) |
| * | Specifies that the character following the * is repeated to fill any unused space in the cell. For example, $**#,##0 places a $ in the leftmost position in a cell, fills any intervening space with *, and right aligns the number in the cell as usual. You see this on computer printed checks. With the $**#,##0 format, the following numbers are formatted as shown:

Entry	Display
45	$*******45
1234	$**** 1,234

You cannot have more than one sequence beginning with an asterisk in one section of a format. |

Formatting
Symbols
(*continued*)
Table 6-1.

Symbol	Usage
%	Specifies that a number is multiplied by 100 and a % placed to the right. For example, the built-in format 0.00% multiplies the number by 100 and places a % after a pair of decimal points. With the 0.00% format, the following numbers are formatted as shown: **Entry** **Display** .07 7.00% .4575 45.75% −0.067 −6.70%
E+ E− e+ e−	Specifies that the scientific format is used if either a # or a 0 precede either E or e. If a − is specified, only negative numbers have a sign. With a +, both positive and negative numbers have a sign. For example, the built-in format 0.00E+00 uses a capital E and both plus and minus signs for the scientific format. With the 0.00E+00 format, the following numbers are formatted as shown: **Entry** **Display** 4567 4.57E+03 −12345 −1.23E+04 .0045 4.50E−03
m mm mmm mmmm	Specifies that a month is displayed as a number without a leading zero (m) or with a leading zero (mm), as a three-letter abbreviation like Apr or Sep(mmm), or as a full name. If m or mm follows h or hh it specifies minutes rather than a month.
d dd ddd dddd	Specifies that a day is displayed as a number (1 - 31) without a leading zero (d), with a leading zero (dd), as a three-letter abbreviation like Tue or Thu(ddd), or as a full name of the day of the week(dddd).

Formatting
Symbols
(*continued*)
Table 6-1.

6

Symbol	Usage
yy yyyy	Specifies that a year is displayed as either a two-digit (94) or four-digit number (1994).
h hh	Specifies that an hour is displayed as a number either without a leading zero (4) or with a leading zero (04).
m mm	Specifies that a minute is displayed as a number either without a leading zero (5) or with a leading zero (05). If the m or mm does not appear after an h or hh, the month is displayed.
s ss	Specifies that a second is displayed as a number either without a leading zero (6) or with a leading zero (06).
AM/PM am/pm A/P a/p	Specifies that time is displayed using a 12-hour clock with AM, am, A, or a (times before noon) and PM, pm, P, or p (from noon to midnight).
[color]	Specifies that the characters in the cell should be displayed in a color. The colors available are black, white, red, green, blue, yellow, magenta, and cyan or [color *n0*] where *n0* is a number from 1 through 56 indicating one of the 56 colors in the custom color palette. For example, the built-in format #,##0_); [Red](#,##0) displays negative numbers in red.
[*condition value*]	Lets you define what values fall in each section of a format code. *Condition* is one of the logical operators < > = <= >= <> (the last operator means *not*) and *value* is any number. For example, using the comma format, if you wanted values above 10,000 to be green, values between 0 and 10,000 to be yellow, and values below 0 to be red, you would use the following format: [Green][>10000]#,##0_);[Yellow][>=0]#,##0_);[Red](#,##0)

Formatting
Symbols
(*continued*)
Table 6-1.

displayed. For example, 0.00;;;@ displays and formats positive numbers and text, but does not display negative numbers and zero values.

General Format
Every time you create a new workbook, all cells are automatically formatted with the General format. The General format displays numbers with a

variable number of decimal places, no thousands separators, a minus sign if the number is negative, and a leading zero if the number is less than 1. If the column is not wide enough to display all of the decimal digits, they are rounded to the nearest digit that can be displayed. If the column is not wide enough to display all of the whole digits to the left of the decimal point, the number is converted to scientific notation.

Here are some examples of General formatting with the standard column width of 8.43 characters:

Entry	Display
1234567.89	1234568
1234567890	1.23E+09
−4567.89	−4567.89
.8956	0.8956

Setting Overall Column Width

6

Excel starts with a standard column width of 8.43 characters. This allows you to display eight or nine text characters or a number with eight characters in it (a blank character always remains on the left of a right-aligned number). A column's width can be set from 0 to 255 characters.

To change the width of a column on a sheet, you can either drag the intersection between two column headings to the right of the column whose width you want to change, or use the Column Width dialog box. You can change single or multiple columns with either method. Try the dialog box next with the following steps:

1. If columns C through H are not currently highlighted (it doesn't matter what rows), drag across C11 through H11.

2. Click on the Format menu, the Column option, and the Width suboption. The Column Width dialog box opens, as shown here:

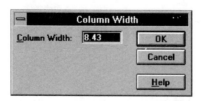

3. Type **10** and press [Enter]. All columns in the C through H range are widened to ten characters, as shown in Figure 6-4.

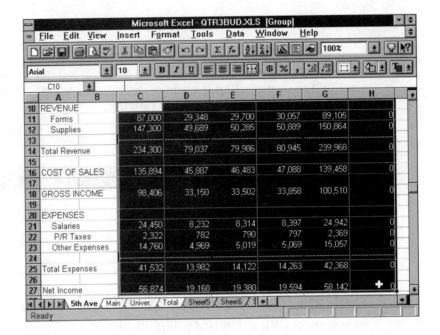

Now compare this dialog box method with dragging the width of multiple columns.

1. Click on the Edit menu and the Undo Column Width option to restore the original width to columns C through H.

2. Drag across the column *headings* (not the individual cells) for columns C through H. Six entire columns will be highlighted.

3. Point on the line between the column headings C and D. The mouse pointer becomes a two-headed arrow with a bar in the middle. This allows you to change the column width.

4. Drag the right edge of column C's heading until "Width: 10.00" appears on the left side of the Formula bar, as shown here:

Columns C through H will be widened to ten characters.

The dragging method is not only slightly easier, but, with Excel 5, you can also see exactly how wide the column will be.

Detail Formatting

You have now set the overall format and column width. Next you will tailor specific areas with the formatting that makes them look best. In the following sections your formatting tasks include recovering the percentages that disappeared, formatting the summary lines in the budget as currency, and centering and embolding the column headings in their columns.

Creating a Percentage Format

The percentages disappeared when the overall format was set with no decimal places. With the General format the percentages were not easy to read. A format with the % symbol, which multiplies a number by 100 and adds a percent sign, is a better way to display percentages. Two areas or groups of cells in the workbook require this kind of format: the percent growth in column H and the assumptions in the upper part of column C. First, though, you will create your own custom format.

Excel comes with two built-in formats for percentages: one with zero decimals and one with two decimals. If you want a percentage format with one decimal place, you must create it. The easiest way to create a format that is only slightly different from a built-in format is to start with the built-in format. Do that now.

6

1. Drag OK from cell H11 through H27 to highlight the first area to be formatted.
2. Press the right mouse button to display the shortcut menu, click on the Format Cells option, and, if necessary, click on the Number tab to display the Format Cells Number dialog box.
3. Click on the Percentage category, and then click on the 0.00% format code.

   Your Number Format dialog box should look like this:

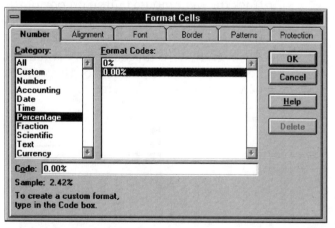

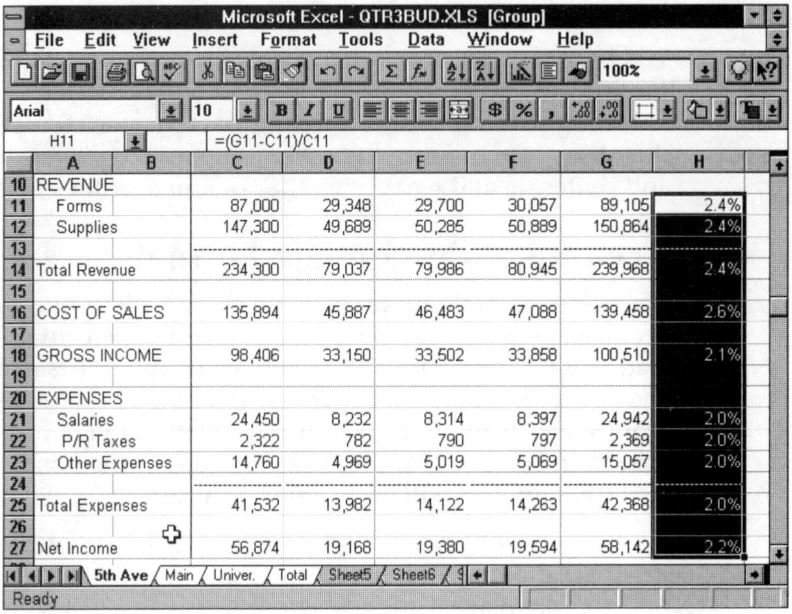

Growth
percentages
formatted with
a single
decimal place
Figure 6-5.

4. Drag across one of the decimal zeros in the lower Code text box and press (Del). You have created a new format with only one decimal place.

5. Click on OK. The Number Format dialog box closes, and the percentage growth numbers in column H are formatted as shown in Figure 6-5.

   The new percent format you created is an additional format now available in this workbook. It does not replace the original format you used to create the new one.

6. Scroll your sheet up and to the left and then select C3 through C5.

7. Click the right mouse button on one of the selected cells to open the shortcut menu and then click on the Format Cells option. The Number tab should already be selected.

8. Click on the Percentage category and double-click on the new single decimal format. The three growth assumptions are formatted into percentages, as shown here:

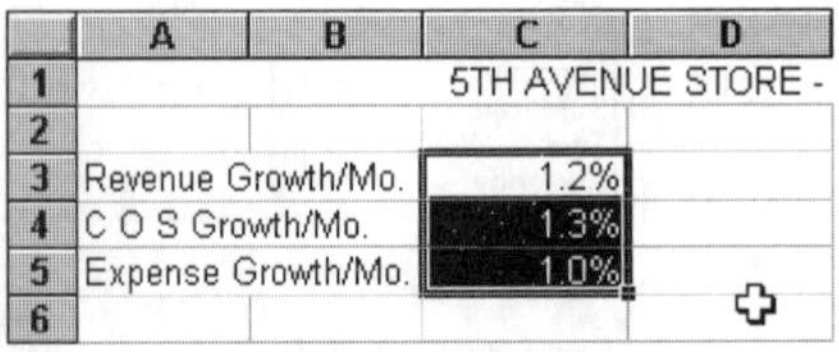

Adding Currency Formatting

To set off the total lines from the rest of the budget, you can format them as currency, which places a dollar sign in front of each number. There are four total lines: Total Revenue, GROSS INCOME, Total Expenses, and Net Income. Use these instructions to format the first of the lines:

1. Drag across C14 through G14. The two quarterly and three monthly totals are highlighted.

2. Click on the Format menu and the Cells option. The Number Format Cells dialog box opens.

3. Click on Currency in the Category list box, as shown here:

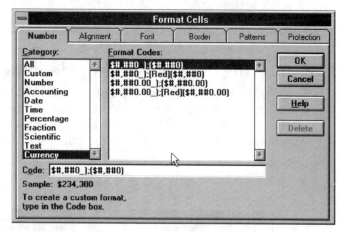

4. Double-click on the first code in the Format Codes list box.

   The Total Revenue amounts are now formatted with dollar signs. Also, notice that the numbers are now shifted one character to the left, leaving a blank space on the right. This is because the formats contain a _) on the right of the positive number section so positive numbers will align with negative numbers that have parentheses around them. Since you don't have any negative numbers in this budget, let's get rid of the space on the right to improve the sheet's appearance. Do that with another custom format by removing the _) from the dollar format you used earlier. (C14 through G14 should still be selected.)

5. Click on the Format menu and the Cells option to again open the Number Format Cells dialog box. The first dollar format should still be selected.

6. Drag across the _) in the Code text box at the bottom of the dialog box, press Del, and then click on OK. When you return to the sheet you will see that the numbers in row 14 are shifted back one character to the right.

You could use the above procedure with your new format to format the remaining "total" lines. Excel 5, though, has a copy format tool, called Format Painter, that allows you to quickly repeat a format you have already applied. Try that now to complete the currency formatting.

7. With C14:G14 still selected, click on the Format painter tool (the paintbrush), a marquee appears around C14:G14 and the mouse pointer now includes a paintbrush.

8. Drag across C18 through G18 and you will see the new format applied.

9. With C18:G18 still selected, again click on the Format Painter tool, and then drag across C25 through G27 (three rows). Both Total Expenses and Net Income are formatted with the custom currency format and your screen should look like the one shown in Figure 6-6.

The Format Painter is extremely powerful and you will find many uses for it.

Centering and Embolding Headings

The final item of detail formatting that you need to do is to center each of the column headings within their columns and make them bold. Remember from Chapter 4 that Excel automatically left-aligns text. Unless you or someone else changed your third quarter budget, all of the headings are left aligned.

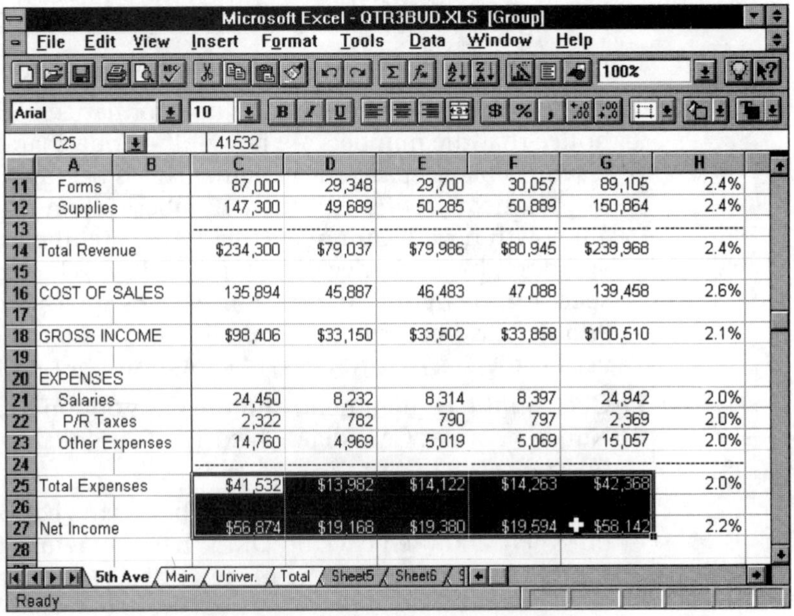

Formatting the totals as currency
Figure 6-6.

Centering the column headings and making them bold improves their look and is easy to do with the Formatting toolbar displayed. Use it now to do this formatting:

1. Scroll the screen up so you can see C7 through H8 and then drag across that range.

2. Click first on the center tool and then on bold (the "B"), as shown here:

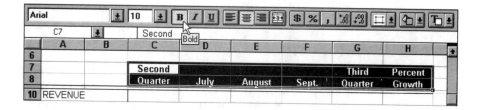

The Formatting Toolbar

6

The Formatting toolbar provides convenient access to many of the common formatting techniques most people often use. You can change the font and font size; apply bold, italic, and underline styles; align the cell contents on the left, center, right or over a group of columns; apply the default currency, percent, or comma format; and increase or decrease the number of decimal digits as well as add background color, cell borders, and type color.

On the faint chance that none of the formatting tools interest you, you can turn off the Formatting toolbar to see more rows of your sheet and make the area above the sheet less "busy." Try the following instructions to remove the Formatting toolbar from the screen.

1. Click the right mouse button on one of the toolbars. The toolbar shortcut menu opens with the Standard and Formatting toolbars checked, as shown here:

2. Click on Formatting. The Formatting toolbar is removed from the screen, and the area displaying your workbook expands by two rows.

3. Repeat the two preceding steps to restore the Formatting toolbar.

4. Click on the Save tool in the Standard toolbar to save your work.

The rest of this book assumes that you have left the Formatting toolbar displayed and can make use of it. Appendix B describes each of the tools in all the toolbars and provides instructions on how to customize a toolbar by adding or deleting individual tools.

AutoFormat

AutoFormat allows you to automatically format your workbook. From a list of 8 formatting styles and a total of 17 formats, you can make choices that will change the appearance of any selected group of cells, or even an entire workbook, to give your work a professionally designed look.

In the previous formatting exercises, you learned how to use and customize built-in formats to give the third quarter budget a more personalized appearance. In this process, you were offered a number of individual options with which to format the workbook. This greater flexibility carries with it the extra burden of the time it takes to design and construct the final appearance of the workbook. AutoFormat provides 17 formats—each of which is a combination of number formats, fonts, alignment, borders, patterns, color, column widths, and row heights—that have been preselected for you. When you select one of the 17 formats, AutoFormat displays a sample of it and allows you to see the immediate effect of changing the formatting combinations.

The best way to appreciate AutoFormat is to use it. In the following instructions you will change your workbook a number of times. In order to restore the workbook to the way it looked before you applied the AutoFormat changes, you will use the Undo feature. Undo is a lifesaver, as you will see. The key is to use it *immediately* after making the change (or mistake). If you do anything that causes Excel to leave Ready mode, Undo undoes only to that point. Note that you can choose Undo from the Edit menu as well as use one of the two shortcuts, [Ctrl]-[Z] or [Alt]-[Backspace]. Try AutoFormat now:

1. Press [Ctrl]-[Home] and then [Ctrl]-[Shift]-[End] to select the entire sheet.

2. Click on the Format menu and choose AutoFormat.

3. The AutoFormat dialog box appears, as shown here:

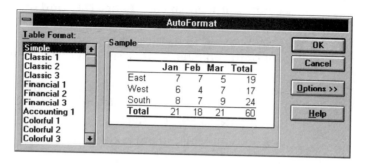

4. Take a moment to click on each format in the Table Format list box and see the different appearances you can choose.

5. Click on the Classic 3 format.

6. Click on the Options button.

Six formats are displayed in the Formats to Apply section, with a check box next to each one, as shown here:

6

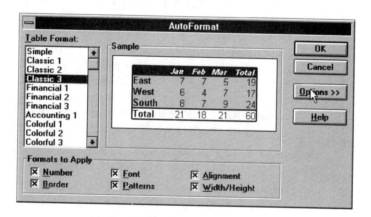

Initially, all formats are selected.

7. Click on the Border check box. Notice how the borders are removed from the sample.

8. Click on the Width/Height check box; the column widths are expanded.

When you clear formats from the Formats to Apply box, Auto-Format deletes the effect of those formats on the Table format and retains any previous formatting you may have applied to the selected group of cells or sheet.

9. Click on Cancel to return to the sheet.

Next see how AutoFormat can change the third quarter budget. Since experimentation with AutoFormat is part of the exercise, your workbook will need to be preserved in its present appearance so you can continue the remainder of the chapter. This is easily done by saving the file now.

1. Click on the File menu and choose Save. The file QTR3BUD.XLS is saved to disk. You can now use AutoFormat freely, without worrying about making unrestorable changes.

2. Click on the Format menu and AutoFormat.

3. Click on Classic 3 and then on OK.

4. When you return to the sheet, click on the View menu and on the Full Screen option. The sheet expands to fill as much of the screen as possible. To see the layout without obstructions, drag the Full Screen button to the right and click in the lower-right corner of your sheet to remove the highlight. Figure 6-7 shows what you should see.

5. Click on the Edit menu and Undo to clear the AutoFormat.

   Continue to experiment with different AutoFormat formats and then try different selected ranges to get a sense of what AutoFormat can and cannot do. Also, turn off Full Screen view and use the Formatting toolbar to customize some of the AutoFormat settings. As you will discover, AutoFormat works best on a simple table, as in the samples. Depending on the structure of your workbook, it may be easier to do the formatting yourself, without using AutoFormat, or by using a combination of individual and automatic formats. Now, to return to the third quarter budget workbook without AutoFormat changes:

6. Click on the File menu and Close. Excel will ask if you want to save changes to QTR3BUD.XLS. Click on No.

7. You will return to a blank SHEET1.XLS. Click on the File menu and then click on the first file in the list of four files at the bottom of the menu. This is the last saved version of file QTR3BUD.XLS.

8. If you haven't already, click on the Full Screen button to return to the normal screen layout.

Changing the Layout

Now you can make some changes to the workbook. The biggest change is deleting column B. To facilitate that, you'll move the assumptions over one column. Then you'll widen column A, narrow column H, and recenter the

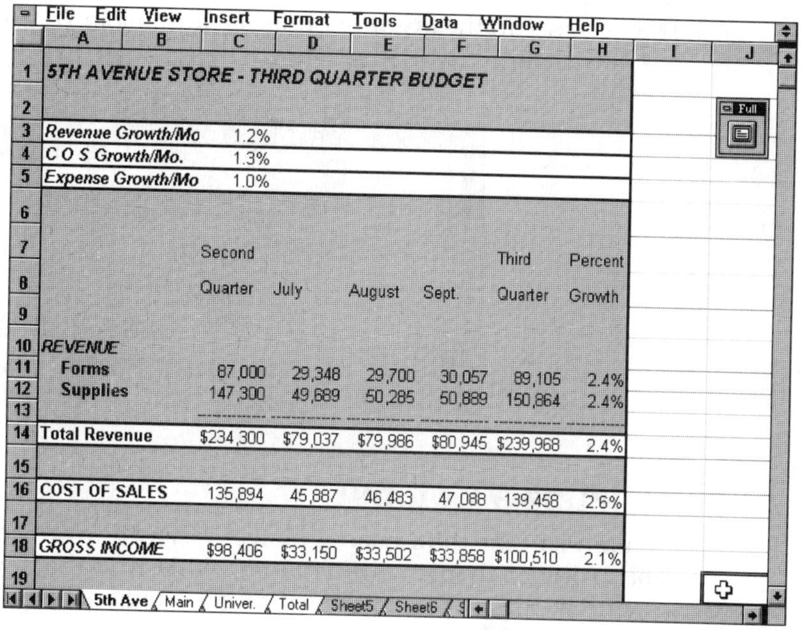

Effect of
applying
AutoFormat
Classic 3
Figure 6-7.

title. To make the formulas more understandable, you'll add some notes to them. Finally, you'll erase the previous month in preparation for the next quarter, but, remembering that you have not printed the workbook yet, you'll undo the erasure.

Moving Formulas

You need to move the growth assumptions from column C to column D so the assumption labels still have enough room when column B is deleted. When the contents of a cell are moved, any formula that refers to that cell is changed to reflect the move, even if it has an absolute reference. This gives you significant flexibility.

1. Drag down C3 through C5. The assumptions are highlighted.

2. Point on the right border of range C3:C5. The cursor turns into an arrow. Drag and drop the range to its new position, D3:D5. The assumptions are moved.

3. Click on D11 to look at the formula.

The reference to the assumption in the formula in D11 used to be $C$3. It has now changed to $D$3, as shown here:

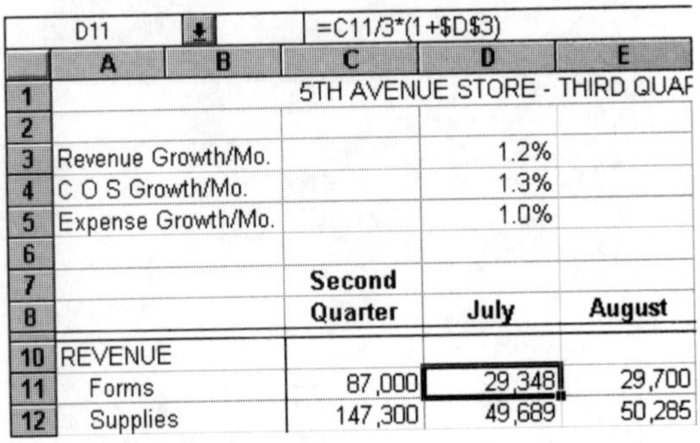

D11		=C11/3*(1+$D$3)		
A	B	C	D	E
			5TH AVENUE STORE - THIRD QUAF	
1				
2				
3 Revenue Growth/Mo.			1.2%	
4 C O S Growth/Mo.			1.3%	
5 Expense Growth/Mo.			1.0%	
6				
7		Second		
8		Quarter	July	August
10 REVENUE				
11 Forms		87,000	29,348	29,700
12 Supplies		147,300	49,689	50,285

Deleting a Column

Column B of the third quarter budget was used to provide room for the row labels without changing the column width. Now that you can change the column width, there is no longer a reason to keep column B. Using these instructions, delete column B:

1. Click on the column heading for column B.

2. Click on the right mouse button to display the shortcut menu and click on Delete.

When column B is deleted, the remaining columns to the right are relettered, as shown in Figure 6-8. Also, all formulas are revised accordingly. Look at several formulas that used to refer to the old column C, and you'll see they now refer to column B.

Adjusting Individual Column Width

Now that column B is gone, you need to widen column A so you can read the row labels. Do that by following these steps:

1. Place the mouse pointer in the column heading, at the intersection of columns A and B. The mouse pointer turns into a two-headed arrow with a line in the middle, as shown here:

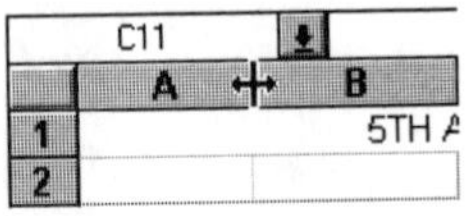

C11		
A	+	B
1		5TH A
2		

2. Drag the column intersection to the right until you are almost over the intersection of columns B and C—you are making column A about equal to the sum of the old columns A and B. Notice in the Formula bar how the column width is increasing. Size the column to 17.57.

The second column sizing you will do narrows the percentage growth column to about seven and a half characters.

1. Place the mouse pointer in the column heading at the intersection of columns G and H.

2. Drag the column intersection to the left until the width in the Formula bar reads 7.57. Your workbook should look like the one shown in Figure 6-9.

Adding Notes to Cells

After a period of time has passed, it is sometimes difficult to remember why you built a formula the way you did, for example, or who gave you a certain figure. This is a problem that becomes more important if you give your workbook to someone else to use. Excel has a feature that allows you to add notes to cells to explain their contents. You can put a note on only one sheet at a time. For the following exercise, you will deselect the four sheets and then reselect the 5th Avenue Store's sheet (Sheet1) on which to place

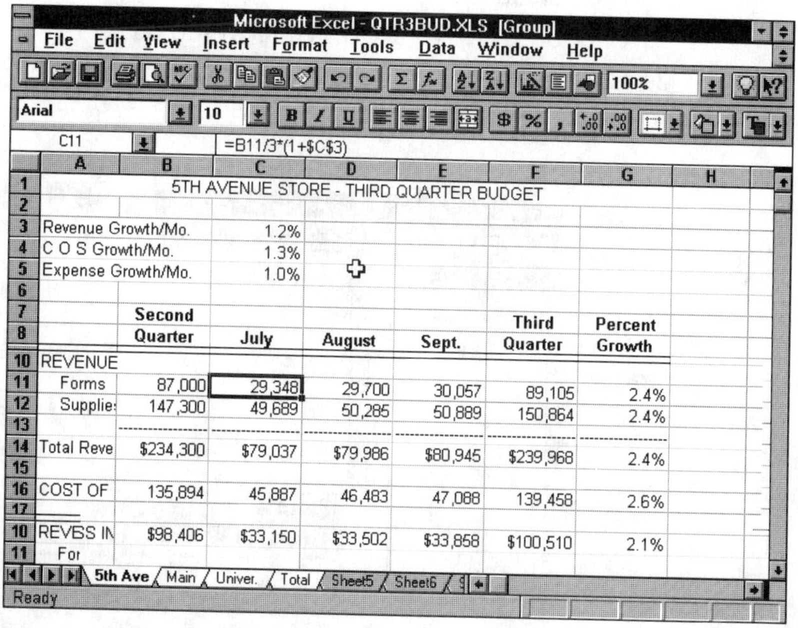

6

The effect of deleting the original column B

Figure 6-8.

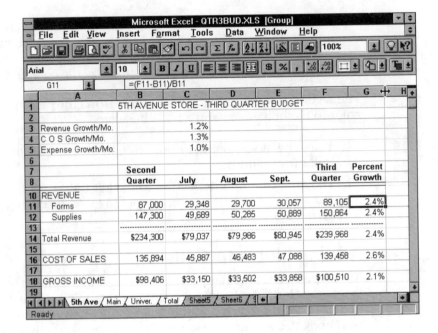

After column
resizing is
completed
Figure 6-9.

the note. Do this with the following steps and then add a couple of notes to
your workbook.

1. Click on the tab for Sheet5 and then click on the 5th Ave tab to select
   just that sheet.

2. Click on C11. The active cell moves to C11.

3. Click on the Insert menu and the Note option. The Cell Note dialog box
   opens, as shown here:

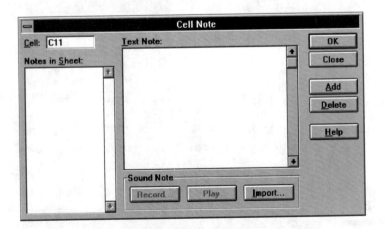

4. Type **Previous Quarter / 3 * (1 + Growth Rate)** and click on OK. This note is added to cell C11.

5. Click on C3. The active cell moves to C3.

6. Click on the Insert menu and the Note option. The Cell Note dialog box opens.

7. Type **From George Brown** and click on OK. This note is added to cell C3.

You can tell that a note is in a cell by the small red (or black on monochrome monitors) mark in the upper-right corner of the cell. To read a note, move the active cell to a cell with a note and press ⟨Shift⟩-⟨F2⟩. The same Cell Note dialog box will open. You can also print notes by selecting the appropriate option on the Sheet tab of the Page Setup dialog box from the File menu.

Excel also allows you to record and play back a sound note and add it to the active cell. To use this feature, you need to be using Microsoft Windows version 3.0 with Multimedia Extensions version 1.0 or later, or Microsoft Windows version 3.1 or later, and have the appropriate hardware installed in your computer. From the Cell Note dialog box, you can choose to record a new sound note, play back an existing note, or import a prerecorded sound.

Erasing a Group of Cells

The third quarter budget is now complete. You can turn it into another quarter's budget by changing the previous quarter's actuals and growth rates. All the formulas are based on those two sets of numbers. A simple way to change the actuals is to erase them and enter new ones. Use the following steps to save the workbook twice, once under its current name and once under a name for the new quarter. Then, in the new quarter's workbook, select the first three sheets (you don't want to erase the totals), and erase the second quarter actuals.

1. Click on the File menu and the Save option. The workbook is saved under its current name, QTR3BUD.XLS.

2. Click on the File menu and the Save As option, type **\sheet\qtrbud**, and press ⟨Enter⟩. The workbook is saved again under the name QTRBUD.XLS.

3. With 5th Ave (Sheet1) selected, press and hold ⟨Shift⟩ while clicking on the Sheet3 (or Univer.) tab to select the first three sheets.

4. Drag down column B from B11 through B27. The second quarter actuals are highlighted.

5. Press ⟨Del⟩. The second quarter actuals disappear, as shown in Figure 6-10.

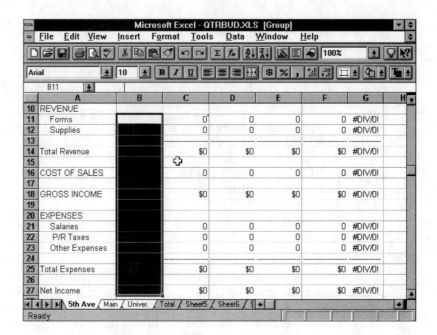

Erasing the
second
quarter actuals
Figure 6-10.

Notice that most of the formulas that depended on the second quarter actuals have changed to 0. The exception is the percentage growth amounts, which changed to #DIV/0!, indicating you are trying to divide by zero. All of the formulas, including the percentages, will change back to legitimate values as soon as you enter a new set of actuals. However, don't do that yet.

Using Undo

We forgot to print the workbook before erasing column B. Luckily, Excel has a feature that can restore the column, as long as you have done nothing since you erased it.

1. Press Ctrl-Z or Alt-Backspace (Undo) now. Your workbook should be restored to the way it was before you erased column B.

   Undo even restores a full workbook erase. (Remember, the key is to use it *immediately* after making a mistake.)

   If, for some reason, your workbook is not restored, restore it from disk by doing the following:

2. Click on the File menu and the Open option, type **qtr3bud**, and press Enter. Your workbook is restored to its original condition.

Printing the Workbook

So far you have seen your budget results only on the screen. The screen version may give you the information you need, but it does not allow you to share the information easily with others—for that you must print the budget. To print you must give Excel information about what and how to print. In other words, you must set some parameters for Excel to use while printing. Once you have set the parameters, you can do the actual printing. The options for both setting parameters and doing the printing are contained on several menus and dialog boxes, discussed in the next several sections. Begin the printing process by determining the area to be printed and by entering the settings on the Page Setup dialog box.

Setting the Parameters

If you specified your printer correctly when you installed Windows, the only required parameter for printing is the area in the workbook that you want to print. To give the printed output the same polish you did to the screen image you can add a heading and check the page margins and length. Excel has a number of other parameters that can be set, but these are the ones most people use.

6

Identifying the Print Area

For this example you'll want to print the first sheet—everything you have done for the 5th Avenue Store. Excel's default is just that—to print everything that has been entered on the currently selected sheet. You do not need to identify what to print here; it's done for you in this case. In other circumstances you might want to print only a section of a sheet. In that case you'll need to specify that specific cells be printed. See how this is done in the following example.

1. Click on the vertical scroll bar to see the top of the Sheet1.
2. Click on the File menu Page Setup option, then on the Sheet tab, and finally in the Print Area text box.
3. If necessary, drag the Title bar of the dialog box so you can see cell A1 of the sheet; then, on the sheet, drag from A1 through G27 to highlight that area. The Page Setup dialog box will reflect this selection as you can see in Figure 6-11.

Whenever possible, print using the default of the entire sheet instead of specifying the print area. The reason for this is that if you modify your workbook by adding columns or rows and you have specified a print area, you will have to modify the print area to incorporate the new columns or

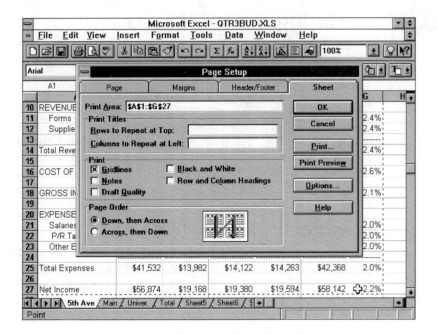

rows. Once you have defined a print area, you can get rid of it by deleting the entry in the Print Area text box of the Page Setup dialog box.

Setting Up a Printed Page

You also use the Page Setup dialog box to specify the major facets of the page to be printed. Through this dialog box you can enter a header and/or footer to be printed on the page, set the page margins, and turn the row and column headings and gridlines on or off.

1. Click on the File menu and the Page Setup option; the Sheet tab of the Page Setup dialog box should again appear.

   Besides the Print Area, you can specify the rows and columns that are repeated on each page by clicking in the text box and dragging on the sheet as you did for the Print Area. The Print option buttons turn on and off the printing of a grid between each cell, the printing of cell notes, and the printing of the row and column headings. The buttons are also used for selecting draft quality and forcing the output to be black and white.

   Additionally, on the Sheet tab you can determine how you print a multipage workbook—*down* the sheet, one page wide until the end and then over to the next set of columns, or *across* the sheet, one page long to the end and then down. For most applications, the default page order of printing down first before moving to the right is what you want to use.

For the third quarter budget, the only change you want to make on the Sheet tab is to turn off the gridlines. Do that next and then open the Page settings of the Page Setup dialog box.

2. Click on Gridlines to turn it off (not checked).

3. Click on the Page tab to display the Page settings shown here:

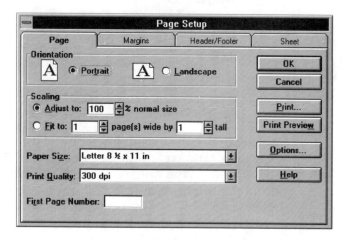

6

Most of the settings under the Page tab are obvious. One of the handiest options, and maybe not so obvious, is the Fit to option under Scaling. If you select this, Excel will automatically scale the area you want to be printed to the number of pages you specify. This is particularly helpful when you find you have a sheet just a little too large for a given number of pages. For the third quarter budget you do not need to change the default settings.

You can also use the settings under the Page tab to change the orientation of what you are printing and the paper size. There are two orientations: *portrait*, in which the long side of an 8.5×11-inch page is vertical (the normal way a page is held), and *landscape*, in which the long side is horizontal. Not all printers can support various paper sizes and/or landscape printing. If yours doesn't, these options will be dimmed or colored light gray.

Entering a Header A *header* is a line of text that is added to the top of every printed page. It often contains a page number, the date of printing, and a descriptive line of text (like a company name). A *footer* is a line of text added to the bottom of every printed page. Excel provides a default header and footer that you can customize, or you can enter your own. In either case you can specify the alignment, use of bold or italic fonts, and the inclusion of such things as the date and page number. Look at the Header/Footer tab next.

1. Click on the Header/Footer tab to display this dialog box:

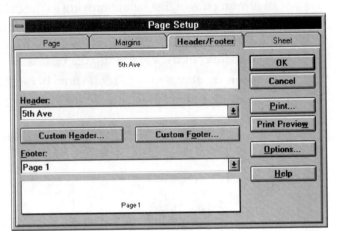

As you can see, the default header is the sheet name shown in the sheet's tab, "5th Ave" in the case of Sheet1 of the quarterly budget. The default footer is the word "Page" and the page number. By clicking on the drop-down list boxes, you can choose several other ready-made headers and footers. Most people though, want to create their own headers and footers, and that is what you will do here.

Add a header containing the date, company name, and page number to the printout of the third quarter budget, as well as a footer that says "Company Confidential" with the following steps:

2. Click on the Custom Header button to display the Header dialog box shown here:

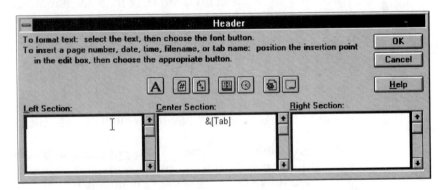

A header or footer can have up to three segments: a left-aligned segment, a centered segment, and a right-aligned segment. Each of the three segments has its own text box or section. All left-aligned text is typed in the Left Section, center-aligned text in the Center Section, and right-aligned in the Right Section.

The seven buttons in the middle of the dialog box perform the following functions in any of the sections:

Button	Name	Function
	Font	Opens the Font dialog box that allows you to change the font, style, and size of text that you have previously selected
	Page	Inserts the current page number
	Pages	Inserts the total number of pages in the document
	Date	Inserts the current date in the computer
	Time	Inserts the current time in the computer
	File	Inserts the workbook filename
	Tab	Inserts the sheet name entered on the sheet's tab

6

Try these buttons next. Note that the insertion point (the blinking vertical line) is in the Left Section so that is where you will begin by placing the date there.

3. Click on the date button (in the middle). In the Left Section, &[Date] appears, telling Excel to place the current computer date on the left of the header when the sheet is printed.

4. Press ⟨Tab⟩ to move the insertion point to the Center Section and highlight the current contents—the sheet (tab) name. Type **MORNINGSIDE SPECIALTIES**. This enters the company name and deletes the existing code. Don't worry that it is on two lines in the text box. It will be on one line when it is printed, unless you make the font size very large.

5. Press (Shift)-(Home) to highlight both words of the company name and then press the font button on the left. The Font dialog box opens as shown here:

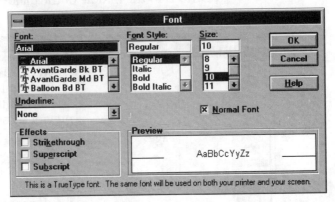

6. Click on bold, scroll the size box until you see 12, and then click on it and finally on OK. The company name is made bold and enlarged to 12 points.

7. Press (Tab) one more time to move to the Right Section. Type **Page**, press (Spacebar) once, and click on the page number button (second from the left). Click on OK.

8. You are returned to the Page Setup dialog box. Click on the Custom Footer button.

9. Press (Tab), and type **COMPANY CONFIDENTIAL** to replace the default footer with these words.

10. Press (Shift)-(Home) to select the words, click on the font button, again select bold and 12 point size, and click on OK twice to complete both the Font dialog box as well as the Footer dialog box.

Your completed Header/Footer tab of the Page Setup dialog box should look like this:

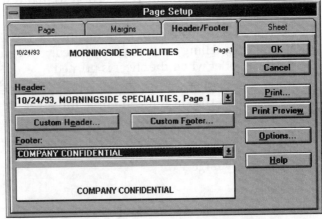

Setting the Margins   Margins are the distances in inches from the edge of the page to the printed data or chart on four sides: top, bottom, left, and right. Look at the Margins tab and set the margins for the third quarter budget with the following steps:

1. Click on the Margins tab. The Page Setup dialog box opens, as you can see next:

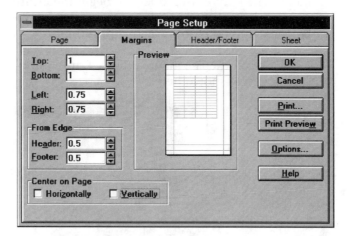

    As can see in the little preview in the center of the dialog box, the default margins cause the sheet you want to print to be offset up and to the left of center. You could change the top and left margins until the sheet was centered, but you can have Excel automatically center it for you by using the Center on Page check boxes in the lower left of the dialog box.

2. Click on Horizontally and on Vertically to center the sheet in both directions. Notice how the little preview in the center mirrors what you do.

3. Click on OK to close the Page Setup dialog box.

Doing the Printing

The actual printing is anticlimactic after setting up the page, but you still must perform several steps, such as readying your printer, setting some final printing parameters, and, finally, telling Excel to print.

The steps to prepare your printer are governed by the printer you are using. All printers must be turned on and placed online. In most printers the paper must be aligned so the upper-left corner is correctly positioned. Also, your printer must be correctly cabled to your computer. Finally, you should have installed your printer with the Windows Setup program or by using the

Windows Control Panel. (If you do not know whether your printer is installed correctly, try printing. If it works, you have an affirmative answer.) If your printer is not installed in Windows, see the section on installing it in Appendix A. Take any other steps necessary to ensure that your printer is ready to print.

Once your printer is ready, start printing with the Print option from the File menu. The Print option does not begin the printing directly but rather opens another dialog box that asks you several more questions. Look at that dialog box next and then do the actual printing.

1. Click on the File menu and the Print option. The Print dialog box opens, as shown here:

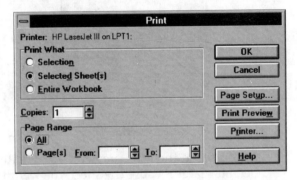

This Print dialog box is for the HP LaserJet III printer. If you are using a different printer, your dialog box may be slightly different but should have most of the options shown. Importantly, this is where you determine what is to be printed: a selected print area, selected sheets, or the entire workbook. Also in this dialog box, you have the ability to specify the number of copies you want, to print all or only selected pages, and to preview the output on your screen. Look at the last of these options first.

2. Click on the Print Preview button. The workbook and dialog box clear from your screen and a small representation of the printed sheet appears, as shown in Figure 6-12.

   On most displays you cannot easily read the image on the preview screen, but you can tell a lot about placement on the page and how good a guess you made on the margins. You can also zoom in and see a particular area. Do that next.

3. Move the mouse pointer, which you notice has become a magnifying glass, to the approximate center of the sheet and click. The image expands to clearly show the center of the sheet, as you can see in Figure 6-13.

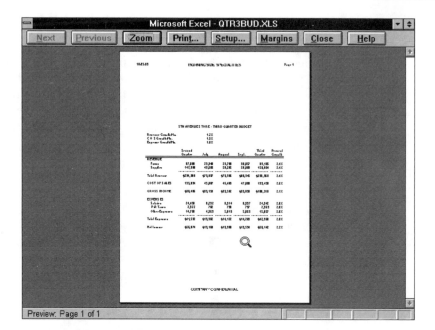

Preview of printed worksheet
Figure 6-12.

6

	Second Quarter	July	August	Sept.	Third Quarter	Percent Growth
Revenue Growth/Mo.	1.2%					
C O S Growth/Mo.	1.3%					
Expense Growth/Mo.	1.0%					
REVENUE						
Forms	87,000	29,348	29,700	30,057	89,105	2.4%
Supplies	147,300	49,689	50,285	50,889	150,864	2.4%
Total Revenue	$234,300	$79,037	$79,986	$80,945	$239,968	2.4%
COST OF SALES	135,894	45,887	46,483	47,088	139,458	2.6%
GROSS INCOME	$98,406	$33,150	$33,502	$33,858	$100,510	2.1%
EXPENSES						
Salaries	24,450	8,232	8,314	8,397	24,942	2.0%
P/R Taxes	2,322	782	790	797	2,369	2.0%
Other Expenses	14,760	4,969	5,019	5,069	15,057	2.0%
Total Expenses	$41,532	$13,982	$14,122	$14,263	$42,368	2.0%
Net Income	$56,874	$19,168	$19,380	$19,594	$58,142	2.2%

Preview zoomed in on the center
Figure 6-13.

4. Use the horizontal and vertical scroll bars to look around the sheet and the header.

   Notice that when you deleted column B you got rid of the vertical line you placed between the old columns B and C. This is what Print Preview is for—it lets you find problems before printing. Go back now and replace the line and then come back and print.

5. Click on Close to return to the sheet. Select the four sheets by pressing and holding [Shift] while clicking on the Total tab, scroll your sheet so you can see rows 10 through 27, and then drag down column A from rows 10 through 27. Open the Borders tool in the Formatting toolbar and select the right-hand border in the top-right corner of the palette. Deselect all but the 5th Ave sheet by clicking on Sheet5 and then on the 5th Ave tab. Finally, again open the Print dialog box from the File menu and click on Print Preview. You now have the vertical line as you intended.

6. With the preview the way you want it, click on the Print command button to actually print. Your final printed output should look like Figure 6-14.

7. If you want to stop printing once you have started, click on the Cancel button in the Printing message box, as shown here:

When you tell Excel to print, it creates a print job in memory, containing all of the information to be printed, and sends it to the Windows Print Manager. You can then go back to work while, in the background, the Print Manager is actually doing the printing. You can have several print jobs in memory waiting to be printed. The Print Manager gives you the ability to cancel a job after it has left Excel and to rearrange the priority of the jobs waiting to be printed. For a small sheet like the one you built here, the advantage of the Print Manager is not very evident, but with a large multipage print job it offers a significant benefit.

Trial and Error

Your printout probably did not come out exactly the way you wanted it—or maybe it did not come out at all. Using a printer is almost always a trial-and-error process. Be persistent, and you should get it to work. To cure

10/25/93 **MORNINGSIDE SPECIALITIES** Page 1

5TH AVENUE STORE - THIRD QUARTER BUDGET

Revenue Growth/Mo.	1.2%
C O S Growth/Mo.	1.3%
Expense Growth/Mo.	1.0%

	Second Quarter	July	August	Sept.	Third Quarter	Percent Growth
REVENUE						
Forms	87,000	29,348	29,700	30,057	89,105	2.4%
Supplies	147,300	49,689	50,285	50,889	150,864	2.4%
Total Revenue	$234,300	$79,037	$79,986	$80,945	$239,968	2.4%
COST OF SALES	135,894	45,887	46,483	47,088	139,458	2.6%
GROSS INCOME	$98,406	$33,150	$33,502	$33,858	$100,510	2.1%
EXPENSES						
Salaries	24,450	8,232	8,314	8,397	24,942	2.0%
P/R Taxes	2,322	782	790	797	2,369	2.0%
Other Expenses	14,760	4,969	5,019	5,069	15,057	2.0%
Total Expenses	$41,532	$13,982	$14,122	$14,263	$42,368	2.0%
Net Income	$56,874	$19,168	$19,380	$19,594	$58,142	2.2%

COMPANY CONFIDENTIAL

Printed sheet
Figure 6-14.

6

several common types of problems, try the following suggestions. (If you leave Excel, choose Save from the File menu to save the workbook on disk before leaving.)

If you could not print at all, try these steps:

1. Start at the printer end. Is the printer plugged in, turned on, and set online? Does it have adequate paper and a ribbon? Is there a cable connecting the printer to the computer?

2. Look at the computer. To which port is the printer connected (LPT1, COM1, COM2)? Do you need a MODE command in your AUTOEXEC.BAT file? (If so, see your operating system manuals.) Are any other devices interfering with the printer port? (For example, are both a printer and a modem connected to the same port?)

3. Open the Windows Control Panel in the Main group. Double-click on Printers, and make sure your printer name is correctly specified and that the port to which it is connected is the correct one.

4. Look at the print settings you have specified. Go through the steps of setting the parameters again, checking each against the figures and illustrations in this book.

If the budget printed but it is not the way you want it, try these steps:

1. Adjust the print settings to fit your particular situation. For example, if the margins are not correct, change them until the sheet is located on the page the way you want it.

2. Make sure your printer is not set through its console for some particular type of printing (for example, compressed printing when you want to print at full size).

3. Adjust the layout and formatting so it pleases you. For example, you may want the title to be bold and a larger or even different font. If so, use the techniques you used earlier with the Formatting toolbar to select the title and make the changes.

4. Click on the Print tool (the printer, fourth from the left) in the Standard toolbar to reprint the sheet until you are satisfied.

Saving the Workbook

When you are satisfied with your printout, you need to resave the workbook to capture the print settings you entered. Click on the Save tool (the disk, third from the left) in the Standard toolbar.

Making a Template

After building the third quarter budget, you can use it for the fourth quarter and other future quarters. None of the formulas needs to be changed. You must change only the titles and the previous quarter actuals. When you make this workbook more general purpose, it becomes a *template* (a type of form or structural pattern) for use with any quarter. The remainder of the chapter discusses how this is done.

Changing Titles

To make the titles general purpose, you need to remove the references to the third quarter. With the following instructions, edit the titles to make them generic:

1. Select just the 5th Ave sheet (if it isn't already selected) by clicking on Sheet5 and then on the 5th Ave sheet (since you have individualized the titles, you must change them one by one).
2. Click on cell A1 and drag across the word "Third" and its following space in the edit area and press (Del). The word "Third" is removed.
3. Click immediately after the word "Quarter," type **LY**, and press (Enter).
4. Repeat this process for the other three sheets and then select all four sheets for the remaining changes.
5. Click on B7. The active cell moves to the first column heading.
6. Type **Previous** and press (Enter). "Second" is changed to "Previous," but remains centered in the column and bold.
7. Press (↓) and (→). The active cell moves to the July column heading.
8. Type **Month 1** and press (Enter). "July" is changed to "Month 1" and centered in the column.

In a similar manner, change the second and third months and the third quarter total, so the column headings are as shown here:

	A	B	C	D	E	F	G	H
1	**5TH AVENUE STORE - QUARTERLY BUDGET**							
2								
3	Revenue Growth/Mo.		1.2%					
4	C O S Growth/Mo.		1.3%					
5	Expense Growth/Mo.		1.0%					
6								
7		Previous				Current	Percent	
8		Quarter	Month 1	Month 2	Month 3	Quarter	Growth	
10	REVENUE							

6

Copying Values—Paste Special

There are several ways to change the previous quarter's actual values. One way is to erase the column and reenter the new numbers. Another way is either to edit or to type over the current numbers. A third way is to copy the current quarter's numbers to the previous quarter. These are not actuals *per se*. If you literally copy column F to column B, you would get a set of formulas that did not have any meaning. What you want to do is to copy the *values* produced by the formulas in F, but not the formulas themselves. To do this, use Excel's Paste Special command. Follow these steps to see how Paste Special works.

1. First deselect the four sheets and reselect only the first three since you do not want to change the Total sheet. Then drag on F11 through F27.

2. Press the right mouse button for the shortcut menu and click on Copy. A blinking marquee appears around the highlighted cells in column F.

3. Scroll your sheet up, and then click on B11, which you want to be the recipient of the copy.

4. Click on the Edit menu and the Paste Special option. The Paste Special dialog box opens, as shown here:

5. Click on Values and OK in the Paste Special dialog box. The dialog box closes. Now only the values in column F are copied to column B. See Figure 6-15 for the result. Note the number in the Formula bar for B11.

6. The F11:F27 copy area is still selected to allow you to paste it in another location. Therefore, deselect it by pressing (Esc).

One of the major benefits of using Paste or Paste Special from the menu (either Edit or shortcut), rather than the keyboard or toolbar, is that it does not deselect the copy area so you can paste multiple times.

Other Modifications

You could make many other changes to this workbook. You could add an assumption for every account by inserting a new column to the left of

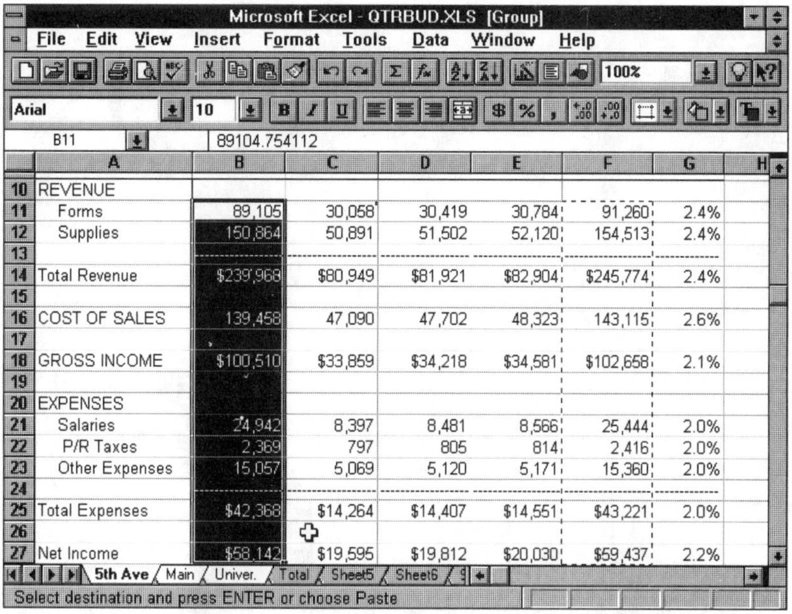

Results of
copying values
Figure 6-15.

column A with the assumptions in it. You could also add more accounts and
subtotals of accounts, or you could add more months and quarterly totals for
a year. Try these on your own if you like.

Saving and Quitting

The last step prior to leaving Excel is to save your work, even if you did it
just a few moments earlier. In this case you want to save the generalized
version of the budget. Use these instructions to do that and then leave Excel:

1. Click on the File menu and the Save As option. The Save As dialog box
    opens and asks you for a filename.

2. If not already shown, type **\sheet\qtrbud**, press [Enter], and click on
    OK. Click on Yes to replace the existing QTRBUD.XLS. The current
    workbook is saved under the name QTRBUD.XLS, replacing the
    workbook you saved under that name earlier.

3. Double-click on the Excel and Windows Control-menu boxes and click
    on OK to leave Excel and Windows and return to the operating system.

6

CHAPTER

7 PRODUCING CHARTS

Excel charts are pictorial representations of data on a spreadsheet. They are another way of displaying the results a spreadsheet produces.

In this chapter you'll work with Excel's charting features. First you'll look at the menus and toolbars containing the charting commands. Then you'll go over the types of charts that are available and their subtypes and peculiarities. Finally, you'll build two types of charts and then you'll see how to edit and customize them.

How a Chart Is Built

Producing charts in Excel is very simple: you create a range on a sheet, highlight that range, and tell Excel, using one of three techniques, to create a new chart. This produces a standard chart based on the defaults set in Excel. You can then change any of these defaults and add many special features to customize the chart. You can creat *chart sheets* that can be printed, viewed, or edited separately, or you can *embed* charts in your sheet so that they become a part of the sheet. Both embedded charts and chart sheets are updated as you change the data on the sheet.

There are three ways to create charts:

✦ The *Default Chart* tool, found on the Chart toolbar, is the easiest way to create an embedded chart. By clicking on the Default Chart tool you can quickly see a chart displayed on the screen based on data you have highlighted. By default (which can be changed) this chart will be a Column (vertical Bar) chart. The Default Chart tool is shown here:

✦ The *ChartWizard* tool, found on both the Standard and Chart toolbars, provides a step-by-step procedure for creating a chart. You can easily switch between 14 different chart types and their subtypes as you create an embedded chart on a sheet. This is what the ChartWizard looks like:

✦ The *Chart* option on the Insert menu displays a submenu which can be used to produce either an embedded chart on an existing sheet or a chart as a separate sheet. This is simply another way of starting the ChartWizard. The Chart option and submenu are shown next:

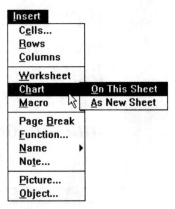

Chart Characteristics

A chart lets you see how data, or numbers on a sheet, look when they are plotted. For Excel to turn the data into a chart, the cells that contain them must adhere to certain guidelines. In addition, charts themselves have common elements that need to be defined.

Guidelines for Charting Data

The data that you intend to chart should be prepared with the following guidelines (use the data in Figure 7-1 as an example):

✦ The data must be in one or more rectangles or ranges (they don't have to be contiguous), with text labels in the topmost row and/or leftmost column. Otherwise, the range may contain numbers and text, but text is interpreted as zeros.

✦ Excel defines the first *data series*—a range of numbers on a sheet that is comprised of related *data points* to be plotted (points that would form, for example, a single line on a chart)—as beginning with the first cell in the upper-left corner of the highlighted range containing a number not formatted as a date and continuing across the rows and columns that are highlighted.

7

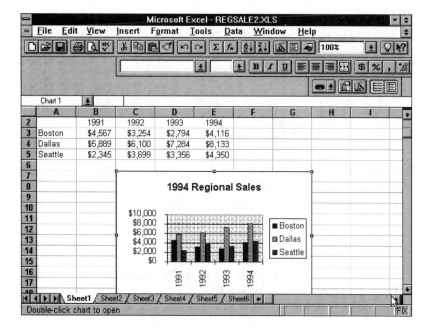

A data range and its resulting chart
Figure 7-1.

✦ Excel determines whether more rows or more columns are highlighted and, with the assumption that there will be more data points than data series, makes the larger of the two the data points. So if you highlight six columns and three rows, each column will be a data point (a single number to be plotted) and each row a data series.

✦ Additional data series can be included in the range by highlighting additional rows or columns, depending on whether you are building a *columnwise* or *rowwise* chart. You can have ten or more data series, but the resulting chart may not be readable.

✦ If the first column or row of the highlighted range contains labels or date-formatted numbers and/or the cell in the upper-left corner is blank, the first column or row—depending on whether the data series are down columns (columnwise) or across rows (rowwise)—is used for the X- or *category axis*.

✦ The numbers on the Y- or *value axis* are formatted with the same format that has been used with the data points on the sheet.

✦ The initial default is to produce a Column or Vertical Bar chart. This and other options can be easily changed.

Figure 7-1 contains a range of rowwise data series that fits the guidelines for a standard chart. Row 2 contains number-formatted dates that are used for the X- (category) axis; the next 3 rows are data series, each containing four numeric data points used to produce the Column chart shown in the lower part of the figure. The legend is taken from the first column.

Elements of a 2-D Chart

Charts have several common elements. Most of the chart elements can be changed or created apart from the creation of the chart itself. Figure 7-2 shows the elements of a 2-D chart; those for a 3-D chart will differ slightly, as you will see. The 2-D chart elements are as follows:

✦ *Y-axis* or value axis, which shows the value of the data points that are plotted.

✦ *X-axis* or category axis, which shows the categories of the data points that are plotted, such as years in Figure 7-2.

✦ *Chart Title*, which can be taken from a cell on the sheet or it can be added directly to the chart.

✦ *Category names*, which identify the individual data points. They may be dates, locations, products, and so forth. The category names are taken from the top-most row or the left-most column, depending on the orientation of the sheet.

◆ *Legend*, which is a set of labels that describe each of the data series. These labels are attached to a symbol, a color, or a pattern that is associated with the series and placed on the chart (initially to the right, but you can move it). It is used to distinguish one data series from another. The text for a legend is taken from a text row or column depending on the orientation of the sheet.

◆ *Data Marker*, which is used to distinguish one data series from another. It is the bar, line, column, or pie wedge on the chart.

◆ *Tick Marks*, which are small lines used to divide the two axes and provide the scaling.

◆ *Gridlines*, which may be displayed for both axes to help read the value of individual data points. Gridlines are scaled according to the values on the axes and can be changed.

◆ *Data Labels*, which are sometimes displayed to show the value of one data point.

◆ *Active Border*, which identifies that a particular chart is active and can be edited. An active border is a thicker gray line as shown in Figure 7-2.

◆ *Selected Border*, which identifies that a chart can be sized, moved, or deleted and contains nodes or handles for that purpose. The chart in Figure 7-1 has a selected border.

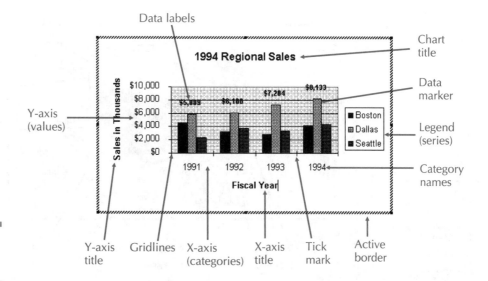

Elements of a
2-D Chart
Figure 7-2.

Elements of a 3-D Chart

3-D charts have the following additional elements which are shown on Figure 7-3:

✦ *Z-axis* or Value axis, which shows the value of the data points.

✦ *X-axis* or Category axis, which is the same as in 2-D charts.

✦ *Y-axis* or series axis, which shows the individual series. It can be considered the depth or inward axis.

✦ *Wall*, which is the background of the plotted area.

✦ *Corners*, which are shown with nodes in Figure 7-3, can be rotated to give you different views.

✦ *Floor*, which is the base upon which the series are plotted.

Each chart element can be accessed and either changed or used to change the chart in some way. You'll learn how later in the chapter.

Chart Tools and Menus

Excel provides an array of helpful tools and menus to build and customize charts. You will look at the more important of these with several hands-on

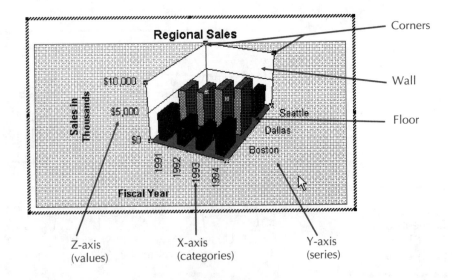

Elements of a
3-D chart
Figure 7-3.

exercises. Prepare for those exercises now by building a simple sheet of data that can be plotted.

1. If you don't have a new workbook on your screen, click on the File menu, and New option to create one now.

2. Type the data on the sheet as presented here:

	A	B	C	D	E	F
1						
2		1991	1992	1993	1994	
3	Boston	4567	3254	2794	4116	
4	Dallas	5889	6100	7284	8133	
5	Seattle	2345	3699	3356	4350	
6						

3. Save the workbook by clicking on the File menu, Save as option, and place it in the SHEET directory, Type the filename **regsales** and press [Enter]. If the Summary Information dialog box appears, press [Enter] to bypass it.

This sheet will be used to demonstrate many of the charting tools and menus. The more complex ones will be explored later in the chapter.

The Insert Menu

To create a new chart sheet or an embedded chart, you can, after selecting the data to be plotted in the chart, use the Chart option on the Insert menu. The two-option submenu will be displayed that you saw earlier in the chapter.

If you select As New Sheet, a new sheet will be created entitled Chart1. You will be led through a series of dialog boxes to fully describe how you want the chart created. You will see how to create a chart sheet later in the section "Creating a Chart."

If you select On This Sheet, the pointer will first turn into a crosshair pointer that you can use in either of two ways to define the area used by the embedded chart. First, you can simply click on the sheet containing the selected data and Excel will lay out the area as it sees fit, but which you can change later. Or second, you can specifically define the chart area by dragging the pointer across the area you want to use. As you drag the pointer, a box will appear which defines the outer perimeter of the new chart. In either case, you will be led through a series of dialog boxes to describe how the chart is to be created. Figure 7-1 shows an embedded chart.

7

The Chart Toolbar

Whenever a chart is displayed on the screen, Excel places the Chart toolbar on the screen. Additionally, you can cause the Chart toolbar to be displayed from either the View or Toolbar shortcut menus. The Chart toolbar provides the following five charting tools:

Tool	Name	Description
	Chart Type	Selects different chart types
	Default Chart	Creates a default chart
	ChartWizard	Starts the ChartWizard
	Horizontal Gridlines	Switches horizontal gridlines on and off
	Legend	Switches a chart legend on and off

Like other toolbars, the name of an individual tool in the Chart toolbar can be seen in a small box beneath the tool whenever the pointer rests on it. Also, the Status bar describes the tool's function. To display the Chart toolbar, follow these steps:

1. From the View menu select the Toolbars option.
2. Click on the Chart check box so that an X appears in it and click OK.

The Chart toolbar will then be displayed. The individual tools on the Chart toolbar are discussed next.

The Default Chart Tool

The Default Chart tool produces a quick look at the selected data range using the default chart type. Initially, the default chart type is the Column chart. Producing a default chart provides a starting point for a customized chart. The default chart is not meant to be a final, presentation-quality chart.

When you click on this tool, the pointer turns into a crosshair which you can then use to precisely define the area in which the chart will be displayed.

Try it now with the sheet you have just entered by following these steps:

1. Highlight the sheet by dragging the pointer from A2 to E5, as shown here:

	A	B	C	D	E	F
1						
2		1991	1992	1993	1994	
3	Boston	$4,567	$3,254	$2,794	$4,116	
4	Dallas	$5,889	$6,100	$7,284	$8,133	
5	Seattle	$2,345	$3,699	$3,356	$4,350	
6						

2. Click on the Default Chart tool. A marquee appears around the selected data and the pointer turns into a crosshair.

3. Maximize your document window if it isn't already, and drag the pointer from C7 to G17, as shown in Figure 7-4.

When you release the mouse button, the default Column chart will be displayed in the area you just defined. Your screen should look similar to Figure 7-1. There will be some differences—your chart will not have a chart title and the x-axis category names may be oriented differently.

7

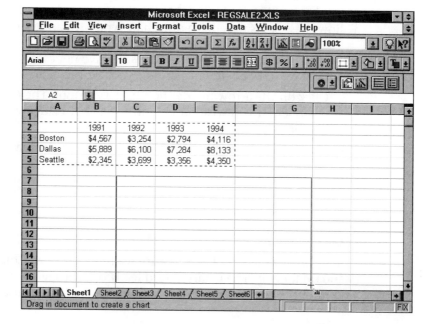

Dragging the pointer across a sheet for a default chart **Figure 7-4.**

The Chart Type Tool

If you would like to see the chart you just produced in another format, then the first tool, the Chart Type tool, is what you need to use. The Chart Type tool opens a tear-off palette that you can leave permanently displayed and which you can drag anywhere in the document window as shown here:

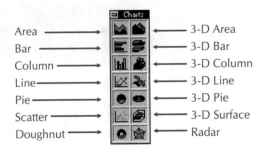

The Chart Type palette presents a choice of 14 chart types from which you can select. The 14 chart types—Area, Bar, Column, Line, Pie, Scatter, Donut, Radar, 3-D Surface, 3-D Pie, 3-D Line, 3-D Column, 3-D Bar, and 3-D Area—are described later in the chapter in "Deciding What to Chart."

You can replace one chart type with another by selecting the chart you want to change and clicking on one of the alternatives in the Chart Type palette. You can tell if the chart is selected if the border has nodes or handles on it. A chart is selected in lieu of an active cell and the reference area of the Formula bar displays the word "Chart" and a number if a chart is selected. Follow these steps to replace one chart type with another:

1. If your chart is not selected (doesn't have nodes or resizing handles), click on it. The reference area of your Formula bar should say Chart1.

2. Click on the arrow beside the Chart Type tool. The Chart Type palette will open. If you wish, drag it off to the right side by dragging on the border.

3. Click on the Line chart type (fourth down in the left column).

The Column chart is immediately replaced by a Line chart, as shown in Figure 7-5. Later you can use this data to explore each of the chart types as they are discussed in the book.

ChartWizard

The ChartWizard, which is the third tool in the Chart toolbar, is also in the Standard toolbar. The ChartWizard leads you through the creation of a chart and prompts you to identify the size of the chart you want to create, the

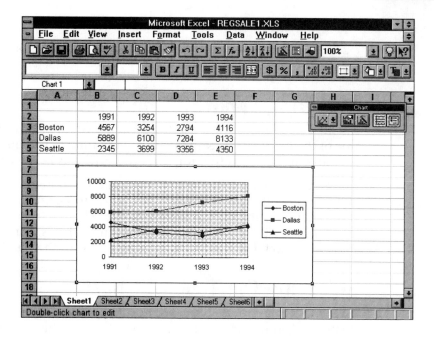

Line chart
replacing the
Column chart
Figure 7-5.

sheet range you want to use to supply the data, the chart type to use, and the descriptive text to add to the chart. You will learn about the ChartWizard in depth later in this chapter.

Horizontal Gridlines Tool

The Horizontal Gridlines tool is an off and on switch which displays horizontal gridlines in the chart or turns them off. Whether gridlines can be displayed depends upon the type of chart being displayed. For example, horizontal gridlines are especially meaningful with charts such as Bar, Column, or Line. They are not meaningful with Pie or Doughnut charts.

To see how this tool works, follow these steps:

1. If your chart is not selected, click on it.
2. Make sure that the chart is either a Line chart or a Column chart.
3. Click on the Horizontal Gridlines tool. The gridlines will disappear. Click again to see the gridlines reappear.

Legend Tool

Similarly, the Legend tool switches the legend in the chart on and off. If you want to turn off the legend, for example, because you are creating a custom legend, you would use these steps:

7

1. Again, insure that your chart is selected.
2. Click on the Legend tool to make the legend disappear. Click on it again to make it reappear.

Deciding What to Chart

The first step in creating a chart is deciding what to chart; this step may be one of the hardest. It is easy to pick a set of numbers to put on a chart, but do those numbers tell the story that you believe is in them?

These questions are not easy to answer, and there are probably several substantially different opinions. The best answer comes from asking yourself if the chart tells the story you are trying to tell. In later sections of this chapter, you will build charts based on simple sheets. For each, you can decide how well the chart tells the story that is in the numbers.

Selecting the Type of Chart

The type of chart to use is as much a subjective decision as what to chart. As mentioned above, Excel offers 14 types of charts plus several variations on each type and the ability to combine types. The choice of which suits your data best depends on what you like, but there are also some rules of thumb. The next sections discuss each of Excel's chart types and when to use them. You also see what variations are available for each type of chart and how each uses particular options in the menus.

Area Charts

An Area chart shows the magnitude of change over time. It is particularly useful when several components are changing and you are interested in the sum of those components. Area charts let you see the change in the individual components as well as the change in the total. For example, in the Area chart shown in Figure 7-6, you can see the change in the sales of three products as well as the change in total sales, which is the sum of the three products.

An Area chart is a Stacked Line chart, with the area between the lines filled in with color or shading. An Area chart plots one data series above another. Assume, for example, that you have two data series in an Area chart. If the first data point of the first series is 50 and the first data point of the second series is 60, the data points would be plotted at 50 and 110. In a normal Line chart, the points would be plotted at 50 and 60. In Figure 7-6, desktop units are added to floor units and laptop units are added to the sum of the first two. The top line on the chart represents total sales, and each layer is that product's share of those sales.

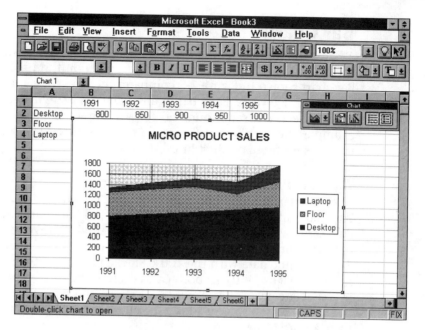

Area chart
showing
product sales
Figure 7-6.

A variation of the Area chart is the 3-D Area chart shown in Figure 7-7. While this chart has a certain "gee whiz" factor, it does not have one of the major features of an Area chart—the ability to show the total as well as the individual components.

7

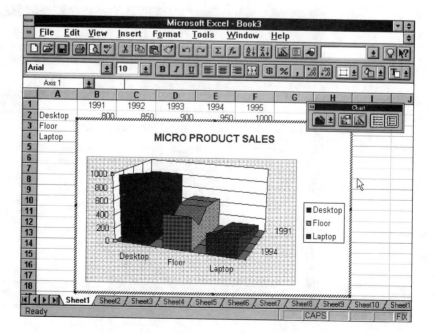

3-D Area
chart showing
product sales
Figure 7-7.

Bar Charts

A Bar chart consists of a series of horizontal bars that allow comparison of the relative size of two or more items at one point in time. For example, the Bar chart shown in Figure 7-8 compares the sales for each of three products in each of five years. Each bar in a Bar chart is a single data point or number on the sheet. The set of numbers for a single set of bars is a data series. For example, the Bar chart in Figure 7-8 contains three data series representing the sales for three product lines.

Bar Chart Variations or Subtypes

The Bar chart has three primary subtypes: the Stacked Bar chart, the 100% Bar chart, and the 3-D Bar chart. The Stacked Bar chart displays additional data series as multiple segments within a single bar. With the product sales data and the Stacked Bar chart variation, you get the chart shown in Figure 7-9. The same data with the 100% Stacked Bar chart type produces the chart shown in Figure 7-10. In both cases each of the three products is contained in a separate data series. Figure 7-11 shows the same data using the 3-D Bar chart type which simply adds depth to a standard Bar chart and does not have a third dimension.

In the Stacked Bar chart, the total length of the bar is the sum of the segments (total company sales, in the example). Therefore, the size of each

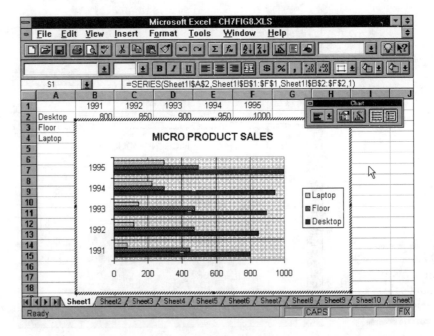

Bar chart
showing
product sales
Figure 7-8.

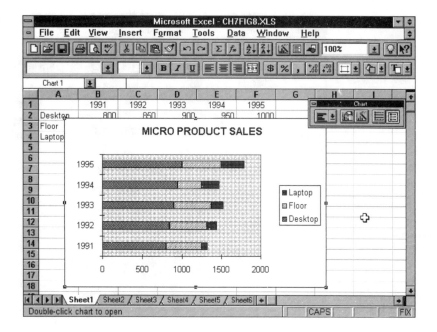

Stacked Bar
chart showing
product sales
Figure 7-9.

segment is relative to both the total and to the other segments. The Stacked
Bar chart has a similar visual effect as the Area chart.

7

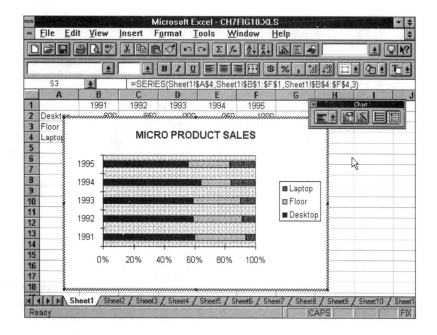

100% Bar
chart showing
product sales
Figure 7-10.

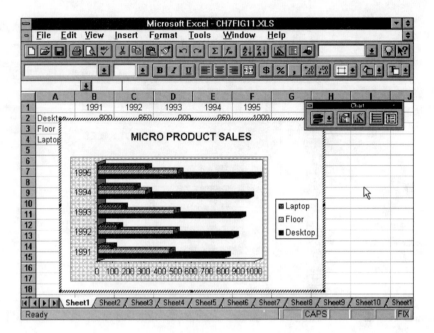

In the 100% Bar chart, all bars become the same height, representing 100 percent. The segments then become their percentage of the total instead of their numerical number, as shown in Figure 7-10. The 3-D Bar chart, in Figure 7-11, provides 3-D markers in place of 2-D horizontal bars.

Column Charts

A Column chart consists of a series of vertical columns that allow comparison of the relative size of two or more items, often over time. For example, the Column chart shown in Figure 7-12 compares annual sales by presenting a column for each year's sales. Each column in a Column chart is a single data point or number on the sheet. The set of numbers for a single set of columns is a data series. For example, the Column chart in Figure 7-12 contains three data series, each bar showing the annual sales for one office.

Column charts have the same variations as Bar charts: Stacked Column, 100% Stacked Column, and 3-D Column, the last of which is shown in Figure 7-13.

Line Charts

A Line chart is used to show trends over time. For example, the Line chart in Figure 7-14 shows that sales and expenses are not following each other, forcing earnings to be negative when expenses are not controlled during

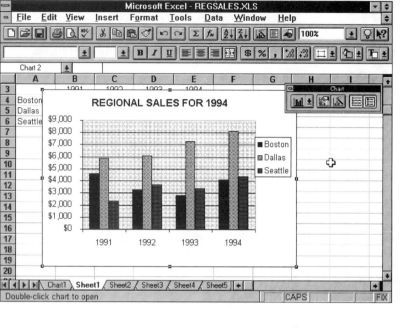

Column chart
showing
annual sales
Figure 7-12.

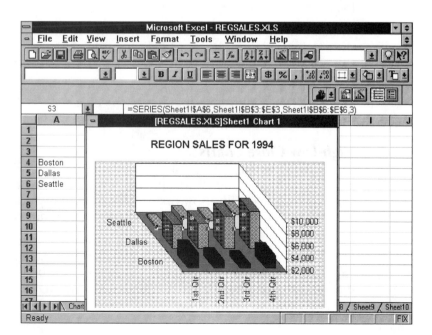

3-D Column
chart showing
annual sales
Figure 7-13.

7

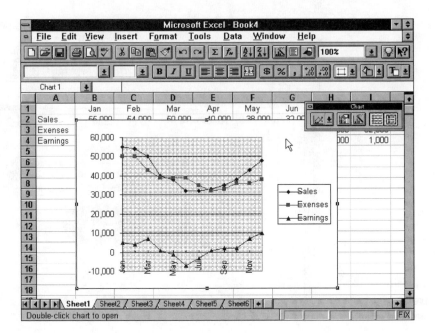

Line chart
showing sales
Figure 7-14.

revenue declines. With Line charts, the reader can make a projection into the future—maybe inappropriately.

In a Line chart, each of the data series is used to produce a line on the chart, with each number in the range producing a data point on the line. There are three data series in Figure 7-14—Sales, Expenses, and Earnings—with 12 data points in each series.

There are two significant variations to the Line chart, a 3-D Line chart, shown in Figure 7-15, and a High-Low-Close chart, discussed next.

High-Low-Close Charts

A High-Low-Close chart is a Line chart with three data series used to display a stock's high, low, and closing prices for a given time period. High-Low-Close charts also work well for commodity prices, currency exchange rates, and temperature and pressure measurements.

Figure 7-16 shows a High-Low-Close chart for stock prices. It contains three data series for the high, low, and closing prices of a stock issue on a given day. The vertical lines are formed by drawing a line between the high and the low data points while the tick mark is the closing price.

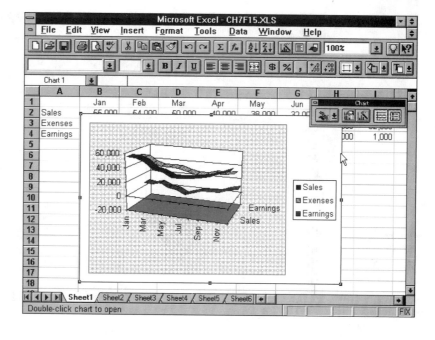

3-D Line chart
showing
monthly sales
Figure 7-15.

7

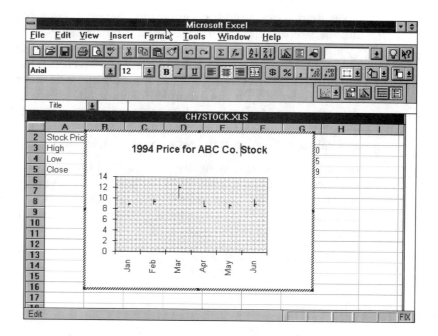

High-Low-Close
chart
Figure 7-16.

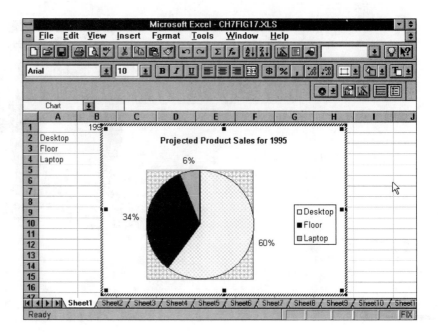

Pie Charts

A Pie chart is best used for comparing the percentages of a sum that several numbers represent. The full pie is the sum, and each number is represented by a wedge or slice. Figure 7-17 shows an example of a Pie chart. Each slice represents the percentage of total sales for a given product category. There is only one data series in a Pie chart. If more than one series is selected, Excel plots the first one. In the example in Figure 7-17, three numbers are in the data series, one for each product category, that represent the sales of each category for one year only. Excel automatically adds the numbers together and calculates the percentages to produce the chart.

In Figure 7-18, you may notice that the Pie chart is *exploded*—that is, one of the slices is separated from the other slices. This is very easy to do. You simply click on the slice and drag it away from the others. When you click on a slice, notice that black selection boxes appear around it, meaning it can be moved, as shown in Figure 7-18.

A 3-D Pie chart, which is the only significant variation, is shown here:

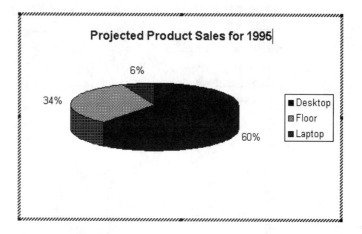

Doughnut Charts

The Doughnut chart is similar to the Pie chart. However, the Pie Chart is restricted to one data series while the Doughnut chart is not. A Doughnut Chart is shown in Figure 7-19.

7

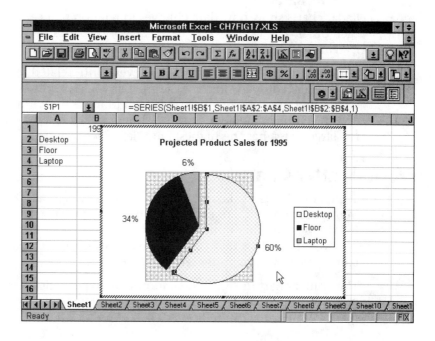

Pie chart with
a selected slice
Figure 7-18.

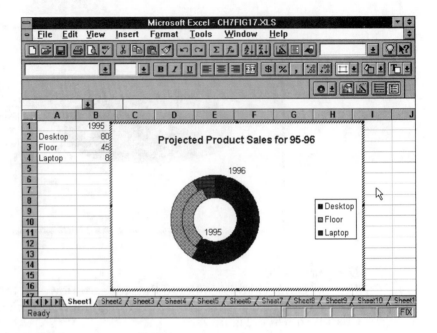

Example of a
Doughnut
chart
Figure 7-19.

Radar Charts

Radar charts show how data changes in relation to a center point and to each other. The value axis of each category radiates from the center point. Data from the same series is connected by lines.

You can use the Radar chart to plot several interrelated series and easily make visual comparisons. For example, if you have three machines containing the same five parts, you can plot the wear index of each part on each machine on a Radar chart, as shown in Figure 7-20. The machine with the largest area has the highest cumulative wear index.

Scatter Charts

Scatter or XY charts show the relationship between pairs of numbers and the trends they present. For each pair, one of the numbers is plotted on the X-axis and the other number is plotted on the Y-axis. Where the two meet, a symbol is placed on the chart. When a number of such pairs is plotted, a pattern may emerge, as shown in Figure 7-21.

The Scatter chart in Figure 7-21 shows the hypothetical correlation between hours of sleep on the X-axis and units of production on the Y-axis. This is a typical example of how a Scatter chart is used.

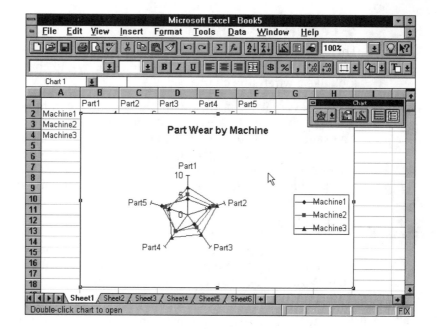

Radar chart
comparing
part wear on
several
machines
Figure 7-20.

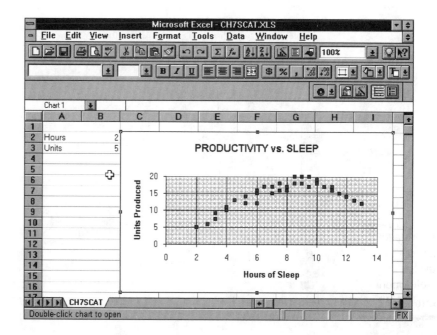

Scatter or XY
chart
Figure 7-21.

7

3-D Surface Charts

There are two types of 3-D Surface charts: color charts that look like a flexible sheet draped over a 3-D Column chart, and charts without color that look like a wireframe chart.

Both types are useful for showing the optimum combinations of two sets of data. On color charts, areas of the same height are shown as the same color. An example of the use of 3-D Surface charts would be bodybuilding: muscle is developed by lifting varying amounts of weight a repetitive number of times. A 3-D Surface chart shows the combinations of weight and repetitions that produce the greatest muscle development, as you can see in Figure 7-22.

Creating a Line Chart

Next, you will create two charts, one as a separate sheet using the Chart option on the Insert menu, and the second as an embedded chart using the ChartWizard. These two exercises will provide you with a good understanding of how a chart is created and what the options are in doing it.

To create these charts, begin with another simple sheet, named SALESCOM.XLS, that shows the sales commissions earned by five sales people. Remembering that a Line chart is best at showing trends, start with a

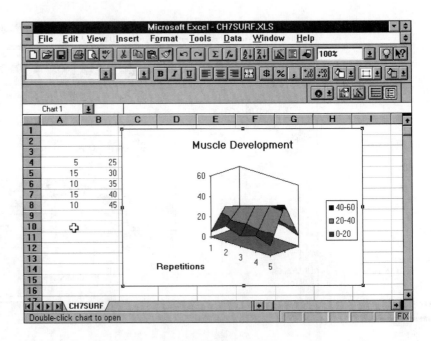

3-D Surface chart of muscle development
Figure 7-22.

Line chart that shows the sales commissions for each sales person for the four quarters of 1994.

1. Click on the File menu, New option. Click OK for the Workbook.
2. Enter the following data on a sheet:

	A	B	C	D	E	F	G
1		1st Qtr	2nd Qtr	3rd Qtr	4th Qtr	Total	
2	Abbott, J	5000	18000	12000	15000	50000	
3	Crowley, C	5000	15000	5500	7000	32500	
4	Gerald, S	3000	10000	5000	7000	25000	
5	Marcus, M	8000	12000	10000	18000	48000	
6	Steel, N	15000	14000	16000	10000	55000	
7							

3. Use the File menu Save As option to save the data with the name SALESCOM.XLS.

Selecting the Ranges to Plot

As you have already seen, your first step in building a chart is to select the range or ranges on the sheet that you want to plot. For this Line chart you want to select the range A1 through E6. Within this range you have five data series, one for each sales person, and each series has four data points, one for each quarter. The category labels for the X-axis are the four quarters in 1994 located in B1 through E1 and the legend labels are the four sales people located in A2 through A6.

1. Select or highlight A1 through E6 (do not include the Total column).

Incidentally, you may find that you have several ranges on a sheet that you want to plot on a single chart, but the ranges are not joined to each other in one unbroken rectangle. Ranges that you are going to plot on a chart may be separated from one another by several intervening rows or columns. These are called *nonadjacent sections*. Even though there several noncontiguous sections, the overall shape of all the sections must still be rectangular. You can select multiple independent ranges by holding down Ctrl as you highlight each range.

Creating a New Chart Sheet with the Insert Menu

To create a new chart sheet you will use the Chart option on the Insert menu. The Chart option gives you two choices, as you will recall. You can either create a chart as a separate sheet or as an embedded chart. Use the following instructions to create a separate chart sheet:

7

1. From the Insert menu, choose Chart. The submenu showing the two options will open.

2. Click on As New Sheet. The first of five ChartWizard dialog boxes will open which verifies that the range is defined as $A$1:$E$6, as shown here:

3. Click on Next. The second ChartWizard dialog box will be displayed.

   The second ChartWizard dialog box asks for the chart type to be plotted and contains 15 alternatives from which you can choose. These are the 14 alternatives that you saw in the Chart Type palette plus one for making combination charts. You want the Line chart type, as shown in Figure 7-23.

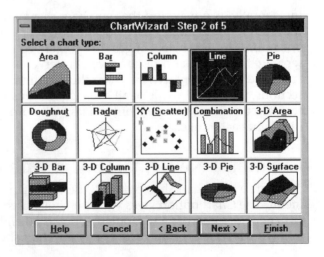

ChartWizard
chart type
dialog box
Figure 7-23.

4. Click on the Line chart and then on Next. The third ChartWizard dialog box will be displayed, as shown here:

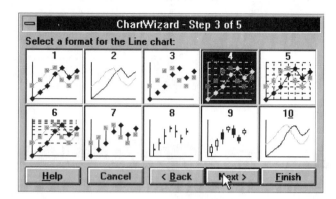

The third ChartWizard dialog box offers ten variations of the Line chart from which you can choose. You want the fourth variation, the format with the gridlines and the plot points, which is the default.

5. Click on Next to accept the default. The fourth ChartWizard dialog box will be displayed.

A sample of the chart is displayed in the fourth dialog box in which you can change the chart's orientation. In other words, this dialog box gives you the opportunity to determine if the Y- and X-axes are correctly labelled and if the legend is correct. In this chart, the orientation and legend are NOT correctly identified. The salesmen are considered to be data points and the quarters are considered to be data series which is reversed from what you want.

You'll remember that one of the items Excel looks at when automatically preparing a chart is whether or not there are more rows or columns in the selected range; Excel assumes that whichever is more are the data points and the other are the data series. If they're the same, Excel assumes the columns are data points and the rows are data series. In this case you fooled Excel by having more series than points.

6. Click on Data Series in Rows. Instantly the chart will be changed and now make more sense, as shown in Figure 7-24.

Now the legend shows the salesmen's names and the category names; the four quarters are on the X-axis. Also, you can tell by quarters which salesman did best and what the trend has been over the year.

7. Click on Next. The last dialog box will be displayed. It allows you to fill in titles and other identifying text.

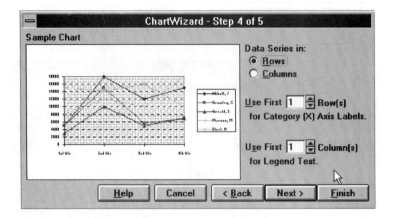

The fourth ChartWizard dialog box allows you to change the chart orientation
Figure 7-24.

At the top of the dialog box you have the opportunity to suppress the legend if you wish. You do not want to do this, so accept the Yes default. You do want to add chart and axis titles, so continue along with these instructions.

8. Press (Tab) to move the insertion point to the Chart Title text box.

9. In the Chart Title text box, type **Salesmen's Commissions For 1994**. You will see the title reflected on the sample chart as soon as you have typed it.

10. Press (Tab) to move the insertion point to the Category Axis Title text box. This is where you enter the text to appear under the X-axis.

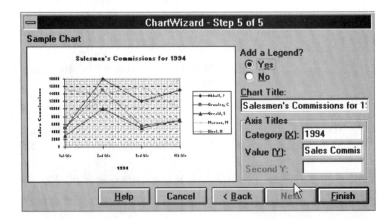

Final ChartWizard dialog box for the Line chart
Figure 7-25.

11. Type **1994** and press `Tab` to move to the Value Axis Title text box. This is where you enter the text to appear to the left of the Y-axis.

12. Type **Sales Commissions**. The completed dialog box is shown in Figure 7-25.

13. Click on Finish. A chart sheet named Chart1 will appear.

Saving, Printing, and Closing

You have now completed the Line chart. Print it, and then save and close it with the following steps:

1. Click on the Save tool in the Standard toolbar to save the workbook with Chart1.

2. Click on the Print tool in the Standard toolbar to print the Line chart. When it is finished, it should look like Figure 7-26. Later you will see how you can use different patterns, markers, orientation, and color to make your chart look different.

Using ChartWizard to Create Embedded Charts

The ChartWizard tool, located on both the Standard and the Chart toolbars, opens the same dialog boxes as the menu approach you just went through. However, you do not have to go through the menu, and, in this case, you will be creating an embedded chart.

Follow these steps to create a Bar chart from the SALESCOM.XLS data:

1. Click on Sheet1 to display that sheet again.

2. If the cells of the sheet are not already selected, select them, A1 to E6; do *not* select the Total column.

3. Click on the ChartWizard tool in the Standard toolbar to begin creating the embedded chart.

4. With the pointer that has become a crosshair, drag over the range in which you want to place the chart, from about B2 to H17.

    When you release the mouse button, the first ChartWizard dialog box will be displayed.

5. Verify that the range of the data is correct, $A$1:$E$6, and click on Next to accept it. The second ChartWizard dialog box will be displayed.

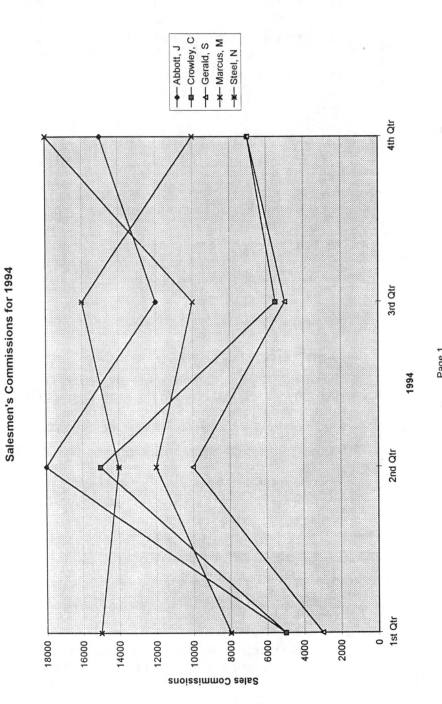

Chart1

Salesmen's Commissions for 1994

Legend:
- Abbott, J
- Crowley, C
- Gerald, S
- Marcus, M
- Steel, N

Sales Commissions

18000
16000
14000
12000
10000
8000
6000
4000
2000
0

1st Qtr   2nd Qtr   3rd Qtr   4th Qtr

1994

Page 1

Printed Line
Chart
Figure 7-26.

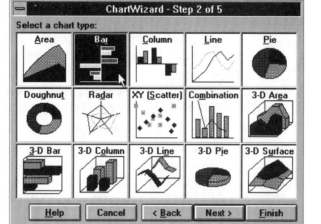

6. Click on the Bar chart option, as shown in Figure 7-27. Then click on
    Next. The third ChartWizard dialog box will be displayed showing the
    several variations of the Bar chart from which you can choose.

7. Click on Next to accept the default format (number 6) that provides
    individual bars and a grid, as shown here:

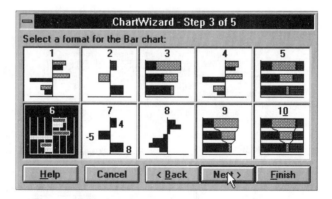

The fourth dialog box will be displayed. It contains a sample of the
chart as it would display right now. This is where you can change the
orientation of the chart by redefining the role of the rows and columns.

You'll notice that again the data series are assumed to be in columns.
You could switch the data series orientation as you did on the line chart
and have the salesmen identified in the legend and have the quarters as

categories. However, it is easier to see the differences between salesmen the way it is.

8. Click on Next to accept the orientation of the chart. The final ChartWizard dialog box will be displayed. On it you can add chart and axis titles.

9. Press `Tab` to move to the Chart Title text box and type **SALES COMMISSIONS FOR 1994**. The title will appear on the sample chart.

10. Click on Finish. The chart will appear on Sheet1 as shown in Figure 7-28.

When you are done creating a chart, you may want to change some parts of it. Excel has considerable capability to edit and modify its charts using the ChartWizard, the Chart toolbar, and special chart menus. You have already seen how the Chart toolbar can be used, so look next at the ChartWizard's ability to edit.

Using ChartWizard to Change the Chart

When you clicked on the ChartWizard to create a chart, five dialog boxes were displayed to guide you through this process. When you click on the ChartWizard with an existing chart selected, you get only two of the dialog boxes: the first one

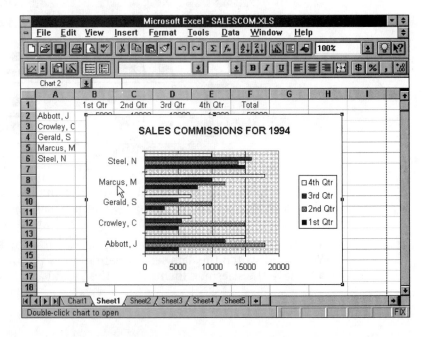

Final embedded Bar chart

Figure 7-28.

in which you can change the definition of the data range and the fourth one in which you can change the chart orientation. Try these now.

1. With the current embedded chart showing, click on the ChartWizard. The first ChartWizard dialog box will be displayed. If you want to add more rows or columns to your sheet, for example, this gives you a quick way to do it.

2. Click on Next for the second dialog box. The second dialog box in Editing mode is the same as the fourth one that appears when you are creating a chart. It allows you to change the orientation of the chart. You can change the references for data series, the X axis, and for legends.

3. Click on OK to accept the original settings.

To make other changes to the chart, you must directly modify the chart itself. In the next section, you'll find out how.

Modifying Charts Directly and With Menus

Once you have a chart defined, you can edit or modify it directly and through menus. In either case, before you can change a chart, it must be *activated*, not merely selected as it has been up until this point.

7

Activating a Chart

A chart must be activated before it can be modified. You will know when a chart has been activated by its border. It has a thicker blue or gray border around it, as compared to the thin border with nodes of a selected chart. Figure 7-28 shows an example of a selected chart, Figure 7-29 shows an activated chart.

Compare selecting and activating a chart with these steps:

1. If the chart is not already selected, click anywhere on the chart to select it. The select nodes or handles will appear.

2. Doubleclick on the chart to activate it (it does not have to be selected first). The border will change to a gray or blue, thicker line.

Now you can edit or change the chart either by using special chart menus or directly. You will first look at what you can do with the menus.

Using the Insert Menu to Change a Chart

Once a chart is activated, the Insert menu contains options for editing it, as shown here:

These special chart options are not available from the menu until a chart has been activated. You will quickly see how you may change the chart with these options.

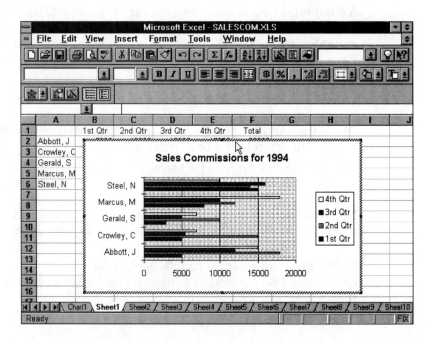

Activated chart
Figure 7-29.

Titles When you click on the Titles option of the Insert menu, you will
see this dialog box:

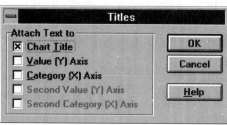

The Titles option allows you to suppress or display a chart or axis title. If the
check box contains a check mark, you will see a title. If there is no check
mark, the title will not be displayed.

To see how this works, turn off the chart title and then redisplay it by doing
the following:

1. Click on the Insert menu and then the Titles option, and the Titles
   dialog box will be displayed.
2. Click on the Chart title check box so that the check mark is no longer
   in the box and then click on OK. The title will disappear from the
   activated chart.
3. Click on the Insert menu, Titles option, and then on the Chart Title
   check box to redisplay a title. Click on OK.

   Now the title, "Title," is displayed. You will change the text later using
   the direct editing method.

Now you will add some data labels to the Bar chart.

Data Labels The Data Labels option on the Insert menu allows you to
place a label (the name of the salesperson) or the value (the quarterly dollar
amount) by each of the bars. Place value labels on the chart with these steps:

1. Click on the Insert menu and then the Data Labels option. This dialog
   box will be displayed:

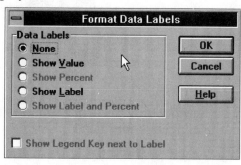

Currently there are no data labels.

2. Click on the "Show Value" check box and then click OK.

The value labels will be placed on the chart. They are difficult to read, but you'll change that shortly.

Next you look at Legends.

Legend   When you select the Legend option on the Insert menu, you are simply telling Excel to display a legend. If no legend is showing and you click on this option, a legend will be inserted in the chart. In this case, the Legend option has no effect since you have a legend already showing.

Axes   When you select the Axes option on the Insert menu, you are shown this dialog box:

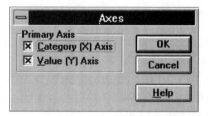

Both the X- and Y-axes labels are showing on the chart and both check boxes are checked in the dialog box. If you remove a check mark by clicking on a check box, the labels for that axis will be removed. You do not want to do that now. If you displayed the dialog box, click on Cancel.

Move on to the Gridlines option.

Gridlines   The Gridlines option on the Insert menu, like the Axes option, allows you to display or remove the gridlines on the chart. If you select the Gridlines option, you will see this dialog box:

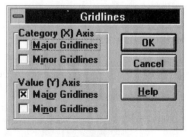

You can see that only the major gridlines for the Y-axis are displayed. Insert minor gridlines also for that axis:

1. Click on the Insert menu and the Gridlines option.
2. Click on Minor Gridlines for the Y-axis so that a check mark is in its box. Click on OK.

   You'll see in the activated chart the effects of the minor gridlines. Now you can more precisely estimate the commissions for each of the sales people.

Picture   The Picture option on the Insert menu allows you to insert a graphic object, such as a logo, into the chart. You do not want to use this right now. However, the dialog box that is displayed simply asks for the directory and filename of the picture file, as you would expect.

New Data   The New Data option on the Insert menu allows you to attach additional data to an existing chart. When you select this option the following dialog box is displayed:

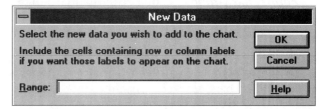

You simply fill in the range of the new data to be added to the chart, or drag across the range on the sheet, and click on OK. The chart will be redisplayed with a new bar appearing with the existing bars.

You have now seen how data can be changed through the Insert menu options. Next, look at how you can change charts through the Format menu options.

Using the Format Menu to Change a Chart
When a chart is active, the Format menu also changes to incorporate several special menu options, as shown here:

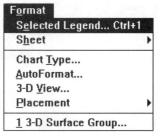

These include changing a selected object, changing the chart type, AutoFormatting a chart, and formatting a particular data group. Start by looking at the Chart Type option.

Selected Object Selected Object is shown as the option if nothing on the chart is selected. In this example the legend on the chart was selected. If you selected another object in the chart, it would be the selected item, such as Selected Axis, or Selected Data Labels. If this menu item is then selected, options pertaining to the selected item would be made available.

Chart Type When you click on this option, you are shown 2-D or 3-D chart types, depending on your current activated chart structure. For the current Bar chart, you see the 2-D alternatives shown in Figure 7-30.

You can change from 2-D to 3-D and see a different selection of chart formats displayed. The alternatives allow you to change the major chart type. If you click the Options button in the Chart Type dialog box, you will open the Format Bar Group dialog box which is also opened by the last option on the Format menu: 1 Bar Group.

Format Bar Group The Format Bar Group dialog box, which is opened either from the Format menu or from the Chart Type dialog box, allows you to access four groups of formatting options that are shown in Figures 7-31 through 7-34.

In Figure 7-31, you can see the major subtypes available for the Bar chart: individual bars, stacked bars, and 100% stacked bars.

By clicking the Series Order tab you get the dialog box shown in Figure 7-32 where you can change the order of how the data series are displayed. For example, instead of displaying the 1st Quarter first, you might want to show the 3rd Quarter first.

Figure 7-33 shows the Axis option, which allows you to change the axis upon which the chart is plotted. In this case you cannot change either (both

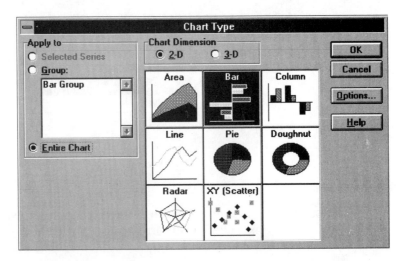

Chart Type selection from the Format menu

Figure 7-30.

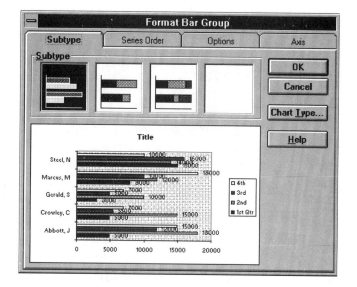

Subtypes tab
of the Format
Bar Group
dialog box
Figure 7-31.

of the axes options are dim) because the chart would have no meaning if an axis were turned off.

Finally, in the Options tab, shown in Figure 7-34, you can vary the distance between bars and how colors are varied.

If you have displayed these dialog boxes on the screen, press Cancel now.

7

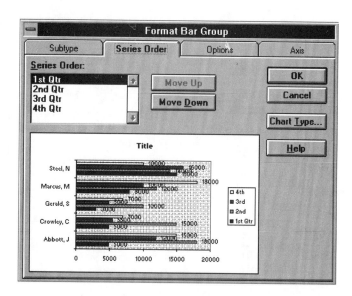

Series Order
tab of the
Format Bar
Group dialog
box
Figure 7-32.

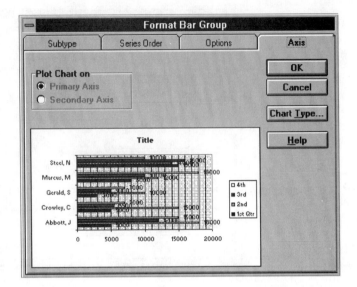

Axis tab of
the Format
Bar Group
dialog box
Figure 7-33.

AutoFormat   *AutoFormat* for charts is like AutoFormat for sheets. Several
formats are predefined for each type of chart and are presented for your
choice. Each format contains selected settings for such elements as label
placement, font and point size selection, titles, colors, gridlines, patterns,

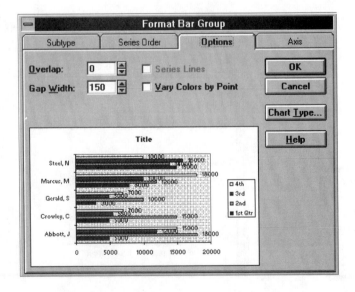

Options tab
of the Format
Bar Group
dialog box
Figure 7-34.

and others. For example, if you select AutoFormat from the Format menu, you would get the dialog box shown in Figure 7-35 that shows the autoformats available for Bar charts. If you were to click on one of the other chart types in the Galleries display box, you would see the autoformats available for that chart type.

You can custom design your own format and save it so that it can be selected just like one of the autoformats.

Changing Charts with Direct Edits

Excel gives you extraordinary direct control over the details of a chart. You can modify or edit all aspects of a chart by simply clicking on the element or area you want changed and then selecting an option or typing text directly onto the chart. Excel refers to the editing or modifications as *formatting*.

When you click on a chart element you select it and, depending on what the element is, you can move, size, or edit the element in that state. If you double-click on an element, a Format dialog box opens and certain options, shown in Table 7-1, become available. Which options are available depends on the element. For example, the Patterns, Font, and Alignment options are available if you double-click on text elements such as titles. For other elements, there are Number, Scale, Placement, Axis, Data Labels, Name and Values, and Y-Error Bars options.

7

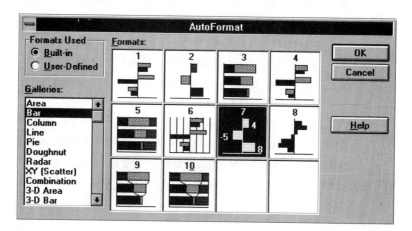

Format menu
AutoFormat
options
Figure 7-35.

Option	Use
Patterns	Changes the border line width, style, and color as well as the foreground and background pattern and color
Font	Selects the typeface, size, style, and color
Alignment	Adjusts the alignment and position of text
Scale	Sets the minimum, maximum, and major and minor increments as well as the type of scales used on each axis
Number	Formats numbers
Placement	Determines the placement of the legend
Axis	Sets the axis on which the data series is plotted
Data Labels	Turns on or off data labels (similar to the Data Label option on the Insert menu)
Names and Values	Selects the sheet ranges that are the sources for the names and values of a particular series
Y-Error Bars	Turns on or off Y-error bars which show the range of possible error in a data point

Format Dialog
Box Options
Table 7-1.

In a 2-D chart you can double-click on ten elements or areas that will result in one or more dialog boxes being displayed. These elements and areas are as follows:

✦ *Chart Title,* which can be formatted for Font, Patterns, and Alignment

✦ *Axis,* which can be formatted for Patterns, Scale, Font, Number, and Alignment

✦ *Axis Title,* which can be formatted for Patterns, Font, and Alignment

✦ *Data Label,* which can be formatted for Font, Patterns, Number, and Alignment

✦ *Legend,* which can be formatted for Font, Patterns, and Placement

✦ *Chart Area,* which can be formatted for Patterns and Font

✦ *Plot Area,* which can be formatted for Patterns

◆ *Data Series,* which can be formatted for Patterns, Axis, Names and Values, Y-Error Bars, and Data Labels

◆ *Data Point,* which can be formatted for Data Labels and Patterns

◆ *Grid Lines,* which can be formatted for patterns and scale

3-D charts have all of the 2-D elements and areas plus the three additional ones: walls, corners, and floors, all of which can be formatted for Patterns.

Next, experiment with some of the formatting capabilities using the Bar chart now on your screen.

Changing Text in Titles and Labels

When you create a chart you are given the opportunity to create titles, legends, and labels. Sometimes you want to change either the text itself or the font and typeface.

Text, as you enter it, is given a default format by Excel. The title is formatted as 12-point bold Ariel. The data values are formatted as 10-point regular Ariel. You can change this formatting as you desire.

Changing the Chart Title   At the top of your screen is a chart title, the original text of which has been replaced with the word "Title." In addition, you can see that the data labels are too big for the chart; they cannot be easily read. You will change the text in the title and the typeface of the data labels. Follow these steps:

1. Make sure Sheet1 is showing with the SALESCOM.XLS workbook and the Bar chart on the screen. The chart should be activated with the distinguishing gray or blue border around it.

2. Click once on the chart title. The word "Title" will be selected and a box with nodes or handles on it will surround it, like this:

3. As you place the pointer inside the box, you'll find that it turns from an arrow to an I-beam. Drag the I-beam pointer across the letters, highlighting all letters of the title, like this:

4. Type **SALES COMMISSIONS FOR 1994**. The Title text will be replaced with the new title.

   Next, add a background for the chart title.

7

5. Double-click on the chart title background. (Be careful. The pointer must be an arrow, not the I-beam, and the area clicked on must be the title area. Otherwise you'll get the Chart Area dialog box, not the Format Chart Title dialog box. It may be easier to deselect the title by clicking somewhere else in the chart and then double-clicking on the title.)

The Format Chart Title dialog box will be displayed.

6. Click on the Patterns tab. The Patterns dialog box will open.

The Patterns dialog box for the chart title lets you place a border around the title, select among a number of alternatives for that border, and select from among a number of colors and patterns for the area behind the title. What you want to do with the Bar chart is place a shadow in the background with the title.

7. Click on the light gray color (second from the right in the second row of the color palette). Click on OK. The title reappears with the gray background as shown here:

You can also change the background of the whole chart in the same way. You can do this by clicking on a blank area of the chart and getting the Format Chart Area dialog box with the same options.

Changing the Data Labels   Currently the data labels are values placed to the right of the bars in the chart. The values are too big to be read. You will make them smaller and boldface.

When you select a data label, you will click on one number, but all numbers for that data series will be selected. Then you will select the numbers for the three other data series as well.

1. Double-click on one of the data labels. The values will be selected and the Format Data Label dialog box will open. Click on the Font tab and the dialog box shown in Figure 7-36 will be displayed.

2. Under Font Style, click on Bold Italic. Under the Size list box, click on 8, as shown here:

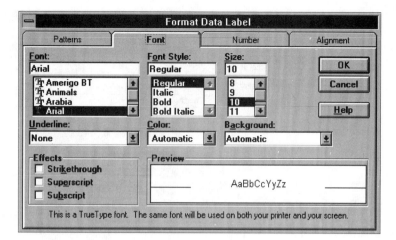

Font tab in the Format Data Label dialog box
Figure 7-36.

3. Click OK. The data labels for that series will be reduced and made bold italic.

4. Select data labels from each of the other three data series and make them 8 points and bold italic as well.

5. Click anywhere in the chart to end the text selection. Figure 7-37 shows the results.

Changing Colors and Adding Patterns   Although you can see the color of the bars perfectly fine on the screen, when they print on your printer, some of the colors will be hard to distinguish. You need to add a pattern to some of the bars. Follow these steps:

1. Double-click on one of the bars that you would like to see changed. Selecting one bar selects all bars for that data series. For example, double-clicking on one of the bottom bars selects all 1st Quarter bars.

   The Format Data Series dialog box opens, offering you a number of options for changing the formats of a data series. You want to change the patterns.

2. Click on the Patterns tab to display the dialog box shown in Figure 7-38.

3. Click on the Pattern drop-down list box and a pop-up palette of patterns and colors will open. Click on the widely spaced dots in the upper-right corner and click on OK.

4. Select another data series by double-clicking on a bar. Then again choose a pattern and click on OK. Figure 7-39 shows one possible way you might reformat your bars.

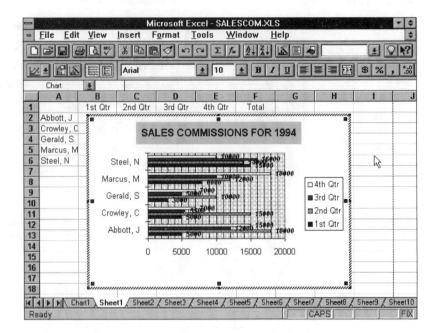

Chart after
changing the
text
Figure 7-37.

You can see how the direct method works. You simply double-click on an
element in a chart and Excel presents a dialog box with choices that you can
use to change the format of the chart.

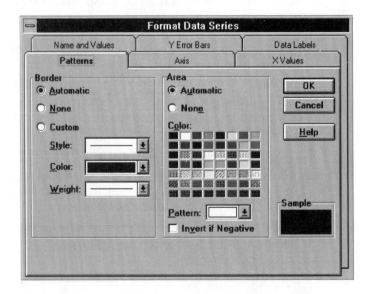

Format Data
Series Dialog
Box, Patterns
tab
Figure 7-38.

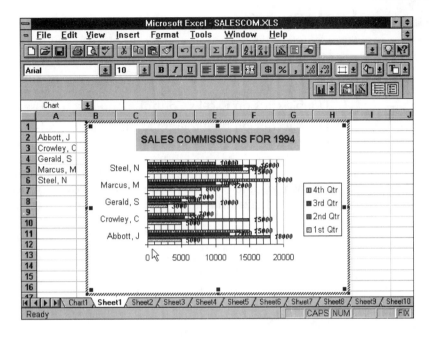

Final Bar chart
as reformatted
Figure 7-39.

Continue to experiment with the chart. Double-click on the chart elements
and see the dialog boxes that are presented to you. When you are finished,
you will need to save and print the chart.

Saving and Printing the Chart

You are now done with the Bar chart, so you need to save it and then print
it. Follow these instructions:

1. Click on the Save tool. SALESCOM.XLS will be saved.
2. Click on the Print tool to print the Bar chart.

Closing a Chart

While you can leave the Bar chart open on the desktop, it serves no real
purpose to do so. Close it by double-clicking on the Bar chart's
Control-menu box. When the Bar chart closes, the previous sheet will be
shown on the screen. You do not have to save it. Double click on its
Control-menu box. When Excel asks whether you want to save the change,
click on No.

Leaving Excel

Since you have saved or released all the sheets used in this chapter, none need to be resaved. You need only leave Excel and Windows. Do that now with these steps:

1. Double-click on Excel's Control-menu box to close Excel.
2. Double-click on the Program Manager's Control-menu box and click on OK to close Windows.

In this chapter you have experimented with the many charting features of Excel. Now try some of these features on your own. In no time at all, your own charts will take on a more professional look.

CHAPTER

8

WORKING WITH A DATABASE

A database is a list—a phone list, a list of products, a list of parts, a list of customers—a set of related information organized into the row-and-column structure of Excel. In this chapter you build two databases or tables. You then sort the tables, summarize them, extract information from them, analyze the information, and build a pivot table and a lookup table.

Databases are the third of Excel's three components (spreadsheets and charts are the other two). A database is a natural adjunct to Excel because Excel's row-and-column structure lends itself to storing information in a database. Each entry in the database, called a *record,* is placed across one row. In a phone list containing names and phone numbers, a record is a single name and phone number combination. Each part of a record (for example, the name or the phone number) is called a *field* and is entered in a column. Thus, a direct relationship exists between rows and columns on a spreadsheet, and records and fields in a database.

A database must be contained on a single sheet. A single sheet can contain several databases, but only one of them at a time may be active and available for performing any of several predefined operations. It is generally better to put separate databases on separate sheets and to separate a database by one blank row and one blank column from other data on the same sheet. This separation allows Excel to automatically select the database. The first row of a database must contain *field names*—the labels in each column of a database that name the field in that column. The maximum size of a database in Excel is 256 fields in 16,383 records (the maximum number of columns in a sheet, and the maximum number of rows less one row to accommodate the field names).

A database can contain any information you want to organize into fields and records. However, it is a good idea to have *at least one blank row at the bottom* of the database to allow for expansion. (You can insert a new record above the last record, and the database range will automatically expand to include the new record.) All of the field names in a database must be unique—they cannot be duplicated—and field names cannot be numbers, logical values, error values, blank cells, or formulas.

Building a Database

Building a database involves little more than typing. You enter a set of field names and then enter the records, and that's all there is to it. Later you will learn some tricks to speed up the entry process, but otherwise it is simply typing. Of course, you can also import data into a database, as you'll see in Chapter 9.

Entering Field Names

The first database for you to build is a list of six sales offices. The record for each office contains an office number, a location, a manager's name, a quota, and a commission rate. The first step in building the database is entering the field names. Your computer should be on and Excel loaded, and you should have a blank workbook on your screen with A1 as the active cell.

1. Type **Number** and press ➡. "Number" is entered in A1, and the active cell moves to B1.

2. Type **Office** and press ➡. "Office" is entered in B1, and the active cell moves to C1.

Complete the remaining field names as shown in the following illustration, using a similar procedure. In column E press (Enter) instead of ➡.

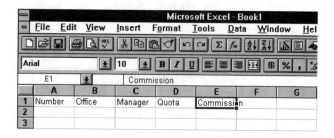

Numbering with a Series

When you have to enter almost any sort of consecutive numbers or dates, you can get help from Excel's Edit Fill Series option. To use this option you must specify the range you want to fill and then enter a start number, an increment or step number, and, optionally, a stop number. For example, if you want a list of numbers from 1 to 10 in column A, beginning in A1, you enter **1** as the start number, highlight the range, and enter (or accept the default of) **1** as the step number. You get 1 in A1, 2 in A2, 3 in A3, and so on to 10 in cell A10.

The start number must be entered on the sheet in the first cell of the row or column you want to fill. Excel uses 1 as the default for the step number and stop number, respectively, if you do not enter them. You can enter any number as the start number, including dates (in a recognizable format), negative numbers, or formulas that evaluate to one of those. The step or stop value must be a recognizable number, not a formula or range name. You can use fractional numbers for the step and stop values, and the stop number may be a date (in a recognizable format).

Either the stop number or the end of the range can stop the series operation. If a stop number stops the series, it does so just before the stop number is exceeded. There are special considerations for series, which are discussed later in this chapter.

Even though you have only six numbers to enter, the Edit Fill Series option makes short work of it. Try it with these steps:

8

1. Click on A2. The active cell moves to A2.
2. Type **250** and press (Enter). The start value of 250 is entered in A2.
3. Highlight the range A2 through A7.
4. From the Edit menu, choose Fill and then select Series from the submenu. The Series dialog box opens, as shown here:

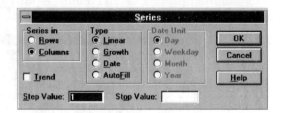

You can see in the Series dialog box that Excel has detected you want the series to go down a column. The default Type setting is Linear, which is what you want. The other Type options are *Growth*, which multiplies the last cell by the step value, *Date*, which produces a series of date values, and *AutoFill*, which will be discussed in the next section. If you choose Date, the Date Unit option becomes available (in the illustrated dialog box this option is grayed) and allows you to choose whether the date increment is Day, Weekday, Month, or Year.

5. Type **5** for the step value and press (Enter). The dialog box closes and the series of numbers appears in column A. Notice that the range size was used to stop the fill operation.

Numbering with AutoFill

AutoFill looks at the values in the highlighted cells and makes an intelligent decision on how to extend those values in a series that fills the remainder of the highlighted cells. As you saw in Chapter 5, AutoFill allows you to create or extend a series either by dragging the fill handle across the sheet in any direction or by selecting an option from the Series dialog box. Creating a series by dragging provides a faster, real-time display of the results, while using the Series dialog box offers greater flexibility in defining the range and incremental values.

To start a series, enter the first two values in two adjacent cells or choose a value with a known increment, such as a date. For example, if you highlight the range C2:D2 and enter **50** in C2 and **100** in D2, you could then simply drag the fill handle of C2:D2 to the right to extend the series. The value 150 would automatically be placed in E2, 200 in F2, and so on. Unlike with the

Series dialog box, there is no way to set a stop value; the series is extended as long as you continue dragging. The Formula bar Reference area displays the prospective values of the active cells as they are dragged. Try the following instructions to see how AutoFill works by dragging the fill handle:

1. Highlight A2:A7 (if it isn't already), press (Del), and click on OK in the dialog box. The series you previously made is deleted.

2. Make sure that Cell Drag and Drop is turned on in the Tools Options Edit dialog box, and then highlight A2:A3. Type **250** in the active cell, A2, and press (Enter).

3. Type **255** and press (Enter) to establish the series increment in cell A3.

4. Drag the A2:A3 fill handle down column A to A7. Notice how the numbers increase in the Formula bar as you drag.

Continue to experiment with AutoFill by dragging the fill handle up and down column A. Click on a single cell in column A. Drag its fill handle to the right. The adjacent cells are filled in with the same values since there is no incrementing detected by AutoFill. When you are through experimenting with AutoFill, erase your experimentation so you have only the field names in the first row and the series in column A.

Entering Records

8

Entering the remaining parts of the records is just simple typing. You can either type down a column or across a row, whichever is easier for you. Do that now, entering all of the information shown in Figure 8-1. If it is easier for you, you may enter the quota figures without the comma and enter the commission amounts as decimals instead of percentages (for example, entering **.04** instead of 4%). If you do enter decimal percentages, they will appear that way on the screen.

Making the Database Easier to Read

The rightmost pair of columns could benefit from formatting, so do that now. If you did not enter the quota with a comma, start with step 1 below, otherwise start with step 4:

1. Drag on D2 through D7.

2. Choose Cells from the Format menu and click the Number tab if necessary. The Format Cells dialog box opens.

3. Click on #,##0 and on OK. The quotas in column D are formatted with a comma.

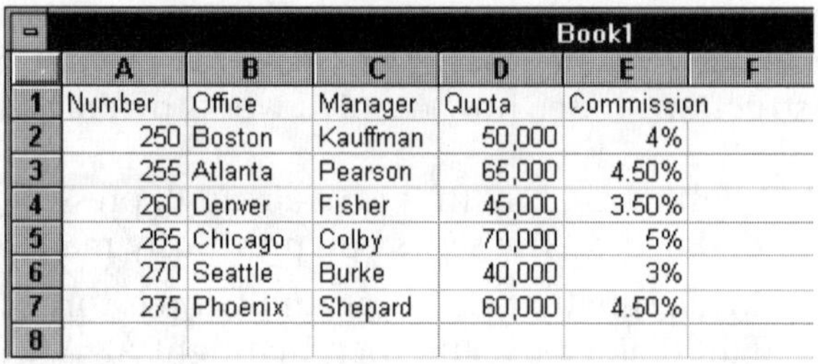

Book1

	A	B	C	D	E	F
1	Number	Office	Manager	Quota	Commission	
2	250	Boston	Kauffman	50,000	4%	
3	255	Atlanta	Pearson	65,000	4.50%	
4	260	Denver	Fisher	45,000	3.50%	
5	265	Chicago	Colby	70,000	5%	
6	270	Seattle	Burke	40,000	3%	
7	275	Phoenix	Shepard	60,000	4.50%	
8						

Completed sales office database
Figure 8-1.

4. Drag on E2 through E7, choose Format Cells from the shortcut menu, and click on the Number tab.
5. Drag across "General" in the Code text box at the bottom of the Number Format dialog box, type **0.0%** to create a single decimal percentage, and press Enter. The percentages in column E are formatted with a single decimal.

The result of formatting the right pair of columns is shown in Figure 8-2.

Sorting a Database

Sorting a database rearranges the records in the database to produce a specific order to the records. You must identify the range or database you want sorted and then specify the key or keys you want to sort on. The keys are one or more fields that you want ordered. Unlike some of the other Data commands, Data Sort does not require the field names, and they should *not* be included in the data range. That means you can sort anything in an Excel workbook, not just a database. When you use Data Sort, each record (which can be a row or a column) within the range you specify is reordered along with the key fields in that record.

Selecting the Sort Range

There are several ways to sort the database you just built; for now, you will consider an alphabetic sort by either office or manager are two ways you consider here. Start by sorting the table by Office. The basic procedure is to

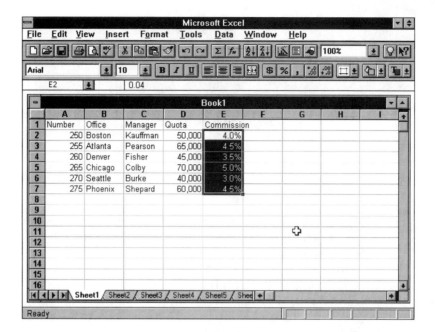

Columns D
and E
formatted
Figure 8-2.

highlight a range of records to be sorted, choose Sort from the Data menu,
enter the keys on which to sort, and start the sort by clicking on OK. Begin
that procedure with these instructions:

1. Select the range A2 through E7, as shown here:

2. Choose Sort from the Data menu. The following Sort dialog box opens:

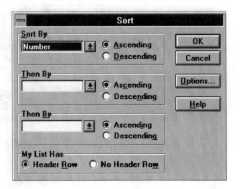

The Sort dialog box shows that Excel has guessed correctly that you have a set of field names (a Header Row) just above the selected range and is using the names in that row to name the column(s) on which to sort. Excel has also assumed correctly that you are sorting by rows. This means that all the cells in one row within the highlight are moved together as the sort is carried out. This makes sense in terms of the database because one row is a single record and, while you want to rearrange the records, you want any given record to remain intact.

Identifying a Sort Key

The sort key, when sorting by rows, is the column containing the field you want sorted. In this example, you want the records sorted by offices, so you want to select Office as the sort key. You can do this by typing **Office** in the first (top) sort key or by opening the drop-down list and selecting it. If necessary, you can move the dialog box to see the sheet.

Click on the top drop-down list box to open it and then click on Office. Figure 8-3 shows how your screen should look.

You have entered the first sort key, which is all you want to sort on in this example. You might wonder what happens in a larger database when you have duplicates in the key you are sorting on. If you specify only one key, duplicates are left in the same order in which they started. But you can specify a second key to sort records with duplicate first keys, and even a third key to sort duplicate second keys. You even can sort on more than three keys by doing more than one sort, using the lowest priority keys first and the highest priority keys last.

Ascending Versus Descending
Once you have specified the sort key, you can specify the sort order—ascending or descending. That is, you indicate whether you want to

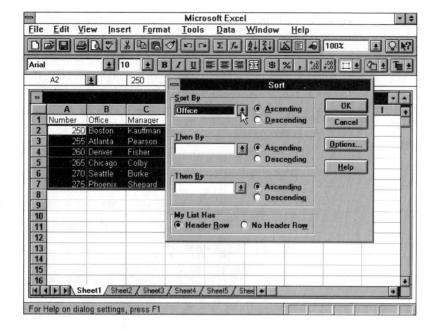

sort in normal *ascending* alphabetical order (A first, Z last) or the reverse of that, *descending* order.

The normal alphabetic sequence (A,B,C,...Z) has been extended to include numbers, blanks, symbols, and logical and error values. Microsoft has established a specific sort order that is followed in all cases. The ascending sequence of this sort order is as follows:

1. Numbers entered as values from the largest negative number to the largest positive number, including dates and times from the earliest to the most recent

2. Text, ignoring capitalization and including numbers entered as text, in this sequence:

   0 1 2 3 4 5 6 7 8 9 Space ! " # $ % & ' ( ) * + , – . / : ; < = > ? @ [\ ] ^ _ '
   { | } ~ (and all other special characters) a b c d e f g h i j k l m n o p q r
   s t u v w x y z

3. Logical values, False first and then True

4. Error values (with no particular sort order)

5. Blank cells

The descending order is the reverse of the order just shown, except that, in both ascending and descending order, blank cells are always sorted last. The ascending sort order for text given above is for United States English and may be different with other languages.

In this example you are dealing with simple alphabetic letters. You want to sort from A to Z, which is ascending order; this is the default and is already selected. If you want to change the sort order, you would click on Descending.

Doing the Sort

The actual sorting is anticlimactic, just click on OK. The dialog box closes, and the database is sorted alphabetically by office, as shown here:

	A	B	C	D	E	F
1	Number	Office	Manager	Quota	Commission	
2	255	Atlanta	Pearson	65,000	4.5%	
3	250	Boston	Kauffman	50,000	4.0%	
4	265	Chicago	Colby	70,000	5.0%	
5	260	Denver	Fisher	45,000	3.5%	
6	275	Phoenix	Shepard	60,000	4.5%	
7	270	Seattle	Burke	40,000	3.0%	
8						

Changing and Re-sorting

Once sorted, the database can be re-sorted on a different sort key in a few quick steps. One reason to have a numbered column in the database is that you can re-sort the list on the numbers and return the database to the original order in which it was entered. You could do that with this database. Instead, sort on the office manager using the sort tools in the Standard toolbar.

The sort tools immediately sort the selected rows in either ascending order or descending order using the active cell to identify the column to sort on. As a matter of fact, you do not even have to select a range you want to sort if the active cell is in the range and there are either sheet edges or blank rows and columns all around the range. Under many circumstances, Excel can even tell if you have a row of field names or not and if you do, they will not be included in the sort. See how is works with these instructions:

1. Click on C1 to deselect the sort range and place the active cell in the column you want to sort on.
2. Click on the ascending sort tool (A to Z). The database is sorted alphabetically by Manager, as shown in Figure 8-4.

The automatic selection of the sort range is impressive, especially the determination of the field names or header row. It is not foolproof, though, and if you want that degree of certainty you should take the extra step of selecting the cells to be sorted.

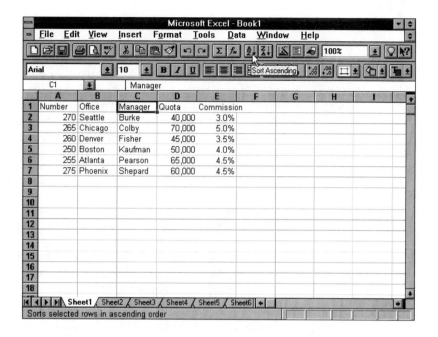

Database
sorted by
Manager
Figure 8-4.

Selecting Information from a Database

A database is primarily an ordered storage place for information. You place information in a database to make it easier to analyze the information or to select particular records. After building a second database, you will spend the remainder of this chapter selecting or analyzing information in one or both of the databases.

8

Building a Second Database

The second database contains the weekly sales amounts for three of the offices for the month of April. The fields will be the office number and name, the week the figures are for, the number of sales, and the total dollar amount of sales. Enter the field names for this table with these instructions:

1. Click on the vertical scroll bar below the scroll box, and click on A21 to move your active cell to A21.

2. Type the five field names shown here, but don't type the dates yet:

	A	B	C	D	E	F
21	Number	Office	Week	Sales	Amount	
22						
23						
24						

Entering Dates as a Series

One of the fields is an identifier for the week of the month for each record. Instead of typing this sequence of dates, you can use the Series dialog box to enter them automatically. For the start number you enter the starting date, for the step number you enter a calendar increment (day, weekday, month, or year), and for the stop number you enter the ending date. The starting and ending dates can be in any recognizable Excel date format. The step number can be a decimal—1.5, for instance. Its units depend on the date units you select: days, weekdays, months, or years. Since you cannot display fractional days without also displaying the time (which you can do), the entries for this database are rounded to the closest whole day.

For the April sales database, enter the weeks in column C, beginning with April 4, 1994, and ending May 2, 1994. Do that with these steps:

1. Click on C22, type **4/4/94** and press Enter. Notice that Excel recognized this as a numeric date because it right-aligned the figure in the cell and changed 94 to 1994 in the Formula bar.

2. Choose Fill Series from the Edit menu, type **7** for a step value of seven days, press Tab to move to the Stop Value field, type **5/2/94,** and click on Columns for the direction of the series. Date and Day have already been selected by Excel, which recognizes that the active cell contains a date. The Series dialog box looks like this when you are done:

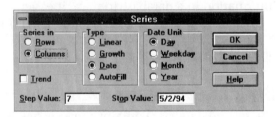

3. Click on OK. The dialog box closes and the dates appear on your sheet like this:

	A	B	C	D	E
21	Number	Office	Week	Sales	Amount
22			4/4/94		
23			4/11/94		
24			4/18/94		
25			4/25/94		
26			5/2/94		
27					

The dates could use a little formatting, so do that next.

4. Select the range C22 through C26.

5. Choose Cells from the Format menu and click on the Number tab if it isn't already selected. The Number Format Cells dialog box opens.

6. Press <kbd>Tab</kbd> twice to highlight the contents of the Code text box, and type **mmm dd**. Your dialog box should look like this:

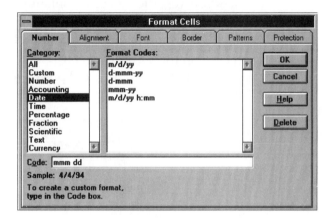

7. Click on OK. The date sequence is formatted as shown here:

	A	B	C	D	E
21	Number	Office	Week	Sales	Amount
22			Apr 04		
23			Apr 11		
24			Apr 18		
25			Apr 25		
26			May 02		
27					

8

Completing Data Entry

The table of sales amounts that you must enter is for five weeks and three sales offices—a total of fifteen entries. The dates that you just entered are for one sales office and therefore need to be copied twice more down column C. Each sales office (Boston, Denver, and Seattle) and its corresponding number must be entered five times, once for each week in the month. Finally, you must enter the sales quantities and amounts. Perform these tasks with the following steps. The week beginning dates should still be highlighted. Begin by copying the dates twice using drag and drop.

1. Press <kbd>Ctrl</kbd> and drag the lower border of C26 to C31. The dates are copied to C27:C31.

2. Again, press [Ctrl], and now drag the lower border of C31 to C36. The dates are copied a second time, as shown in Figure 8-5.

Next, copy the sales office number and name.

3. Click on the vertical scroll bar above the scroll box so you can see row 5, and drag across the two cells containing "250 Boston" (A5:B5 if the first database is still sorted by manager).

4. Press [Ctrl]-[C] to copy "250 Boston" to the clipboard.

5. Again click on the vertical scroll bar—this time below the scroll box—drag A22 through B26, and press [Enter]. "250 Boston" is copied five times, as shown here:

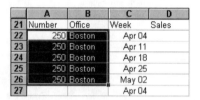

	A	B	C	D
21	Number	Office	Week	Sales
22	250	Boston	Apr 04	
23	250	Boston	Apr 11	
24	250	Boston	Apr 18	
25	250	Boston	Apr 25	
26	250	Boston	May 02	
27			Apr 04	

6. Repeat steps 3 through 5 to copy "260 Denver" to A27:B31 and "270 Seattle" to A32:B36.

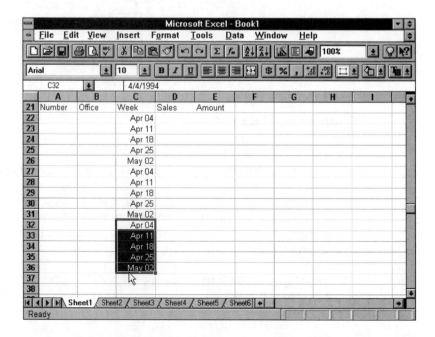

Dates as copied

Figure 8-5.

Enter and copy a formula to calculate the sales amount from the sale units, and then enter those units to complete the database.

7. Click on E22, type **=D22*145.95**, press (Enter), and format E22 with a comma and no decimals (#,##0) by clicking on the Comma format tool and the Decrease Decimal tool twice. (Since 145.95 is the average value of a sale, you can derive the total sales amount by multiplying the number of sales by this average. You'll enter the sales figures in column D in a minute.)

8. Drag the E22 fill handle through E36 to copy the formula down the column.

9. Type the sales figures in D22 through D36 as indicated in Figure 8-6, which shows the finished database.

Carefully check your work against Figure 8-6. This April Sales database is used for the remainder of the chapter. Entry errors could cause considerable confusion in subsequent sections. When you are satisfied with your database, save it before going on.

10. Choose Save As from the File menu, type **c:\sheet\salesapr**, and press (Enter). The file is saved. If you are using a different directory, make the appropriate changes.

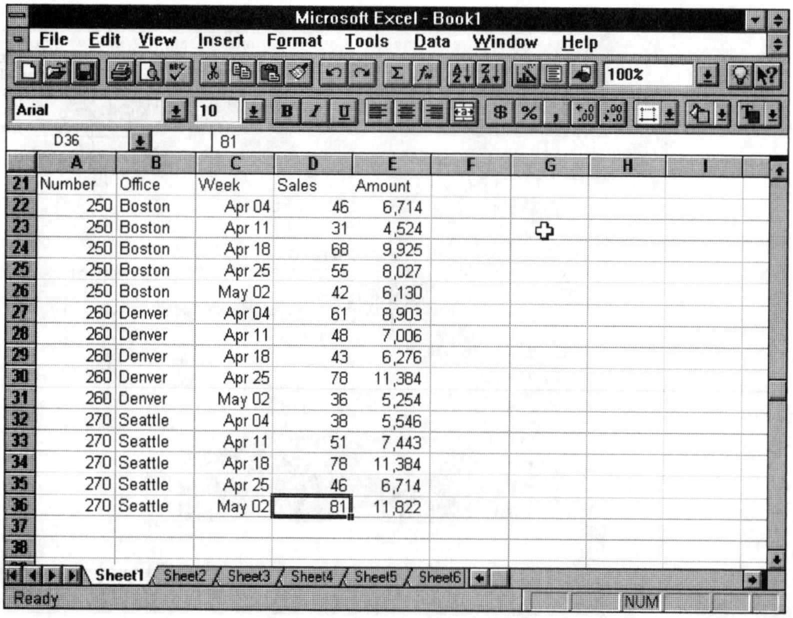

8

Completed
April Sales
database
Figure 8-6.

Subtotalling a List

The first thing you want to do with the April Sales database is find the monthly total for each sales office. You could go through, insert blank rows, and add SUM functions yourself. Excel, though, has the ability to do this for you and in the process, put the list or database in an Excel outline that allows you to see just the subtotals. Try that next with these instructions (the active cell should be in the April Sales database):

1. Open the Data menu and choose Subtotals. The April Sales database is automatically selected and the Subtotal dialog box appears as shown in Figure 8-7.

You can see from the dialog box that Excel has figured out a lot for you. First, it has looked at your database and seen that the first column periodically changes and guessed that you might want to subtotal on that. Since the first column is the office number and you want to subtotal by office, subtotaling on the first column is fine. You could also subtotal on the second column with the same result. Second, since the SUM function is the one most frequently used, Excel has guessed that using SUM is what you want to do here. You could also count, or calculate the average, among many other functions. Finally, Excel has guessed that you want to subtotal the Amount field. This is a good guess. In this case, you want to also subtotal

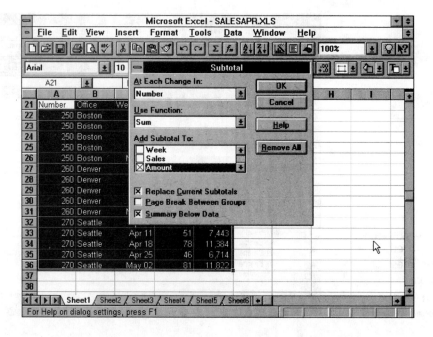

Subtotalling automatically selects the list with the active cell and opens the Subtotal dialog box
Figure 8-7.

on the Sales field. The only change you need to make is to additionally select Sales in the Add Subtotal To list.

2. Click on Sales in the Add Subtotal To list and then click on OK.

3. Choose Full Screen from the View menu to see all the subtotals. Your screen should look like Figure 8-8.

Totals have been added in new rows for the total sales and amount in each office as well as a grand total. Just as valuable, your list has been placed in an Excel outline that allows you to display just the subtotals or grand total. You will see how the outline works in a moment. First make the one following change to your list.

The subtotals would be more informative if they showed the city (office) name instead of the number. Make that correction next.

4. Again open the Data menu and the Subtotal dialog box. In the top drop-down list, select Office. Make sure that Replace Current Subtotals is checked at the bottom of the dialog box and then click on OK.

The subtotal headings change to now reflect the city instead of the number, making them more understandable.

8

	A	B	C	D	E	F	G	H	I
21	Number	Office	Week	Sales	Amount				
22	250	Boston	Apr 04	46	6,714				
23	250	Boston	Apr 11	31	4,524				
24	250	Boston	Apr 18	68	9,925				
25	250	Boston	Apr 25	55	8,027				
26	250	Boston	May 02	42	6,130				
27	250 Total			242	35,320				
28	260	Denver	Apr 04	61	8,903				
29	260	Denver	Apr 11	48	7,006				
30	260	Denver	Apr 18	43	6,276				
31	260	Denver	Apr 25	78	11,384				
32	260	Denver	May 02	36	5,254				
33	260 Total			266	38,823				
34	270	Seattle	Apr 04	38	5,546				
35	270	Seattle	Apr 11	51	7,443				
36	270	Seattle	Apr 18	78	11,384				
37	270	Seattle	Apr 25	46	6,714				
38	270	Seattle	May 02	81	11,822				
39	270 Total			294	42,909				
40	Grand Total			802	117,052				
41									
42									
43									
44									
45									

Outline
structure and
subtotals
added
Figure 8-8.

Using an Excel Outline

The outline structure produced by Excel is very powerful. By simply clicking on the little buttons, you can hide or display various levels of the outline. Try that with these instructions:

1. Click on the minus button to the left of row 27, the Boston total. The Boston detail is hidden like this:

	File	Edit	View	Insert	Format	Tools	Data	Window
		A	B	C	D	E	F
	21	Number	Office	Week	Sales	Amount	
+	27		Boston Total		242	35,320	
·	28	260	Denver	Apr 04	61	8,903	
·	29	260	Denver	Apr 11	48	7,006	
·	30	260	Denver	Apr 18	43	6,276	
·	31	260	Denver	Apr 25	78	11,384	
·	32	260	Denver	May 02	36	5,254	

2. Click on the second level button at the top-left of your screen. All of the detail records are hidden leaving only the subtotals and total, as you can see here:

	File	Edit	View	Insert	Format	Tools	Data	Window
		A	B	C	D	E	F
	21	Number	Office	Week	Sales	Amount	
+	27		Boston Total		242	35,320	
+	33		Denver Total		266	38,823	
+	39		Seattle Total		294	42,909	
−	40		Grand Total		802	117,052	
	41						

3. Click on the first level button and everything is hidden except the grand total.

4. Click on the third level button and it is all redisplayed.

   Click on the various outline buttons until you are comfortable with the operation. (It is a very useful feature of Excel.) When you are done, leave the outline fully displayed.

5. Again choose Subtotals for the Data menu and click on Remove all to return April Sales to the database you entered. Also click on the Full Screen button to return to the normal Excel display.

Adding a Full Screen Tool

The full screen view is useful and deserves its own tool to quickly switch to that view. As an example of how you can customize the toolbars to your own needs, remove the Text Box tool and replace it with the Full Screen tool. The Text Box tool allows you to position a floating box, in which you can insert text, anywhere on the sheet. You won't be using the Text Box tool in this book so it is a good candidate for replacement. Also, at the end of this section, you'll see how to restore your toolbars to their original content (since the Text Box tool provides the only way to do what it does, you'll need to restore it).

1. Click with the right mouse button on a toolbar to open the Toolbar shortcut menu and click on Customize. The Customize dialog box will open as you can see here:

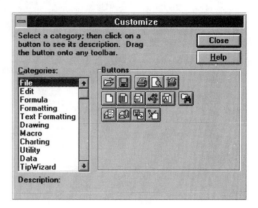

While the Customize dialog box is open, you can drag tools on and off toolbars that are displayed. The dialog box itself displays tools in categories that you can add to the displayed toolbars. You can find out what a tool in the dialog box does by clicking on it and looking at the description at the bottom of the dialog box.

2. Drag the Text Box tool off the top of the Standard toolbar. The Text Box tool disappears.

3. Click on Utility in the Categories list box. In the lower-right of the set of tools or buttons you will see what looks like a tiny screen. Click on it and you will see the description "Toggles Full Screen."

4. Drag the Full Screen tool up to the Standard toolbar, to the approximate location from which you removed the Text Box tool. The tools under and to the right of where you drag the new tool will move to the right to provide room for it as shown in Figure 8-9.

5. Click on Close to close the Customize dialog box.

If you want to restore the Standard toolbar to its original configuration, you can do so very easily with these steps:

1. Click the right mouse button on a toolbar to open the Toolbar shortcut menu and click on Toolbars. The Toolbars dialog box opens as you saw above.

8

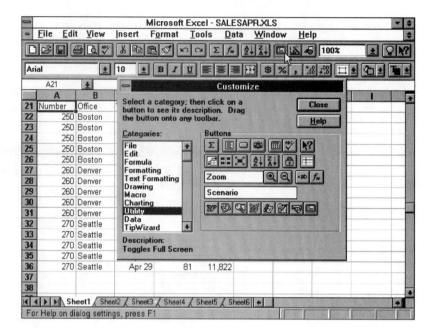

Full Screen
tool added to
the Standard
toolbar
Figure 8-9.

2. Click on Reset and the Text Box tool reappears and the Full Screen tool disappears.

Appendix B discusses all of the toolbars and their tools and further describes how to customize them.

Filtering a Database

Most databases are built with the objective that users will be able to find or select information they contain. In Excel the process of finding and selecting information is called *filtering*. You create a filter that removes (hides—it's still in the workbook) all the information you don't want and leaves only what you want. Excel provides an AutoFilter for doing this simply and an Advanced Filter that handles more complex situations in a manner similar to how Excel worked prior to Version 5. In this and the next sections you will try both of these techniques. Begin by looking at the AutoFilter with these instructions:

1. Click anywhere in the April Sales database (A21:E36) to move the active cell there if it isn't already.

2. Open the Data menu, choose Filter, and then click on AutoFilter from the submenu that opens. Drop-down list arrows appear next to each of field names like this:

	A	B	C	D	E	F
21	Number ±	Office ±	Week ±	Sales ±	Amount ±	
22	250	Boston	Apr 04	46	6,714	
23	250	Boston	Apr 11	31	4,524	
24	250	Boston	Apr 18	68	9,925	

3. Click on the drop-down arrow next to Week. A drop-down list box opens with all the weeks as you see here:

	A	B	C	D	E	F
21	Number ±	Office ±	Week ±	Sales ±	Amount ±	
22	250	Bostor	(All)	46	6,714	
23	250	Bostor	(Custom...)	31	4,524	
24	250	Bostor	Apr 04 / Apr 11	68	9,925	
25	250	Bostor	Apr 18	55	8,027	
26	250	Bostor	Apr 25 / May 02	42	6,130	
27	260	Denve	(Blanks)	61	8,903	
28	260	Denver	Apr 11	48	7,006	

4. Click on Apr 04. All database entries but the three for the week of April 4th disappear as shown here:

	A	B	C	D	E	F
21	Number ±	Office ±	Week ±	Sales ±	Amount ±	
22	250	Boston	Apr 04	46	6,714	
27	260	Denver	Apr 04	61	8,903	
32	270	Seattle	Apr 04	38	5,546	
37						

You have created a filter based on the Weeks field and selected only the entries with "Apr 04" in that field. The other entries were then hidden so you see only the entries you want. This is a very quick way to select just the entries for that one week.

8

5. Again click on the drop-down arrow next to Week and, after scrolling to the top of the drop-down list box, click on All to redisplay all of the entries in the database.

6. Click on the drop-down arrow next to Sales and click on Custom in the drop-down list box that appears. The Custom AutoFilter dialog box opens like this:

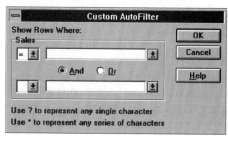

The Custom AutoFilter dialog box lets you create a filter or a *criteria* for selecting other than an existing cell entry. For example, picking one cell entry in the Sales field, like 61, would not have much meaning, but specifying a range of sales, like all weekly sales above 60, would be meaningful. Try that and see.

7. Click on the drop-down arrow on the top-left and a list box opens with various relational operators. Click on greater-than (>).

8. Press ⟨Tab⟩ to move to the text box on the right, type **60**, and press ⟨Enter⟩. The dialog box closes and you see the list filtered to show only those entries with sales above 60 as shown here:

	A	B	C	D	E	F
21	Number	Office	Week	Sales	Amount	
24	250	Boston	Apr 18	68	9,925	
27	260	Denver	Apr 04	61	8,903	
30	260	Denver	Apr 25	78	11,384	
34	270	Seattle	Apr 18	78	11,384	
36	270	Seattle	May 02	81	11,822	
37						

The relational operators that you can use in the Custom AutoFilter dialog box have the following meanings:

Operator	Meaning
=	equal to
>	greater than
<	less than
>=	greater than or equal to
<=	less than or equal to
<>	not equal to

These operators can be used with both text and numbers, and the sort order discussed earlier in the chapter determines the relationship of text. Numbers are matched without regard to their format. For example, the number 54 matches $54, 5400%, 5.40E+01, and 54.00. With text you can use wildcard characters (? for any single character and * for any group of characters) to find inexact matches. For example, entering **pea**? as the criterion selects "peak," "peal," and "pear," while entering **for*** selects "for," "foray," "forecast," and "forest." You can combine wildcard characters. For example, AM??DC* might be used with part numbers in an inventory system to select all parts from a given manufacturer (the AM) for a particular machine (the DC).

You can enter two criteria in the Custom AutoFilter dialog box and combine them with either AND or OR. If you use AND, both criteria must be met but with OR only one of the criteria has to be satisfied. For example, if you want all the records with sales above 50 but below 70 you would use AND between the criteria: >50 AND <70. If you want all the records of sales in either Boston or Seattle, you would use OR with the criteria: =Boston OR =Seattle.

9. Open the Sales drop-down list box and click on Custom. In the Custom AutoFilter dialog box, type **50**, click on And, select < in the bottom-left drop-down list, press ⌊Tab⌋, type **70**, and click on OK. You get a new selection that looks like this:

	A	B	C	D	E	F
21	Number	Office	Week	Sales	Amount	
24	250	Boston	Apr 18	68	9,925	
25	250	Boston	Apr 25	55	8,027	
27	260	Denver	Apr 04	61	8,903	
33	270	Seattle	Apr 11	51	7,443	
37						

10. Open the Data menu, choose Filter, and click on AutoFilter to turn it off. Your database is restored to its original appearance without the drop-down arrows.

Using the Advanced Filter

8

As powerful as AutoFilter is, there are situations where you have complex criteria, especially computed criteria, with which AutoFilter will not work. In those instances you must use the Advanced Filter option. To use the Advanced Filter you must identify two or three ranges. The first range is the database itself and is required by all operations using the Advanced Filter. The database (or list) range is the source for selecting records on which you will operate. The second range is the criteria range and is also required. The criteria range contains the criteria on which the selections are made. The third range is the copy-to range and is required only if you want to copy the selected records to a location different from the original database. The copy-to range will contain a new database of the selected records.

Defining the Database   To define the database, you have the choice of selecting or highlighting it either before or after you start the Advanced Filter or of typing the coordinates or a range name into the Advanced Filter dialog box. The database range must contain the full set of records from which you want to select, as well as the field names for those records. Since you will be using this range in many operations throughout the chapter, it is best to name the range now and have it over with. If you name the range

"Database," Excel will automatically identify the first row as a set of field
names. To create a name, you can use either the Name Define option on the
Insert menu or type the name in the reference area on the left of the
Formula bar. Define the database range for the April Sales database using the
insert menu and these steps:

1. Drag from A21 through E36 to highlight the database.

2. Choose Name from the Insert menu and click on Define in the
   submenu. The Define Name dialog box will open.

3. Type **Database** as the name in the dialog box, as shown in Figure 8-10.

4. Click on OK. The highlighted range is given the name "Database," and
   you are returned to Ready mode.

You can tell that the database has been named, because, as long as it is
selected, the name will appear in the reference area of the Formula bar.

Establishing the Selection Criteria   Establishing the selection criteria
requires that you identify a criteria range in the workbook. The criteria range
is a small database. The first row of the criteria range must contain some or
all of the field names from the database you want the criteria to work with.
The rest of the criteria range contains the criteria that will be the basis of
your selection.

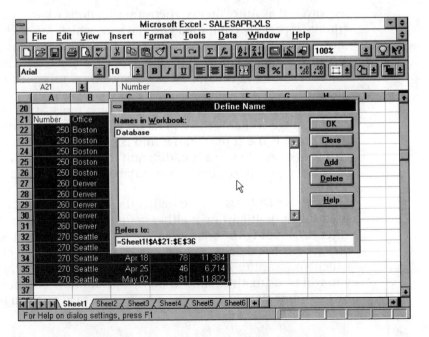

Defining the
name of the
April Sales
database
Figure 8-10.

You can build the criteria range in any blank area of the workbook, but it is usually best not to build it directly below the database so there is room for the database to expand. The field names in the criteria range must be exact copies of the field names in the database. Frequently the full set of field names is copied from the database with the Copy option.

The criteria directly relate to the field name under which they are entered. For example, if you want to select all of the records for the Boston sales office in the April sales database, you'll build a two-cell criteria range. The top cell has the field name "Office"; the bottom cell contains "Boston." The selection process searches for "Boston" in the Office field. This process gives you the matches between the criterion and the records in the database. A criterion of "Boston" also gives you a match with "Bostonian." If you want just "Boston" you must enter the formula ="=**Boston**", including the quotation marks. You can use text, numbers, or formulas as criteria for matching.

You can also use text, numbers, or formulas that cause Excel to search for records that are not matches. For example, if you want all records from the April Sales database that have more than 60 sales, as you did with the AutoFilter, you build a criteria range with Sales as the field name and >60 as the criterion. Do that now, and identify it as the criteria range with the following instructions. Since you want the field name in the criterion to be exactly the same as the field name in the database, copy the database field name.

8

1. Click on D21, click on the Copy tool in the Standard toolbar, click on G21, and press ⟨Enter⟩. The word "Sales" is copied from D21 to G21.

2. Click on G22, type **>60**, and press ⟨Enter⟩. The field name and criterion are entered.

3. Drag on G21 through G22, click in the reference area of the Formula bar, type **Criteria**, and press ⟨Enter⟩. The criterion is identified as shown here:

F	G	H
	Sales	
	>60	

Like the AutoFilter, the >60 criterion entered in the example is just one of many ways to specify criteria. Some rules on specifying criteria follow:

✦ Use relational operators, numbers, text, and wildcard characters as defined for the AutoFilter.

✦ Formulas that refer to fields in the database range should use relative addresses. Formulas that refer to fields outside the database range should use absolute addresses. For example, the formula =SALES>=AMOUNT/150 is the same as =D22>=E22/150 and uses relative addressing to refer to fields within the database range of the April sales database. On the other hand, =SALES>=$H$23 uses absolute addressing to refer to an address outside the database range.

✦ Usually a criterion refers to the field name under which it has been entered. If the criterion is a formula that relates to the total record instead of a specific field (as =SALES>= AMOUNT/150), then you need to use a field name in the criteria not used in the database. For example, "Formula" might be such a field name.

✦ You can use the database field names in a criterion formula (for example, =SALES>=AMOUNT/150) without defining them with the Formula Define Names option. You will get the error message #NAME? in the criterion cell, but the formula is utilized correctly for database selection. An example of an error message resulting from a field name formula is shown here:

F	G	H
	Formula	
	#NAME?	

✦ If you put criteria in multiple columns but only one row of a criteria range, *all* of the criteria must be satisfied for a record in the database range to be selected. It is as if you had put a logical AND between the fields. For example, if you create a criteria range with field names of "Sales" and "Amount" and enter **>60** under Sales and **>8000** under Amount, only records that have both greater than 60 in sales and greater than $8,000 in the amount are selected. If either of those conditions is not met, the record is not selected. This is an AND criteria range:

F	G	H
	Sales	Amount
	>60	>8000

✦ If you put criteria in multiple rows of a criteria range, satisfying *either* of the criterion causes a record in the database range to be selected. It is as if you had put a logical OR between the fields. For example, if you enter **>60** under Sales in row 1 and **>8000** under Amount in row 2, records that satisfy either criterion are selected. This is an OR criteria range:

F	G	H	I
	Sales	Amount	
	>60		
		>8000	

✦ If you have a blank row in a criteria range, all of the records in the database are selected. You can combine as many rows and as many columns as necessary to specify the criteria you need, but do not include a blank row unless you want to select all records.

✦ You can select records that fall within a range for a given field. For example, select all records that have greater than 50 sales and fewer than 70 sales by creating two criteria columns (both with the same field name) and entering the **>50** in one column and **<70** in the other, as shown here:

F	G	H	I
	Sales	Sales	
	>50	<70	

Selecting Records   Once you have specified both the database range and the criteria range, you can use the Advanced Filter to identify selected records in the database range that meet the criteria. Try the Advanced Filter with the following instructions (your criteria should still be Sales, >60):

8

1. Click outside both the database and criteria ranges so the active cell is not in either.
2. Open the Data menu, choose Filter, and click on Advanced Filter. The Advanced Filter dialog box opens with the correct ranges identified, as shown in Figure 8-11.
3. Click on OK and the database is filtered just as it was with the AutoFilter. (Don't worry about row 22 disappearing—it will return in a minute.)
4. Open the Data menu, choose the Filter option, and click on Show All to return the database to its original state.

Copying Selected Records   If you wish, with the Advanced Filter you can copy or extract selected records and selected fields from the database and place them in another location on the sheet. To do this you must define a range to receive the selected records. Like the criteria range, this copy-to range must have a row containing one or more field names that exactly

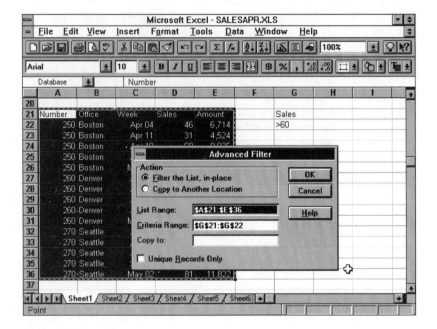

Advanced
Filter dialog
box with the
database and
criteria ranges
identified
Figure 8-11.

match the field names in the database range. If you want to limit the
number of rows that Excel can fill with selected records, then you need to
highlight that number of rows in addition to the row of field names when
you define the copy-to range. If you want Excel to define the number of
rows it needs, then highlight only the row of field names when you define
the copy-to range. With the following steps, define a copy-to range, change
the criteria to a more complex one, and then use the Advanced filter to copy
selected records the range you defined with these steps:

1. Click on G26, type **Office**, press ⊡, type **Week,** and press (Enter). The
   labels "Office" and "Week" will be placed in G26 and H26, respectively.

2. Drag G26 through H26 to highlight the cells to be used as the range,
   click in the reference area of the Formula bar, and type **Extract**.

3. Click on G21, type **Formula**, press ⊡, and type **=Amount*.05>$I$22**
   to look for commissions that are greater than the amount in I22, and
   press (Enter) to redefine the criteria.

4. Click on I22, type **500**, and press (Enter) to enter the reference value for
   the criteria.

5. Choose Filter from the Data menu and click on Advance Filter. The
   Advanced Filter dialog box opens.

6. Click on Copy to Another Location option button, click in the Copy to text box and drag across the G26:H26 (if the reference isn't already there), as shown in Figure 8-12.

The Advanced Filter dialog box allows you to select all records that match the criteria or only unique records, thus eliminating duplicates. Here you select all records.

7. Click on OK. The copy-to operation executes, placing information extracted from three records in the copy-to range, as shown in Figure 8-13.

If you select a fixed area beneath the Copy-to field names and the copying selects more records than can fit in that area, you get an error message to that effect. Enlarge the area or highlight only the field names and repeat the process.

Be aware that if you specify only a one-row Copy-to range and thereby allow Excel to use as much room as it needs for selected records, any other information in the rows under the field names of this range is cleared or written over. *All rows below the Copy-to range are cleared, whether or not they are used for extracted data. You cannot undo the Advanced Filter Copy operation!*

8

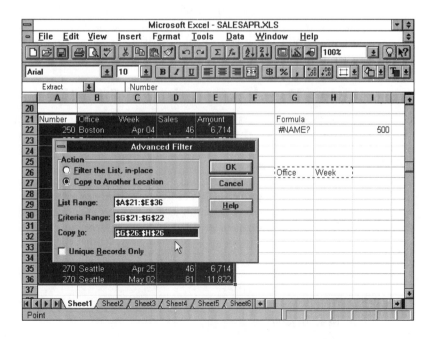

Defining the Copy to range in the Advanced Filter

Figure 8-12.

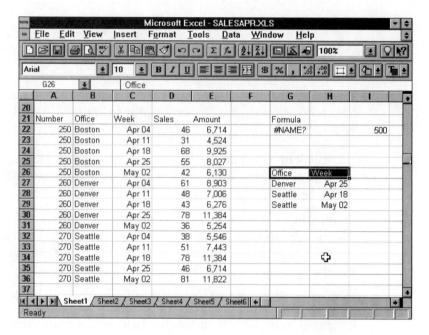

Results of
copying
selected
records to
another range
Figure 8-13.

Analyzing Information from a Database

In addition to selecting and extracting information, the other primary
reason for building a database is to analyze the information it contains.
Analyzing includes summarizing, averaging, counting, grouping, and
calculating the standard deviation and variance. The next few sections cover
several functions and options within Excel that are used for analyzing
information in databases.

Using Database Statistical Functions

In previous chapters, you used the SUM function to add a set of numbers in
a range. SUM has the general form, or syntax, of

SUM(*reference*)

where *reference* is any set of reference names or addresses. Other functions
include AVERAGE, which calculates the average of a reference; COUNT,
which counts the number of items in a reference; and MIN and MAX, which
identify the minimum and maximum numbers in a reference. They have
similar syntaxes:

AVERAGE(*reference*)
COUNT(*reference*)
MAX(*reference*)
MIN(*reference*)

Excel has another set of functions called *database statistical functions*. Among them are DSUM, DAVERAGE, and DCOUNT. They have the same general purposes as statistical functions: they sum, average, and count. Database statistical functions, however, are meant to operate on specific fields in a database and to perform only on records that match criteria. Each database statistical function has a syntax similar to

DSUM(*database,field,criteria*)

where *database* is a range in the workbook containing the field, *field* identifies a field name or column in the database on which you want to operate (sum, average, count), and *criteria* is a criteria range used to select the particular records you want to use in the calculation.

The primary difference between SUM and DSUM or between statistical and database statistical functions is that statistical functions operate on a group of cells without any selection. Database statistical functions select both a particular column (field) within a larger range and particular records (cells in the column) on which to operate. DSUM is the same as SUM if the database is a single column you want to sum and the criteria range is blank.

All of the information you have learned about database ranges and criteria ranges as they apply to the Advanced Filter applies to database statistical functions. The *database* can be the addresses of a range in the workbook (A21:E36, for example) or the name of a range you have defined with Insert Name or by typing a name in the reference area.

The *field* can be a field name, a field number, or the address of a cell that contains a field name or number. If a field name is used, it should be in quotation marks and should match the field name in the database range exactly. The number determines the column within the database table, beginning with the leftmost column as 1. The number for the second column is 2, and so on.

The *criteria* can be the addresses of a range in the workbook (G21:G22, for example) or a name you have defined with Insert Name or by typing a name in the reference area.

All of the following formulas do the same thing: sum the selected sales units in the April Sales database you entered into A21:E36 using the criteria you entered into G21:G22.

```
=DSUM(A21:E36,4,G21:G22)
=DSUM(Database,"Sales",Criteria)
=DSUM(April,D21,Top) if you have defined the names "April" as
A21:E36 and "Top" as G21:G22
```

8

Creating Names

You have already named the database and criteria ranges of the April Sales database using the Insert Name option and by typing in the reference area of the Formula bar. Once you have created a name, you can use it anywhere to represent a group of cells in the current workbook. You can have only one range with a given range name, so you can have only one range named "Database" and one range named Criteria. As you work with database statistical functions, you are going to want to use ranges other than those defined as Database and Criteria. For these other ranges you can use either addresses or names.

There are two and sometimes three reasons to use names over addresses. First, and most compelling, is that a name always accurately reflects changes you make to a workbook. When you use a name in several functions, all those functions are updated when you change the range referred to by the name. Secondly, names are often easier to remember and almost always more recognizable than the addresses they represent. Third, in some cases a short name is easier to enter than a long set of addresses. Since you will be building several database statistical functions with the same database and criteria ranges, get some practice naming a couple of ranges even though you could use the name already attached to one of those ranges. Use these instructions for that purpose:

1. Highlight the range A21:E36 (the database), open the Insert menu, choose Name, and click on Define. The Define Name dialog box opens, as shown here:

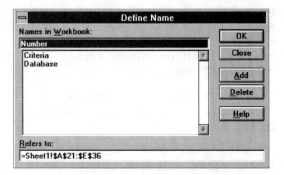

Notice that Criteria and Database are listed as names already existing in the workbook. Also the range that you highlighted is shown as the range to which the new name you enter will be attached. "Number," which came from the first cell of the highlighted range, is shown as a default name, but you want a different name for the range.

2. Type **April** and press ⟨Enter⟩. The database is now named April, as well as Database.

3. Highlight the range A38:A39, which you will use as a second criteria range, click in the reference area on the left of the Formula bar, type **Loc** (short for location), and press ⟨Enter⟩ to name the range.

Next, prepare an area on the sheet for entering database statistical functions by entering several titles.

4. Click on A38 and type **Office**. Press ▸ twice to move to C38 and type **Number**. Press ▸, type **Total #**, press ▸, type **Total $**, press ▸, type **Average #**, press ▸, type **Average $**, and then press ⟨Enter⟩.

The bottom few lines of your screen should look like this:

37						
38	Office		Number	Total #	Total $	Average #	Average $
39		✥				
40						

Building the Formulas

Under each of the titles (Number, Total #, and so on) you will enter a database statistical function. (Use Office as a criteria range field, not a title for a database statistical function.) The titles are not necessary for the database statistical functions, but they are informative. After the formulas are entered, only their result is displayed. The formulas you enter are DCOUNT, to count the number of nonblank cells in a field in the records in the database range that match the criteria; DSUM, to sum a field in the records of the database range that match the criteria; and DAVERAGE, to average a field in the records of the database range that match the criteria. Initially, you leave the criteria blank to select all of the records in the database range.

When you enter a function you can either type the function or use the Function Wizard to lead you through it. If you type the function, do not include spaces anywhere except in a literal enclosed in quotation marks. Also, be sure to include the = symbol and both parentheses (although in many cases the last parenthesis will automatically be provided for you). With these rules in mind, enter several database statistical functions with the following steps.

1. Click on C39. The active cell moves to C39.

2. Type **=dcount(april,"number",loc** and press ⟨Enter⟩. The result, 15, appears in C39, as shown in Figure 8-14. The DCOUNT function counts

the number of nonblank cells in the Number field of the April database that match the criteria in Loc.

When typing a function, it is a good idea to use lowercase letters. That way you can tell if Excel recognizes what you are typing. If it does, the functions automatically change to all uppercase, and range names change to leading caps. Excel acts like a spelling checker.

3. Click on cell D39 and then click on the Function Wizard tool next to AutoSum in the Standard toolbar. The Function Wizard dialog box opens as you can see here:

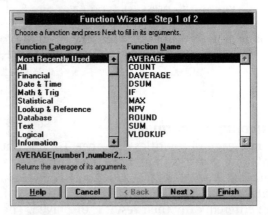

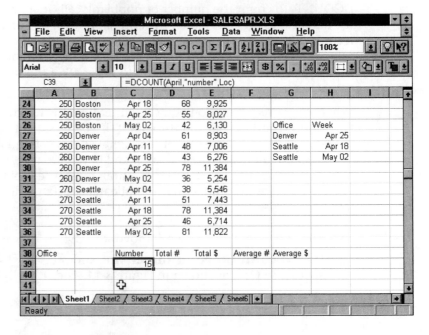

DCOUNT function completed **Figure 8-14.**

4. Click on Database in the Function Category list, click on DSUM in the Function Name list, and click on Next. The second Function Wizard dialog box opens like this:

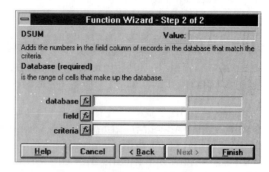

5. Type **april**, press ⌨Tab, type **"sales"** including the quotation marks, press ⌨Tab, and type **loc**. Notice that as you are typing, as soon as Excel recognizes the name it appears on the right of the text box. Also, as soon as you complete typing the criteria, the value appears in the upper right of the dialog box as shown here:

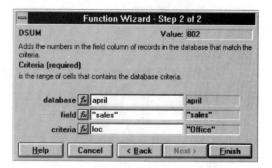

8

6. Click on Finish and the result, 802, appears in D39. This DSUM function adds all the numbers in the Sales field of the April database that match the criteria in Loc.

The Function Wizard does three things for you: first, it presents the list of functions from which you can choose; second, it saves you a little typing by supplying the equal sign, function name, parentheses, and commas; third, and probably most important, it provides a list of arguments for you to fill in. Depending on how good your memory is and how often you use functions, you may or may not find the Function Wizard helpful.

7. Click ⊣ and in the next three cells use the Function Wizard, or type the following formulas. Press ⊣ after the first two and (Enter) after the last.

```
=dsum(april,"amount",loc)
=daverage(april,"sales",loc)
=daverage(april,"amount",loc)
```

8. Drag across C39:G39, click on the Comma tool, and then click twice on the Decrease Decimal tool in the Formatting toolbar. The row of database statistical functions is formatted with the comma format and no decimal places. Figure 8-15 shows the results.

You are now in a position to change the criteria and immediately see the result—called a *what-if* situation. The formulas in C39:G39 reflect the criterion in A39. Enter a new criteria, and the formulas reflect the result. Currently, the blank criteria range means that the formulas are utilizing the entire database range. If you enter **Boston** in the criteria range, the formulas utilize only records with Boston in the Office field. Try that next with these instructions:

9. Click on A39, type **Boston**, and press (Enter). "Boston" is entered in the criteria range, and the formulas recalculate to reflect that, as shown here:

	A	B	C	D	E	F	G
37							
38	Office		Number	Total #	Total $	Average #	Average $
39	Boston		5	242	35,320	48	7,064
40							
41							

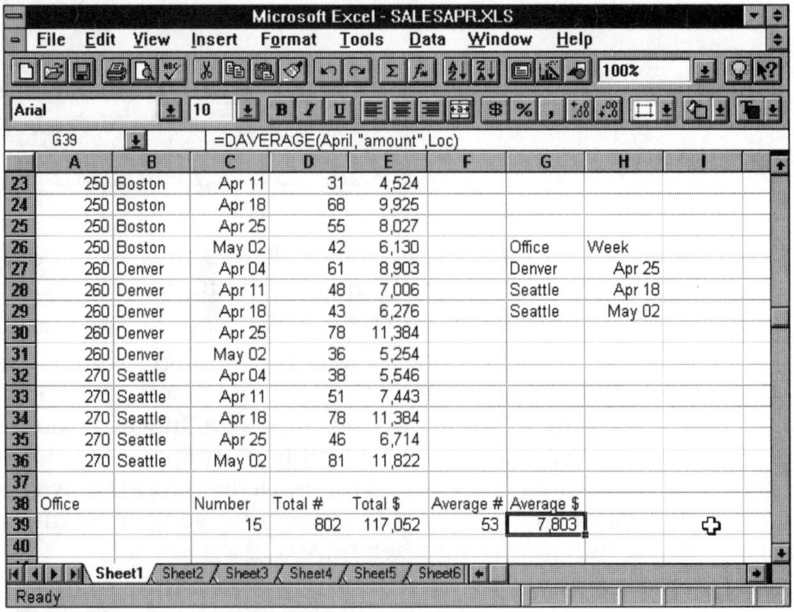

Database statistical functions entered and formatted
Figure 8-15.

Note that the criteria is not case-sensitive. You could enter **boston** or **BOSTON** and get the same results. Also note that amounts in the Total # and Total $ fields are the same as the Boston subtotals shown in Figure 8-8.

Creating a Data Table

As powerful as the criteria-and-formula combination is, Excel has a better way to perform its task—a *data table*. A data table shows the results of one or more formulas when one or two variables in the formulas are varied. As an example, a data table can show the results of the five database statistical functions entered in the last section for all of the three sales offices at one time. The variable in this case is the criteria, and the three offices are the variations. This is known as a *one-input data table*.

A one-input data table is a specially configured range on a sheet. It can be configured in rows or columns, but rows are most common. For the row configuration, the top row contains as many formulas as you want to use. C39:G39 would be such a row. Then, in the column to the left of the first formula and beginning one row beneath it, enter as many variables as you want applied to those formulas. Here you will enter the three cities **Boston**, **Denver**, and **Seattle**. Each formula needs to refer to one cell where the variable is substituted. This cell is known as the *input cell* and is A39 in this example. Build this data table now, and observe how it works. A39 should still be the active cell.

1. Press ⌨Del⌨. The criterion (Boston) is erased, and the database statistical functions once again show the totals in the database range.

2. Click on B40 and type **Boston**, **Denver**, and **Seattle**, pressing ⌨↓⌨ after the first two and ⌨Enter⌨ after the last.

3. Highlight B39 through G42 as your data table range, which is shown here:

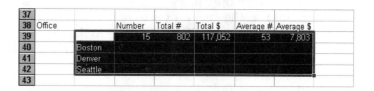

	Office		Number	Total #	Total $	Average #	Average $
37							
38	Office		Number	Total #	Total $	Average #	Average $
39			15	802	117,052	53	7,803
40		Boston					
41		Denver					
42		Seattle					
43							

4. Choose Table from the Data menu. The Table dialog box opens, as shown here:

8

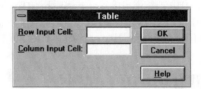

The Table dialog box asks you for a row input cell and/or a column input cell. Since you have only one variable and it is in a column, you only need to enter a column input cell.

5. Press (Tab) to move from Row Input Cell to Column Input Cell, click on A39 (or type **$A$39**), and click on OK. The data table is then calculated, as shown here. (Although A39 is blank, it is used by Excel during the calculation of the table to hold each of the criteria as they are used.)

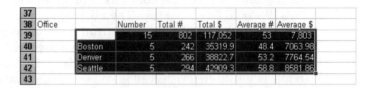

	Office		Number	Total #	Total $	Average #	Average $
37							
38	Office		Number	Total #	Total $	Average #	Average $
39			15	802	117,052	53	7,803
40	Boston		5	242	35319.9	48.4	7063.98
41	Denver		5	266	38822.7	53.2	7764.54
42	Seattle		5	294	42909.3	58.8	8581.86
43							

6. Format the data table with the comma format and no decimal places as you did with the original database statistical functions above.

Working with Two-Input Data Tables

The data table you just used is called a one-input data table because there is one variable (the criteria). It can have multiple formulas but only one variable. The other type of data table is a *two-input data table*. It has two variables but only one formula. In a *two-input data table*, one variable is in a column, as the sales offices were in the previous example, and the other variable is in a row. The formula is in the upper-left corner cell that is the intersection between the row variables and the column variables.

For an example of a two-input data table, assume you are a sales manager and want to look at the kind of money your sales people can earn with varying commission rates and varying monthly sales. The formula for this would be to multiply the monthly sales by the commission rate by 12 to get annual income. The two variables are commission rates, which vary from 3 percent through 6 percent, and monthly sales, which normally fall between $40,000 and $100,000. The steps to build such a table follow:

1. Click on the vertical scroll bar beneath the scroll box. You get a blank area on your sheet.

2. Click on C45, type **Commission Rate**, press ⬇, type **Monthly Sales**, and press (Enter).

3. Click on B48, type **3%**, press (Enter), choose Fill from the Edit menu, click on Series, type **.5%** for the step value, press (Tab), type **6%** for the stop value, and press (Enter). The row variables appear across columns B through H.

4. Highlight B48 through H48 and click once on the Increase Decimal tool in the Formatting toolbar. The row variables are now formatted.

5. Click on A48, type **=e45*e46*12**, and press ⬇ to enter the formula you want to vary.

6. Type **40,000**, press (Enter), choose Fill from the Edit menu, click on Series, type **10,000**, press (Tab), type **100,000**, click on Columns, and click on OK. The column variables are entered.

7. Highlight A48 through H55, choose Table from the Data menu, click on E45 for the row input cell, press (Tab), click on E46 for the column input cell, and click on OK. Your commission table is produced.

8. Format the body of the commission table with the comma format and no decimal places and move the active cell to A48. You screen should look like that shown in Figure 8-16.

This table is equivalent to repeating the formula 49 times (seven rates and seven amounts). As you can see, a data table is a valuable analysis tool.

8

Creating Pivot Tables

A *pivot table* is a table in which you can interactively exchange the rows and columns to look at the data in different ways. Normally, the table shows summary information that is grouped in several ways with row and column totals and grand totals, like this:

	A	B	C	D	E	F	G	H	I
57									
58			Week						
59	Office	Data	4/4/94	4/11/94	4/18/94	4/25/94	5/2/94	Grand Total	
60	Boston	Sum of Sales	46	31	68	55	42	242	
61		Sum of Amount	6,714	4,524	9,925	8,027	6,130	35,320	
62	Denver	Sum of Sales	61	48	43	78	36	266	
63		Sum of Amount	8,903	7,006	6,276	11,384	5,254	38,823	
64	Seattle	Sum of Sales	38	51	78	46	81	294	
65		Sum of Amount	5,546	7,443	11,384	6,714	11,822	42,909	
66	Total Sum of Sales		145	130	189	179	159	802	
67	Total Sum of Amount		21,163	18,974	27,585	26,125	23,206	117,052	
68									
69									

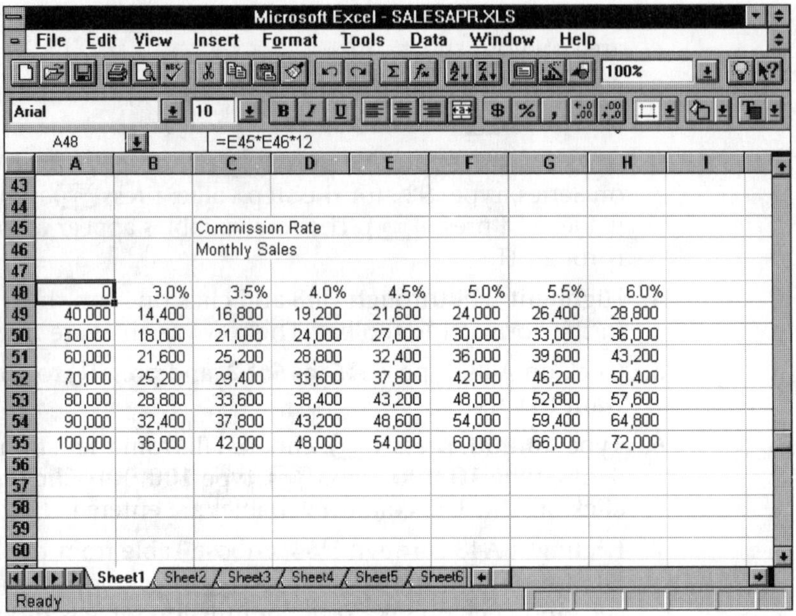

Completed
two-input data
table

Figure 8-16.

Excel has a PivotTable Wizard that will help you build a pivot table from an existing Excel or external database if you tell the Wizard various facts about the data. For your April database, a pivot table might total each office by week and then total each weekly figure to get the office total for the month. At the same time, you can get a total each week for all sales offices and do this for both sales and sales amounts. In this, each major row is a sales office and each column is a week, as shown in the previous illustration. Each cell totals the sales or the sales amounts for an office in a week. The total of each row is the total for an office in April, and the total for a column is the weekly total for all sales offices. The grand total is the total sales for all offices for the month. See for yourself how the PivotTable Wizard works with these instructions:

1. Open the Data menu and choose PivotTable. The PivotTable Wizard's first dialog box appears as shown in Figure 8-17.

In the PivotTable Wizard's first dialog box you select the source of the data for the pivot table. In this case you want the default already selected—a single Excel database. The alternatives are an external (non Excel) database, multiple Excel databases or ranges, or another pivot table.

2. Click on Next. The second PivotTable Wizard dialog box opens, that you can see here:

Excel has identified the range named Database as the potential range from which to build the pivot table. Since that is what you want, you have nothing to do in this second dialog box.

3. Click on Next. The third PivotTable Wizard dialog opens as shown in Figure 8-18.

The third dialog box allows you to drag the various database fields to where you want them in the table. See how that is done and it will become clearer what this means.

4. Drag the Office button to the ROW area so that offices become row headings.

5. Drag the Week button to the COLUMN area so that weeks become column headings.

8

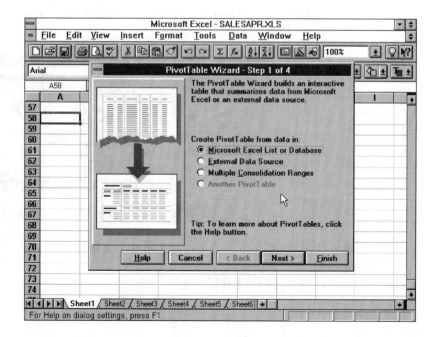

PivotTable Wizard's first screen

Figure 8-17.

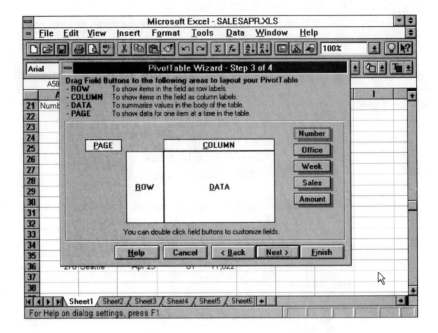

PivotTable's
third dialog
box
Figure 8-18.

6. Drag first the Sales and then the Amount buttons to the DATA area so they become the body of the table. Your completed third dialog box should look like Figure 8-19.

7. Click on Next. The final PivotTable Wizard dialog box opens, as shown here:

8. Click on A58 (scroll your screen first if necessary) to identify the starting cell for the pivot table. You want all the other options that are already selected, so click on Finish.

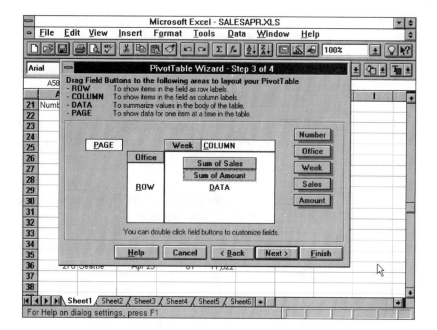

PivotTable's
third dialog
box completed
Figure 8-19.

The pivot table is displayed, as you can see in Figure 8-20. The dates across the top of the pivot table are text, so you cannot reformat them; if you want to change them, you must reenter them. The numbers in the pivot table can be formatted for better readability. If you use the comma format with no decimal places, you will get the pivot table report shown at the beginning of this section. The problem is that the formats will go away each time you refresh the data (see below for how this is done). You can get around this by applying an autoformat to the table that will automatically get reapplied each time you refresh the data. Unfortunately, though, there is no autoformat that matches what you want here (those available have dollar signs and/or decimal points where you don't want them).

The PivotTable Wizard saves you a great deal of work in building what is in essence a summary sheet. If you want to do that in your work, it would be worthwhile to try the Wizard on your own.

Using a Pivot Table

As powerful as the PivotTable Wizard is, the real power in a pivot table is in what you can do with it after it is built. Notice in the completed pivot table that there are three buttons: one for Weeks, one for Data, and one for Office. By dragging these buttons, you can reorder the pivot table. Try that next.

8

1. Drag the Office button up so it is on top of the Week button. The table is reordered like this:

	A	B	C	D	E	F	G	H	I	J
56										
57										
58		Office	Week							
59		Boston					Boston Total	Denver		
60	Data	4/4/94	4/11/94	4/18/94	4/25/94	5/2/94		4/4/94	4/11/94	4/18/94
61	Sum of Sales	46	31	68	55	42	242	61	48	4
62	Sum of Amount	6713.7	4524.45	9924.6	8027.25	6129.9	35319.9	8902.95	7005.6	6275.8
63										
64										

2. Drag the Week button to the other side of the Office button. Again the table is reordered as you see here:

	A	B	C	D	E	F	G	H	I	
56										
57										
58		Week	Office							
59		4/4/94			4/4/94 Total	4/11/94			4/11/94 Total	4/1
60	Data	Boston	Denver	Seattle		Boston	Denver	Seattle		Bo
61	Sum of Sales	46	61	38	145	31	48	51	130	
62	Sum of Amount	6713.7	8902.95	5546.1	21162.75	4524.45	7005.6	7443.45	18973.5	9
63										
64										

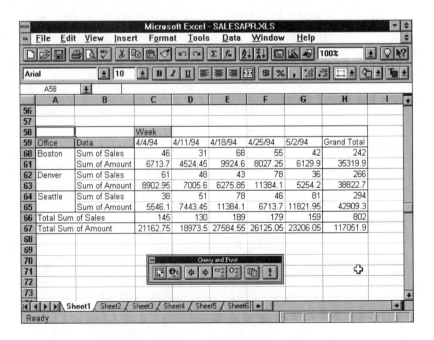

Completed pivot table
Figure 8-20.

3. Drag the Week button down so it is on top of the Data button. The table is reordered for a final time. Your screen should look like that shown in Figure 8-21.

There are, of course, several other combinations of the three buttons that you can try out on your own. The point is that there is exceptional flexibility in a pivot table that allows you to look at data in any way that you want; all you have to do is drag elements around with the mouse.

In addition to dragging the buttons around the pivot table, you can get rid of either Office or Week by simply dragging them off the table—a large "X" appears in them as you drag them off. You can also go back to the PivotTable Wizard and revise your selections either by again choosing PivotTable from the Data menu or by clicking on the PivotTable Wizard tool on the left of the Query and Pivot toolbar that appears with a pivot table.

You can reorder the table through a dialog box instead of dragging by first selecting the field to change and then either choosing PivotTable Field in the Data menu or clicking on the second tool in the Query and Pivot toolbar. In the PivotTable Field dialog box that appears and on the next pages, you can determine in which position the field is to appear, how it is to be subtotalled, and whether any of the entries are to be hidden.

8

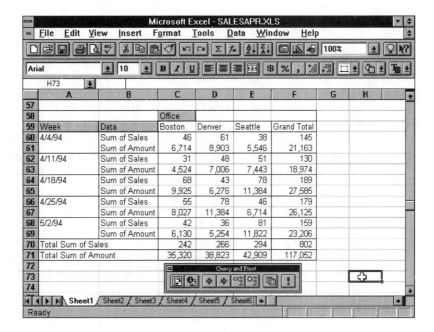

Pivot table after it has been reordered for the third time

Figure 8-21.

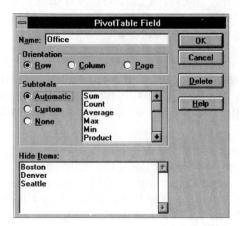

You can create groups of items by simply dragging across the items to
highlight them and then clicking on the Group (right arrow) tool in the
Query and Pivot toolbar. For example, if you wanted to group the weeks of
April 4 and April 11 together, you would drag across these dates and click on
the Group tool. You will get a new level as shown here:

	A	B	C	D	E	F	G	H	I
57									
58			Week2	Week					
59			Group1		4/18/94	4/25/94	5/2/94	Grand Total	
60	Office	Data	4/4/94	4/11/94	4/18/94	4/25/94	5/2/94		
61	Boston	Sum of Sales	52	31	68	55	42	248	
62		Sum of Amount	7589.4	4524.45	9924.6	8027.25	6129.9	36195.6	

After grouping and creating a second level, you can get rid of the original
level by dragging it off the table. If you want to restore the original level and
ungroup what was grouped, click on the Ungroup (left arrow) tool in the
Query and Pivot toolbar. If you want to just hide the detail within one
grouping instead of dragging an entire level off the table, select the items to
be hidden and click on the Hide Detail (minus sign) tool in the Query and
Pivot toolbar. You can reverse that operation with the Show Detail (plus
sign) tool.

There is an additional level, called Pages, that is available with a pivot table
but not used in the example shown in this chapter. If you use that
additional level, you still see only one page on a sheet but you have a
drop-down list box to select the other pages. If you want to print the other
pages, you need to display each of them on a sheet and then select those
sheets to be printed. To do that, select the location for receiving a page from
the table and then click on the Show Pages (sheets of paper) tool in the

Query and Pivot toolbar. A dialog box will open and you can select the page to be placed on the current sheet.

A pivot table is not directly tied to the source data by formulas on the sheet. In other words, the numbers that you see are values not formulas that reference the original data. If you make a change to the original data, your pivot table will not automatically be updated; you will need to update or *refresh* the numbers in the pivot table. You can do that either by choosing Refresh Data in the Data menu or by clicking on the Refresh Data (exclamation point) tool in the Query and Pivot toolbar.

Using Lookup Functions

Excel has two functions that, while not database functions, are related to using databases. These are the horizontal and vertical table lookup functions HLOOKUP and VLOOKUP. You use these two functions to search a two-dimensional range for an item, based on finding a match in another item that is in the first row (horizontal lookup) or the first column (vertical lookup) and an index that tells Excel how many rows down (horizontal lookup) or across (vertical lookup) to move to find the sought-after item. These functions have three arguments:

✦ A value (x) to look for in the first row or column

✦ A range or database in which to look

✦ An index to determine how far down or across to look in the range to find the item sought

The formats of these functions are

HLOOKUP(*x,range,index*)

where x is the value to look for in the first row, and

VLOOKUP(*x,range,index*)

where x is the value to look for in the first column.

Use the vertical lookup function with the second database you built (April Sales) to calculate commissions earned based on the commission rates in the first database you built. The function uses the office number in each record of the second database as the value to search for in the leftmost column of the first database, which is the range of the function. An index of 5 is used since the commissions are in the fifth column. The values in the first column must be in numerical order, so the first step is to re-sort the first database by office number. Do that and then build the formulas with vertical lookup functions using these instructions:

1. Press Ctrl-Home to go to the top of the sheet so you can see the first database you built.

2. Highlight A2 through E7, choose Sort from the Data menu, select Number to sort by, and click on OK to accept the remaining defaults. Your database is sorted.

3. Click on the vertical scroll bar below the scroll box and click on F22.

4. Type **=e22*vlookup(a22,a2:e7,5)** and press Enter. The formula is calculated with the result of 268.548 (4% of 6,714), as shown here:

	F22		=E22*VLOOKUP(A22,$A$2:$E$7,5)					
	A	**B**	**C**	**D**	**E**	**F**	**G**	**H**
20								
21	Number	Office	Week	Sales	Amount		Formula	
22	250	Boston	Apr 04	46	6,714	268.548	#NAME?	
23	250	Boston	Apr 11	31	4,524			

The lookup function took the office number (250) in A22, searched the left column (because you used the vertical function) of the first database (A2:E7), and then, in the row in which it found 250, it went over five cells to find 4%. The 4% was then multiplied by the amount in E22. In searching for the 250 in the first database, Excel picks the first value that equals or exceeds the value for which it is searching. For that reason it is imperative that the range be sorted on the first column or row. The A2:E7 range needs to be absolute because you will be copying it down the database and you do not want it to vary, as you do A22 and E22. To complete the April Sales database, format cell F22 and copy it to the remaining entries in the database.

5. Format the number with a comma and no decimal places.

6. Drag the F22 fill handle through F36. The formula is copied down the rest of the database, as shown in Figure 8-22.

To be sure that the lookup function is working, check several of the numbers. For example, Denver's April 11 sales of 7,006 times 3.5% is 245, and Seattle's April 18 sales of 11,384 times 3% is 342. Remember that both the sales amount and the commission are rounded to the nearest whole number. You should find that the vertical lookup function is working perfectly.

Like several other features of Excel's database capabilities, the vertical and horizontal lookup functions are very powerful. As you have seen in the

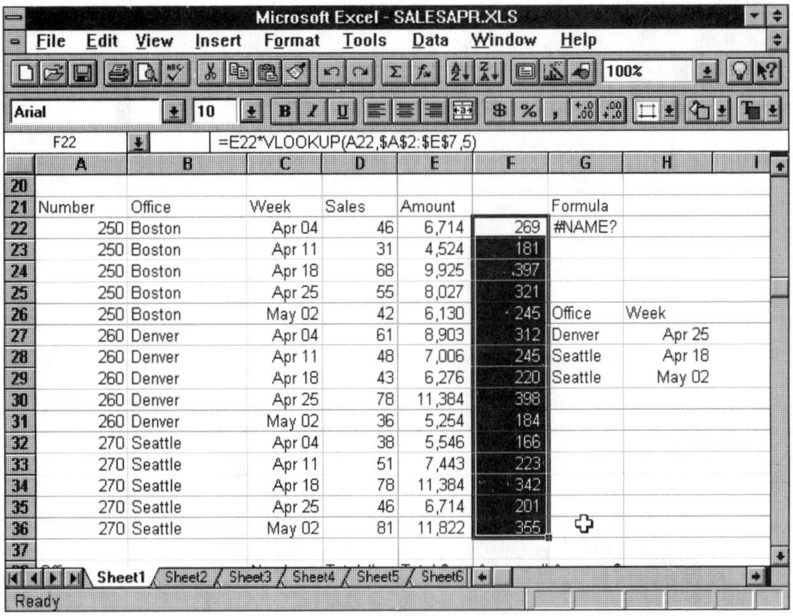

Vertical
lookup
commission
calculation
Figure 8-22.

example here, they allow you to combine two databases to perform certain functions.

As a final step in this chapter, save your workbook and, if you wish, leave Excel and Windows by following these steps:

1. Choose Save from the File menu. The file is saved under its current name, replacing the version previously saved.

2. Double-click on both Excel's and the Program Manager's Control-menu box, and click on OK to leave Windows. Excel and Windows close and return you to the operating system.

C H A P T E R

LINKING WORKBOOKS AND USING EXTERNAL FILES

Establishing a link to and exchanging information between workbooks is the major topic in this chapter. The chapter covers the process of combining several workbooks into one, including using external-reference formulas, copying from one workbook to another, adding ranges from different workbooks, and linking workbooks with external-reference arrays. Also, the procedure for exporting and importing non-Excel text and number files is discussed.

Linking Workbooks

Even with Excel's multiple-sheet capability, there are many instances where you will want to use information in another workbook or transfer information between workbooks. Any time different people create and contribute information to a central organization or project, as in a budgeting process, for example, this capability is needed. Each department or other company segment can create and maintain its own workbook, which can then be combined at the corporate level.

Another common situation is where you are working on a large project and it is easier and safer to compartmentalize various aspects of the project in separate workbooks and then combine their results in still another workbook. Multiple workbooks have a safety aspect. With a single large workbook, you have to worry about what effect inserting and deleting rows, columns, and sheets will have on surrounding sections of the workbook. With multiple workbooks, you have a physical separation that protects you. Additionally, the multiple workbook structure often makes intuitive sense and simplifies the layout of a complex project. Build a multiple workbook project now, and see for yourself.

Creating Multiple Workbooks

In the examples in this chapter you use a set of simple departmental budgets for the marketing area of a corporation. Three departments—customer relations, public relations, and advertising—are summed into the total marketing budget. Each department and the total have exactly the same workbook format. You can, therefore, build one master workbook, copy it to the other three, and then come back and customize each of them. They could very easily be separate sheets in one workbook, but since you want to work with separate books in this chapter, you'll put each department in a separate book. Prepare these workbooks now with the following instructions. Your computer should be on, Windows and Excel loaded, and a blank workbook on your screen.

1. Enter, center, and make bold the titles and column headings across columns A to G as shown here (column A has been widened to 17 spaces, or approximately two normal column widths):

	A	B	C	D	E	F	G	H
1			QUARTERLY BUDGET					
2								
3								
4	Description	Assump.	1st Qtr	2nd Qtr	3rd Qtr	4th Qtr	Total	
5								
6								

2. Select the column headings and, using the Borders tool on the right of the Formatting toolbar, add a double bottom border with the leftmost style in the second row of the Borders palette.

3. Maximize the workbook, enter the row headings, and make them bold, as shown in Figure 9-1.

   These departmental budgets are based on a head count, which varies by department; on an assumption (Assump.) for the average cost per head for each of the expense items, which also varies by department; and on a quarterly growth percentage, which is common to all departments. The formula, then, for all expense items, is head count times assumption times 1+ growth.

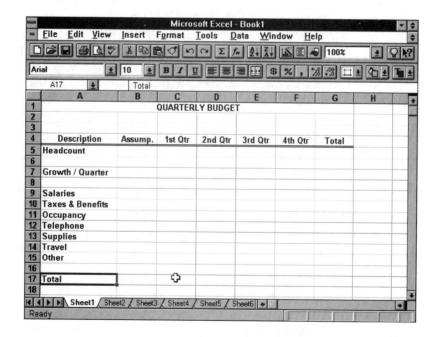

Row headings and double bottom border

Figure 9-1.

9

4. Enter the three growth percentages in D7:F7, format them with a single decimal place, and enter the first formula in C9 as **=C\$5*\$B9*(1+C\$7)**, as shown here:

	A	B	C	D	E	F	G	H
			C9	±X√ f_x =C\$5*\$B9*(1+C\$7)				
1			QUARTERLY BUDGET					
2								
3								
4	Description	Assump.	1st Qtr	2nd Qtr	3rd Qtr	4th Qtr	Total	
5	Headcount							
6								
7	Growth / Quarter			1.5%	3.0%	5.0%		
8								
9	Salaries		=C\$5*\$B9*(1+C\$7)					
10	Taxes & Benefits							

Note the mixed references on all the cell addresses. These are very important since you will be copying this one formula to all the other quarters and expense items. Remember that the easiest way to get absolute and mixed references is by pressing F4 immediately after pointing to or typing a cell address. The first time you press F4 you get an absolute reference (\$C\$5), the second time you press F4 you get a mixed reference with the row fixed (C\$5), and the third time you press F4 you get a mixed reference with the column fixed (\$C5). You do not have to remember the order because you can continue to press F4 until you get the reference you want.

5. By dragging on the AutoFill handle in the lower-right corner of the cell, drag C9 down to C15. Then, again with the AutoFIll handle, drag C9:C15 to F9:F15 to copy the formula in C9 to the other quarters and expense items.

6. Select C9:G17 and click on the AutoSum tool to build the totals in G9:G15 and C17:G17 in one very swift stroke.

7. Select B9:G17 and format it with the Comma format and no decimals. When you are done your master workbook should look like Figure 9-2.

Copying Across Workbooks

With the master workbook complete, follow these steps to build the other three workbooks and copy the master workbook to each of them.

1. Select Sheet2 through Sheet16 (click on Sheet2, press and hold Shift and click on the End-sheet button just to the left of the Sheet2 tab and then on Sheet 16), click the right mouse button on a sheet tab to open the Sheet tab shortcut menu, click on Delete, and click on OK to delete the extra sheets. Since you are using only one sheet, there is no sense in carrying the extra baggage with you.

2. Open the Tools menu, choose Options, and click on the General tab. Then drag across the Number of Sheets in New Workbook, type **1**, and click on OK. This way the new workbooks you create will have only one sheet.

3. Select A1:G17 and choose Copy from the Edit menu (or press Ctrl-C).

4. Click on the New Workbook tool in the far left of the Standard toolbar, click on the Paste tool also in the Standard toolbar, and click on column A and widen it to 17 spaces.

5. Repeat step 4 for a third and fourth workbook. When you are done, click on the document window Restore button to reduce the size of your workbooks so you can see all of them; your screen will look like Figure 9-3.

Handling Multiple Workbooks

The display that you have on your screen and that is shown in Figure 9-3 is one of several ways to look at multiple workbooks. This current display is called overlapping workbooks. If you see only one window, it is probably because you still have a maximized view—see Step 5 immediately above.

Remember that one way to get around with multiple workbooks is by clicking on the book you want to go to. The default display, shown in Figure 9-3, provides the ability to click on all the other books if you are looking at Book4, but you cannot click on any other book if you are looking

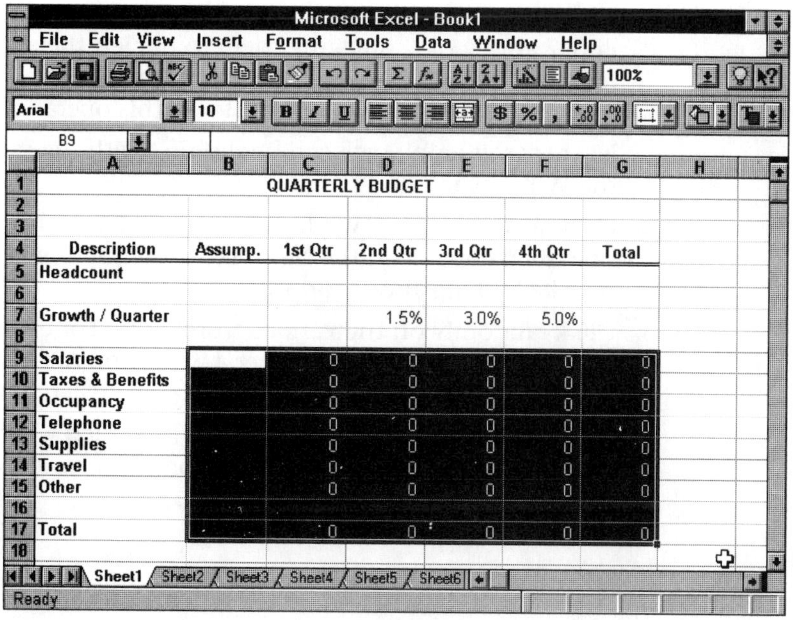

Completed
master
workbook
Figure 9-2.

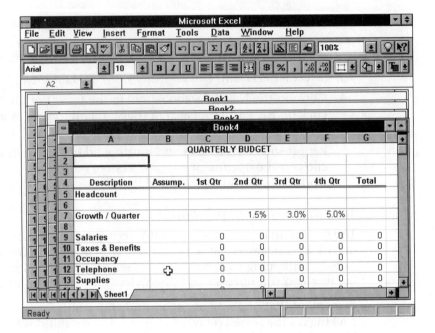

Four
workbooks
with base
information
Figure 9-3.

at Book1. The first step, then, is to pull the right edge of each workbook to the left so they are stair-stepped in the reverse order, as shown in Figure 9-4.

1. Drag the upper-right corner of Book3 to the left approximately the width of the vertical scroll bar on Book4. Repeat this procedure for Book2 and Book1, dragging them to the left the approximate width of the previous workbook's scroll bar. Alternatively, use the Size option on each workbook's Control menu to do this operation with the keyboard.

    Next try switching between books, first with the mouse and then with the Window menu.

2. Click successively on workbooks 3, 2, and 1. Notice how the books are now stair-stepped on the right. Had you not done step 1, you would now be looking at only Book1.

3. Click randomly on the various workbooks. For example, click on Book3, Book4, Book1, and Book2. After a while you can tell which is which by their heights and if they are showing on the left or right.

4. Click on the Window menu. Notice how each workbook is listed and that the last workbook you clicked on, the *active workbook,* has a check mark beside it, as shown here:

5. Choose one or two of the workbook options from the Window menu. Notice how this method works exactly like clicking on a workbook. The benefits of using the menu are that there is never any question which workbook you are going to and the workbook does not have to be visible.

All of your work so far has been with overlapping windows. Another type of window view is called a *tiled view,* which basically gives each window a small part of the screen. Look at that now.

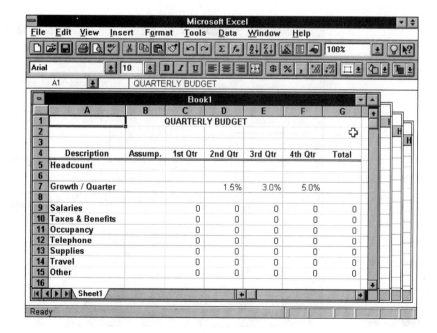

Stair-stepping
the right edge
Figure 9-4.

6. Choose Arrange from the Window menu. The Arrange Windows dialog box appears as shown:

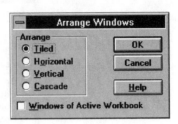

7. If it isn't already selected, click on Tiled in the Arrange list and then click on OK. The windows are resized so that a portion of all the windows you have open are displayed on the screen, as shown in Figure 9-5.

With the tiled view you can easily see what workbook you want to use, and then you can click on the Maximize button to actually use the workbook. When you restore the workbook to its original size with the Restore button or the Restore option on the workbook's Control menu, you return to the

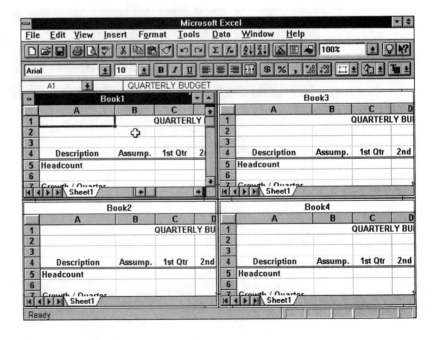

Tiled view of
worksheets
Figure 9-5.

tiled view. If you want to get back to the overlapped view, you can choose a range from the Window menu and then click on Cascade.

Customizing Individual Workbooks

Using the tiled view, customize each workbook by following these three steps:

1. If it isn't already the active sheet, click on Book1 to make it so, and then click on its Maximize button so Book1 fills the Excel work area.
2. Enter the title, head count, and assumptions on Book1, as shown in Figure 9-6. For the Taxes & Benefits assumption, enter **=14.5%*B9** in place of the amount shown in Figure 9-6. Click on Restore to return Book1 to its original size.
3. Repeat step 2 for Book2 and Book3, using Figures 9-7 and 9-8 for title, head count, and assumptions.

If your Taxes & Benefits quarterly amounts are three or four dollars different than those shown here, you missed changing the assumption to =14.5%*B9.

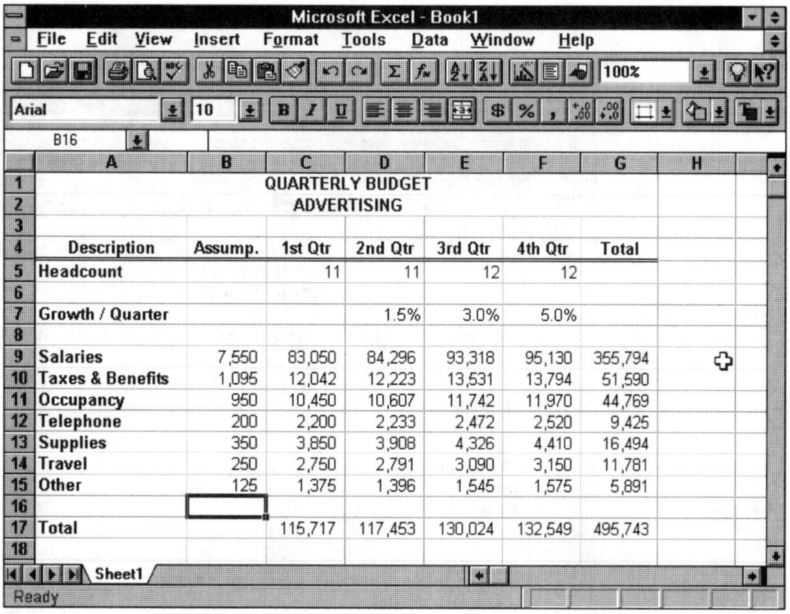

QUARTERLY BUDGET
ADVERTISING

Description	Assump.	1st Qtr	2nd Qtr	3rd Qtr	4th Qtr	Total
Headcount		11	11	12	12	
Growth / Quarter			1.5%	3.0%	5.0%	
Salaries	7,550	83,050	84,296	93,318	95,130	355,794
Taxes & Benefits	1,095	12,042	12,223	13,531	13,794	51,590
Occupancy	950	10,450	10,607	11,742	11,970	44,769
Telephone	200	2,200	2,233	2,472	2,520	9,425
Supplies	350	3,850	3,908	4,326	4,410	16,494
Travel	250	2,750	2,791	3,090	3,150	11,781
Other	125	1,375	1,396	1,545	1,575	5,891
Total		115,717	117,453	130,024	132,549	495,743

Headcount and assumptions for Book1
Figure 9-6.

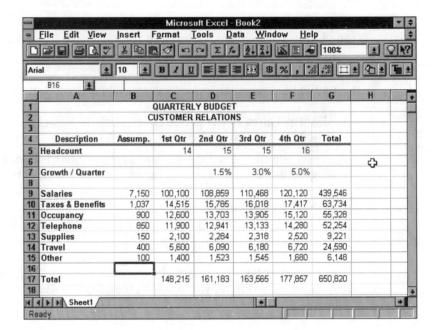

Microsoft Excel - Book2

	Description	Assump.	1st Qtr	2nd Qtr	3rd Qtr	4th Qtr	Total
	QUARTERLY BUDGET						
	CUSTOMER RELATIONS						
5	Headcount		14	15	15	16	
7	Growth / Quarter			1.5%	3.0%	5.0%	
9	Salaries	7,150	100,100	108,859	110,468	120,120	439,546
10	Taxes & Benefits	1,037	14,515	15,785	16,018	17,417	63,734
11	Occupancy	900	12,600	13,703	13,905	15,120	55,328
12	Telephone	850	11,900	12,941	13,133	14,280	52,254
13	Supplies	150	2,100	2,284	2,318	2,520	9,221
14	Travel	400	5,600	6,090	6,180	6,720	24,590
15	Other	100	1,400	1,523	1,545	1,680	6,148
17	Total		148,215	161,183	163,565	177,857	650,820

Microsoft Excel - Book3

	Description	Assump.	1st Qtr	2nd Qtr	3rd Qtr	4th Qtr	Total
	QUARTERLY BUDGET						
	PUBLIC RELATIONS						
5	Headcount		8	8	8	8	
7	Growth / Quarter			1.5%	3.0%	5.0%	
9	Salaries	7,700	61,600	62,524	63,448	64,680	252,252
10	Taxes & Benefits	1,117	8,932	9,066	9,200	9,379	36,577
11	Occupancy	1,000	8,000	8,120	8,240	8,400	32,760
12	Telephone	600	4,800	4,872	4,944	5,040	19,656
13	Supplies	250	2,000	2,030	2,060	2,100	8,190
14	Travel	600	4,800	4,872	4,944	5,040	19,656
15	Other	200	1,600	1,624	1,648	1,680	6,552
17	Total		91,732	93,108	94,484	96,319	375,643

Creating Linking Formulas

Book4 will be the total of the other three workbooks. You therefore want to replace the standard formulas in Book4 with formulas that sum the other three workbooks. The tiled view and the mouse make short work of this. Follow these steps:

1. If you are not there already, return to the tiled view so you can see all four workbooks.

2. If necessary, scroll the books so that the first quarter head count is visible in each window, and click on C5 in Book4 to make it the active cell and workbook, as shown in Figure 9-9.

3. Type **=**, double-click on C5 in Book1, and press F4 three times to make the reference relative. Type **+**, double-click on C5 in Book2, and press F4 three times. Type **+** again, double-click on C5 in Book3, press F4 three times, and press Enter.

   You have created an *external reference formula,* shown in Figure 9-10. Each part of the equation references a cell in a different workbook. This is accomplished by including the full book name in square brackets followed by the sheet name, an exclamation point (!), and the cell reference. You need it to be relative so you can copy the same formula to the other head count and expense cells.

9

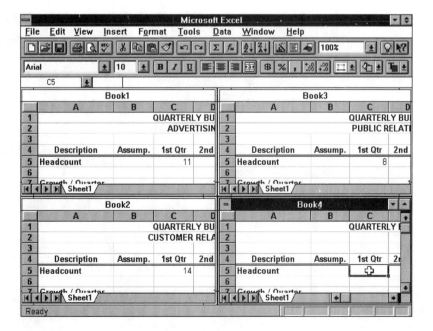

Each book displaying the 1st Qtr Headcount
Figure 9-9.

4. Maximize Book4 and use AutoFill to copy the equation to the remaining head count cells.

5. With C5:F5 still selected, press Ctrl-C to copy the selected cells, select C9:C15 on Book4, and press Enter or press Ctrl-V to paste the formulas into the expense cells.

6. Drag across the column headings for columns C through G, widen the columns slightly, and then reformat C9:F15 with the Comma format and no decimal places, as shown in Figure 9-11.

7. Type the title **MARKETING DEPARTMENT** in A2, make it bold, and center it across A2:G2 to finish the summary workbook.

Saving Multiple Workbooks

When you have a series of linked workbooks as you do here, it is very important that you save them in the proper sequence to maintain the linked formulas. Currently, the formulas have Book1, Book2, and so on for the filenames. If you were to save and close Book4 before saving Book1, Book2, and Book3, you would lose all your references. On the other hand, if you save Book1, Book2, and Book3 before saving Book4, the workbook references in Book4 automatically are replaced with the filenames. Excel has a fast way to do that with the Save Workspace command; it saves the group of

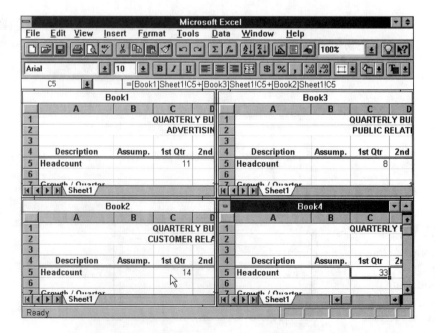

External reference formula
Figure 9-10.

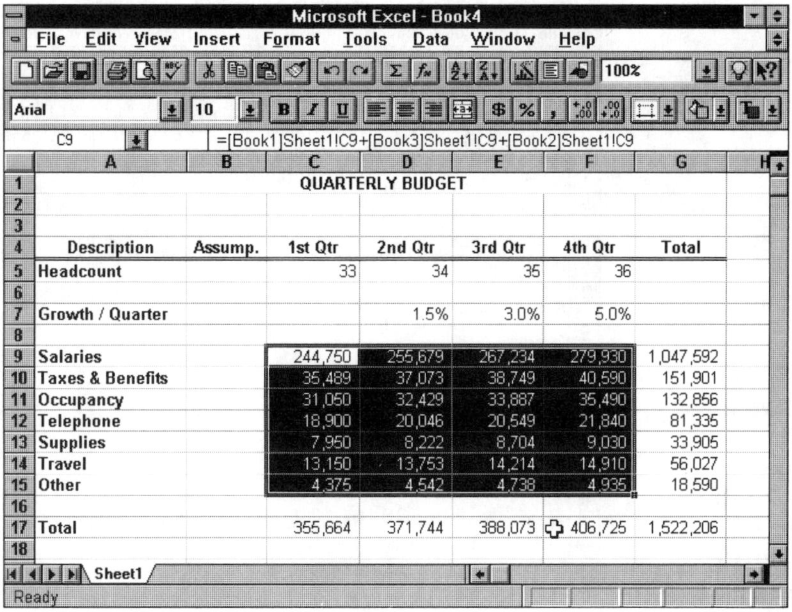

	A	B	C	D	E	F	G
1			QUARTERLY BUDGET				
2							
3							
4	Description	Assump.	1st Qtr	2nd Qtr	3rd Qtr	4th Qtr	Total
5	Headcount		33	34	35	36	
6							
7	Growth / Quarter			1.5%	3.0%	5.0%	
8							
9	Salaries		244,750	255,679	267,234	279,930	1,047,592
10	Taxes & Benefits		35,489	37,073	38,749	40,590	151,901
11	Occupancy		31,050	32,429	33,887	35,490	132,856
12	Telephone		18,900	20,046	20,549	21,840	81,335
13	Supplies		7,950	8,222	8,704	9,030	33,905
14	Travel		13,150	13,753	14,214	14,910	56,027
15	Other		4,375	4,542	4,738	4,935	18,590
16							
17	Total		355,664	371,744	388,073	406,725	1,522,206
18							

Completed summary formulas
Figure 9-11.

workbooks and in the process prompts you to save the individual workbooks in the appropriate order. Try that next with the following steps:

1. Open the File menu and choose Save Workspace. In the dialog box that opens, select the C:\SHEET directory, type **qtrbud** for the filename, and click on OK.
2. When you are prompted about saving changes in Book1, click on Yes, type **qtrbudad** for the filename, and press Enter to save Book1 as QTRBUDAD.
3. In a similar manner save Book2 through Book4 as QTRBUDCR, QTRBUDPR, and QTRBUDTO, respectively.
4. Click on C5 and on QTRBUDTO or Book4 and look at the formula, which is also shown in Figure 9-12. Notice how the formula has been changed to reflect the new filename.
5. Restore QTRBUDTO to tile size and then close each book (double-click on the Control-menu box) in the same order (start with QTRBUDAD or what was Book1, and end up with QTRBUDTO or Book4 last).

After closing QTRBUDAD (Book1), notice that the head count value in QTRBUDTO (Book4) remains 33. If you look at the formula in QTRBUDTO after closing the other two workbooks you see it is still correct and now includes the full path name as well as the filename. All of the values on the workbook are also still correct, which means they are getting their information off your hard disk.

One consideration with external references is that names are even more important than they are in other workbook formulas. External reference formulas are not updated if you insert or delete rows or columns or move or cut cells in the workbook being referenced. If you use a range name, the range name is adjusted for the changes to the workbook and the external reference is correct.

Combining Files

There are two other ways of combining workbooks: adding external ranges and linking external ranges. These are the two ends of the technology spectrum. Adding external ranges is the original way that several spreadsheets were combined, and linking external ranges uses the newest object linking technology. Using external reference formulas, as you did in the first part of the chapter, is somewhere in the middle of the spectrum. Look at both the adding and linking techniques in the following sections.

Adding External Ranges

Excel provides the means to mathematically combine a range in one workbook with a similar range in another workbook using the Paste Special option from the Edit menu. In other words, you can select and copy a range in one workbook and then, through the Paste Special option, combine it with a similar range on another workbook. The important phrase is *similar range*. More accurately, the two ranges must be exactly alike, cell for cell, because one entire range is overlaid on the other. The two workbooks also have to be in memory together, although you can combine six workbooks and have only two of them in memory at one time.

See how this works using the three workbooks created earlier in this chapter with a new total workbook. Build the new total workbook first with the normal Copy and Paste options and these steps:

1. Open the advertising department workbook QTRBUDAD, maximize it, select the range A1:H17, and click on the Copy tool in the Standard toolbar.

2. Create a new workbook, press (Enter) or click on the Paste tool, widen column A, delete the formulas in the range B5:F15, change the title to COMBINED TOTAL, and save the new workbook as QTRBUDCO in the SHEET directory.

   You now have a blank workbook, as shown in Figure 9-13, with the exact layout of the other three workbooks you built. You can use this new workbook to add the other three with the Paste Special option.

3. From the Window menu, activate QTRBUDAD, select C5:F15, and click on the Copy tool.

4. Activate QTRBUDCO, select C5, and choose Paste Special from the Edit menu. The following dialog box opens:

The Paste Special option allows you to paste only parts of the range you copied (the options on the left of the dialog box) and then to add, subtract, multiply, or divide the cells you copied to, from, by, or into the cells being pasted. As you are pasting, you can skip blank cells in the copied range so that you do not blank the contents of cells in the pasted

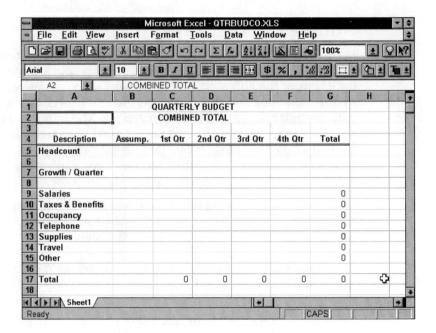

range; you can also transpose rows and columns. In this example, you want to paste *only* the values, and you want to *add* them.

5. Choose Values and Add in the dialog box and click on OK. Your QTRBUDCO workbook now looks like Figure 9-14.

6. To make this example real, close the QTRBUDAD workbook by activating it and choosing Close from its Control menu. You do not need to save any changes to QTRBUDAD.

   Note that you cannot close QTRBUDAD before choosing Paste Special. If you do close QTRBUDAD, the Paste Special option will no longer have the ability to mathematically combine ranges.

7. Open QTRBUDCR, select C5:F15, choose Copy, activate QTRBUDCO, select C5 as the active cell, choose Paste Special, and then choose Values, Add, and OK. The second workbook is added to the contents of the first.

8. Close QTRBUDCR, open QTRBUDPR, and follow the same procedure outlined in Step 7.

9. Delete the range C6:F8 on QTRBUDCO since the added percentages are not meaningful. Drag across the column headings for columns C through G and then widen them slightly so all your numbers display. Your final Combined Total workbook looks like Figure 9-15.

10. Close QTRBUDPR and save QTRBUDCO a second time.

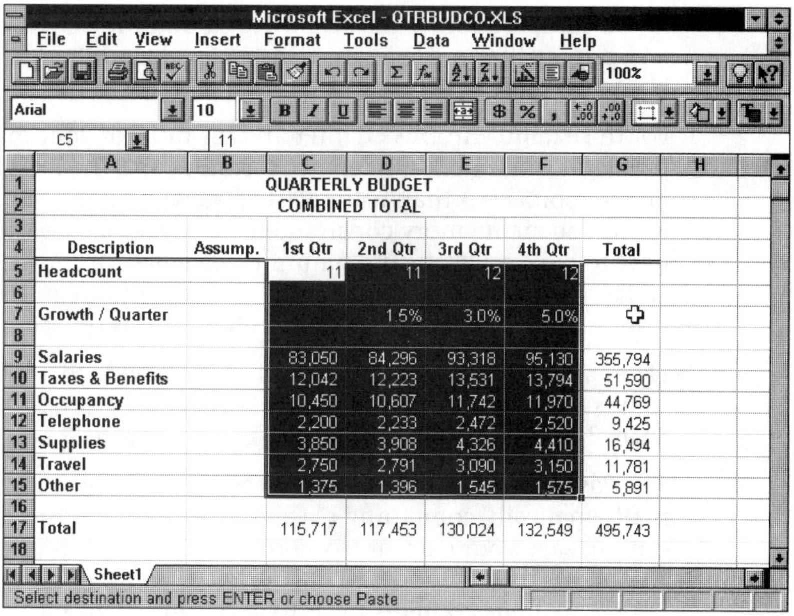

Results of
pasting the
first workbook
Figure 9-14.

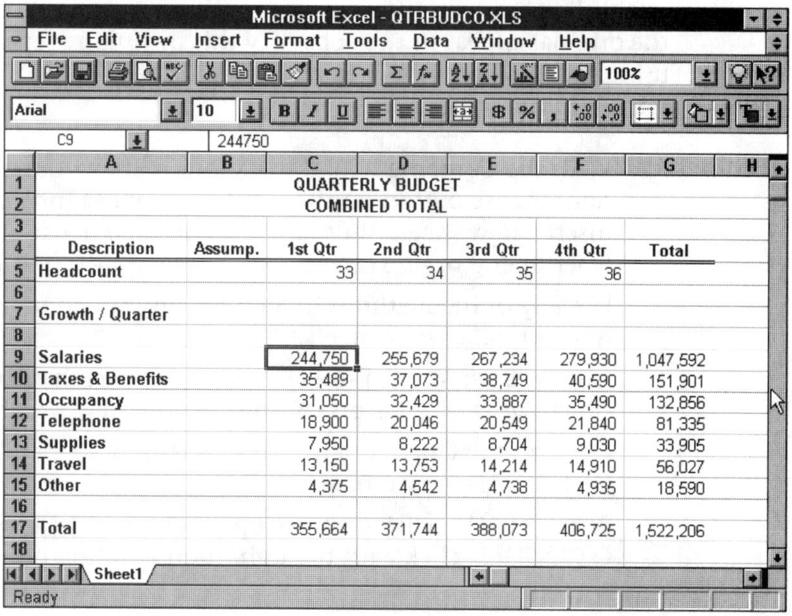

9

Final
Combined
Total
workbook
Figure 9-15.

If you compare this QTRBUDCO workbook with QTRBUDTO in Figure 9-12, you can see they are the same except for the growth percentages, which have been deleted in QTRBUDCO.

For the example in this chapter and for most of your multiple workbook problems, the external reference formulas and the linking of ranges are better approaches than using Paste Special. Paste Special should be used only when you are memory constrained. Paste Special is easier in that you do not have to build and copy the summing formulas. Of course, the big disadvantage is that the files must have exactly the same file layout. The numbers you want to add must be in the same cell positions on each workbook.

Dates and times generally should not be combined with Paste Special; the results are not meaningful. Also, blank cells are considered to be 0 by Paste Special unless you select Skip Blanks in the Paste Special dialog box.

The Paste Special option changes the current workbook by copying over or mathematically combining with its cells. Before using the Paste Special option, save your current workbook and carefully position the active cell. Also, if used soon enough, Edit Undo ([Ctrl]-[Z]) can restore the current workbook to its contents prior to executing Paste Special.

Linking External Ranges

Linking external ranges consists of the copying of an external range and then pasting it in its own area in another workbook. In the process, a link is established between the original range and its copy, so that any changes in the original appear in the copy. Try this by linking separate Excel workbooks using the files you have created earlier in the chapter and following these instructions:

1. With the Combined Total workbook still on your screen, click your right mouse button on the sheet tab, choose Insert, and click on OK to insert a new sheet. Alternatively, you can choose Worksheet from the Insert menu or press the shortcut keys [Shift]-[F11] or [Alt]-[Shift]-[F1].

2. Use any of the methods in Step 1 to insert two more sheets. You should have a total of four sheets.

3. Choose Save As from the File menu, type **qtrbudle** (for *linked* and *embedded*), and click on OK to save your new workbook.

4. Click on the Open tool in the Standard toolbar and double-click on QRTBUDAD.XLS to open it.

5. Select A1:G17, click on the Copy tool, press [Ctrl]-[Tab] to switch to QTRBUDLE, click with the right mouse button on cell A1 on Sheet4 of

QTRBUDLE, and then choose Paste Special from the Edit menu. The same Paste Special dialog box opens that you saw above.

6. Click on Paste Link. The range appears on Sheet4 as shown in Figure 9-16. Note the formula in A1 (you may have to click on A1 to see the formula). It is a group reference (or an *array*) to the source workbook. With it, any changes made to the source will appear here. The data needs a little formatting, but it is all here.

7. Press (Ctrl)-(Tab) to return to QTRBUDAD window, double-click on the document Control-menu box to close QTRBUDAD.XLS, answering No to saving changes to QTRBUDAD and to saving the large Clipboard.

8. The range A1:G17 on Sheet4 of QTRBUDLE should still be selected and visible to you. Select sheets 4, 3, and 2 so the formatting you do will apply to all three detail sheets.

9. From the Tools menu, choose Options, click on View, click on Zero Values to turn off the display of zeros, and click on OK.

10. Widen column A to 17, make the data in column A and row 4 bold, format D7:F7 as percents with one decimal, and format B9:G17 with the Comma format and no decimals.

Unfortunately you cannot center the two titles across columns A through G because the limitations of an array won't allow it. You also

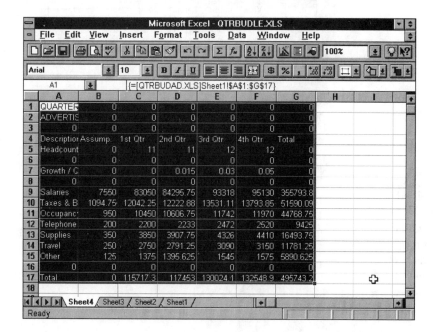

Pasted data linked to the original workbook
Figure 9-16.

cannot do any editing within an array—you must go back to the original workbook for that.

11. Repeat steps 4 through 7 to paste links from QTRBUDCR.XLS and QTRBUDPR.XLS to sheets 3 and 2, respectively, of QTRBUDLE.

12. Click on Sheet1, click on C5, click on the AutoSum tool, click on Sheet4, press and hold (Shift) while clicking on Sheet2, click on C5 again, and press (Enter). The sheet summing formula will be produced.

13. Use the AutoFill handle to copy C5 to D5:F5. Leaving C5:F5 selected, press and hold (Ctrl) while dragging across C9:F15, and then choose Fill and then Down from the Edit menu.

14. Select C9:F15 and format it with commas and no decimals. You have created a third copy of the departmental total, as shown in Figure 9-17.

This third technique of summing linked sheets is probably the best for most applications where you need to combine workbooks. It is particularly effective across a network for summing information produced in several departments of a company. Every time you open QTRBUDLE it will be updated for any changes in the linked sheets. Try that now.

Combined
Total
produced by
summing
linked sheets
Figure 9-17.

	Microsoft Excel - QTRBUDLE.XLS						
_ File Edit View Insert Format Tools Data Window Help							
Arial	10	B I U			$ % ,		
C9		=SUM(Sheet4:Sheet2!C9)					
	A	B	C	D	E	F	G	H
1			QUARTERLY BUDGET					
2			COMBINED TOTAL					
3								
4	Description	Assump.	1st Qtr	2nd Qtr	3rd Qtr	4th Qtr	Total	
5	Headcount		33	34	35	36		
6								
7	Growth / Quarter							
8								
9	Salaries		244,750	255,679	267,234	279,930	1,047,592	
10	Taxes & Benefits		35,489	37,073	38,749	40,590	151,901	
11	Occupancy		31,050	32,429	33,887	35,490	132,856	
12	Telephone		18,900	20,046	20,549	21,840	81,335	
13	Supplies		7,950	8,222	8,704	9,030	33,905	
14	Travel		13,150	13,753	14,214	14,910	56,027	
15	Other		4,375	4,542	4,738	4,935	18,590	
16								
17	Total		355,664	371,744	388,073	406,725	1,522,206	
18								

Sheet4 / Sheet3 / Sheet2 \ Sheet1

Ready

15. Save and close QTRBUDLE. Open QTRBUDAD, change C5 to 14, save and close QTRBUDAD, and reopen QTRBUDLE. You will get this message box:

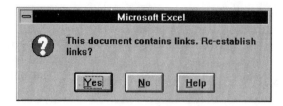

16. Click on Yes and QTRBUDLE will open. If you look on Sheet4 you will see the change. Close QTRBUDLE one last time.

17. Open the Tools menu, choose Options, and click on the General tab. Then drag across the number of Sheets in New Workbook, type **16**, and click on OK to return this to its default setting.

Saving a Workbook as a Text File

Sometimes you want to get a range or a complete file out of Excel to use in another program. Most other programs cannot read an Excel file, but they can read a file that is written in the ASCII (American Standard Code for Information Interchange) format. Excel uses the File Save As option to accomplish this. The Save As dialog box has a Save File as Type list box. When opened, the list box displays 23 different file formats in which you can save Excel files. These file formats are summarized in Table 9-1.

9

File Type	Description
Excel Workbook	Saves an entire workbook in the normal Excel 5 .XLS file format.
Template	Saves an entire workbook in an Excel 5 .XLT template file format. A template, which is a pattern for future workbooks, forces you to rename the file when you use it, so you do not write over the template.
Formatted Text	Saves only the active sheet in the Lotus .PRN space delimited text file format.

The Various File Formats in Which You Can Save Excel Files
Table 9-1.

File Type	Description
Text	Saves only the active sheet in the ASCII .TXT file format with tabs between columns and carriage returns at the end of each row. This format is primarily used to bring a workbook into a word processing package. All formulas are replaced by their values and, if a cell has a comma or a tab in it, the cell's value is enclosed in quotation marks.
CSV (Comma Separated Values)	Saves only the active sheet in the ASCII .CSV file format with commas between columns in place of tabs. Otherwise it is the same as a text file. This is primarily used by database packages. It is sometimes called an *ASCII delimited file*.
Excel 4.0 Workbook	Saves sheets, chart sheets, and Excel 4 macro sheets in the Excel 4.0 .XLW file format.
Excel 4.0 Worksheet	Saves only the active sheet in the Excel 4.0 .XLS file format.
Excel 3.0	Saves only the active sheet in the Excel 3.0 .XLS file format.
Excel 2.1	Saves only the active sheet in either the Excel 2.1 for Windows or the Excel 2.2 for OS/2 .XLS file format.
WK3, FM3	Saves all sheets and chart sheets in the Lotus .WK3 format used with Lotus 1-2-3 Release 3.x.
WK1, FMT (ALL)	Saves only the active sheet in the Lotus .WK1 format used with Lotus 1-2-3 versions 2, 2.01, and 2.2.
WKS	Saves only the active sheet in the Lotus .WKS format used with Lotus 1-2-3 version 1A.
WQ1	Saves only the active sheet in the QuattroPro for DOS .WQ1 format.
DBF 4	Saves the currently defined database range in the format used by dBASE IV.
DBF 3	Saves the currently defined database range in the format used by dBASE III.

The Various File Formats in Which You Can Save Excel Files (*continued*)
Table 9-1.

File Type	Description
DBF 2	Saves the currently defined database range in the format used by dBASE II.
Text (Macintosh)	Saves only the active sheet in a tab delimited text format readable on the Apple Macintosh.
Text (OS/2 or DOS)	Saves only the active sheet in a tab delimited text format readable in either OS/2 or DOS.
CSV (Macintosh)	Saves only the active sheet in a comma delimited text format readable on the Apple Macintosh.
CSV (OS/2 or DOS)	Saves only the active sheet in a comma delimited text format readable in either OS/2 or DOS.
DIF	Saves only the active sheet in the Data Interchange Format used by VisiCalc. This format does not transfer formulas, only values.
SYLK	Saves only the active sheet in the SYLK (Symbolic Link) format used to transfer information among Microsoft workbook packages, including Multiplan.

The Various File Formats in Which You Can Save Excel Files (*continued*)

Table 9-1.

For your purposes here, you want either the Text or CSV format. For use in the body of a word-processed document, you use Text and then set tab stops in the word processor to re-create Excel's columns. For use in a database other than dBASE or for mail merging with word-processed documents, you use CSV. Save the QTRBUDCO file in both of these formats, and then exit Excel and look at the results by following the next set of instructions.

1. Open QTRBUDCO.XLS and then choose Save As from the File menu, open the Save File as Type list box, click on Text (Tab delimited), and click on OK. The file QTRBUDCO.TXT is written to your active (SHEET) directory.

2. Choose Save As from the File menu, open the Save File as Type list box, click on CSV (Comma delimited), and click on OK.

9

You have now created two new files: one in the ASCII text format with the filename extension .TXT and the second in ASCII comma delimited format with the extension .CSV. Next close Excel and look at these files with Windows Write.

3. Double-click on the Excel Control-menu box to close it.

4. If necessary, open the Windows Accessories Group by double-clicking on its icon and then double-click again on Write to open that program. Click on the Maximize button to expand Write to full-screen size.

5. Choose Open from the File menu, change the directory to \SHEET\ (or the directory you are using for Excel files), replace the *.WRI in the filename text box with the filename QTRBUDCO.TXT, and click on OK.

6. Choose Convert from the dialog box that asks you if you want to convert to the Write format (although it really does not make any difference). The quarterly budget combined total workbook opens, as shown in Figure 9-18.

At this point the text file does not look great, but with very little work it can be markedly improved.

7. Choose Replace from the Find menu, type " in Find What, and click on Replace All. This removes all quotation marks. Double-click on the Control-menu box of the Replace dialog box to close the dialog box.

Quarterly
budget in Text
format as
displayed by
Windows
Write
Figure 9-18.

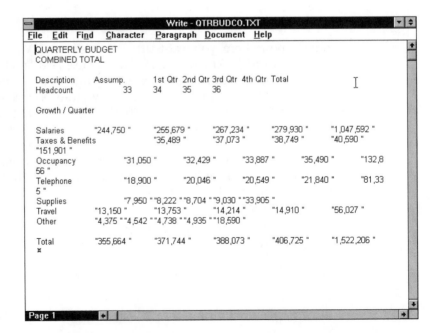

8. Choose Ruler On from the Document menu, click on the decimal tab icon (the second tab icon with the upward arrow and a period), and click in the space just below the ruler at 1.75", 2.5", 3.25", 4", 4.75", and 5.5" to set decimal tab stops at those locations.

   All of a sudden the exported workbook looks pretty good, as shown in Figure 9-19. Additionally, since it uses tabs instead of spaces, the workbook can be printed with a proportionally spaced font and not be thrown out of alignment.

9. Choose Save As from the File menu, change the filename extension to .WRI, change the Save File as Type to .WRI, and click on OK. The word processing file will be saved with the normal .WRI Write extension.

10. Choose Open from the File menu, type **qtrbudco.csv**, click on OK, and click on No Conversion. The second text file opens, as shown in Figure 9-20.

You can see that the CSV file has replaced tabs with commas, but otherwise it looks very similar to the text file when you originally brought it in. The big difference is that you cannot simply set some tab stops and get a CSV file to line up properly. What you must do is replace the commas with tabs, which will cause a problem with commas used as the thousands separator in a number. In a word processing package, the CSV format is not very useful

9

```
Write - QTRBUDCO.TXT
File   Edit   Find   Character   Paragraph   Document   Help

QUARTERLY BUDGET
COMBINED TOTAL

Description      Assump.     1st Qtr    2nd Qtr    3rd Qtr    4th Qtr     Total
Headcount                        33         34         35         36

Growth / Quarter

Salaries                     244,750    255,679    267,234    279,930   1,047,592
Taxes & Benefits              35,489     37,073     38,749     40,590     151,901
Occupancy                     31,050     32,429     33,887     35,490     132,856
Telephone                     18,900     20,046     20,549     21,840      81,335
Supplies                       7,950      8,222      8,704      9,030      33,905
Travel                        13,150     13,753     14,214     14,910      56,027
Other                          4,375      4,542      4,738      4,935      18,590

Total                        355,664    371,744    388,073    406,725   1,522,206

Page 1
```

Text file in Write after tabs have been inserted

Figure 9-19.

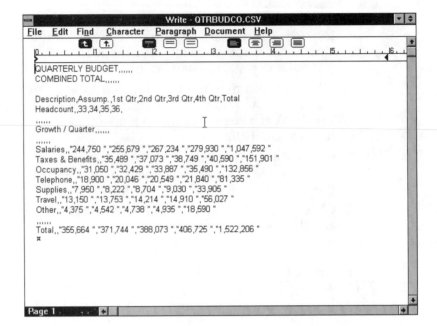

except for mail merge. The standard text format with tabs is much more useful. The CSV format is primarily used for transferring files to database packages.

Importing ASCII Text Files

Just as you may need to get data out of Excel for use in other programs, you may need to get data into Excel from other programs in a format other than the Excel standard file format. The most common format is ASCII text in one of two types: nondelimited ASCII files that are continuous text strings and delimited ASCII files. A delimited ASCII file includes delimiters, usually commas, between fields or columns and often quotation marks around text. Delimiters can also be tabs for Excel's use, but most other programs recognize only commas or semicolons. Using ASCII delimited files with commas and quotation marks is the most common means of exchanging information among database programs. Many word processing programs can also read ASCII delimited files and use them with their mail merge function.

Look at how Excel brings in each of the two text files (both the .TXT and the .CSV files) as well as a nondelimited text. While you are still in Windows Write, create the nondelimited file from QTRBUDCO.CSV, which should still be on your screen.

1. Delete the first four lines down to but not including the Headcount line (select the lines and use the Cut option in the Edit menu or the ⌊Del⌋ key), delete the three lines between Headcount and Salaries, and delete the line between Other and Total as well as any leading space in front of Total.

2. Select all of the remaining text, open the Character menu, choose Fonts and then select Courier New or Courier from the Font list box to change from a proportional-spaced font to a fixed-spaced font. Click on OK.

3. Select the full Headcount line, choose Replace from the Find menu, type , (comma) in Find What, press ⌊Spacebar⌋ six times in Replace With, and click Replace Selection to replace all commas in the first line with six spaces. Click on Close.

4. Select the remainder of the text below the Headcount line. Using the Replace dialog box, change ,," to two spaces. Next change all remaining commas to nothing by typing , in Find What, pressing ⌊Del⌋ in the Replace With text box, and clicking Replace All. Change "" to two spaces, and change the remaining " to nothing. Click on Close.

5. Add and delete spaces so the numbers line up to the right, as shown in Figure 9-21. Then use Save As to save the file as text only with the filename TEST.TXT and change the Save File as Type to Text files.

6. Double-click on Write's Control-menu box to close it. Finally, double-click on the Excel icon to reopen Excel.

9

Write - QTRBUDCO.CSV					
Headcount	33	34	35	36	
Salaries	244750	255679	267234	279930	1047592
Taxes & Benefits	35489	37073	38749	40590	151901
Occupancy	31050	32429	33887	35490	132856
Telephone	18900	20046	20549	21840	81335
Supplies	7950	8222	8704	9030	33905
Travel	13150	13753	14214	14910	56027
Other	4375	4542	4738	4935	18590
Total	355664	371744	388073	406725	1522206

Nondelimited ASCII text file in Write after being cleaned up
Figure 9-21.

Opening Tab and Comma Delimited Text Files

Both the .TXT and .CSV files that you created are delimited text files. The .TXT file is delimited with tabs, and the .CSV file is delimited with commas. Both files have quotes around numbers that contain comma formatting so the commas will not be treated as delimiters. Bring each of the two delimited files back into Excel and see how they are split up into rows and columns with the following steps.

1. Click on the Open tool from the Standard toolbar, select C:\SHEET as your directory, choose Text Files in the List Files of Type, and double-click on QTRBUDCO.TXT in the File Name list box.

   The first Text Import Wizard dialog box opens as shown in Figure 9-22. The little black rectangles in the text are the delimiters (tabs in this case).

2. Click on Next. The second Text Import Wizard dialog box opens, showing you what it has determined to be the delimiters and how the text would be divided into columns.

3. Click on Next. The third Text Import Wizard dialog box opens allowing you to select the overall formats by column.

4. Click on Finish to accept the default formatting. Figure 9-23 displays the tab delimited file back in Excel. When you click in individual cells, you see that everything is in place. About the only things you lost are the formulas and the centering and bold text formatting.

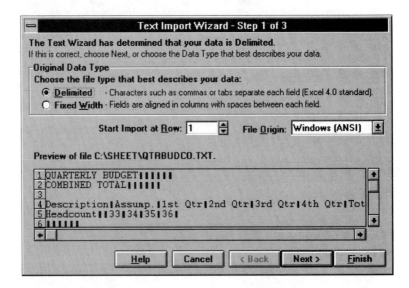

First Text
Import Wizard
dialog box
Figure 9-22.

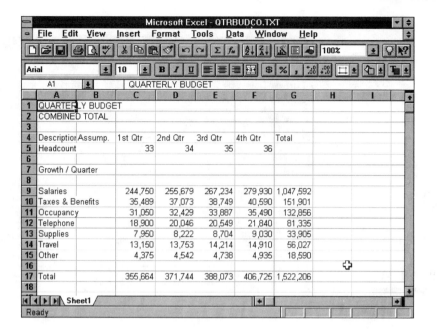

5. Double-click on the Control-menu box to close the file called QTRBUDCO.TXT, and double-click on QTRBUDCO.CSV in the File menu.

The CSV file is brought in immediately and everything is in its correct cell, with all that's lost being only the formulas, the title and column centering, and the extra width in column A, as it was with the tab delimiter. The ease with which these files come in is not deceptive. Any ASCII delimited file will come in as easily and as well behaved. If you are using commas as delimiters, use the .CSV extension when saving the file in another application. Excel will not as easily split the text into columns without this extension.

6. Double-click on the Control-menu box to close the QTRBUDCO.CSV file.

Opening Nondelimited Text Files

Bringing in a nondelimited text file into Excel, which used to be a major headache, is not much harder than a delimited file thanks to the Text Import Wizard. See for yourself by bringing in the TEST.TXT file you created in Write.

1. Choose Open from the File menu, if necessary reselect Text Files from the List Files of Type list, and double-click on test.txt.

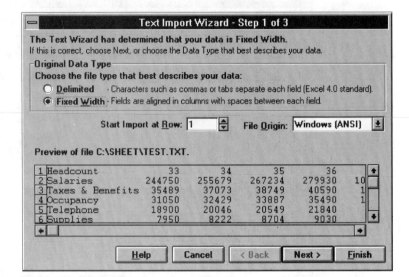

First Text
Import Wizard
dialog box
with a
nondelimited
file
Figure 9-24.

The first Text Import Wizard dialog box opens, as shown in Figure 9-24. Note that the file has been correctly identified as a fixed-width file instead of delimited as you saw before. The dialog box is correct in all aspects.

2. Click on Next. The second Text Import Wizard dialog box opens as you can see in Figure 9-25.

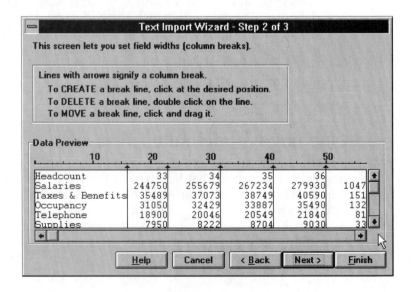

Second Text
Import Wizard
dialog box
Figure 9-25.

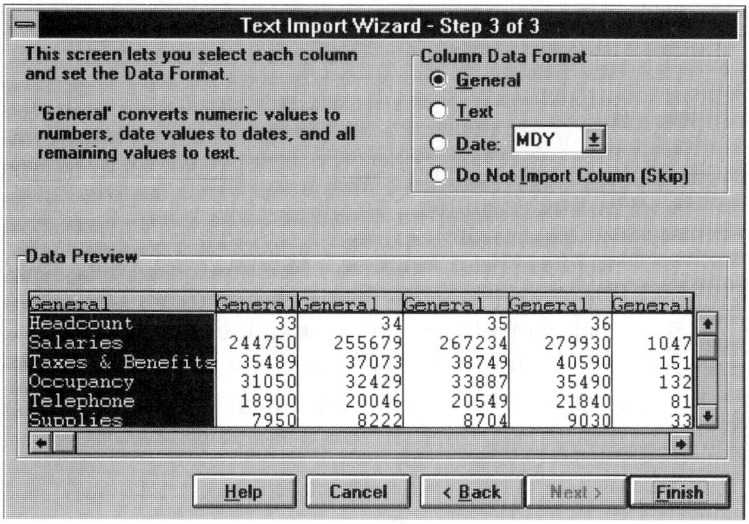

Third Text
Import Wizard
dialog box
Figure 9-26.

This dialog box lets you add, delete, and move column breaks. In this case, though, all the column breaks are OK as is.

3. Click on Next. The third Text Import Wizard dialog box will open like that shown in Figure 9-26.

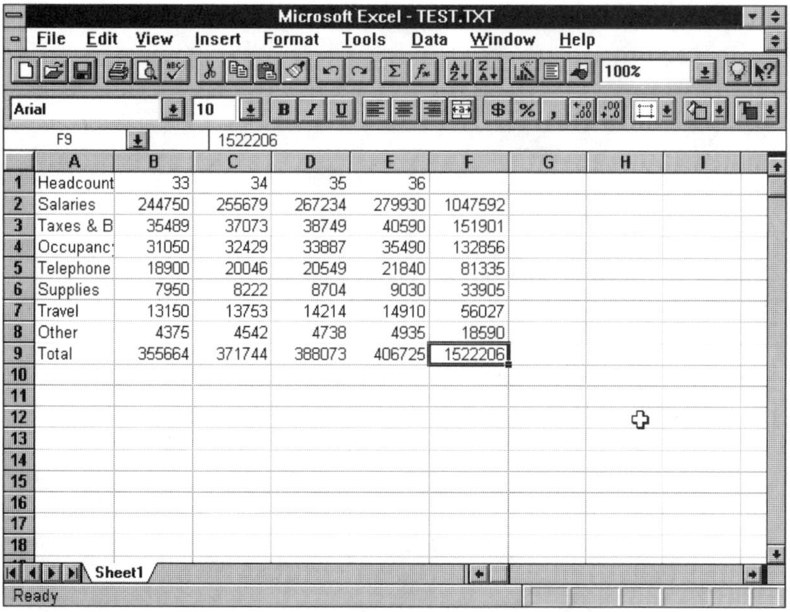

Nondelimited
text brought
into Excel
Figure 9-27.

9

The final dialog box allows you to set the overall formatting of each column and to skip (not bring in) a column if you wish. Once again all the assumptions are correct as is.

4. Click on Finish.

The file comes into Excel perfectly laid out in rows and columns, as shown in Figure 9-27. Look at several cells in column A and then in other columns. You can see that each cell contains just the information (text or numbers) that it is supposed to and that numbers are such since they are right-aligned. If you wanted, you could do arithmetic operations on them and format them. The key to this was the alignment work that you did in Windows Write. The Text Import Wizard was able to look at this text and quickly see what to do with it.

5. Double-click on the document's Control-menu box to close the TEST.TXT file. There is no need to save it.

CHAPTER

10

DATES, FUNCTIONS, AND MACROS

This chapter brings together three subjects that do not fit easily into any other category: dates and times, functions, and macros. These three subjects need a forum of their own, in which it can be shown how their finishing touches—the "icing on the cake"—make a good spreadsheet a great spreadsheet.

Using Dates and Times

From schedules and dates on reports to time-related financial calculations, dates and times are important aspects of the problems Excel addresses. The sections that follow discuss how Excel handles dates and times internally, various ways Excel formats dates and times, and the date and time functions and arithmetic operations.

Dates and Excel

Dates do not form a nice, neat, linear progression: you cannot add 12 days to April 28th and get with certainty the proper date in May without knowing how many days there are in April. Microsoft has solved this problem by establishing a date serial number scheme. This scheme allocates one number for every day from January 1, 1900 (date serial number 1) to December 31, 2078 (date serial number 65380). Microsoft also provides formatting and formulas to convert the date serial number to a specific calendar date. Internally, Excel uses the unformatted date serial number. You can format the date serial number in several ways and get a normal looking calendar date from a serial number. For example, when formatted with the first Excel date format, the serial number 34567 becomes 8/21/94, as shown here:

B2		8/21/1994	
A	**B**	**C**	**D**
1			
2	8/21/94		
3			
4			

In other words, simply typing 34567, pressing (Enter), and formatting the number with the date format m/d/yy produces the date 8/21/94. The following instructions demonstrate several date entry procedures. Your computer should be on, Excel should be loaded, and you should have a blank workbook on your screen.

1. Select B2:F2, choose Cells from the Format menu, click on the Number tab, select the Date category and the m/d/yy format, and click on OK. The range B2:F2 is formatted as m/d/yy dates.

2. Type **34567** and press →. The date 8/21/94 appears in B2.

3. Type **30638** and press →. The date 11/18/83 appears in C2.

4. Type **1**, press →, type **65380**, and press (Enter). The date 1/1/00 appears in D2, and E2 contains 12/31/78 as you can see here:

E2	↓		12/31/2078			
	A	B	C	D	E	F
1						
2		8/21/94	11/18/83	1/1/00	12/31/78	
3						
4						

Note that when you are working with dates in the next century, the two-digit year format can be confusing. Change the format next. (E2 should still be the active cell.)

5. Choose Cells from the Format menu, click on the Number tab, click after the last "y" in the Code text box, type **yy**, and click on OK. E2 fills with #'s because the date is now too big for the cell.

6. Drag on the intersection of columns E and F in the heading to widen the column slightly. The date 12/31/2078 appears in E2, like this:

E2	↓		12/31/2078			
	A	B	C	D	E ↔ F	
1						
2		8/21/94	11/18/83	1/1/00	12/31/2078	
3						
4						

There is one abnormality in Microsoft's date scheme. The year 1900 was not a leap year, even though the year was evenly divisible by four. Therefore, Excel assigns a date serial number to February 29, 1900, which didn't exist. The only impact of this is that date arithmetic spanning February 28, 1900, through March 1, 1900, is off by one day. All date serial numbers and calculated dates from March 1, 1900, onward are correct.

Times and Excel

Microsoft has also developed a scheme for calculating time: the time is added to the date serial number as a decimal fraction of a 24-hour day. Therefore, midnight is 0.000000, noon is 0.500000, and 11:59:59 PM is 0.999988. When the decimal fractions are formatted with Excel as times, they produce normal looking time numbers on either a 12-hour or 24-hour basis. The following steps show how several times are entered.

1. Select B2:F2, choose Clear from the Edit menu, and click on All to erase both the contents and formats of B2:F2.

10

2. Choose Cells from the Format menu, click on the Time category, select the first time format, h:mm AM/PM, and click on OK. The range B2:F2 is formatted with the first time format.

3. Type **.65** and press ➡. Cell B2 contains 3:36 PM, as shown here:

	A	B	C	D
1				
2		3:36 PM		
3				

4. Type **.45** and press ➡. Cell C2 contains 10:48 AM.

5. Type **0**, press ➡, type **.9999**, and press ⌈Enter⌋. Cells D2 and E2 contain 12:00 AM and 11:59 PM, as you see here:

E2	↧		11:59:51 PM		
	A	B	C	D	E	F
1						
2			3:36 PM	10:48 AM	12:00 AM	11:59 PM
3						
4						

Dates and times are stored in one number. For example, 9:21:36 PM August, 21 1994, is stored as 34567.89 (the date on the left side of the decimal, the time on the right). In a single cell you can display this as a date, as a time, or both, depending on the formatting.

Formatting Dates and Times

There are four date formats, seven time formats, and one combined date and time format built into Excel. The date formats use the integer part of a date serial number, and the time formats use the decimal part. The decimal part of a number is ignored by a date format, and the integer part of a number is ignored by a time format. If a date format encounters a number that is negative or greater than 65380, the cell fills with #'s. If a time format encounters a negative number, the cell fills with #'s.

The 12 built-in date and time formats are shown in Figure 10-1. You can, of course, make your own. The components needed to construct your own formats are shown in Chapter 6. Some examples of custom date and time formats are shown in Figure 10-2.

The choice of which format to use is one of personal taste. Some formats require wider columns than others, which may have some bearing on your decision. Also, there is no reason you cannot mix formats in a workbook.

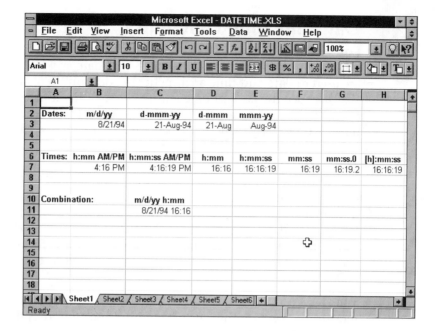

Built-in date
and time
formats
Figure 10-1.

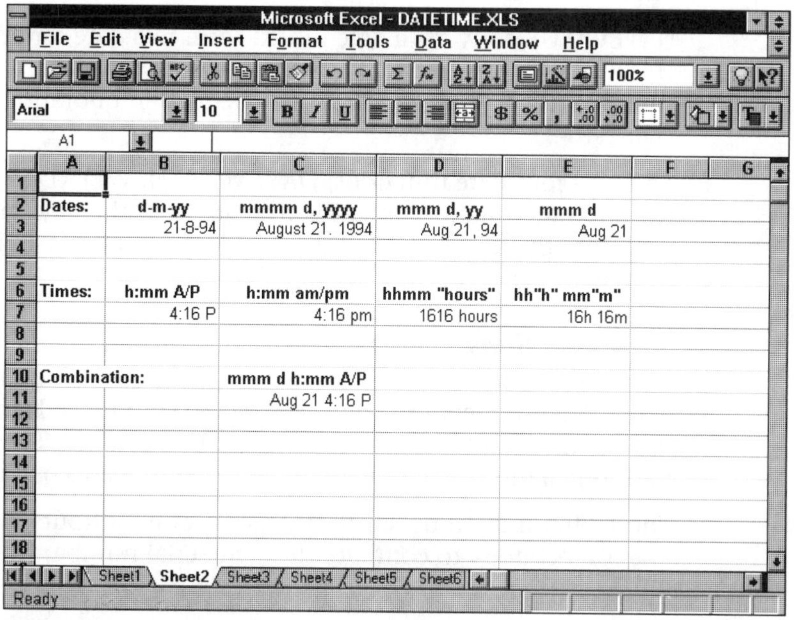

Examples of
custom date
and time
formats
Figure 10-2.

10

Date and Time Functions

Date and time functions use the date serial number to calculate various date- and time-related numbers. There are seven date and five time functions that are used in date and time arithmetic. In addition there are two functions that produce the current date and/or time. Of the fourteen functions, five produce a date or time serial number that must be formatted in order to be displayed properly. Any of the formats may be used with the functions.

Date Functions

The seven date functions are shown in Figure 10-3. The first two produce date serial numbers, shown in the middle column of Figure 10-3, that can be formatted as dates, shown in the third column. The next four functions transform a date serial number into part of a date. Note that a date for a day can be formatted into the name of the day with the format code dddd. The last function calculates the number of days between two dates using a 360-day year.

The DATE function takes three integers—one for the year, one for the month, and one for the day—and with these computes the date serial number. As with all functions, the three arguments (year, month, and day) can be integers that are entered directly into the function, or they can be addresses or reference names that refer to cells containing or computing integers suitable for the function. The DATE function is used when you break out a date for sorting or to use as a database criterion and you want to display the date that results from the combined parts.

DATEVALUE converts a date in text form to a date serial number. DATEVALUE looks for text as an argument. Therefore, a date that is directly entered into the function must be enclosed in quotation marks, as shown in Figure 10-3.

The next four date functions, DAY, MONTH, WEEKDAY, and YEAR, perform the opposite function of DATE: they split out the day, month, weekday, or year from the date serial number. WEEKDAY returns an integer from 1 for Sunday to 7 for Saturday.

Time Functions

The five time functions are shown in Figure 10-4. The first two produce the date serial numbers shown in the middle column of Figure 10-4, which can be formatted as the times shown in the third column. The last three functions transform a time serial number into the components of a time designation.

The TIME function uses three integers—one for hours, one for minutes, and one for seconds—to compute the time serial number (the decimal portion of

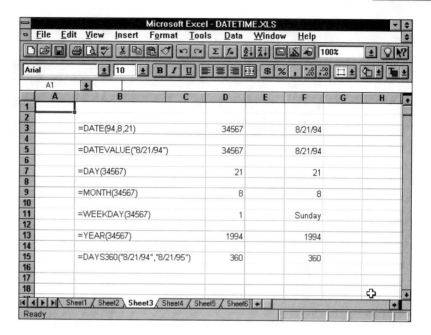

Date functions
Figure 10-3.

a date serial number). TIME is used when you break out a time for sorting or for use as a database criterion and you want to display the time that results from the combined parts.

You use TIMEVALUE to convert a time that is entered as text to a time serial number. TIMEVALUE looks for a text as an argument. Therefore, a time that is directly entered into the function must be enclosed in quotation marks, as shown in Figure 10-4.

The next three date functions, HOUR, MINUTE, and SECOND, perform the opposite function of TIME: they split out the hour, minute, or second from the time serial number.

Current Date and Time Functions

The functions used to produce the current date and/or time are NOW and TODAY. Examples of their use are shown in Figure 10-5. These functions use the internal clock-calendar in your computer to determine the current date and time. NOW produces both the integer and decimal components needed for both date and time display. If you are using the current date in a formula or with another function, use TODAY to obtain the integer part of the current date. The decimal (time) part of NOW can cause inaccuracies in date calculations. If you simply are displaying the date, NOW by itself works. Date formats ignore the decimal part of the number.

10

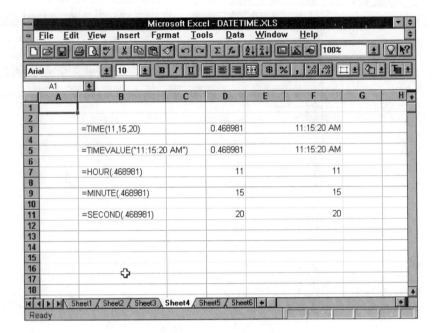

Time functions
Figure 10-4.

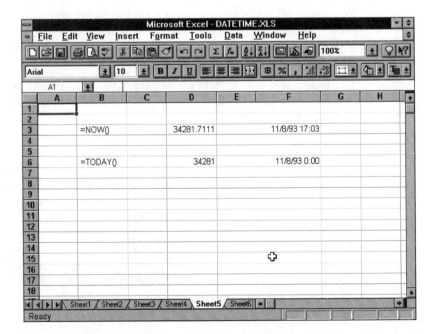

Current date
and time
functions
Figure 10-5.

Entering and Generating Dates and Times

You have just seen how you can enter dates and times either by entering the date serial number (which is not very practical because you don't know what it is in most instances) or by using one of the functions that convert a date or time to the date serial number. Also, you have seen how to generate the current date and/or time. You have two other ways to get dates and times into Excel. First, just typing a date or time on a sheet in an Excel format produces a date or time serial number. Second, the Data Series option generates a sequence of dates or times.

Direct Entry of Dates and Times

You can enter a date or time directly into Excel in any recognized format and get a date or time serial number. It does not have to be one of the built-in formats. When you enter a date or time, it is automatically formatted as the first date or first time format, respectively. The following instructions provide some examples of direct entry of dates and times:

1. Choose New from the File menu, and click on OK for a new workbook.

2. Move the active cell to B3.

3. Type **8/21/94**, and it goes in the edit area, as shown here:

4. Press (Enter). The date, 8/21/94, is converted to 34567, and the cell is automatically formatted as m/d/yy.

5. To confirm that 8/21/94 is in fact the date serial number 34567, click on B2, type **=B3**, and format B2 with the General format. Your results will look like this:

6. Click on E3, type **8-21-94**, and press (Enter). The date is converted to 34567 and automatically formatted as 8/21/94 even though 8-21-94 is not a built-in format.

If you want to enter a formula that looks like a date, you must put an equal sign in front of it.

7. Click on B5, type **3:45 pm**, and press (Enter). The time, 3:45 PM, is converted to 0.65625, and the cell is automatically formatted with h:mm AM/PM.

8. Prove that 3:45 PM is 0.65625 by clicking on B6, typing **=B5**, and formatting B6 with the general format.

9. Click on E5, type **3:45 p**, and press (Enter). The time, 3:45 p, is converted to 0.65625, and the cell is automatically formatted as 3:45 PM even though 3:45 p is not a built-in format, as shown here:

E5	↓		3:45:00 PM		
A	**B**	**C**	**D**	**E**	**F**
1					
2	34567				
3	8/21/94			8/21/94	
4					
5	3:45 PM			3:45 PM	
6	0.65625				
7					

Generating a Series of Dates

In Chapter 8, you saw how you can generate dates with the Edit Fill Series option, which is a very capable and flexible tool. From any starting date to any ending date within the 178-year range of Excel's date scheme, you can generate as many dates as you can hold in the memory of your computer. If you are generating dates, you can increment them by a number of days, weekdays, months, years, or fractions thereof.

The following steps give several examples of generating dates and times with the Data Series option:

1. Delete what you entered above, or choose New from the File menu and click on OK to create a new workbook, or click on a different sheet.

2. Select B2:F13, choose Format Cells from the Cell shortcut menu, select the Date category, the m/d/yy format, and click on OK to format the selected area.

3. Click on B2, type **1/31/94**, press (Enter), select B2:B13, choose Fill from the Edit menu, and click on Series. In the Series in and Type fields, Columns and Date should already be selected. Select Month for the unit and type **12/31/94** as the stop value. One month is the default step value, as shown here:

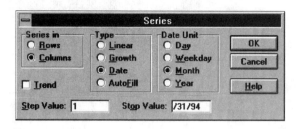

4. Press (Enter). B2:B13 fills with a series of dates that are one month apart, from 1/31/94 through 12/31/94.

   This series provides the actual month-end date, 1/31, 2/29, 3/31, 4/30, and so on, not just 30- or 31-day intervals. It can be a very useful capability.

5. Click on D2, type **1/31/94**, press (Enter), select D2:D13, choose Fill from the Edit menu, click on Series, and type **7** for the step value. Seven days or one week is the intended step value.

6. Press (Enter). D2:D13 fills with a series of dates that are one week apart, from 1/31/94 through 4/18/94.

7. Click on F2 and do a third data series, using years as the increment from 1/31/94 to 1/31/2005. You also must reformat the column to display the dates in the next century.

When you are done, your screen should look like Figure 10-6. Column B shows a progression by month, column D shows a progression by week, and column F shows a progression by year.

Generating a Series of Times

Generating times with Excel is not much different from generating dates. Although there are no ready-made increments like hours, minutes, and seconds, you can use the standard time notation of hh:mm:ss to indicate a step value. For example, a step value of one second would be 00:00:01, one minute would be 00:01:00, and one hour would be 01:00:00.

10

The following steps demonstrate several data series that produce times:

1. Delete what you entered above, or choose New from the File menu and click on OK to create a new workbook, or click on a different sheet.

2. Select B3:F15, choose Format Cells from the Cell shortcut menu, select the Time Category, h:mm:ss AM/PM, and click on OK. The selected range is formatted with the second time format.

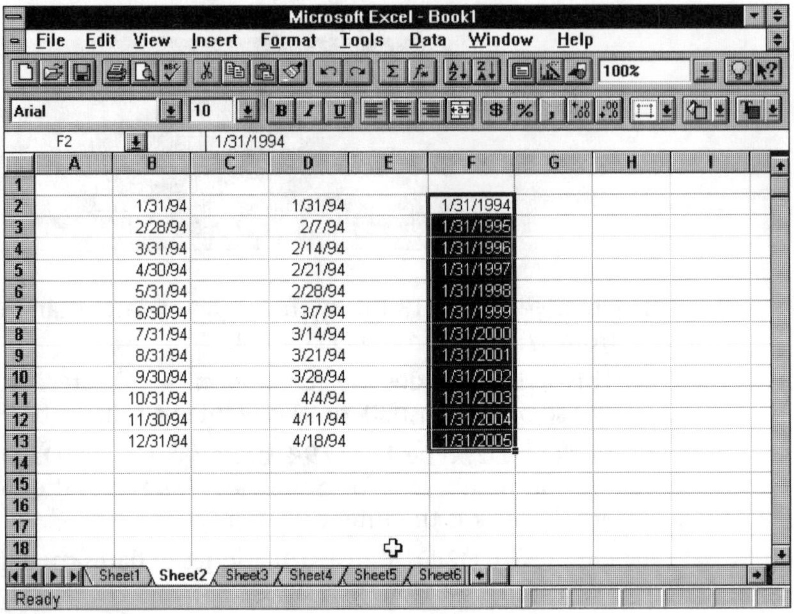

Date series by
month, week,
and year
Figure 10-6.

3. Choose Column and then Width from the Format menu, type **12** for the new width, and click on OK. Columns B through F widen to 12 to handle the full time format.

4. Click on B3, type **11:00:00**, press (Enter), select B3:B15, choose Fill from the Edit menu, click on Series, type **00:00:01** as the step value, and press (Enter). B3:B15 fills with a series of times that are one second apart, from 11:00:00 through 11:00:12.

5. Click on D3, type **11:00:00**, press (Enter), select D3:D15, choose Fill from the Edit menu, click on Series, type **00:01:00** as the step value, and press (Enter). D3:D15 fills with a series of times that are one minute apart, from 11:00:00 through 11:12:00.

6. Click on F3, type **11:00:00**, press (Enter), select F3:F15, choose Fill from the Edit menu, click on Series, type **01:00:00** as the step value, and press (Enter). F3:F15 fills with a series of times that are one hour apart, from 11:00:00 AM through 11:00:00 PM.

When you are done, your screen should look like Figure 10-7. Column B shows a progression by second, column D shows a progression by minute, and column F shows a progression by hour, all formatted for a 12-hour clock.

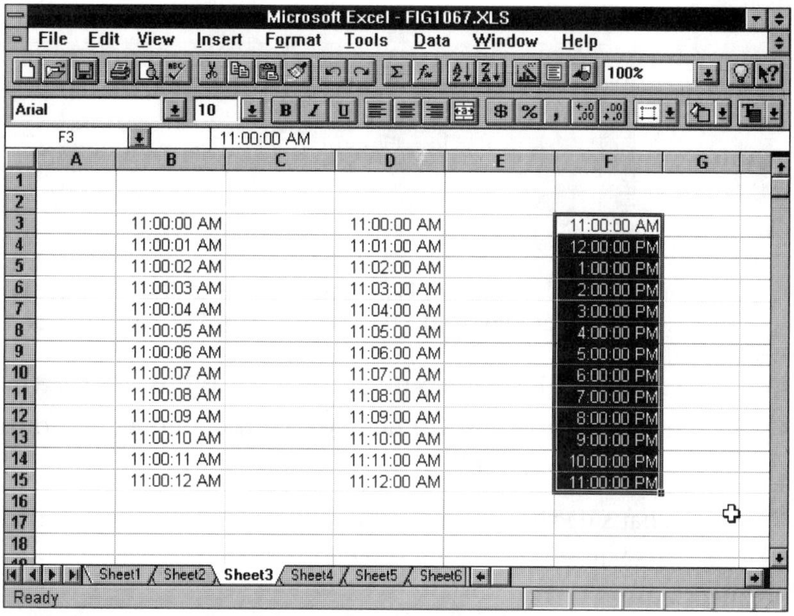

Time series by
second,
minute, and
hour
Figure 10-7.

Generating a List of Months or Weekdays

Often you find that you want a list of months or days of the week. For
example, you might want months for row headings in a financial
performance summary, as shown here:

		Sales	Expense	Net Income
January		1,805	1,516	289
February		4,368	3,669	699
March		7,330	6,157	1,173
April		9,449	7,937	1,512
May		8,956	7,523	1,433
June		6,961	5,847	1,114
July		6,000	5,040	960
August		2,807	2,358	449
September		7,692	6,461	1,231
October		3,182	2,673	509
November		9,272	7,788	1,484
December		2,553	2,144	408
Total		70,374	59,114	11,260

Alternatively, you might want days of the week for a daily lunch menu, like this:

	A	B	C	D	E	F	G	H
1								
2								
3			Monday	Tuesday	Wednesday	Thursday	Friday	
4		Menu	Hamburgers	Pizza	Spaghetti	Hot dogs	Fish & chips	
5								
6								

You could, of course, type the months or days of the week, but Excel has a much easier way to do it with the AutoFill handle. Use these steps:

1. Type the first month or day, such as **January** or **Monday**, and press ⟨Enter⟩.
2. Drag the AutoFill handle over the number of months or days you want the series to fill.

That's it! The month and weekday lists are stored in the Custom Lists tab of the Options dialog box that you open from the Tools menu, shown next:

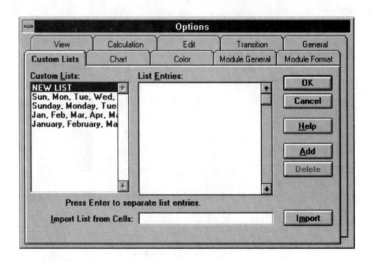

As you see, you can use the full name of the month and day of the week or their three-letter abbreviation.

You are not limited to these lists. You can build your own, either on a sheet and import it into the dialog box, or you can build it in the dialog box. Your lists can include a list of products, a list of sales people, a list of accounts, or virtually anything you repeatedly use. For example, if you have a list of sales people who you frequently use, you might enter their names in the dialog box, as shown here:

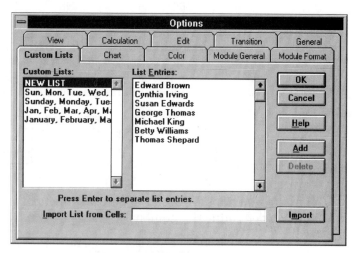

Then, by typing the first name (you must type the full name as you entered it) and dragging the fill handle, you will get a list of names like this:

	A	B	C
1			
2		Edward Brown	
3		Cynthia Irving	
4		Susan Edwards	
5		George Thomas	
6		Michael King	
7		Betty Williams	
8		Thomas Shepard	
9			

10

Date and Time Arithmetic

One of the primary reasons Microsoft developed the date serial number was to allow easy date and time arithmetic. For example, you can add 1 to a date and get the day following, as shown in the next illustration:

C2		=B2+1		
	A	B	C	D
1				
2		4/30/94	5/1/94	
3				

You can add 30 days and get the appropriate day in the next month:

D2	±		=B2+30	
A	**B**	**C**	**D**	**E**
1				
2	4/30/94	5/1/94	5/30/94	
3				

You can also subtract two dates and get the number of days between them.

E2	±		=D2-C2		
A	**B**	**C**	**D**	**E**	**F**
1					
2	4/30/94	5/1/94	5/30/94	29	
3					

The date functions are useful in date arithmetic. For example, you can use YEAR to determine the number of years between two dates, as shown here:

D2	±		=YEAR(C2)-YEAR(B2)	
A	**B**	**C**	**D**	**E**
1				
2	6/7/89	5/15/94	5	
3				

Time arithmetic is a little more complex in that you must add fractions. For example, the way to add one hour is to add 1/24th, as shown here:

C2	±		=B2+1/24	
A	**B**	**C**	**D**
1			
2	9:25 AM	10:25 AM	
3			

Adding ten minutes requires the fraction 10/(24*60):

D2	±		=B2+10/(24*60)	
A	**B**	**C**	**D**	**E**
1				
2	9:25 AM	10:25 AM	9:35 AM	
3				

Time functions are useful in time arithmetic. For example, you can determine the number of hours between two times with two HOUR functions, as shown here:

E2	±		=HOUR(C2)-HOUR(B2)		
A	**B**	**C**	**D**	**E**	**F**
1					
2	9:25 AM	10:25 AM	9:35 AM	1	
3					

Functions

In earlier chapters you gained some familiarity with statistical functions, database statistical functions, and lookup functions, and you just learned about date and time functions in this chapter. Excel has six other types of functions: financial, mathematical (including matrix and trigonometric), text, logical, informational, and command. These will be discussed in this chapter, but first look at how functions are used and created.

Using Functions

Functions are ready-made formulas. They perform a previously assigned task that usually involves a calculation but may also include a nonarithmetic operation. Functions always produce a result in the cell in which they are entered. For example, SUM produces a value that is the arithmetic addition of a set of numbers, and UPPER produces a text string that is all uppercase. Functions provide a faster alternative to standard ways of accomplishing many tasks. For example, using SUM(*reference*) is quicker than adding each individual cell in the reference if the reference contains three or more cells. Functions are also the only way some tasks can be accomplished. For example, using NOW or TODAY are the only ways you can read your computer's clock-calendar with Excel.

Specifying Arguments

In order to perform their tasks, many functions require specific pieces of information (for example, the reference in the SUM(*reference*) function). These pieces of information are called *arguments*. The number of arguments in a function varies between 0 and 14, and the length of all arguments in a function is limited to 255 characters, including any quotation marks.

Arguments can be numbers, text, arrays, references, and logical or error values, as outlined here:

✦ Numbers used as arguments in a function can be numerals, numeric formulas, or addresses or reference names for cells that contain numbers or numeric formulas.

✦ Text is any sequence of letters, numbers, spaces, or symbols. Text in a function can be literal text enclosed in quotation marks, a text formula, or an address or reference name for a cell that contains literal text or a text formula.

✦ An array is a rectangular set of values (a range) that is treated in a special way. An array is enclosed in braces, { }, and has a semicolon between rows. For example, the array {5,6,7;3,4,5;1,2,3} is a 3-by-3 array, with three rows that each contain three columns. Arrays used as arguments in a function can be entered directly, result from a formula that evaluates

10

to an array, or be a set of addresses or a reference name for a reference that contains an array or a formula that evaluates to an array.

✦ References can be addresses, reference names, or any formula that evaluates to an address or reference name.

✦ A logical value is either True or False. You can enter **True** and **False** in either uppercase or lowercase letters, but Excel converts them to uppercase. In a function, logical values may be entered directly, result from a logical formula that evaluates to either True or False, or be in a cell referenced by an address or reference name. A logical formula is one that contains one of these logical operators:

=	Equal to
>	Greater than
<	Less than
>=	Greater than or equal to
<=	Less than or equal to
<>	Not equal to

✦ Error values include #DIV/0!, #N/A, #NAME?, #NULL!, #NUM!, #REF!, and #VALUE!. In a function, error values may be entered directly, result from a formula, or be contained in a cell referenced by an address or reference name. A brief meaning of each of the error values is given here:

#DIV/0!	You tried to divide by zero
#N/A	Not available
#NAME?	Excel does not recognize a name
#NULL!	Two group of cells you expected to intersect do not
#NUM!	Excel has a problem with a number
#REF!	Excel cannot find a reference to a cell or group of cells
#VALUE!	You used the wrong type of operand or argument

Entering Functions

There are many different functions, but they all have the same structure, or syntax. A *syntax* is a set of rules for consistently doing something in an orderly manner—in this case, entering functions. The syntax for entering functions is as follows:

✦ Every function begins with the = symbol, unless it is inside a formula (that is, not the first element of the formula) or another function.

◆ Functions can be entered in either uppercase or lowercase letters. They are displayed in uppercase by Excel. If you type a function in lowercase letters and Excel does not change it to uppercase, you know that you misspelled the function name or made some other mistake.

◆ Spaces cannot occur anywhere in a function, except within a literal string enclosed in quotation marks or immediately after a comma between arguments.

◆ The arguments of a function must be enclosed in parentheses. If one or more functions are used as arguments for other functions, the parentheses must be nested, with complete left and right sets of parentheses for each function. Even functions that do not have arguments must have a set of parentheses. For example, NOW().

◆ Two or more arguments within a function are separated by commas. You should not have more commas than there are arguments or two arguments without a comma between them.

◆ Blank cells referenced in a function are assigned the value 0.

◆ Functions can be used by themselves as a formula or as a part of another formula, function, or macro command.

Functions may be directly entered by typing them in a cell, following the syntax just described, or you can have Excel build the formula using the Function Wizard. To do the latter, make the cell in which you want the function placed the active cell, and then click on the Function Wizard tool in the Standard toolbar. The first Function Wizard dialog box opens, as shown here:

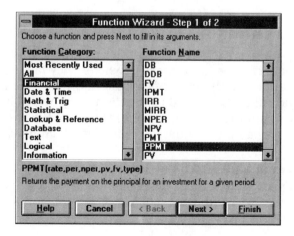

10

In the first Function Wizard dialog box, functions are listed alphabetically, within 13 categories that include All and Most Recently Used. You can use the scroll bar to select first a category and then a function, or you can type the first letter of a function to quickly jump closer to it. Once you have chosen a function, click on Next to open the second Function Wizard dialog box, like this:

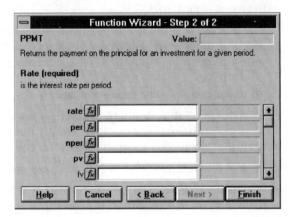

The second Function Wizard dialog box lists all the arguments and provides an explanation of those that are not obvious. You can enter a value, a reference, or another function for each argument by typing the value or reference or by clicking on the Function Wizard tool next to the argument name. Arguments that are required are bold, and those that are optional are not. When you are done entering the arguments you want to use, click on Finish and the completed function is transferred to the sheet.

Additional Functions

The next several sections of this chapter discuss some of the functions that have not been discussed elsewhere. They fall into five groups: financial, mathematical, text, logical, and informational. Because there are so many, not all of the individual functions are covered here. The following sections contain tips and suggestions for each of the five groups, along with one or two examples of functions within each group.

Financial Functions

Financial functions such as the following calculate amounts used in financing, budgeting, and depreciation. Optional arguments to the functions are in square brackets.

FV(*rate,term,payments*[*,pv,type*])	Returns the future value, given a series of equal payments, the interest rate, and the term. Optionally, you can enter the present value and/or whether the payment is made at the end of the period (the default, *type* = 0) or at the beginning of the period (*type* = 1).
IRR(*reference*[*,guess*])	Returns the internal rate of return for a series of cash flows contained in the reference. A guess may speed up the calculation. If you don't enter a guess, Excel uses 10%.
NPV(*rate,reference*)	Returns the net present value of a series of cash flows contained in the reference at a given interest rate.
PMT(*rate,term,principal*[*,fv,type*])	Returns the payment required for a loan amount (principal) given the interest rate and loan term. Optionally, you can enter the future value and/or whether the payment is made at the end of the period (the default, *type* = 0) or at the beginning of the period (*type* = 1).
PV(*rate,term,payment*[*,fv,type*])	Returns the present value, given a series of equal payments, the term, and the interest rate. Optionally, you can enter the future value and/or whether the payment is made at the end of the period (the default, *type* = 0) or at the beginning of the period (*type* = 1).
SLN(*cost,salvage,life*)	Calculates depreciation expense for an asset using the straight-line depreciation method.

When you use financial functions, the term and interest rate must be in the same time units. For example, if you want a result in months, the term must be in months and the interest rate must be in months. (See the first example in the "Examples" section that follows.)

The interest rate can be entered in a financial function as either a decimal (.108) or a percent (10.8%). Also, in many financial functions you must distinguish between cash outflow, which should be a negative number, and cash inflow, which should be a positive number (see the examples that follow).

Where a series of payments is used in a function, the payments are assumed to be equal and paid regularly at the end of each period. This is known as an *ordinary annuity*. If you want to change the payment to the beginning of the period, use the optional *type* argument with a value of 1.

Examples   To calculate the prospective monthly mortgage payment on a $140,000 30-year loan at 7.8% interest, use the following function:

```
=PMT(.078/12,30*12,140000)   returns -$1,007.82/month
```

To calculate the annual rate of interest necessary for a $10,000 investment to grow to $24,000 over 10 years with monthly compounding, use the following function:

```
=RATE(10*12,0,-10000,24000)*12   returns 8.79%/year
```

Mathematical Functions

Mathematical functions such as the following calculate general, matrix, and trigonometric values.

ABS(*x*)	Returns the absolute value of a number
ATAN(*x*)	Returns the arctangent of a number
MINVERSE(*array*)	Returns the inverse of a matrix or array
RAND()	Returns a random number between 0 and 1
ROUND(*x,n*)	Rounds a number off to a specific number of decimal places
SIN(*x*)	Returns the sine of an angle
SQRT(*x*)	Calculates the square root of a number

Angles used as arguments for COS, SIN, and TAN must be expressed in radians. To convert degrees to radians, multiply the degrees by PI/180. The angle that results from ACOS, ASIN, ATAN, and ATAN2 is in radians. To convert radians to degrees, multiply the radians by 180/PI.

Example   To calculate the length of a guy wire that is supporting a 150-foot antenna when the guy wire, attached to the top, makes a 55-degree angle with the ground, use the following function:

```
=150/SIN(55*PI/180)   returns 183.12 feet
```

Text Functions

Text functions convert, parse, and manipulate text strings. Some of the text functions are as follows:

CHAR(*x*)	Returns the ASCII character corresponding to the number x
EXACT(*string1,string2*)	Compares two text strings and returns True if the two strings are the same and False if they differ
LEN(*string*)	Returns the number of characters in a text string
MID(*string,start-number,n*)	Returns the specified number of characters from within a text string beginning at a specified position
PROPER(*string*)	Converts the first character in each word of a text string to uppercase and the rest of the characters to lowercase, as in a proper name
TEXT(*x,format*)	Converts a number to text with a given numeric format

The offset number used in string functions always begins at 1. The first character in a string is 1, and the last character is the length of the string. Blank cells in a string function are still considered text, have a length of 0, and do not return an error code.

Example   To convert the date 4/19/94 in A1 to a text string that can be used in a title, use the following function:

```
=TEXT(A1,"mmmm d, yyyy")
```

This function returns April 19, 1994, which is text, not a value.

Logical Functions

Logical functions such as the following perform tests to determine if a condition is true.

AND(*condition 1,condition 2,...*)	Returns True if all conditions or logical statements are true
IF(*condition,true-result,false-result*)	Evaluates an equation or condition for true or false and takes one action for a true result and another action for a false result
TRUE	Returns a logical True

Example When you calculate percentages, there are situations that result in dividing by 0, which produces a #DIV/0! error. To replace a possible error value with 0 in the formula =E15/C15, use the following formula in its place:

```
=IF(ISERR(E15/C15),0,E15/C15)
```

Informational Functions

Informational functions such as the following provide information about cells and areas of the workbook, including the number of rows or columns in a reference, the formatting of a cell, and whether a cell is blank, contains text, or is a logical value.

COLUMNS(*reference*)	Returns the number of columns in a reference
ISBLANK(*value*)	Returns the logical value True if the value or cell is blank
ISTEXT(*value*)	Returns the logical value True if the value or cell is text
ROW(*reference*)	Returns the row number (not the number of rows) of the first row in the reference or an array of row numbers for all of the rows in the reference

Example Often it is helpful to know the column width of a cell. You can choose Column Width from the Format menu, or you can use the function CELL("width"). CELL("width") returns a value that is rounded to the nearest whole number. For example, =CELL("width") returns 8 for the standard cell width of 8.43.

Macros

A *macro* is a shortcut. It is a way of accomplishing a set of Excel commands with fewer steps and a way to automate or speed up repetitive procedures. A macro is also a way to guide a less knowledgeable user through a complicated workbook.

There are two kinds of macros in Excel. A *command macro* is a series of Excel commands, and a *function macro* is a custom function that returns a result. An example of a command macro is one that saves your workbook, while an example of a function macro is one that calculates your local sales tax. You can have Excel execute a command macro by pressing only two keys. A function macro is executed by putting it in a workbook cell and recalculating the workbook. Almost all commands that you can perform from the keyboard, the mouse, or a menu can be stored in a macro and can be activated as you choose. In addition to keyboard and menu commands, a set of *macro commands* lets you perform built-in programming functions, such as repeating a sequence or accepting input from the keyboard. With macro commands you can build custom menus and automate a workbook. You can see that command macros, which are custom procedures that you create to perform some function, and macro commands, which are used in command macros and supply the programming capability, are distinct—although they can be easily confused.

Anything that you do on a repetitive basis is a candidate for a macro. You can even create a library of macros that you can use with many workbooks, a way of making macros even more useful.

There are two ways in Excel 5 to create macros: using Visual Basic and using the Excel 4 macro language. Visual Basic is the wave of the future and is covered in considerable detail in Chapters 12 and 13. For the balance of this chapter you'll see how the Excel 4 macro language gives you the ability to create many macros.

Excel 4 Macro Basics

You have seen earlier in this book that formatting a number is important, but if your preferred number format is not preassigned to a tool in the Formatting toolbar, it requires six mouse clicks (the Format menu, the Cells option, the Number tab, the category, the format code, and OK) or 11 keystrokes ([Alt]-[O], [E], one or more arrow keys to select the tab, [Alt]-[C] and several arrow keys to select the category, [Alt]-[F] and several arrow keys to select the format code, and [Enter]). This is not a lot of effort, but when you repeat it several times a day, it begins to add up. If you could replace the actions with easy keystrokes like [Ctrl]-[e], a single option in the Tools menu, or, better yet, a single tool in a toolbar, it would make a difference. Applying your preferred number format, then, is a candidate for a macro.

Recording a Macro

Built into Excel is the capability to record whatever you are doing on an Excel sheet and to store those steps on a macro sheet. Once stored, you can "play back" the steps and repeat what you were doing. The steps that are stored on the macro sheet comprise the macro, and playing them back is called *running the macro*. You turn on the Excel macro recorder by choosing Record Macro from the Tools menu. Do that now and record a macro that formats a preselected area of a workbook with these instructions:

1. Choose New from the File menu and click on OK to open a new workbook.

2. From the Tools menu choose Record Macro and then select Record New Macro for the submenu that opens. The Record New Macro dialog box opens, as shown here:

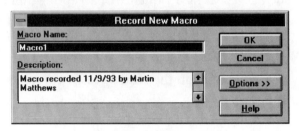

In this dialog box you can name the macro (which cannot contain spaces) and enter or edit a description. Here, you do want to name the macro, and you also do need to enter some other options.

3. Type **Format_Number** in the Macro Name text box and then click on Options to open the rest of the dialog box, as shown here:

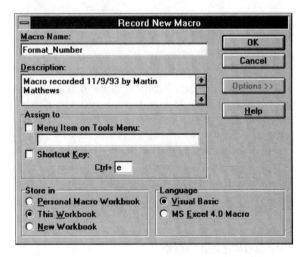

There are three ways you can store macros: in a special Personal Macro Workbook, on a macro sheet in the current workbook, or on a macro sheet in a new workbook. The Personal Macro Workbook is automatically opened each time you start Excel. This is generally the workbook to use for simple, frequently used utility macros because Excel will name, open, and save the workbook for you. If you use the current workbook, the macros are only available with it. If you create a new workbook, you will have to manually open it both to record to it and to run the macros once they are recorded and you will have to save the workbook. Here, you will create and record a macro using the Personal Macro Workbook.

4. Click on Menu Item on the Tools menu and click in the text box under that and type **Format Number** to place the macro in the Tools menu.

5. Click on Shortcut Key and accept the Ctrl-e that is shown. If you accept the keys that are shown, you will not use a shortcut key that is already assigned as Ctrl-a through Ctrl-d are.

6. Click on Personal Macro Workbook in the Store In list box, click on MS Excel 4 Macro, and click on OK. The dialog box closes, and the Recording status message comes on in the Status bar.

The name of a macro can be any legitimate Excel name. It must start with a letter, can be up to 255 characters long, and can contain any combination of letters, numbers, and underlines. It should not look like a reference (either D3 or R3C4) and cannot contain spaces or punctuation marks. Since you cannot use spaces, underlines are used as word separators. An Excel name can be entered in either uppercase or lowercase letters—Excel does not distinguish between the two.

The shortcut key can be any single uppercase or lowercase letter. Uppercase and lowercase letters are considered two different characters and will not conflict with one another. You cannot use numbers as shortcut characters. If you use a shortcut key that has been previously assigned, you will be alerted to that fact, and you can choose whether to reassign the key. The shortcut keys you can possibly reassign include the ones like Ctrl-C for copying and Ctrl-S for saving. So you want to think carefully about doing this.

7. Choose Cells from the Format menu and then click on Number. Select the Currency category, click on the second currency format code, and click on OK. These are the steps you want to record.

8. Click on the Stop Recorder tool in the little one-tool Stop Recorder toolbar that looks like this:

The Recording message disappears as does the Stop Recorder toolbar.

9. From the Window menu, choose Unhide. The Unhide dialog box opens as shown here:

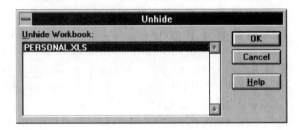

10. Double-click on PERSONAL.XLS. The Personal Macro Workbook that was automatically created in the previous steps becomes the active sheet, as shown here:

	A	B	C
1	Format Number (e)		
2	=FORMAT.NUMBER(		
3	=RETURN()		
4			
5			

PERSONAL.XLS

The Personal Macro Workbook looks just like a normal sheet except that the columns look a little wider. The macro itself is in the upper-left corner, in cells A1:A3. A1 contains the name and shortcut key you gave the macro. A2 and A3 are the macro commands that format the selected cells and return control to you. Macro commands are formulas—they always begin with an equal sign (=). A macro sheet always displays formulas, not the results they produce. Displaying formulas is an option on a normal sheet, but normally a sheet displays the results a formula produces. You can use the View tab in the Options dialog box reached from the Tools menu to turn off the formulas display on a macro sheet, but the resulting values are generally not informative. In this case, your macro commands in rows 2 and 3 are replaced with the word "FALSE."

When you are displaying formulas instead of their results, their placement on the sheet is left-aligned and cannot be changed with the Format alignment option. Otherwise, all formatting works on a macro sheet as it does on a sheet.

Documenting a Macro

As you create macros, you may find that after a while you forget what they do. Also, you may want to give one or more macros to someone else, who will need to know what the macros do. For this reason you must document your macros when you create them.

You can document a macro in several ways. You have used a form of documentation already—giving the macro a descriptive name. Other ways include formatting the macro name on the Personal Macro Workbook so it stands out, adding one or more cell notes, and, most importantly, adding some comments beside the macro commands. Add some comments and format the macro name with these steps:

1. With A1 as the active cell, click on the Bold button in the Standard toolbar. The macro name should be made bold.

2. Click on B1, type **Formats selection**, press ⬇, type **Second $ format**, and press (Enter). After widening column A, the upper-left corner of your macro sheet now looks like this:

	A	B	C
	PERSONAL.XLS		
1	**Format_Number (e)**	Formats selection	
2	=FORMAT.NUMBER("$#,##0_);[Red]($#,##0)")	Second $ format	
3	=RETURN()		
4			
5			

Running a Macro

Now that you have a finished and documented macro, you can run it in one of three ways. First and most simply, you can press (Ctrl)-(e), the shortcut key. Second, the Macro dialog box, reached by choosing Macro from the Tools menu, lists all the macros available on open macro sheets, so you can select the macro you want and click on OK. Third, the Tools menu now contains a new option named Format Number that you can choose. Try all of these methods using the following instructions:

1. From the Window menu, choose Book1, type several numbers to format and make one of them negative, use the AutoFill handle to copy those numbers to four more rows so you have five sets of numbers, and then select the first set of numbers.

2. Press Ctrl-e. The numbers are formatted.

3. Select the second set of numbers. Then, from the Tools menu, choose Macro. The Macro dialog box opens, as shown here:

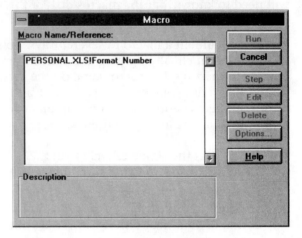

The Macro dialog box lists the macro you have just created. By clicking on the entry in the list box and then on Run, you can run the macro. You can also just double-click on the entry.

4. Double-click on the entry. The second set of numbers are formatted.

5. Select the third set of numbers. Then, open the Tools menu. Notice a new option appears at the bottom of the menu, like this:

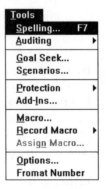

6. Click on Format Number and the third set of numbers are formatted.

If you had any fears about macros, you can now set them aside. You have successfully created and run a macro!

7. Activate the Personal Macro Workbook by choosing it from the Window menu.

8. Close the Personal Macro Workbook by choosing Hide from the Window menu. When you exit Excel, a dialog box will ask if you want to save changes to the Personal Macro Workbook; click on Yes and the Personal Macro Workbook will be hidden, but working, in future Excel sessions.

If you exit Excel without both hiding the Personal Macro Workbook again and choosing Yes to save the change to it, the Personal Macro Workbook will appear every time you start Excel until you choose to hide it and to save the change on exiting.

Attaching a Macro to a Tool on a Toolbar

There is one more way to run a macro and that is to attach it to a tool on a toolbar. The tool can either be a custom tool that is not currently assigned to a function or an existing tool that has a built-in function it performs. For example, the Currency Style tool on the Formatting toolbar has a slightly different format from the one you choose in the macro. Assume that most of your currency formatting will be the new format, so you want to attach your macro to the Currency Style tool (you can easily reset it back to its original format). See how that is done with these steps.

1. Select the fourth set of numbers and click on the Currency tool in the Formatting toolbar. The numbers are formatted with the built-in format.

2. Click the right mouse button on a toolbar to open the Toolbar shortcut menu and choose Customize.

3. Click on the Currency Style tool to select it.

4. From the Tools menu, choose Assign Macro. The Assign Macro dialog box opens as shown here:

10

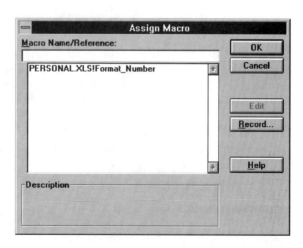

5. Double-click on the Format_Number macro and click on Close in the Customize dialog box.

6. Select the fifth set of numbers and click on the Currency Style tool. The numbers are once more formatted like this:

$34,568	($87,654)	$53,479
$34,568	($87,654)	$53,479
$34,568	($87,654)	$53,479
$ 34,567.89	$ (87,654.32)	$ 53,478.97
$34,568	($87,654)	$53,479

Attaching macros to tools is one of the most powerful features in Excel. By doing this, you can customize the toolbars to your needs. You can reset the tool to which you attached the macro in two ways: one restores just one tool to its original function, and the other resets all tools to their original function and tool face. If you want to reset all the tools, choose Toolbars from either the View menu or the toolbar shortcut menu and click on Reset. If you want to restore just one tool to its original function, use these steps:

1. From the toolbars shortcut menu, choose Customize.

2. Drag the tool to which you assigned the macro (Currency Style in this case) off the top of the screen.

3. From the Customize dialog box, select the category from which you want to select a tool (Formatting here) and then drag the tool you want from the Customize dialog box to the toolbar to which it belongs. The function of the tool will be restored.

Creating Additional Macros

Create several more simple and general-purpose macros. This time, however, watch the macros being built by reducing the size of the workbook you are working on and exposing most of the macro sheet, as shown in Figure 10-8. Do that with these steps:

1. Choose Unhide from the Window menu. The Unhide dialog box appears. Highlight PERSONAL.XLS, click on OK, and the file is opened.

2. Scroll the PERSONAL.XLS sheet to the left so column C is active. Widen the column to 20.

3. Drag the upper-left corner of the Book1 window to reduce it to approximately the size shown in Figure 10-8.

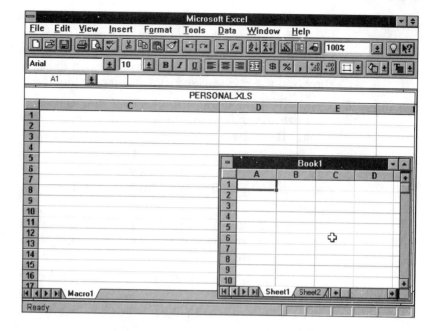

A small workbook window for watching macros being built

Figure 10-8.

When you create a second macro, Excel places it at the top of the next available column of the current macro sheet, unless you tell Excel otherwise (you'll see how in a minute). Since you have used columns A and B, the next macro you create is placed in C1.

Move Macro

Assume that you have a number of entries on an Excel sheet that you want to move to the right by three columns. These entries are not all in one column so you can't easily move them together, you can't simply delete and insert columns to make it happen, and dragging won't work. There are enough cut and paste operations to make it worth a macro. To accomplish this task quickly, make sure that Book 1 is the active book and then record a macro to handle it, with these instructions:

1. From the Tools menu, choose Record Macro, then choose Record New Macro, type **Move_Selection**, click on Options, click on Shortcut Key, accept the suggested Ctrl-h, click on Personal Macro Workbook, click on MS Excel 4 Macro, and click on OK. The Recording message comes on in the Status bar, and the name and shortcut key appear in C1 on the macro sheet.

   If you cannot see the Move_Selection macro name on your macro sheet, it is probably because you did not click on Personal Macro Workbook in

Step 1. It could also be that you did not set up your screen as described in the previous section. In either case, stop the macro recording by clicking on the Stop Recorder tool, exit Excel *without* saving either the Personal Macro Workbook or Book1, restart Excel, set up your screen as shown in the previous section, and repeat Step 1.

2. Press Ctrl-X to cut the current selection to the Clipboard. The blinking marquee appears around A1 (or whatever cell you are pointing at) in Book1. The macro command =CUT() appears in C2 on the macro sheet.

3. Click three columns to the right in Book1 (D1 if you started in A1) and press Enter to complete the steps you want to record. The macro commands =SELECT("R1C4") and =PASTE() appear in C3 and C4 on the macro sheet.

4. Click on the Stop Recorder tool. The macro command =RETURN() appears in C5 on the macro sheet. Your screen should look like that shown in Figure 10-9.

5. Click on cell C1 in the macro sheet. Click on the Bold tool in the Standard toolbar.

6. Click on D1, type **Copies selection**, and press Enter. Your second macro is documented. Next try it out.

7. From the Window menu, choose Book1. Type something in A4, press Enter and press Ctrl-h. What you typed in A4 has moved to D1.

   The concept for this macro was to move the contents of the selected cells to the right three columns. In other words, move the contents of A4 to D4, not D1 as just happened. You therefore have a problem.

   The reason for this is that the =SELECT macro command gave you an absolute reference ("R1C4"). The R1C4 stands for "row 1, column 4" and is the same as $D$1. If you want a relative reference, as you do when moving an active cell relative to its current position, place [] around the numbers. For example, =SELECT("RC[3]") moves the active cell three columns to the right without changing the row and =SELECT("R[−2]C[2]") moves the active cell up two rows and to the right two columns. If you want all your recorded references to be relative addresses, you can choose the Use Relative References suboption from the Record option of the Tools menu.

8. Click on the macro sheet to activate it and then double-click on C3. Change R1C4 to RC[3] and press Enter.

9. From the Window menu, choose Book1. Type something in A4, press Enter and press Ctrl-h. Now, what you type in A4 is moved to D4, as shown in Figure 10-10 and as you wanted.

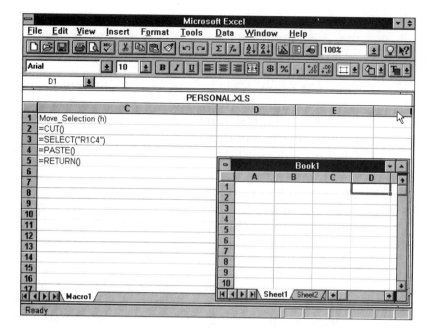

Move macro
added to the
macro sheet
Figure 10-9.

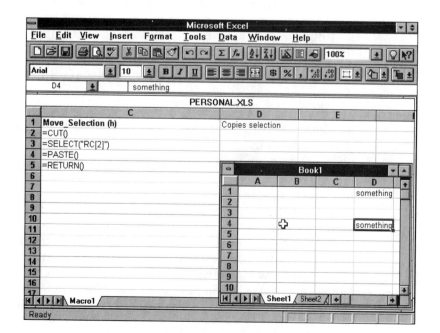

10

The results
of the
Move_Selection
macro
Figure 10-10.

These steps of trying out and correcting a macro are called *debugging*—the trial and error process of correcting problems in a macro.

Setting a Recording Area

Your next macro would be placed in E1, unless you tell Excel otherwise. Since that is off the screen, tell Excel you want it to begin in C8. You do that by clicking on this starting cell (C8 in the macro sheet), choosing the Mark Position for Recording suboption under Record Macro on the Tools menu, and then using the Record at Mark suboption from the regular sheet for the actual recording.

If you select a single cell in which to start the macro, Excel fills as many cells below that cell in the same column as necessary to complete the macro. If the macro reaches the bottom of the column, Excel redirects the macro to the top of the next vacant column with a GOTO macro command and then continues the macro in the next column. If you select a single cell and the single cell is not blank, Excel finds the last nonblank cell in the column and begins recording immediately below it. If the last nonblank cell has the RETURN macro command in it, RETURN is replaced by the first macro command of the new macro. In this way you can stop recording a macro and then later restart where you left off.

If you select an area in which to record a macro, the area becomes the limits within which the macro is contained. Excel starts the macro in the upper-left corner and continues to the lower-right corner, placing GOTO functions at the bottom of each column. If Excel reaches the limits of the area without completing the macro, you get a message that the area is full. Unlike when selecting a single cell, if you select an area and the upper-left cell in the area is not blank, Excel displays a message saying the area is full and cannot be used.

Set the starting cell for recording the next macro with these instructions:

1. Click on C8 of the macro sheet.
2. Choose Record Macro from the Tools menu and click on Mark Position for Recording.
3. Choose Book1 from the Window menu to return to your regular sheet.

Once you have set where you want to place your next macro, you must start the macro with the Record at Mark suboption of the Record Macro option of the Tools menu. Record at Mark, though, is meant to be used for adding to the last macro you have entered. Record at Mark does not ask you to name or enter a shortcut key for a macro. You can use it only if you have already used Record New Macro within an Excel session (after your most recent starting of Excel) or if you have used Mark Position for Recording to establish a starting cell. If you have started a macro with Record New Macro, you can use Stop Recorder to quit macro recording and then restart with Record at Mark as if you had never quit; you need not use Mark Position for Recording.

Percentage Macro

The custom percent format 0.0% deserves a macro for quick use. Build it next and give it the shortcut key Ctrl-j.

1. Choose Record Macro from the Tools menu and click on Record at Mark.

2. Choose Cells from the Format menu, click on the Number tab, click on Percentage, select 0.00%, delete one decimal zero in the text box, and click on OK.

3. Choose Stop Recorder from the Macro menu to complete the macro. Your macro sheet should look like this:

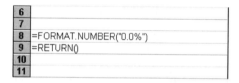

6	
7	
8	=FORMAT.NUMBER("0.0%")
9	=RETURN()
10	
11	

You can see your new macro does not have a title or shortcut key as it should. Supply these next.

4. Click on the macro sheet to make it active, click on cell C7, type **Percent_Format (j)**, press Enter, and make it bold.

5. Open the Insert menu, choose Name, and then click on Define to open the Define Name dialog box shown here:

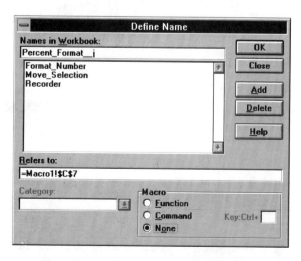

6. Drag across the __j in the Names in Workbook text box and press ⌈Del⌉. Click on Command under Macro, type **j** in the Key text box, and click on OK. Your percentage macro is defined.

   If you ever want to delete an Excel 4 macro, you must do it from the Define Name dialog box. You cannot do it from the Macro dialog box. The Delete button in the Macro dialog box works only with Visual Basic macros.

7. Click D7 in the macro sheet, type **0.0% Format**, and press ⌈Enter⌉ to document the macro. Now try it out.

8. Click on Book1 in the Window menu, type a decimal number (**.345**) in the active cell, press ⌈Enter⌉, and press ⌈Ctrl⌉-⌈j⌉ to format it. Your screen should look like Figure 10-11.

Date/Time Stamp Macro

You will often want to add the date and/or time to a sheet. To do so manually, you must type **=NOW( )**, format the cell, and then use Copy and Paste Special to convert the function to a permanent value that does not change every time the sheet is recalculated. It is easier to look at your watch or calendar and type the numbers as text so they do not have to be formatted. A macro takes this process down to two keystrokes that format

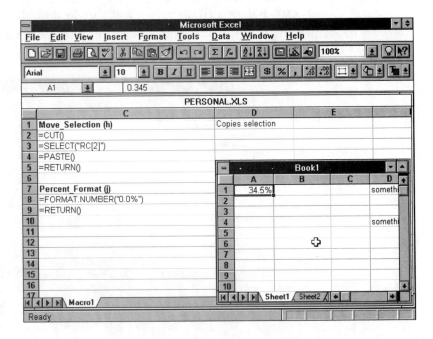

Percentage macro and its results
Figure 10-11.

the cell, enter the function, and convert it to a value. Create the macro following these steps:

1. Click on A3 in Book1 to make it the active cell.

2. Choose Record Macro from the Tools menu, click on Record New Macro, type **Date_Time_Stamp**, click on Option and Shortcut Key, accept ⓚ as the shortcut key, click on Personal Macro Workbook, click on MS Excel 4 Macro, and click on OK. The name appears in E1 of the macro sheet.

3. Type **=now()** and press Enter. The date and time appear and are automatically formatted the way you want them.

4. Widen column A of the sheet by dragging on the intersection between columns A and B until column A is about half-again as large.

5. Click on the Copy tool, choose Paste Special from the Edit menu, click on Values and OK, and press Esc. The =NOW( ) formula is converted to a value and the copy marquee removed.

6. Click on the Stop Recorder tool. Click on the macro sheet, widen column E so you can see all of the macro, and make that column the leftmost one in the window. Then make the macro name bold and document your macro as shown in Figure 10-12.

   Now try out this macro.

7. Choose Book1 from the Window menu, click on B3, and press Ctrl-ⓚ.

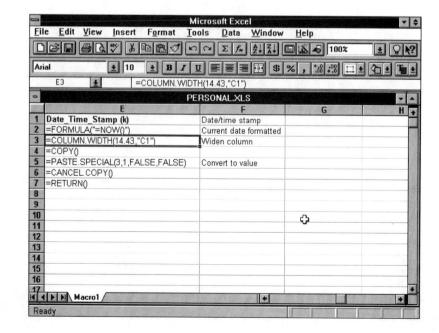

Date/Time
Stamp macro
Figure 10-12.

The date and time are placed in B3, but the column is not widened. Go back to the macro sheet and see why.

8. Click on the macro sheet and click on E3, which contains the COLUMN.WIDTH macro command.

   The COLUMN.WIDTH macro command has two arguments: the width itself (your width may be different due to variations in dragging), and an optional reference to the column to be widened. The reference shown here, C1, does not mean column C, row 1, but rather "column 1." This is the problem. To make the Date/Time Stamp macro flexible, you need to remove the column reference. Then the COLUMN.WIDTH macro command will refer to the current selection, which is what you want. If your width value is a number with many decimal places, edit by rounding it to an even 14.

9. Edit E3 so that it contains =COLUMN.WIDTH(14).

10. Return to Book1 and try the macro again in C5. It now works the way it should, as you can see in Figure 10-13.

Entering Macros

All the macros you have created so far have been recorded. You modified two of the recorded macros to give you what you want. You can also directly type in a macro. You can either use an existing macro sheet or create a new one. You simply pick an area on the macro sheet and start typing the

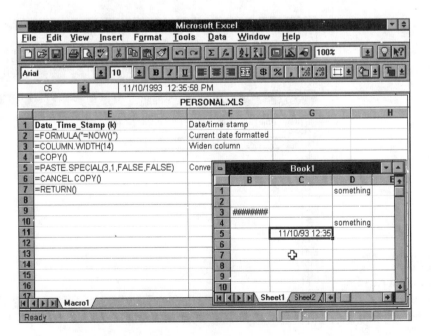

Final results of the Date/Time Stamp

Figure 10-13.

necessary macro commands. Doing this, of course, takes some familiarity with the macro commands and their arguments. Once you have written the macro, you can name it with the Name Define option on the Insert menu. Try that next by writing a macro to apply the #,##0 format. You can use the Percent macro as a model.

1. Click on the macro sheet and on C11. Type **Comma_Format (l)** and press ⬇.

2. Type **=format.number("#,##0")**, press ⬇, type **=return()**, and press ⬆ twice.

3. Choose Name from the Insert menu, click on Define, drag across the __l and press `Del`, click on Command as the macro type, press `Tab`, type **l** as the shortcut key, and click on OK.

4. Format the name on the macro sheet to make it bold, and enter the documentation as shown here:

10		
11	Comma_Format (l)	#,##0 Format
12	=FORMAT.NUMBER("#,##0")	
13	=RETURN()	
14		

5. Try out the macro by returning to the Book1 sheet, typing **62503.60**, pressing `Enter`, and pressing `Ctrl`-`l`. It works!

You can see that while you can type in a macro, it is much easier to use the recorder. Even if you need to do some heavy modification, building an initial structure with the recorder is a substantial benefit. It not only saves time, but it also gives you the correct macro command name and argument set and saves you from having to look either of these up.

Rules for Macro Entry

All parts of a macro can be typed in either uppercase or lowercase. Excel converts it to uppercase if it is spelled correctly. A macro can occupy as many cells in a column as necessary. You can use both sheet functions and macro commands. Placing one function or command per cell makes the macros easier to read on the screen and easier to edit. As Excel is executing a macro and completing the instructions in one cell, it automatically goes to the cell immediately below and continues macro execution. Excel continues down a column in this manner until it reaches a terminating or redirecting macro command such as RETURN, GOTO, or HALT. During macro execution, Excel ignores a blank cell.

If a macro refers to one or more cells, it is better to name the reference than to use addresses. An address in a macro is not updated if the sheet is changed. A reference name, on the other hand, continues to track an address

10

through changes in the workbook. Also, if you are working with multiple files, it is a good idea to precede a reference name with the filename in square brackets ([*filename*]).

Debugging Macros

When a macro does not behave the way you expect, you need to *debug* it, or correct it. Debugging can be as simple as correcting an obvious spelling error in a reference name. In many instances, however, the error is not so obvious, as with the COLUMN.NUMBER problem in the Date/Time Stamp macro.

Debugging begins by looking carefully at what happened when the macro was run. Were there any error messages, and what did they say? What happened on the sheet? Do you get the same result each time you run the macro?

Next, look at the macro itself. Are there any misspellings? Are there missing arguments, periods, or macro commands? If you recorded the macro, did the recorder supply some arguments you do not want? Did you use absolute addressing when you wanted relative or vice versa? Have you defined the reference and macro names you are using?

Finally, go back and record the macro again to see if you get the same macro commands a second time. Carefully note all of your actions while you are recording the macro.

In most instances these steps identify the problem. If not, there is one further thing that can be done. You can use the Step command in the Macro dialog box to execute a macro one step (one macro command) at a time. Excel pauses after each step so you can see the effects of that step, and continues only when you give the command to do so. The Step command also allows you to permanently halt the macro after any step, so you can more fully explore the partial results of a macro.

Try the Step command now by choosing the DATE.TIME.STAMP macro from the Macro dialog box. Click on Step and the Single Step dialog box appears like this:

Arrange your screen so you can see both the Single Step dialog box and Book1. Keep clicking on Step Into to see the macro execute one step at a time.

Macro Commands

A macro command, when executed, performs a predefined function that may be available from the keyboard, the menus, or the mouse. Some macro commands, however, are for purposes of further automating a process and are not available in any other form. These macro commands cause the macro to accept input from the user, wait while the user does something, make a choice among several things, or loop through a set of macro commands multiple times. These are programming macro commands, which, due to the advent of Visual Basic, are replaced by it and discussed in Chapters 12 and 13.

Macro commands have a common syntax that must be followed in order for Excel to understand what to do. This syntax is exactly the same as that for sheet functions described earlier in this chapter.

Function Macros

Function macros are custom functions you create on a macro sheet and then use on a regular sheet to return a value or other result. You can distinguish function macros from command macros in two ways. First, command macros take some action like formatting, copying, or saving. Function macros take no action, but rather produce a result, as you might get from a calculation. Second, a command macro is wholly contained on the macro sheet and is executed with the shortcut key or the Macro option on the Tools menu. A function macro is created on a macro sheet, but to use it you must enter the resulting function on a regular sheet.

Function macros are generally calculations you have to perform over and over. They have arguments through which you supply values, and they use formulas and regular functions to calculate a result based on the values you supply. When you build a function macro, you must use three special macro commands that handle the arguments and the result. These commands, in the order in which they must be used, are described in the final three sections of the chapter.

RESULT

The RESULT command is used only if you need to change the data type of the result. The RESULT command has one argument, the data type number. If you have not used a RESULT command to change it, the data type is

10

assumed to be a number, text, or a logical value. The possible data type numbers are listed here:

1	Number
2	Text
4	Logical
8	Reference
16	Error
64	Array

Data type numbers can be added together except for the reference and array types. For example, the default of number, text, or logical is a type 7 (1+2+4) and the default RESULT command looks like this:

```
=RESULT(7)
```

ARGUMENT

You must have one ARGUMENT command for each argument in the function macro you are building, and the arguments must be in the order in which they are presented in the function macro. The ARGUMENT command can have up to three arguments of its own: a name, a data type, and a reference. You must have either a name or a reference. Whichever you specify, the other is optional. The data type is always optional. The name must be a legitimate Excel name and becomes defined by the ARGUMENT command. It can then be used by the formulas and regular functions that follow. If you do not specify a data type, Excel assumes it to be a number, text, or a logical value. If the value received by the ARGUMENT command is not a default type and you have not used the data type argument to change that, you will get a #VALUE! error. The reference argument is a reference to a cell or cells on the macro sheet where the value received by the ARGUMENT command is placed. If you use both a name and a reference, the reference is given the name and can be referred to by it. A typical ARGUMENT command with a name and a data type looks like this:

```
=ARGUMENT("amount",1)
```

RETURN

All function macros must end with the RETURN command. The RETURN command has one argument in a function macro—the cell on the macro sheet that contains the result.

The formulas and regular functions to be used in a function macro must be placed after the last ARGUMENT command and before the RETURN command. Any formulas and regular functions must result in a value being placed in a single cell that is referred to by the RETURN command. A typical RETURN command looks like this:

```
=RETURN(A9)
```

Function macros must be directly entered—they cannot be recorded. Build an example to see how they work. The example, call it Tax, calculates sales tax. It has two arguments: the amount on which to calculate the tax, and the tax rate. Enter the tax function macro on the open macro sheet in A6.

1. Click on the macro sheet and in A6. Type **Tax** and press Enter. Format it as bold.
2. From the Insert menu, choose Name, and click on Define. Click on Function at the bottom and on OK.
3. Click on cell A7. Then type **=argument("amount",1)**, press ⬇, and then type **=argument("rate",1)**. Press ⬇ again.
4. Type **=amount*rate**, press ⬇, type **=return(a9)**, and press Enter.
5. Click on Book1 in the Window menu, and click on A5.
6. Click on the Function Wizard, and the first Function Wizard dialog box will open.
7. Scroll the Function Category list box and click on User Defined. The name you want, PERSONAL.XLS!Tax, is already selected, so click on Next. The second Function Wizard dialog box will open.
8. Type **100**, press Tab, type **8.1%**, and press Enter.

The result, 8.1, appears in A5 in Book1, as shown in Figure 10-14. If an argument is missing when a function macro is used, the ARGUMENT command for that argument passes a value of #N/A to the formulas and functions that follow. To allow for optional arguments, you must trap the #N/A with an IF(ISNA()) function. For example, if you want to include a default 8.1% rate and make the entry or a tax rate optional in the function macro you just built, you must change the formula in A9 to:

```
=amount*IF(ISNA(rate),8.1%,rate)
```

This way, if the rate is not entered, 8.1% would be used.

As you are going back and forth between the macro sheet and a regular sheet, be aware that the regular sheet is not recalculated by simply activating it. You must either make an entry to or edit a cell, or press F9, the Calculate Now key.

10

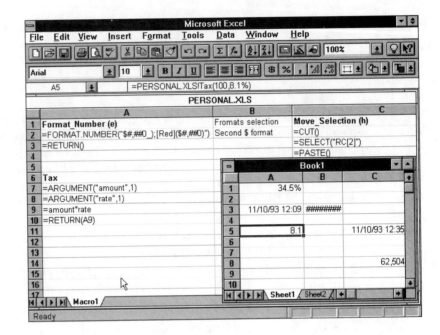

Function
macro for
calculating
sales tax
Figure 10-14.

Depending on who is going to use your macros, especially function macros, you must consider their error-handling capability. If you are the only one who will be using them, they can probably be fairly insensitive to errors. If novice Excel users are going to handle them, the function macros must work with many different error conditions. You are now in the position of many programmers whose hardest job is probably to figure out all the ways someone can use their programs. A basic ground rule is that if it can happen, it will, and if it cannot happen, it might anyway. Chapters 12 and 13 deal with writing macros in Visual Basic to automate a workbook so a novice can use it (and they do *not* consider every possible error that could occur!).

You are now left with a number of open sheets. Only the macro sheet has potential value. Save it (if you want and exit both Excel and Windows) by telling Excel you do not want to save the other sheets.

CHAPTER

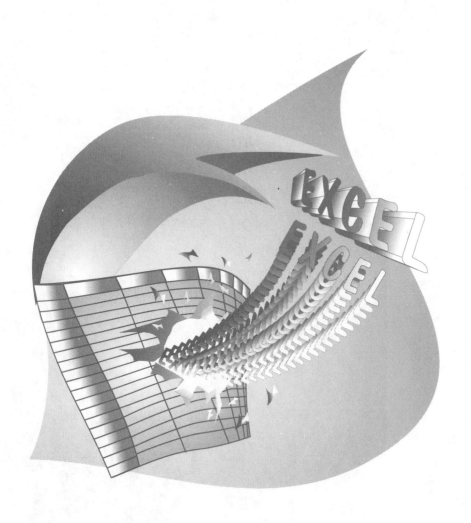

11

SOLVER AND OTHER ANALYSIS TOOLS

One of the real powers of an electronic spreadsheet is the ability to change a number and have that change almost instantly reflected in all related numbers. This makes it possible to look at many alternatives for a given situation. Keeping track of the alternatives and finding the "best" one, though, can still be a difficult job. Excel provides several tools to make such an analysis easier for you. These tools can help you quickly cycle through and organize different sets of values or scenarios. They can also help you determine what values will achieve a certain result. These tools are:

✦ *Goal Seek*, which finds a solution for a formula by changing a single variable.

✦ *Scenario Manager*, which keeps track of different sets of values for you.

✦ *Solver*, which finds a solution for a formula by changing multiple variables, and it allows you to set constraints on the variables. Solver also allows you to create several reports.

These tools will help you answer such questions as: How much money should I spend on advertising in order to maximize profit? If I only have a certain amount of dollars to spend on advertising, how should I allocate that money on a monthly basis in order to get the biggest return? What if the monthly growth ratios are different? How will that difference affect sales and income? Each of these tools will be discussed in the following sections.

Preparing for Analysis

Before you can use Excel's analysis tools, you need to set up a workbook on which the tools will operate. The workbook should contain formulas that express a situation. Make your workbook as easy to use and as understandable as possible. Write clear formulas and use a simple layout. It is helpful to name variables so they are easy to identify.

The workbook that you created in Chapters 5 and 6 can be used after you make a few modifications. You will change the formula for the monthly sales of forms to be dependent on advertising expense and a monthly growth ratio. It is important to have the cells that you are defining as variables related, either indirectly or directly through formulas, to the cell or cells for which you are trying to find values. Without this relationship, the analysis tools will not work.

1. Open the workbook QTR3BUD.XLS. Your screen should look like Figure 11-1. (You may need to scroll up the screen before you see the same rows.)

2. Click on C11. Type the formula **=290*(C3 * 100)*(C23 + 3000)^0.5** and press Enter. This formula relates sales of forms (C11) to a monthly growth ratio (C3) and advertising expense (C23). You will change C23 to represent advertising shortly.

3. Select the range C11:E11.

4. Choose Fill from the Edit menu and then Right from the submenu. Cells D11 and E11 will change to zero. You will fix that next.

5. Click on D3. Type **1.4%** and press →. You are entering a monthly growth ratio for August.

6. Type **1.2%** and press Enter. This is the monthly growth ratio for September.

7. Select D3:E3. Format as 0.0% by clicking on the Decrease Decimal tool in the Formatting toolbar.

8. Scroll your screen and click on A23. Indent (press Spacebar four times), type **Advertising**, and press Enter.

9. Click on C23. Type **5000** as the beginning advertising value. Press Enter.

10. Select C23:E23. Choose Fill from the Edit menu and Right from the submenu.

11. Click on the File menu and the Save As option.

12. Type **SOLVEREX** in the File Name box and press Enter. Press Enter again to bypass the Summary Info dialog box.

Your workbook should now look like Figure 11-2. Now that you have prepared your workbook, with cells related through formulas, you are ready to explore Excel's analysis tools.

11

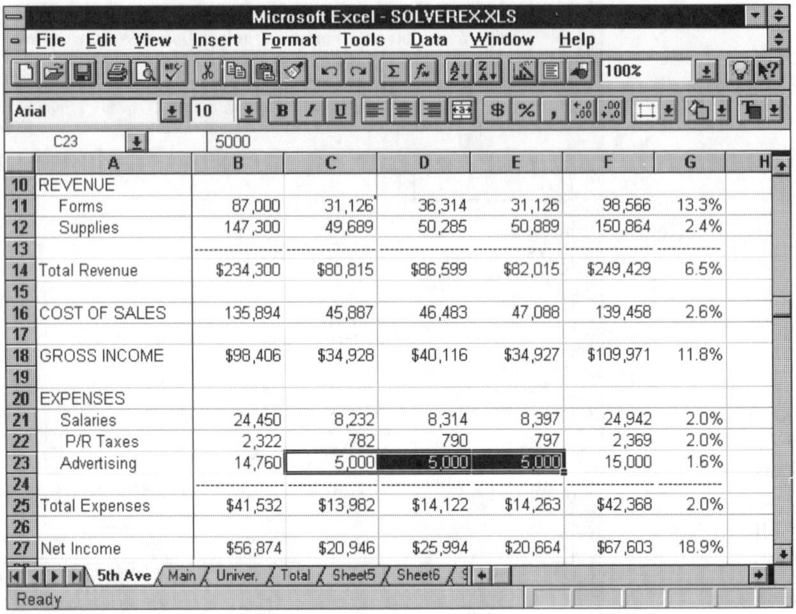

	A	B	C	D	E	F	G
10	REVENUE						
11	Forms	87,000	31,126	36,314	31,126	98,566	13.3%
12	Supplies	147,300	49,689	50,285	50,889	150,864	2.4%
13							
14	Total Revenue	$234,300	$80,815	$86,599	$82,015	$249,429	6.5%
15							
16	COST OF SALES	135,894	45,887	46,483	47,088	139,458	2.6%
17							
18	GROSS INCOME	$98,406	$34,928	$40,116	$34,927	$109,971	11.8%
19							
20	EXPENSES						
21	Salaries	24,450	8,232	8,314	8,397	24,942	2.0%
22	P/R Taxes	2,322	782	790	797	2,369	2.0%
23	Advertising	14,760	5,000	5,000	5,000	15,000	1.6%
24							
25	Total Expenses	$41,532	$13,982	$14,122	$14,263	$42,368	2.0%
26							
27	Net Income	$56,874	$20,946	$25,994	$20,664	$67,603	18.9%

Workbook prepared for analysis
Figure 11-2.

Goal Seek

Goal Seek is one of Excel's simplest analysis tools. When you want a formula to equal a particular value, you specify a cell on which the formula is dependent; Goal Seek varies the value of that cell until the formula is the value you want. Goal Seek is useful when you want to solve a formula dependent on one variable. To see how Goal Seek works, use the workbook you just prepared to find out how much you need to spend on advertising in order to sell $40,000 worth of forms in July. In this case, the variable is cell C23 (advertising expense for July), and the formula we want to equal $40,000 is in cell C11 (sales of forms for July).

If you haven't already, scroll your workbook so you can see cells C11 and C23 simultaneously. Notice that C11 (sales of forms for July) contains the value 31,126. Notice also that C23 (advertising for July) contains the value 5,000.

1. Click on cell C11.
2. Open the Tools menu and choose the Goal Seek option. The Goal Seek dialog box opens, as shown in the following illustration. Set cell is automatically $C$11 because C11 is the active cell on the current sheet.

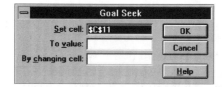

3. Press Tab and type **40,000** in the To value box.

4. Press Tab and type **C23** (advertising for July) in the By changing cell box. Click on OK.

5. If necessary, move the Goal Seek Status dialog box so that you can see both C11 and C23.

   Notice that C11 now contains the value 40,000, and cell C23 now contains 10,212, as seen in Figure 11-3. You now know that you would have to spend $10,212 on advertising in July to increase your sales of forms to $40,000 (assuming that the formula is valid!).

6. Click on the Cancel button to restore values to what they were before. If you click on OK, the new values are saved in your workbook. If you

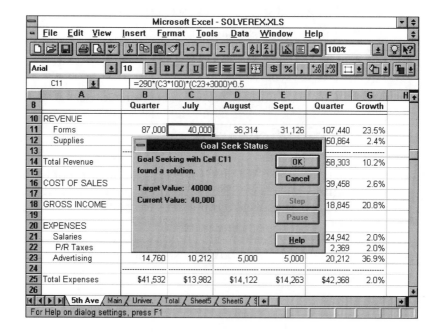

Workbook
after Goal Seek

Figure 11-3.

11

choose OK by accident, and you want to restore your old values, immediately choose Undo Goal Seek from the Edit menu.

Goal Seek is useful if you want to know what a single value needs to be in order to cause a single formula to result in a particular value. Solver, discussed later in this chapter, is useful if you want to solve a problem with multiple variables.

Scenario Manager

Scenario Manager allows you to store different values for variables in your workbook. With Scenario Manager you must explicitly enter all *sets* (specific combinations) of values you want to represent. Each combination or set of values is a *scenario*. You can have as many different scenarios for your workbook as you like. Each scenario is named and is a convenient way to organize your sets of values. Once you have entered all the scenarios in your workbook, you can print a report that compares the different scenarios by listing all the sets of input values and any affected cells you would like to appear on the report. With this report, you can easily compare the various scenarios you are analyzing. In summary, Scenario Manager allows you to

◆ Name and store as many scenarios as you like

◆ View existing scenarios

◆ Modify existing scenarios

◆ Delete scenarios

◆ Create a summary report of the different scenarios

Creating Scenarios

First, you'll want to create several scenarios in your workbook. You must explicitly enter a scenario for every combination of input values you want to examine. Make sure SOLVEREX.XLS is your active workbook and C3 your active cell, then follow these steps to create three new scenarios:

1. Open the Tools menu and choose the Scenarios option. The Scenario Manager dialog box opens, as shown here:

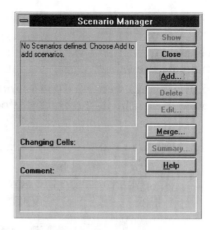

2. Click on Add. The Add Scenario dialog box opens:

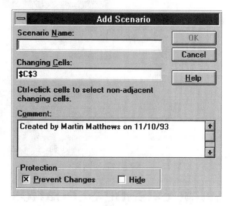

3. In the Scenario Name box, type **Scenario1**.

4. In the Changing Cells box, type **C3:E3**. Click on OK.

   The Scenario Values dialog box will be displayed where you identify the values of the changing cells, as shown here:

11

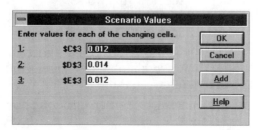

You want to retain the default values for this first scenario.

5. Click on Add. The first scenario is stored. Now you can add other scenarios in the same way. You will repeat filling in the name and changing the value for each scenario.

6. For the second scenario, type **Scenario2** in the Name box. The cells are correctly identified—no change is needed. Click on OK.

7. Type **0.011** in the $C$3 box and click on Add.

8. Type **Scenario3** in the Name box. Click on OK.

9. Type **0.015** in the $D$3 box and click on OK. The Scenario Manager dialog box reappears with the new scenarios that you just defined listed in the Scenarios list box, like this:

Viewing Existing Scenarios

You just added three scenarios. You can view the different scenarios by choosing the Show option in the Scenario Manager dialog box. When you show a scenario, Scenario Manager substitutes the values associated with that scenario into the variables in your workbook. Any cells containing formulas dependent on those variables are updated to new values. Follow these steps to see how this works:

1. Click on Scenario2, then click on the Show button.

   Watch how the values you assigned to the three variables in Scenario2 affect your workbook. You may need to move the dialog box. Now look at a different scenario.

2. Click on Scenario1, then click on Show. Examine the results in your workbook.

3. Click on Scenario3, then click on Show.

4. Practice going back and forth between the scenarios using Show.

You can see how easy it is to substitute sets of values into cells and to examine the effect they have in your workbook.

Modifying a Scenario

Scenario Manager provides a convenient way of storing and reviewing different scenarios. You can modify an existing scenario very easily. For example, you can change the value of E3 in the Scenario3 you just created by following these steps:

1. Click on Scenario3 in the Scenario Manager, then click on the Edit button. In the Edit Scenario dialog box, click on OK.

2. In the Scenario Values dialog box, change the value of $E$3 to 0.011 and click on OK.

3. Back in the Scenario Manager, click on the Show button to see the effect of your change.

Creating a Summary of Your Scenarios

Next create a summary report of your three scenarios. The summary report not only lists your various input values for your variables, it also allows you to specify other cells in the workbook you want included in the report, such as the cells that will change in each scenario. This gives you a convenient way to compare how different inputs give you different results.

1. Click on the Summary button.

2. The Scenario Summary dialog box appears, as seen here:

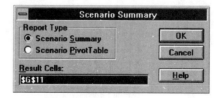

You want a Scenario Summary, which is the default report.

3. In the Result Cells box, type **C11:F11, C27:F27**. These cells, for forms sales and net income, respectively, contain formulas that are dependent on the values in cells C3:E3.

4. Click on OK.

11

A summary report is created on a new sheet in the workbook, as seen in Figure 11-4. You can save this summary as a separate workbook and print it out if you wish. You may want to chart the summary report to give you a comparison between the scenarios. Refer to Chapter 7 for information about how to build a chart. Figure 11-5 shows an example of a chart created from a Scenario Manager summary report. You can see at a glance the relationship between different growth ratios and sales figures.

5. When you have finished looking at the summary, activate SOLVEREX.XLS again, if you are not already in it, by clicking on the 5th Ave sheet tab.

Creating Other Reports

You can also create reports with the different scenarios using the Print Report option on the File menu. The Print Report option is an add-in and will only appear on the File menu if it has been installed. If it does not appear on your File menu, you can look at the Add-ins from the Tools menu to see if it is there. If Print Report is on the Add-in list, you can simply click on it and then click on OK and Print Report will be installed and appear on the File menu. If it is not on the list, you will have to install it from the Excel 5 distribution disks using SETUP.

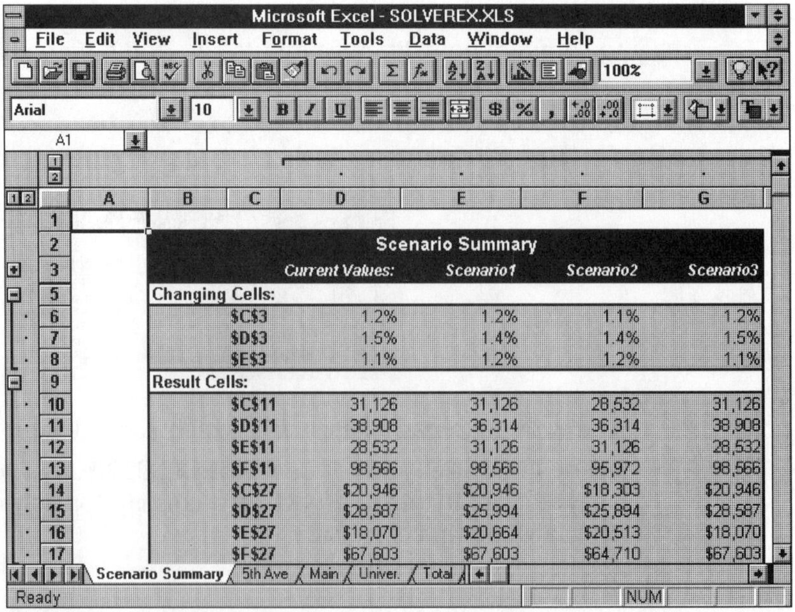

Printout of the
Summary
Report
Figure 11-4.

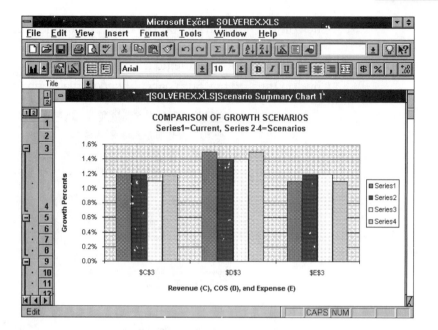

Using Print Report, you can print a single view (or scenario) of your workbook, or you can print a series of views in one step. Use the following directions to print out a single view of your workbook using the Print Report option.

1. Open the File menu and choose the Print Report option.
2. On the Print Report dialog box, click on Add. The Add Report dialog box will be displayed, as shown here:

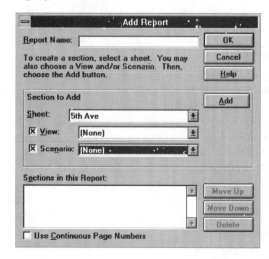

11

3. Click on the down arrow on the right end of the Scenario box, and click on Scenario1.

4. Click on the Report Name box, and type **Report1**.

5. Click on the Add button. Your Add Report dialog box should look like this:

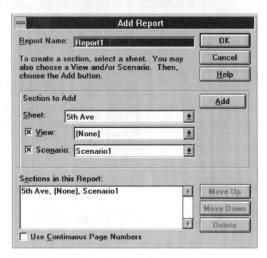

6. Click on OK. On the Print Report dialog box, click on Print, then click on OK in the Print dialog box for one copy. A report is generated as shown in Figure 11-6.

The power of the Print Report feature is realized when you have many scenarios set up for your workbook and you want to print out a copy of your workbook for each scenario. Because this option allows you to print them all at once, it will save you a great deal of time.

Solver

Solver, another Add-in, is Excel's most sophisticated analysis tool. If you want to find a solution to a formula that has multiple variables, Solver is the right tool to use. Solver allows you to specify up to two hundred variables. It also allows you to define up to one hundred constraints on those variables. A *constraint* limits the values a variable can take on. For example, you could constrain a variable to be an integer, to be greater than zero, or no larger than a certain value. Solver tries to solve the formula to equal the value you specify by trying different values for the variables you defined within the constraints. Instead of specifying a single value you want the formula to equal, you can indicate that the formula should be a maximum or a minimum value.

The following example shows how to use Excel's Solver to maximize income for the quarter by figuring out how to best spend advertising dollars on a

11/11/93	MORNINGSIDE SPECIALITIES					Page 1

Revenue Growth/Mo.		1.2%	1.4%	1.2%		
C O S Growth/Mo.		1.3%				
Expense Growth/Mo.		1.0%				

	Second Quarter	July	August	Sept.	Third Quarter	Percent Growth
REVENUE						
Forms	87,000	31,126	36,314	31,126	98,566	13.3%
Supplies	147,300	49,689	50,285	50,889	150,864	2.4%
Total Revenue	$234,300	$80,815	$86,599	$82,015	$249,429	6.5%
COST OF SALES	135,894	45,887	46,483	47,088	139,458	2.6%
GROSS INCOME	$98,406	$34,928	$40,116	$34,927	$109,971	11.8%
EXPENSES						
Salaries	24,450	8,232	8,314	8,397	24,942	2.0%
P/R Taxes	2,322	782	790	797	2,369	2.0%
Advertising	14,760	5,000	5,000	5,000	15,000	1.6%
Total Expenses	$41,532	$13,982	$14,122	$14,263	$42,368	2.0%
Net Income	$56,874	$20,946	$25,994	$20,664	$67,603	18.9%

11

COMPANY CONFIDENTIAL

Printout of
Report1
Figure 11-6.

monthly basis. Make sure 5th Ave is the active sheet. Since Solver is an Add-in, you will have to make sure it has been installed in the same way as Print Report above.

1. Scroll your workbook up, if necessary, click on C3, type **1.1%** if it isn't that value already, and press ⏎.
2. Type **1.2%** and press ⏎.
3. Type **1.4%** and press (Enter). You just entered three new monthly growth ratios for this exercise.

Your workbook should now look like the one pictured in Figure 11-7.

4. Click on File, then click on Save. If you make a mistake in the following exercises, you can return to this point and start over.

Setting Up Solver

You are now ready to set up Solver.

1. Scroll your workbook so you can see C23:F23 and cell F27, as shown in Figure 11-8.

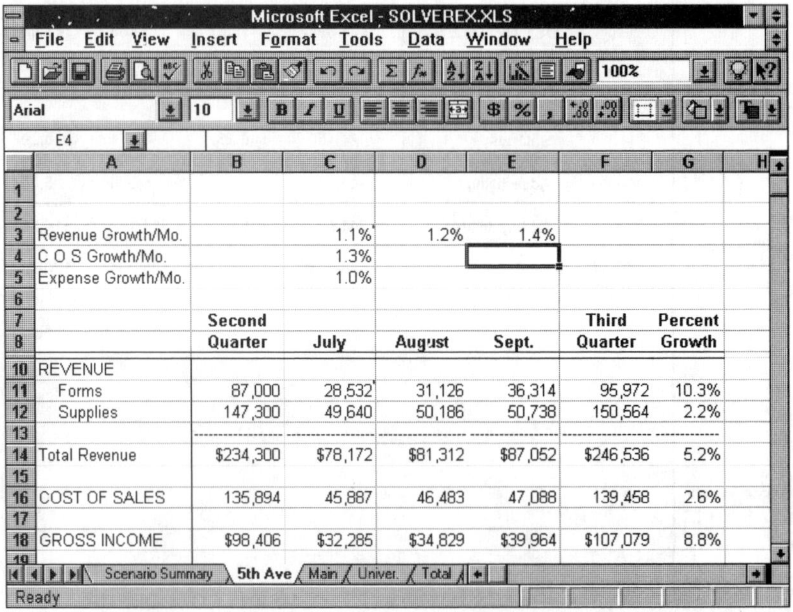

Workbook
with new
monthly
growth ratios
Figure 11-7.

	A	B	C	D	E	F	G	H
1								
2								
3	Revenue Growth/Mo.		1.1%	1.2%	1.4%			
4	C O S Growth/Mo.		1.3%					
5	Expense Growth/Mo.		1.0%					
6								
7		Second				Third	Percent	
8		Quarter	July	August	Sept.	Quarter	Growth	
10	REVENUE							
11	Forms	87,000	28,532	31,126	36,314	95,972	10.3%	
12	Supplies	147,300	49,640	50,186	50,738	150,564	2.2%	
13								
14	Total Revenue	$234,300	$78,172	$81,312	$87,052	$246,536	5.2%	
15								
16	COST OF SALES	135,894	45,887	46,483	47,088	139,458	2.6%	
17								
18	GROSS INCOME	$98,406	$32,285	$34,829	$39,964	$107,079	8.8%	

	Microsoft Excel - SOLVERE1.XLS						
	A	B	C	D	E	F	G	H
10	REVENUE							
11	Forms	87,000	28,532	31,126	36,314	95,972	10.3%	
12	Supplies	147,300	49,640	50,186	50,738	150,564	2.2%	
13								
14	Total Revenue	$234,300	$78,172	$81,312	$87,052	$246,536	5.2%	
15								
16	COST OF SALES	135,894	45,887	46,483	47,088	139,458	2.6%	
17								
18	GROSS INCOME	$98,406	$32,285	$34,829	$39,964	$107,079	8.8%	
19								
20	EXPENSES							
21	Salaries	24,450	8,232	8,314	8,397	24,942	2.0%	
22	P/R Taxes	2,322	782	790	797	2,369	2.0%	
23	Advertising	14,760	5,000	5,000	5,000	15,000	1.6%	
24								
25	Total Expenses	$41,532	$14,013	$14,103	$14,194	$42,311	1.9%	
26								
27	Net Income	$56,874	$18,272	$20,725	$25,770	$64,767	13.9%	

Workbook
ready for
Solver
Figure 11-8.

2. Open the Tools menu and choose Solver. The Solver Parameters dialog box opens, as shown here:

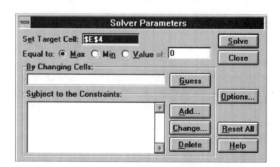

3. Type **F27** (net income for the quarter) in the Set Target Cell box. You want to maximize net income, and since Max is the default Equal to option button you can Tab past the Equal to option.

4. Type **C23:E23** (monthly advertising expense) in the By Changing Cells box.

5. Click on the Solve button.

Notice that the values Excel is using to try to solve for in cell F27 appear in the Status bar. It may take several seconds. Once a solution is found, the Solver Results dialog box appears as shown here:

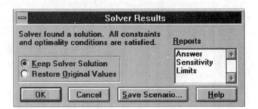

This dialog box allows you to restore the original values, keep the new values, store the values using Scenario Manager, or print reports. For now, you want to look at what happens when you keep the new values.

6. Make sure the Keep Solver Solution button is on, and click on OK.

Your workbook should now look like Figure 11-9. Compare Figure 11-8 with Figure 11-9. Figure 11-8 shows what your workbook looked like before using Solver, and Figure 11-9 shows your workbook after using Solver. Pay special attention to cells C11:F11 (sales of forms), C23:F23 (advertising expenses), and C27:F27 (income). Because all of these cells are related either directly or indirectly through the formula in cell F27, when Solver maximized F27 by changing advertising expenses, it also caused the sales for forms to increase. In this example, instead of spending $5,000 a month on advertising, Solver found that you could make the most money if you spend $22,440 in July, $27,276 in August, and $38,209 in September for advertising.

On the basis of the information you provided in your workbook, you have just determined how to make the most money possible by spending $87,925 on advertising. You could have used trial and error in order to determine this result, but that would have been a very tedious and time-consuming undertaking, with no guarantee that the answer you found would be the optimal solution. Solver is an extremely efficient and accurate problem solver that will provide you with invaluable information.

Constraining Variables

It's nice to say you can make the most money if you spend $87,925 on advertising, but what happens if you don't have $87,925? You need to set an upper limit, a *constraint* on the advertising budget. You can constrain a Solver problem in several ways. You can constrain variables to take on particular values, not to exceed or go lower than certain values, to be integers, to be positive numbers, and so on. You can also constrain the

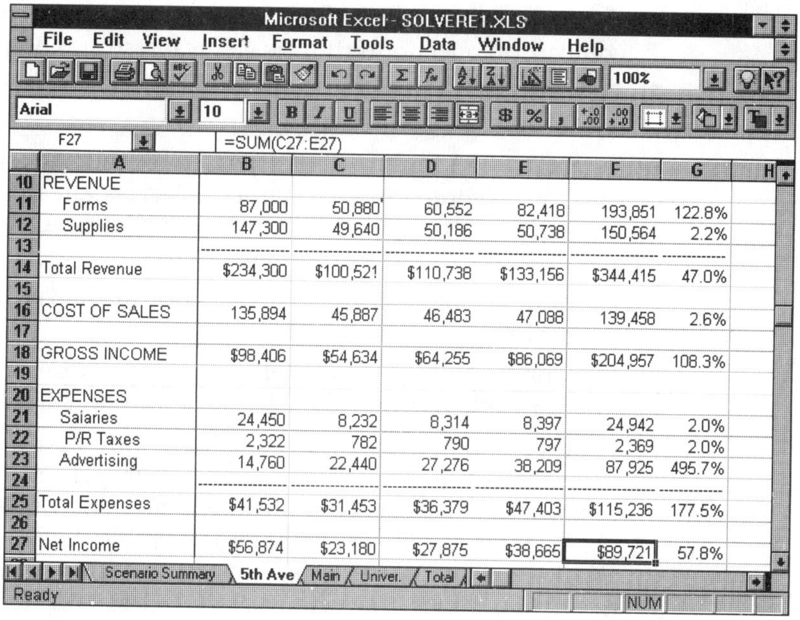

	A	B	C	D	E	F	G
10	REVENUE						
11	Forms	87,000	50,880	60,552	82,418	193,851	122.8%
12	Supplies	147,300	49,640	50,186	50,738	150,564	2.2%
13							
14	Total Revenue	$234,300	$100,521	$110,738	$133,156	$344,415	47.0%
15							
16	COST OF SALES	135,894	45,887	46,483	47,088	139,458	2.6%
17							
18	GROSS INCOME	$98,406	$54,634	$64,255	$86,069	$204,957	108.3%
19							
20	EXPENSES						
21	Salaries	24,450	8,232	8,314	8,397	24,942	2.0%
22	P/R Taxes	2,322	782	790	797	2,369	2.0%
23	Advertising	14,760	22,440	27,276	38,209	87,925	495.7%
24							
25	Total Expenses	$41,532	$31,453	$36,379	$47,403	$115,236	177.5%
26							
27	Net Income	$56,874	$23,180	$27,875	$38,665	$89,721	57.8%

After Solver is run

Figure 11-9.

problem by limiting the time Solver can take to come up with a solution. If Solver takes too long to solve a problem and you want to interrupt the process, you can stop Solver by pressing Esc.

If your advertising funds are limited, you can constrain the problem to take this into consideration. Say you are going to limit the amount of money you allocate to advertising to $20,000 for the quarter; now, let Solver determine how best to spend this money on a monthly basis in order to maximize profits.

1. Open the Tools menu and choose the Solver option.
2. Type **F27** in the Set Cell box (if $F$27 isn't already there).
3. Make sure the Max button is selected.
4. Type **C23:E23** in the By Changing Cells box (if it isn't there already).
5. Click on the Add button to add a constraint. The Add Constraint dialog box appears, as shown here:

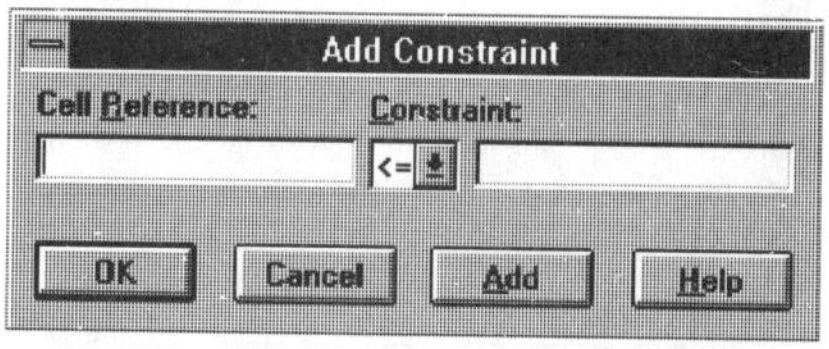

11

6. Type **F23** in the Cell Reference box. The <= (less than or equal to) comparison operator is the one you want, so you don't need to change it.

7. Type **20,000** in the Constraint box. Click on Add to add a second constraint.

8. Type **C23:E23** in the Cell Reference box and click on the arrow to display the comparison operators. Select >= (greater than or equal to), type **3,000** in the Constraint box, and click on OK to add the constraint and close the Add Constraint dialog box.

The Solver Parameters dialog box is now displayed. It shows the constraints you have now set up.

9. Click on the Solve button. Solver again searches several seconds for a solution. When it finds one, the Solver Results dialog box reappears.

Your workbook should now look like Figure 11-10. Notice that Solver determined how to optimally spend your quarterly advertising budget in order to maximize your income. If you don't enter the second constraint (C23:E23 >= 3,000), it is possible that the formulas in C11:E11 will go negative. Since you cannot take the square root of a negative number (the formulas in C11:E11 take the square root), you will get an error condition that will stop the Solver.

Instead of saving the solution in the workbook, try using the Scenario Manager option instead.

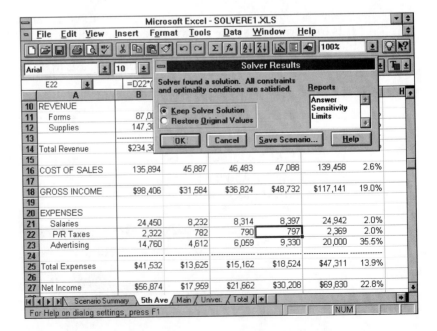

Results with
constraints
Figure 11-10.

10. Click on the Save Scenario button.
11. Type **adv20000** in the Scenario Name box.
12. Click on OK.
13. Back in the Solver Results dialog box, click on the Restore Original Values button, then click on OK.

Using Solver and Scenario Manager Together

If you create another scenario, you can see how you can use Solver and Scenario Manager together. Follow the steps below to create an additional scenario where the advertising budget is constrained to $30,000. This example will also show you how to modify an existing constraint.

1. Click on the Tools menu, then click on Solver.
2. Click on the $F$23 <= 20,000 constraint to select it, and click on the Change button.
3. In the Change Constraints dialog box, type **30,000** in the Constraint box and click on OK.
4. Click on Solve.
5. Once Solver finds a solution, click on the Save Scenario box.
6. Type **adv30000** in the Name box, then click on OK.
7. Click on the Restore Original Values box, then click on OK.

Now you can take a look at the scenarios you created with the Solver by using the Scenario Manager option.

1. Click on the Tools menu, then click on Scenarios.
2. Click on adv20000, then on Show to see one of the scenarios; then click on the other scenario, and click on Show again.
3. Click on Summary to create a summary report.
4. On the Scenario Summary dialog box, make sure the Scenario Summary button is on and then click OK.

    A summary report is created and appears as shown in Figure 11-11. Use the scroll bars to see it all.
5. To return, click on the 5th Ave sheet tab.

Saving a Model

When you save a workbook, the latest settings you defined for Solver are saved with the workbook. If you want to set up several problems and save

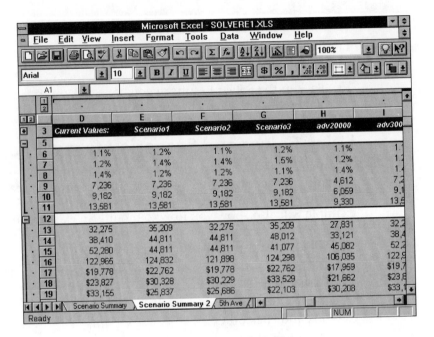

Summary
report
Figure 11-11.

them for later viewing, you can use the Save Model option. You must find a range in your workbook where you can store the settings. Follow these steps to save the current problem.

1. Open the Tools menu and choose Solver.

2. Click on the Options button. The Solver Options dialog box opens, as shown here:

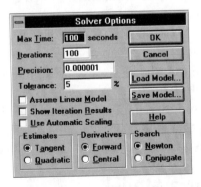

3. Click on the Save Model button. The Save Model dialog box opens, as shown here (your default range of cells may be different):

It is asking for a range of cells as a destination for the save parameters. You want the range away from the data, but close enough to be easily found. The destination range should be empty.

4. Highlight $E$22:$E$26, type **J1:P8**, and click on OK.

5. Click on OK again to close the Solver Options dialog box, and click on Close to close the Solver Parameters dialog box.

The information you need in order to load the solution has been stored in your workbook, as shown in Figure 11-12.

To load the model, follow these steps:

1. Open the Tools menu and choose Solver.

2. Click on the Options button. The Solver Options dialog box opens.

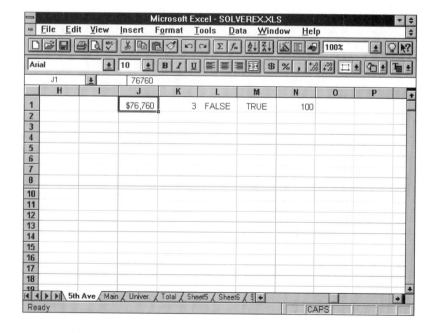

Solution data stored in the workbook
Figure 11-12.

11

3. Click on the Load Model button. The Load Model dialog box opens:

4. Type **J1:P8** in the Select Model Area box and click on OK. Note that you must enter the complete range. Click on OK to "reset previous Solver cell locations" and click on OK again to leave the Solver Options dialog box. The Solver Parameters dialog box opens with all the parameters you set for the model loaded.

5. Click on Close to close the Solver.

Solver is a potent tool with many features—only some of which have been covered here. Along with the other tools presented in this chapter, Solver will save you hours of time by helping you organize your work, create meaningful comparative reports, and solve problems.

CHAPTER

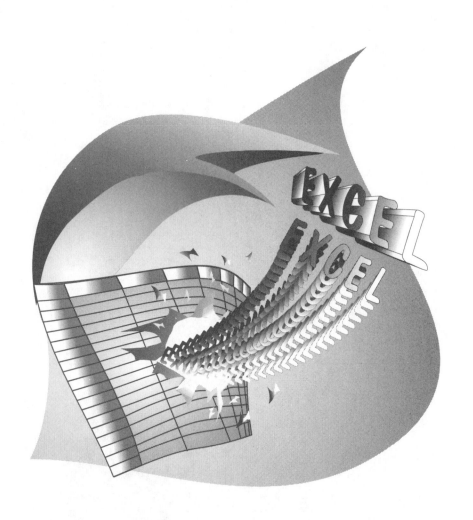

12

USING VISUAL BASIC WITH EXCEL

Visual Basic is a programming language, one of the newest, easiest to use, and most fully featured of programming languages. With it, you can write programs that direct Excel and your computer to carry out tasks that you would have to otherwise do manually. Once a program is written, you can repeat it, time after time, and never vary a step. Alternatively, a program can be made either to ask for instructions or to look at the situation and tailor itself accordingly each time it runs.

You don't even have to do much of the programming. As you saw in Chapter 10, you can have Excel record many steps and produce Visual Basic commands or statements. Like the Excel 4 macro language, then, the Visual Basic programming language is just a way to communicate with a computer and with Excel and to tell them what to do.

This chapter gives you an overview of using the Excel Implementation of the Visual Basic Programming System, Applications Edition (or Visual Basic for Applications). The terms *Visual Basic for Excel* and *Visual Basic* will be used to refer to this programming system.

Date/Time Stamp in Visual Basic

To get a quick look at Visual Basic and compare it to the Excel 4 macro language, rerecord the Date/Time Stamp macro that you recorded in Chapter 10, but in this case record it in Visual Basic. With your computer on, Windows and Excel loaded, and a blank workbook on your screen, follow these instructions:

1. Choose Record Macro from the Tools menu, click on Record New Macro, type **VB_Date_Time_Stamp**, click on Options, click on Shortcut Key, accept "m", the default key, click on Personal Macro Workbook, accept Visual Basic as the language, and click on OK. "Recording" will appear in the Status bar.

2. Type **=now()** in the currently active cell (it doesn't matter which one) and press (Enter).

3. Widen the column that contains the active cell to 14.

4. Click on the Copy tool, choose Paste Special from the Edit menu, click on Values and on OK, and press (Esc) to turn off copying.

5. Click on Stop Recorder and, if it is not hidden, click on PERSONAL.XLS in the Window menu. If you don't see PERSONAL.XLS in the Window menu, click on Unhide in the Window menu and double-click on PERSONAL.XLS in the Unhide dialog box. The PERSONAL.XLS will appear on your screen.

6. Click on the Module 1 tab and the Visual Basic Date/Time Stamp macro will appear as shown in Figure 12-1.

When you record an Excel macro and choose Visual Basic as the Language option, the resulting macro is in the form of Visual Basic statements or *code* stored on a module sheet. You can then inspect and modify this code directly. An excellent (and recommended) way to supplement your reading of this chapter is to record numerous short macros (as you did in Chapter 10) and inspect the resulting Visual Basic code. As you explore various

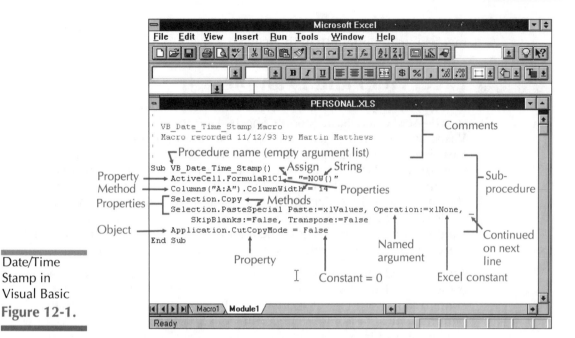

Date/Time
Stamp in
Visual Basic
Figure 12-1.

aspects of the Visual Basic programming language, you might want to
modify your recorded macros to see the effect of changes made directly to
the code. An essential part of learning any programming language is actually
writing programs, so you are encouraged to experiment. In Chapter 13,
you'll have a chance to fully practice this by creating an order entry system
with Visual Basic and Excel.

In the remaining sections of this chapter each element of the Visual Basic
language is discussed. As you are reading about them, come back and look at
Figure 12-1, and the many items designated there will be more meaningful.
Also, as you are looking at Visual Basic statements, think about how different
ways of reading them would help them make more sense. For example, the
first line within the subprocedure might be read as follows: "the active cell
contains a formula in R1C1 style which has a value of the string =NOW()."
Sometimes it helps to read the line from right to left. For example, the
second line of the subprocedure could be read as follows: "14 is assigned to
the column width of the columns in the current selection." You'll find after
you do this a bit that Visual Basic statements are much clearer than they
originally seemed. Also, don't be confused by the many element names, like
object, method, and property. They are just ways of identifying parts of the

language so they can be classified and discussed. How these elements work is much more important than the name.

Excel Help and Examples

If you press F1 while in a module sheet (where Visual Basic code is stored—see "Visual Basic Module Sheets" later in this chapter), you get the Visual Basic Reference help window. If the insertion point is on a Visual Basic *keyword* (a word recognized by Visual Basic), you get the help topic for that particular keyword. If Visual Basic does not recognize the word at the insertion point, you also get the Visual Basic Reference Index window, as shown in Figure 12-2. You might find it handy to keep these windows open while reading this chapter and working with your Visual Basic code. These windows allow you to quickly find additional information on most Visual Basic topics, as well as code examples that you can copy and use.

Another good source of code that you can study and copy for your own use is the SAMPLES.XLS workbook, included with Excel. This example workbook contains an assortment of short Visual Basic routines (or macros) that perform typical tasks in Excel. SAMPLES.XLS also contains several routines that are shown in both Visual Basic and the Excel 4 macro language so that you can compare and contrast the two programming languages. When you look at these samples, you will probably agree that the Visual Basic language

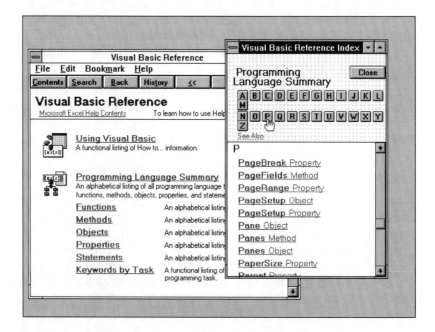

The Visual Basic Reference and Visual Basic Reference Index windows
Figure 12-2.

is easier to understand than the Excel 4 macro language, especially if you have programmed in a procedural language (such as Basic, Pascal, or C) before.

Objects in Visual Basic for Excel

The understanding of *objects* is fundamental to programming in Visual Basic for Excel. You manipulate objects in your Visual Basic code in order to automate tasks in Excel. There are a large number of objects provided for your use, ranging from the Excel application itself (an Application object), and individual sheets (Worksheet objects), to details like the floor of an Excel chart (a Floor object). Other examples of objects include windows, workbooks, dialog boxes, ranges, charts, and so on. The Visual Basic Reference Index for Objects (click on Objects in the Visual Basic Reference window) provides a complete list of every Excel object along with its properties and methods (properties and methods are discussed next). The Object Browser, discussed later in this chapter, is an additional resource for working with objects.

Excel objects can contain other objects. *Container objects* are often themselves contained by yet another object, so nesting of objects is common. For example, a Range object is contained in a Worksheet object, which is contained in a Workbook object, which is contained in an Application object. In writing Visual Basic code, when you need to differentiate between objects in different containers, write the container's name first, followed by a period and the contained object's name. For example, to refer to a chart named "Widget_Sales" in a particular sheet named "October," the expression might look like October.Widget_Sales. This expression would be useful in differentiating between Widget_Sales charts that exist in multiple sheets.

Some Excel objects consist of sets of objects. These objects are *collections*, and the individual members of each collection are *elements*. Common collection objects include Charts, Sheets, and Workbooks. All objects, whether collections or individual objects, have properties, which are discussed next.

The Properties of Objects

The *properties* of an object are characteristics that determine the appearance or behavior of the object. For example, the TextBox object has a Text property, which is the text contained in the text box. You refer to an object's property by following the object name with a period and the property name, as in *object.property*. Some properties have optional object names that can be omitted. For example, the Application object is optional for the ActiveWorkbook and ActiveSheet properties. Commonly used properties include ActiveWorkbook, ActiveSheet, ActiveCell, Column, Row, ColumnWidth, RowHeight, Height, Width, Selection, Value, Bold, and Italic. Most properties apply to more than one object; for instance, the Height property applies to nearly 50 objects.

Properties come in two general classes: Read-only and Read/Write.

✦ **Read-Only** properties allow you to examine a particular aspect of an object by returning the value of the property. You can read the value of any property, but you cannot assign a new value to a read-only property. For example, the ActiveSheet property is a read-only property of Workbook objects, and the expression MyWorkbook.ActiveSheet returns the active sheet (an object) in MyWorkbook.

Read/Write properties can have their values changed as well as examined. You can change the condition of the object by changing (or *setting*) the value of a read/write property. For example, the Name property is a read-write property of Worksheet objects. The expression

MyWorkbook.ActiveSheet.Name

returns the name of the active sheet in MyWorkbook, and the expression

MyWorkbook.ActiveSheet.Name = "MyWorksheet"

sets the name property of the active sheet in MyWorkbook to "MyWorksheet".

The Methods of Objects

In addition to properties, most objects have one or more *methods* that you can use to cause a specific task or action to be performed on the object. Methods and properties are related, because the action of a method sometimes results in a corresponding change to a property. For example, when you remove an item from a Listbox object with the RemoveItem method, the value returned by the List property changes. As with properties, many methods are used by more than one object. Commonly-used methods include Activate, Select, Calculate, Offset, Clear, Copy, and Sort.

You refer to an object's method by following the object name with a period and the method name, as *object.method*. For example, the expression MyWorkbook.Activate makes MyWorkbook the active workbook.

You can pass additional information to some methods in the form of *arguments* (sometimes called *parameters*). When you use a method that takes one or more arguments, you add the arguments after the method name (separated from the method name by a space), as *object.method arguments*. If there are multiple arguments, separate them from each other by commas (or the list separator for the Language/Country you specify in Tools Options

Module General). For example, MyWorksheet.Cells(3,4) returns a range object consisting of the single cell in row 3, column 4 of MyWorksheet. Some methods return a value, as the Cells method just mentioned. If you want to save the return value of a method, enclose the arguments (if any) in parentheses. If the method does not return a value or if the return value is to be discarded, do not use parentheses around the arguments, as in MyWorksheet.PrintOut 1,4,3, which prints 3 copies of the first 4 pages of MyWorkbook.

Methods can take named arguments instead of the conventional arguments just shown. Named arguments can be passed in any order and are easier to understand. For example, the expression ActiveWorkbook.Close True, "SALES.XLS" (which saves the active workbook as SALES.XLS, then closes it) could be written ActiveWorkbook.Close fileName := "SALES.XLS", saveChanges := True to make it easier to understand.

Visual Basic Module Sheets

As mentioned earlier, when you record a macro the generated Visual Basic code is stored on a *module sheet*, which is similar to a regular sheet, but dedicated to storing and displaying Visual Basic code. The location of the module sheet is determined by the settings you choose in the Record New Macro dialog box, as shown in Figure 12-3. If you specify Store in This Workbook, you will find the new module sheet at the bottom of the stack of sheets in the active workbook's window, as shown in Figure 12-4.

If you are unsure of the location of a particular macro, you can view a list of all the currently available macros by choosing Macro from the Tools menu. Highlight the desired macro in the list, then choose the Edit button to bring up the module sheet containing that macro.

You can also manually insert a new module sheet in the current workbook by choosing Macro from the Insert menu and clicking on Module.

Visual Basic Procedures

All *executable* code (capable of being run) must be contained in *procedures* (declarations, discussed later in this chapter, are not executable and can be outside procedures). A procedure is a series of instructions or *statements* that is executed as a unit. Each statement accomplishes one kind of action or declaration. Generally, a procedure accomplishes some well-defined and easily understood task, such as formatting a range of cells or calculating and returning a value. Excel 5 macros and user-defined functions are actually two different types of Visual Basic procedures, and both are stored on module sheets.

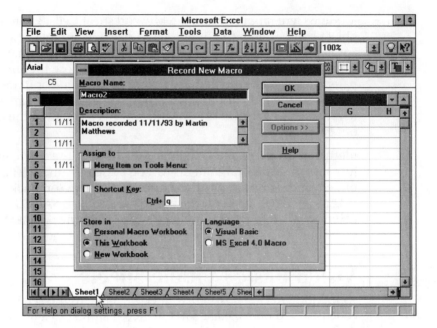

Record New
Macro dialog
box expanded
to show
Options
Figure 12-3.

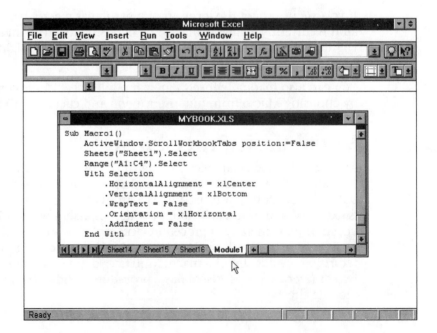

Macro sheet
under sheet 16
Figure 12-4.

In Excel 5, macros are Visual Basic *Sub* procedures, and user-defined functions are *Function* procedures (the *Property* procedure is a third, but less commonly used type of procedure). The following example of a Sub procedure applies the Italic font style to a range of cells:

```
Sub ItalicFont()
    Range("A2:A10").Font.FontStyle = "Italic"
End Sub
```

The following example of a Function procedure calculates and returns the area of a rectangle from the length and width arguments:

```
Function Area(Length, Width)
    Area = Length * Width
End Function
```

Sub and Function procedures are quite similar, but they do have some important differences. You can create some Sub procedures by recording a macro, but you must create all Function procedures manually, by typing code into a module. In addition, Function procedures always return a value while Sub procedures never do. Sub procedures generally accomplish some action by manipulating objects, while Function procedures usually do not perform actions (except calculating and returning a value). A Function procedure can be used exactly like a built-in Excel function (if it does not alter the sheet in any way). Both Sub and Function procedures have the same general structure, which consists of the following parts:

✦ The first line begins with "Sub" or "Function." If the procedure is to return a value (as all functions do, whether built-in or user-defined), then "Function" must be used.

✦ Following "Sub" or "Function" (on the same line) is the procedure's name. Names must begin with a letter, can contain up to 40 letters, numbers, and the underscore (_) character, but cannot contain punctuation or spaces. Function procedure names cannot resemble a cell reference (like A1 or R1C1) and cannot be any Visual Basic reserved words.

✦ After the name (still on the same line) come the arguments, if any, enclosed in parentheses. Arguments are values that the procedure needs in order to accomplish its tasks, and are passed to the procedure each time it is called (run). Both Sub and Function procedures can take arguments. You can specify the data types of arguments and the data type of the value that a Function procedure returns by adding As clauses (see "Declaring Variable Data Types" later in this chapter).

◆ Additional lines of Visual Basic code follow. These are the statements that accomplish the task or tasks of the procedure. In addition to assignment statements (Area = Length * Width), such lines may be used for executing built-in statements and functions (Open "MYFILE" For Input As #1), executing methods (Cells(1,3).Select), setting properties (ActiveSheet.Name = "MyWorksheet"), and using control structures (If Score > 50 Then . . .), and so on.

◆ A Function procedure always contains at least one statement that assigns a value to the function name (Count_Function = Count). This is its return value.

◆ The procedure's last line contains either End Sub or End Function.

Calling Procedures

Sub procedures can be called with the Call statement, followed by the Sub procedure name, followed by the arguments enclosed in parentheses. The parentheses are required for the Call statement, even if no arguments are passed. More commonly, the word Call and the parentheses are omitted when calling Sub procedures. For example, to call a Sub procedure named Apply_Bold that takes two arguments (Row_num and Col_num), you could use either of the following statements:

```
Apply_Bold 2,3

Call Apply_Bold(2,3)
```

Like the arguments for methods (discussed earlier in "Methods"), you can use named arguments when calling procedures to make your code easier to write and read. When using named arguments, they can appear in any order. The Apply_Bold procedure could be called using named arguments as follows:

```
Apply_Bold Col_num := 3, Row_num := 2
```

Function procedures can be called in exactly the same way as Sub procedures if you don't want to save the return value. Normally, however, the return value is saved by assigning the Function call to a variable (discussed next). Following are two ways to call the Area Function procedure shown earlier and assign it to a variable named Size:

```
Size = Area(10, 20)

Size = Area(Width := 20, Length := 10)
```

Using Variables

The Area function shown earlier takes two arguments (the length and width of a rectangle). An argument in a procedure represents a value passed to the procedure when it is called, and is itself a type of *variable*. Variables are simply names that represent stored values or objects. You can modify the value assigned to a variable while your program runs. The use of variables is a convenient way to store values, and helps make your code more understandable. Here's an example of the use of variables in a Function procedure:

```
Function B&O_Tax(Gross, Deductions)
    Taxable = Gross - Deductions
    If Taxable < 3000 Then
        B&O_Tax = 0
    Else
        B&O_Tax = Taxable * 0.0213
End Function
```

In this example, Taxable is the name of a variable used as a temporary storage location for the amount that is taxable. Gross and Deductions, which are arguments of the B&O_Tax function, are also variables within the function—names of temporary storage locations that are used to hold amounts. In the same sense, B&O_Tax, which is the name of the function, is also a variable that stores the result of the function.

Declaring Variables

You can identify a variable or argument before you use it in your Visual Basic code by *declaring* it. Although it is not necessary to use declarations, there are several advantages to doing so, including the following:

✦ Your code will generally run faster.

✦ Less memory will be used by your code when it runs.

✦ Visual Basic can check for spelling and data type errors in the use of your declared variable or argument.

Variables are typically declared with the Dim statement. The above procedure looks like this when the Taxable variable is declared before being used:

```
Function B&O_Tax(Gross, Deductions)
    Dim Taxable
    Taxable = Gross - Deductions
    If Taxable < 3000 Then
        B&O_Tax = 0
```

```
    Else
            B&O_Tax = Taxable * 0.0213
End Function
```

The Dim statement declares Taxable as a variable that is to be used within the B&O_Tax function. Without the Dim statement, if another variable named Taxable already exists when B&O_Tax is called, its value could be changed by the code in the B&O_Tax function. See "Scope and Lifetime of Variables and Constants" later in this chapter for more information on declaring variables.

To enable Visual Basic to check for errors in your spelling of variable names, include the statement Option Explicit at the top of your module. If you include this statement, you must declare all variables before you use them in your procedures. Then, if you misspell a variable name, Visual Basic will display an error message as the code is run (the misspelled name appears as an undeclared variable).

Note, you can have Visual Basic automatically include Option Explicit in all new modules by checking Require Variable Declaration in the Module General Options, as described in "Setting Options for Visual Basic" later in this chapter.

Declaring Data Types

Variables can hold various types of data. The basic data types available in Visual Basic for Excel are Boolean (true or false), Integer (whole numbers), Long (large whole numbers), Single (decimals), Double (large decimals), Currency, Date, Object, and String (characters). In addition, an Array type is a set of sequentially indexed data, a User-defined type is a combination of types that you define, and a Variant type is a general-purpose data type that can accommodate any data (except User-defined types).

In the variable declaration examples shown earlier, the variables are automatically given the Variant data type. You can also specify a specific data type for a variable when you declare it. This can enable Visual Basic to check for errors in assigning values to the variable as well as make your code run more efficiently. For example, to specify the Currency type for the Taxable variable in the earlier example, use the following declaration:

```
Dim Taxable As Currency
```

In addition to variables, you can declare arguments, functions, and constants (discussed next) with specific data types by adding the As clause.

For example, the earlier example could have the function's return value and the arguments all declared as the Currency type:

```
Function B&O_Tax(Gross, Deductions As Currency) As Currency
```

Using Constants

You can often improve the readability and maintenance of your code by using *constants*. Like a variable, a constant is a name that represents a value. The constant can be used in your code wherever the value is called for. Unlike a variable, however, the value of a constant cannot be changed as your program runs—it *is* constant. Excel and Visual Basic provide many constants, and you can define your own.

To declare a constant, use the Const statement in the same way that you use the Dim statement to declare a variable, for example:

```
Const TAXRATE = 0.0213
```

The names you give your constants must conform to the same naming rules as apply to variable, argument, and procedure names. Traditionally, however, all uppercase letters are used for constant names. In addition, since the built-in Excel and Visual Basic constants begin with "xl" or "vb," you should avoid using these characters to begin the names you give your constants.

You will usually want to declare a constant at the top of the module, outside all procedures. This makes the constant available to all the procedures in the module. The TAXRATE constant could be used in the earlier B&O_Tax example to improve readability and make tax rate changes easier:

```
Const TAXRATE = 0.0213
Function B&O_Tax(Gross, Deductions)
    Dim Taxable
    Taxable = Gross - Deductions
    If Taxable < 3000 Then
        B&O_Tax = 0
    Else
        B&O_Tax = Taxable * TAXRATE
    End If
End Function
```

Scope of Variables and Constants

The *scope* of a variable or procedure refers to its visibility within all modules and workbooks. Scope determines whether a variable or procedure can be used from a particular procedure in a particular module. In addition, each variable and procedure has a lifetime that determines when it can be used.

Procedures can have Public or Private scope. Public is the default scope of procedures. Public scope makes the procedure available to all procedures in all modules. Private scope makes the procedure available only to other procedures located in the module where it is declared. Procedures can be made to have a Static lifetime, which means that all the variables declared within the procedure retain their values between calls to the procedure. Static lifetime can be combined with either Public or Private scope.

Variables and constants can have Local, Module, or Public scope. Variables declared within a procedure have local scope, that is, they are available only within that procedure. A variable declared within a procedure can be given Static lifetime, so that it retains its value between calls to the procedure. Variables declared outside all procedures at the top of a module have Module scope, that is, they are available only to the procedures within that module. Module-level variables can be declared with the Private (preferred) or Dim statements. Variables can also be given Public scope, which makes them available to all procedures in all modules. This is accomplished by declaring them at the top of the module, outside all procedures, and using the Public statement.

Entering and Editing Visual Basic Code

As you enter lines of code in a module, they are automatically formatted for you (unless you have this feature turned off). Your code is also checked for the correct syntax as you enter it. Entering and editing code in a module is accomplished using the typical Windows text editing techniques.

Each line is usually a single Visual Basic statement, but you can include multiple statements on a single line or extend a single statement over multiple lines, if needed. To include multiple statements on one line, separate them with a colon (:). Use this feature sparingly, since it can make your code harder to read. More typically, you might want to split a long statement into multiple lines for improved readability. You can accomplish this by adding an underscore (_) to the end of each line that is continued on the next line. The underscore must be preceded by a space when used this way.

Using Comments in Your Code

You should liberally include comments in your code to remind yourself (and others who might later read or modify your code) what it does. A comment is text that is ignored when your procedure runs. Precede your comment text with an apostrophe (') or "rem" (for "remark") and a space. Comments can occupy an entire line or can appear to the right of a statement (if the rem form is used to the right of a statement it must be preceded by a colon). The apostrophe is most often used for comments and is typically used like this:

```
Const TAXRATE=0.0213     'TAXRATE is the current B&O tax rate.
'This is a full line comment that introduces the following code.
```

You will see numerous comments in the examples that appear in the online Visual Basic Reference and the SAMPLES.XLS workbook.

Using Control Structures (Decision Making)

Visual Basic for Excel contains statements that enable your code to run different statements based on the results of a test. These *control structures* can add important flexibility and power to your procedures because they can change the order in which your statements are run. If you do not use these decision or control structures, your code can run the statements only in the order in which they appear on the module sheet—from top to bottom. Following is a brief discussion of each type of control structure, along with examples.

If. . .Then. . .Else

The If. . .Then. . .Else control structure first tests the expression that follows "If." If it is True, the statements following "Then" are executed. Otherwise, the statements following "Else" are executed. For example:

```
If Taxable < 3000 Then
    B&O_Tax = 0
    Print_Check = False
Else
    B&O_Tax = Taxable * TAXRATE
    Print_Check = True
End If
```

If you have a single statement to conditionally execute, you can use a single-line form and omit "End If," as follows:

```
If Print_Check Then MsgBox "Load checks into the printer."
```

On the other hand, if you have multiple conditions to check, you can add an ElseIf statement for each test, as follows:

```
If Print_Check = False Then
    MsgBox "No Tax is Due."
ElseIf Printer = BUSY Then    'Print_Check is True and Printer is BUSY.
    MsgBox "The printer is busy; can't print B&O tax check now"
```

```
Else                             'Print_Check is True and Printer is not BUSY.
    MsgBox "Load checks into the printer."
End If
```

Select Case

If you want to compare the same expression to several different values, use the Select Case control structure instead of If. . .Then. . .ElseIf control structure to make your code more efficient. Select Case evaluates the test expression once, then compares its value to each case in the structure. If a match is found, the associated statements are executed. For example:

```
Select Case Print_Job          'Print_Job is evaluated once
    Case "Checks"              'Does Print_Job = "Checks"?
        MsgBox "Load checks into the printer."
    Case "Reports", "Charts"   'Does Print_Job = "Reports" or "Charts"?
        MsgBox "Load Report paper into the printer."
    Case "LetterHead"          'Does Print_Job = "LetterHead"?
        MsgBox "Load Letterhead paper into the printer."
    Case Else                  'Print_Job does not match any of the cases.
        MsgBox "Load plain paper into the printer."
End Select
```

As you can see in the above example, a Case expression can be a list of items separated by commas. The statements associated with the first matching Case statement are executed. The Case Else statement is optional and executes if no match is found in the earlier Case statements.

Do. . .Loop

The Do. . .Loop control structure is used to repeatedly execute (or loop through) a series of statements. The loop continues while or until a test condition is True. There are several different forms of the Do. . .Loop, as follows:

✦ **Do While. . .Loop** evaluates the test condition *before* it executes the statements in the loop. This means that if the test condition is initially False, the statements are never run. For example:

```
Loop_Count = 0                 'Initialize Loop_Count.
Do While Amount < 100          'Exit loop when Amount = 100 or more.
    Amount = Amount + 1        'Increment Amount.
    Loop_Count = Loop_Count + 1  'Increment Loop_Count.
Loop
MsgBox "Amount =" & Str(Amount) & " after" & Str(Loop_Count) & " loops."
```

The message box displays a value of 0 for Loop_Count if Amount had an initial value of 100 or more.

◆ **Do. . .Loop While** executes the statements in the loop at least once, because the test condition is located at the bottom of the loop:

```
Loop_Count = 0                      'Initialize Loop_Count.
Do
    Amount = Amount + 1             'Increment Amount.
    Loop_Count = Loop_Count + 1     'Increment Loop_Count.
Loop While Amount < 100             'Exit loop when Amount = 100 or more.
MsgBox "Amount =" & Str(Amount) & " after" & Str(Loop_Count) & " loops."
```

This example increments the value of Amount at least once, even if Amount has an initial value of 100 or more.

◆ **Do Until. . .Loop** is identical to the Do While. . .Loop control structure, except that it loops as long as the test condition is False. The following example produces the same results as the Do While. . .Loop example shown earlier, because the test condition is logically reversed:

```
Loop_Count = 0                      'Initialize Loop_Count.
Do Until Amount >= 100              'Exit loop when Amount >= 100.
    Amount = Amount + 1             'Increment Amount.
    Loop_Count = Loop_Count + 1     'Increment Loop_Count.
Loop
MsgBox "Amount =" & Str(Amount) & " after" & Str(Loop_Count) & " loops."
```

◆ **Do. . .Loop Until** is identical to the Do. . .Loop While control structure, except that it exits the loop when the test condition is True. The following example produces the same results as the Do. . .Loop While example shown earlier:

```
Loop_Count = 0                      'Initialize Loop_Count.
Do
    Amount = Amount + 1             'Increment Amount.
    Loop_Count = Loop_Count + 1     'Increment Loop_Count.
Loop Until Amount Not(< 100)        'Exit loop when Amount = 100 or more.
MsgBox "Amount =" & Str(Amount) & " after" & Str(Loop_Count) & " loops."
```

For. . .Next

The For. . .Next control structure is similar to Do...Loop, but is used when you know the number of times you want the loop statements executed. For. . . Next loops automatically increment or decrement a counter to keep track of the number of loops performed. The following example sets the value in the first ten cells of column 1 to the row number:

```
For Row_Count = 1 To 10
    ActiveSheet.Cells(Row_Count, 1).Value = Row_Count
Next Row_Count
```

You can add the Step clause to specify the value added to the counter variable each time through the loop. If you specify a negative number, the value is decremented, and looping stops when the counter is less than the specified end value. Otherwise, the looping ends when the counter is larger than the specified end value. The following example decrements the counter variable by 2 each time through the loop:

```
For Row_Count = 10 To 2 Step -2   'Decrement counter by 2 each iteration.
    'Copy the formula from the cell in the next column.
    Cells(Row_Count, 1).Formula = Cells(Row_Count, 2).Formula
Next Row_Count
```

For Each. . .Next

The For Each. . .Next loop executes a series of statements for each element in a collection or an array. For example, the following example calculates each sheet in the collection of sheets:

```
For Each Sheet in Worksheets 'Sheet represents each sheet in turn.
    Sheet.Calculate           'Calculates the sheet.
Next Sheet
```

Exit

You might want to exit directly from a Do or a For loop structure, perhaps if you find a value for which you are searching. The Exit Do and Exit For statements end the looping immediately when they are executed, which can speed up your code. The following example illustrates the use of the Exit Do statement:

```
Row_Count = 1                           'Initialize Row_Count variable
Do
    If Cells(Row_Count, 1).Value = 99 Then
        MsgBox "99 was found in row " & Str(Row_Count)
        Exit Do
    End If
    Row_Count = Row_Count + 1
    Continue = MsgBox ("Continue Searching?", vbYesNo)
Loop While Continue = vbYes
```

The following example illustrates the use of the Exit For statement:

```
For Char = 1 To Len(A_String)              'A_String contains a string
    If Mid(A_String, Char, 1) = "*" Then    'Searching for *
        MsgBox "* was found in position " & Str(Char)
        Exit For
    End If
Next Char
```

Constructing Expressions

You use *expressions* in your procedures to manipulate characters (strings), perform numerical calculations, and test data of various kinds. Following are a few examples of common types of expressions:

```
Amount < 100

StrComp(String1, String2)

4 + 5

IsNumeric(Cells(2,2).Value)

A Or B

Not C
```

Expressions can contain combinations of Visual Basic and Excel keywords, operators, variables, and constants. Keywords are those words that are recognized by Visual Basic as part of the programming language, and include functions, properties, and methods. The key thing to remember about expressions is that they always *yield a value*, such as a string, number, or object. The next section briefly discusses operators.

Operators

Operators act on data and objects to perform calculations, comparisons, and logical operations and to combine strings. There are four general types of operators:

✦ **Logical** operators are used to compare logical (true or false) expressions. The result is itself a logical expression. The logical operators are And, Eqv, Imp, Not, Or, and Xor. The following examples show how these operators are used and the rules for evaluating the resulting expressions.

```
Logical_expr1 And Logical_expr2
```

The And expression is True if both Logical_expr1 and Logical_expr2 are True, otherwise it is False.

```
Logical_expr1 Or Logical_expr2
```

The Or expression evaluates to False only when Logical_expr1 and Logical_expr2 are both False.

```
Logical_expr1 Eqv Logical_expr2
```

The Eqv (equivalence) expression is True if Logical_expr1 and Logical_expr2 are logically the same, otherwise it is False.

```
Logical_expr1 Xor Logical_expr2
```

The Xor expression evaluates to False when Logical_expr1 and Logical_expr2 are logically the same, otherwise it is True.

```
Logical_expr1 Imp Logical_expr2
```

The Imp (implication) expression evaluates to False only when Logical_expr1 is True and Logical_expr2 is False.

```
Not Logical_expr
```

The Not expression evaluates to the opposite (negation) of Logical_expr.

✦ **Arithmetic** operators are used to perform mathematical operations. They include + (addition), – (subtraction), / (floating-point division), \ (integer division), × (multiplication), ^ (exponentiation), and Mod (remainder).

✦ **Comparison** operators are used to compare two expressions, and evaluate to True or False. They include the following: < (less than), > (greater than), <= (less than or equal), >= (greater than or equal), <> (not equal), and = (equal). In addition, the Is operator tests whether two variables refer to the same object, and the Like operator compares two strings.

✦ **Concatenation** operators join two strings (a series of characters). The concatenation operators are & and +. You should use the & operator for concatenation, since the + operator is also an arithmetic operator, so its action depends on the data types of the two expressions used with it.

Debugging Your Code

A *bug* is an error of some sort in your code that causes it to run incorrectly (or not run at all). When your code does not perform as you intend, usually the hardest task is to determine *where* the error is located in your lines of code. Visual Basic detects most errors in syntax (grammatical form and spelling) immediately, unless you turn off this debugging feature (see *Setting Options for Visual Basic* later in this chapter). Other types of errors occur when your code is run and result in *run-time errors* (and an error message from Visual Basic) or simply incorrect results.

Generally, your code will be easier to debug if you include comments that explain what the code is doing, and use meaningful and consistent names for variables. If you can't spot the error in your code by browsing through it (you might want to print out your code), you can use the debugging tools provided by Visual Basic to look inside your code.

Setting Breakpoints

You can suspend execution of your procedure at a particular statement by setting a *breakpoint*. When you run your procedure, execution is suspended at the statement with the breakpoint, but the statement is not executed. You can then examine the values of variables, properties, and statements, observe which procedures have been called, change variable and property values, and step through your code line by line.

To set a breakpoint in your procedure, place the insertion point on the line where you want execution to suspend, then press (F9) or choose Toggle Breakpoint from the Run menu. You can also click on the Toggle Breakpoint button on the Visual Basic toolbar, as shown in Table 12-1.

Visual Basic Toolbar Tools
Table 12-1.

Tool	Name	Function
	Insert Module	Adds a new Visual Basic module sheet to the current workbook
	Menu Editor	Opens the Menu Editor dialog box

Tool	Name	Function
	Object Browser	Opens the Object Browser dialog box allowing you to see the objects, properties, methods, and procedures in the current workbook
	Run Macro	Opens the Macro dialog box where you can choose a macro to run
	Step Macro	Opens the Macro dialog box where you can choose a macro to step through
	Resume Macro	Continues the operation of a macro that has been paused
	Stop Macro	Stops the current macro or stops the recording of a macro
	Record Macro	Opens the Record New Macro dialog box where you can start the recording of a macro
	Toggle Breakpoint	Adds or removes a breakpoint from a Visual Basic line of code which causes execution to pause at that point
	Instant Watch	Opens the Instant Watch dialog box where you can see the value of a selected expression
	Step Into	Executes the next line of Visual Basic code and then pauses; called procedures are also executed one at a time, pausing between each
	Step Over	Executes the next line of Visual Basic code and then pauses; called procedures are fully executed before pausing

Visual Basic Toolbar Tools (*continued*) Table 12-1.

Use the same technique to clear the breakpoint from a line: place the insertion point on the line and press F9 or click on the Toggle Breakpoint button. You can clear all breakpoints in the application by choosing Clear All Breakpoints from the Run menu.

Using the Debug Window

When program execution reaches a breakpoint, it switches to Break mode and automatically opens the Debug window, as shown in Figure 12-5.

The Debug window has two halves: the lower part is the *code pane* in which your procedure code is displayed, and the upper part can be either the Immediate pane or the Watch pane. These upper panes are used to observe the values of your variables and expressions, to execute statements, and to display debug messages. The first time you use the Debug window the Immediate pane appears, as shown in Figure 12-5. In the Immediate pane you can type statements just as you do in your modules, but these statements are immediately executed when you press (Enter). This enables you to evaluate expressions, assign new values to variables, or test procedures.

If you include Debug.Print statements in your code, they are displayed in the Immediate pane when your procedure runs. You can also type the Print method statements directly into the Immediate pane. For example, Figure 12-6 shows the results of typing Print Amt into the Immediate pane.

If you want to monitor the value of a variable or property automatically, you can add a *watch expression* that will be displayed in the Watch pane. To add a watch expression, first select the expression in your code, then choose Add Watch from the Tools menu. The Add Watch dialog box appears, as shown

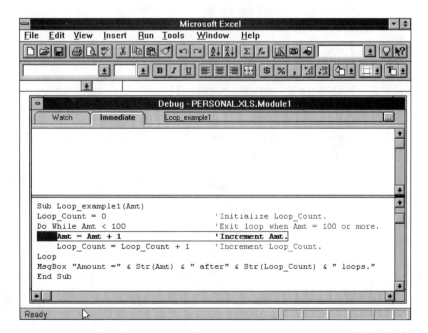

Program execution is halted at the breakpoint on the Amt = Amt + 1 line
Figure 12-5.

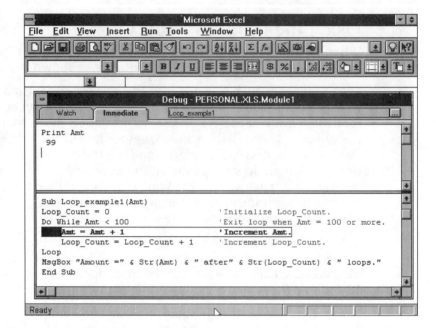

The results of
the Print
statement
appear on the
next line
Figure 12-6.

in Figure 12-7. In the Add Watch dialog box you can also type the expression directly into the Expression text box. Additional options allow you to specify the scope for which the expression will be evaluated (see "Scope of Variables and Constants" earlier in this chapter) and to specify that execution should halt when the expression's value changes or is True.

To edit or delete a watch expression, double-click on the watch expression or select it then choose Edit Watch from the Tools menu.

You can also check the value for an expression and add a watch expression for it using Instant Watch. To get the Instant Watch dialog box, first select the expression then press Shift-F9, click on the Instant Watch button, or choose Instant Watch from the Tools menu. The expression and its current value are displayed, as shown here:

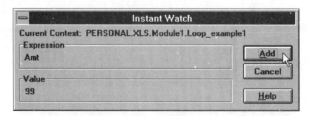

Click on the Add button to add a watch for the expression.

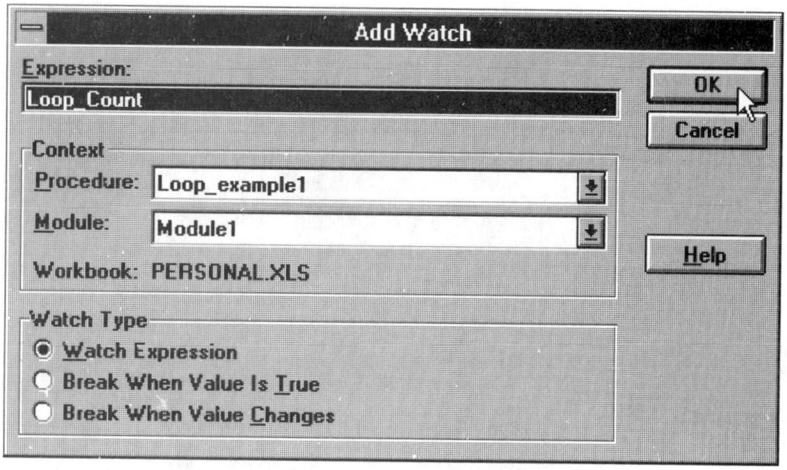

Adding a
Watch
Expression for
Loop_Count
Figure 12-7.

Stepping Through Your Code

While execution is halted in Break mode, you can execute one statement at a time by clicking on the Step Into button, or by choosing Step Into from the Run menu. Step Into takes you into the code of any called procedures, so you can follow execution wherever it goes. If you want to go to the next statement rather than stepping into the code of a called procedure, use Step Over instead of Step Into.

Step Over behaves identically to Step Into until it gets to a statement that calls a procedure. At that point, Step Over executes the call but does not take you into the called procedure's code. Instead, you go to the statement after the procedure call. This saves time when you are not interested in stepping through a called procedure.

Setting Options for Visual Basic

You can customize the Visual Basic environment in various ways, including the font and size of the text in modules and the Debug window, the colors used for code elements, whether code is automatically indented to the same level as the previous line, the width (number of spaces) of tabs, whether your code is checked for correct syntax as you enter it, whether Break mode is entered when an error is encountered, and whether variable declarations are

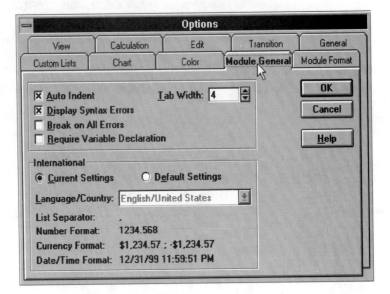

The Module
General Tab
in the Options
dialog box
Figure 12-8.

required. To set options for modules, choose Options from the Tools menu.
The Options dialog box appears, as shown in Figure 12-8. Choose the
Module Format tab to customize the font and colors, or the Module General
for other options.

CHAPTER

13

AUTOMATING A WORKBOOK

In this chapter you will build an automated workbook or application to be used by people who know very little about Excel. This application provides the means of entering, editing, and printing sales orders. All of these functions are as complete as they would be in an actual application. At the same time, there are many enhancements you could add to the application to give it even more features. These enhancements are discussed at the end of the chapter.

Building the application takes several steps. The first is to plan it. You must determine what the application will do and how it will be laid out in the workbook. The second step is to build the working part of the workbook, the title screen, and the database list. Next, you will build a sophisticated dialog box that will be used for data entry. Finally, you will build and test the macros necessary to guide a user through the application. The macros produce a custom menu, accept data from the dialog box, update a database list, and print the list.

Building an application is a detailed process that requires concentration. The reward is to watch the application operate once you finish it. The results in a business environment can be very powerful. With applications like this you can have people who know very little about Excel doing sophisticated things with it.

Planning an Application

Planning an application entails answering questions in five general areas. First: What will the application do and how is the data manipulated? What are the inputs and what are the outputs? Second: How do these requirements translate into operations performed by Excel? Third: How will the workbook be laid out? Which parts will go where in the workbook? Fourth: What is the logic path for operating the application? How do you logically work through all of its functions and cleanly start and stop it? Fifth: How does the logic path translate into Excel capabilities (dialog boxes, menus, and Visual Basic procedures/macros)?

While all five of these steps are important, most applications built with Excel do not go through such a formal process. They generally result from the "build some, try it out, and when it works, build some more" philosophy. This chapter covers only what the application will do, how that translates to Excel, and how it is laid out in the workbook.

What the Application Will Do

Before determining what an application will do, it is important to remind yourself to "keep it simple" and define the minimum set of things that you want to do. It is very easy to describe the Taj Mahal if you ignore what it will take to build it.

Here is the minimum set of things this application should do:

1. Automatically prepare the workbook and display its custom menu.
2. Accept sales orders entered with the customer name, salesperson, product description, quantity, unit price, and sales tax rate.

3. Build a database list of these items with the tax calculated and the order totaled.

4. Provide for editing of the database list items, including changing individual fields and deleting items.

5. Print the database list with a heading.

6. Save the workbook and leave Excel.

This translates well into Excel. You can use a custom dialog box for order entry, a database list to store the orders, and print just the list range in the workbook. Excel's custom dialog box options enable you to create a dialog box specifically designed for this ordering system, and the Data Form option works well for editing and deleting existing records in the database list. The conclusion to be drawn is that Excel can handle all of the specified tasks.

How the Application Will Be Laid Out

You could lay out this application in a number of ways. You must follow only one rule: don't put anything under the database list; it should be able to grow without interference.

The layout adopted for this example is shown in Figure 13-1. The sheet can be broken into three vertical segments. The left segment is used for two screens—one that serves as a title screen and the other that serves as a backdrop for entering the sales orders and other information. The middle segment contains the database list, with column headings. The right segment contains the list of products. As you can see, the one layout rule was adhered to in forming this layout.

In addition to the order sheet, this application has one dialog sheet for the order entry dialog box and one module sheet for the Visual Basic code for the automation.

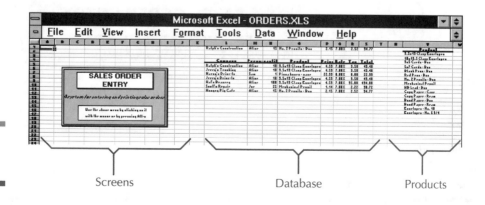

Layout of the order sheet
Figure 13-1.

Screens   Database   Products

13

Building the Order Sheet

There is no right or wrong place to start. Here, you'll start with the screens and then do the database.

Building Screens

The order entry application you will create utilizes the left part of the sheet for display purposes. At the top is the title screen that is used at startup and whenever the user completes an operation. This screen contains a graphic object that contains the name of the application and an instruction for using the menu. The title screen is shown in Figure 13-2 in its finished form. The area below the title screen on the sheet is a blank area that is used as a backdrop for the order-entry dialog box. The normal row and column headings, gridlines, scroll bar, Formula bar, Status bar, Sheet tabs, and various toolbars usually seen on an Excel screen are turned off when this application runs, leaving the simple screen shown in Figure 13-2.

Load Excel, open a new workbook and use the following instructions to build the title screen:

1. Double-click on Sheet1's tab and rename it OrdSheet. Delete the remaining sheets (as many as 15) to simplify things and save a little disk space, then save the file as ORDERS.XLS.

   You can now create the title screen graphic, which consists of three text boxes and one rectangle.

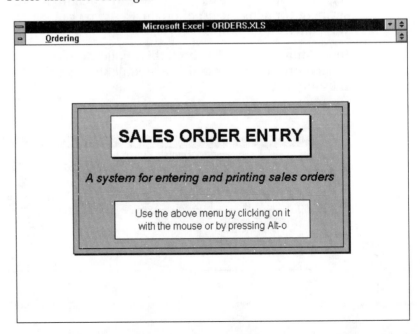

Title screen in its finished form

Figure 13-2.

2. Maximize both the Excel and the workbook windows by clicking on their maximize buttons. Click on the Drawing tool next to the Zoom text box in the Standard toolbar to display the Drawing toolbar.

3. Drag the bottom of the Drawing toolbar down until the toolbar becomes a long, narrow window, and then drag the toolbar to the right side of the screen.

4. Click on the Text Box tool, the third from the right in the Drawing toolbar.

5. Move the crosshair mouse pointer to the upper-left corner of B3 and then drag diagonally to the lower-right corner of H16 to form the outer boundary of the box. Your text box should look like the one shown in Figure 13-3 (after you click once on the border box to select it).

   Notice that the mouse pointer is a single-headed arrow when it is on the border. You can move the box by dragging it with the single-headed arrow. Also notice that the selected box has small "handles" in each of the corners and in the center of each side. When you move the mouse pointer onto one of these handles it changes to a double-headed arrow. You can resize the box by dragging with the double arrow.

6. Adjust your text box until it is the size you want. It is not necessary that it look precisely as shown in Figure 13-3. You will have to adjust the centering of the title box later when the borders and bars are turned off.

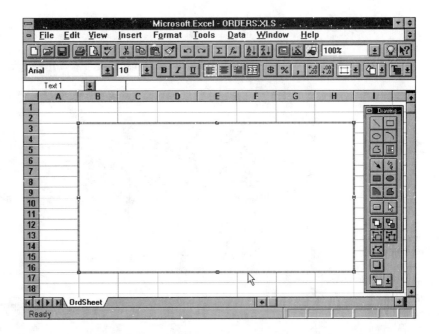

You can move
the box when
the mouse
pointer looks
like this
Figure 13-3.

13

7. Click on the border of the text box to select it if you haven't already, then click the right mouse button and choose Format Object.

8. In the Format Object dialog box, click on the Font tab, then choose Italic for the Arial font style and 14 point for the font size. Click on the Alignment tab and choose Center for both the horizontal and vertical text alignment. Finally, click on the Patterns tab. Notice that the current fill is indicated by a dashed border around a colored square (the default color is white), and a sample is shown in the Sample box at the lower-right corner. Click on the gray color (second row, second from the right) or any other color that you want for your title box. Click on OK to close the Format Object dialog box.

9. While the text box is still selected, click on the Drop Shadow tool (second from the bottom on the left of the Drawing toolbar).

10. Click anywhere inside the text box to place the insertion point in the center, then type **A system for entering and printing sales orders**. Your text box should now look approximately like the one shown in Figure 13-4.

11. Click on the Text box tool again and create a second text box on top of the first, by dragging *approximately* from the upper-left corner of C4 to the lower-right corner of G7.

12. Double-click on the border of the new text box to open the Format Object menu and give the new text box the Bold font style, 20 point font size, centered horizontal and vertical text alignment and specify

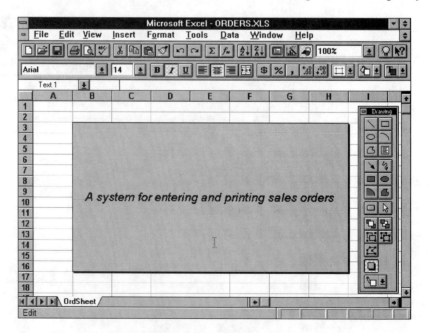

First text line
added to the
text box
Figure 13-4.

white (or your choice) for the fill. Click OK to close the Format Object dialog box.

13. Give the new text box a Drop Down Shadow and then click in it and type **SALES ORDER ENTRY**. If necessary, resize the text box to display the text on a single line as shown here:

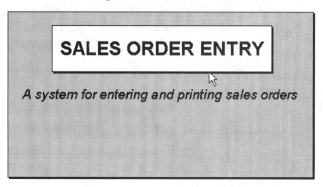

14. Once more click on the Text box tool and create a third text box in the lower part of the main text box, extending from approximately the upper-left corner of C12 to the lower-right corner of G15.

15. From the Format Object dialog box, give the new text box the Regular font style, 12 point font size, centered horizontal and vertical text alignment, and specify white (or your choice) for the fill. Close the dialog box and resize the text box, if necessary.

16. Type **Use the above menu by clicking on it**, press ⏵Shift⏴-⏵Enter⏴ to go to the next line and then continue typing: **with the mouse or by pressing Alt-o**.

17. Select the open Rectangle tool in the top right of the Drawing toolbar and create a rectangle by dragging the tool from the upper left to the lower right just inside the main text box so that the resulting rectangle looks like this:

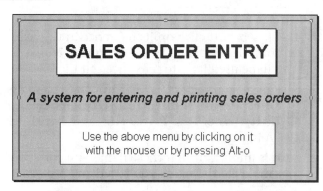

13

18. Once your text boxes and rectangle look the way you want them, hold down (Shift) while you click on each of the four objects (three text boxes and the rectangle) in turn. Then, while they are all selected, choose Placement from the Format menu and then click on Group.

    This enables you to move the entire graphic as a unit, for fine-tuning the centering after the borders and bars are turned off.

19. Click on the Control-menu box of the Drawing toolbar to turn it off and then click on the Save tool to save your work.

That completes the title screen. Next, you will prepare the orders and product lists.

Preparing the Orders Database

To prepare for the Orders database list, you need to enter a set of headings, adjust the column widths, and apply formats to the columns.

1. Scroll your screen so that L1 is in the upper-left corner.

2. Widen columns L and O to 25, and narrow columns P, Q, and R to 7. You can hold down (Ctrl) while selecting the columns with the mouse to do L and O together and then do P, Q , and R together.

3. Enter the headings in row 4 that are shown next, plus headings of **Tax** in R4 and **Total** in S4. Center them, make them bold, and put a bottom border under them using the three appropriate tools on the Formatting toolbar.

	L	M	N	O	P	Q	
1							
2							
3							
4	Company	Person	Quantity	Product	Price	Rate	
5							
6							

4. Click on L1, click on its reference in the name box (at the left end of the Formula bar), then type **Company_Name** and press (Enter). This name will be used later to reference cell L1.

5. Repeat step 4 for cells M1 through S1, and assign them the names **Salesperson_Name**, **Quantity_Ordered**, **Product_Descrip**, **Unit_Price**, **Tax_Rate**, **Tax**, and **Total**. Be sure to press (Enter) after typing each name.

    It is important that these names are correct. If you make a mistake, you can delete the name you typed and replace it in the Define Name dialog box, which is reached from the Name option on the Insert menu and is shown here with the correct names:

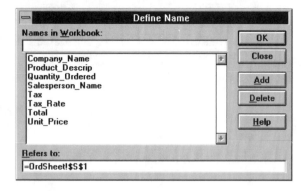

6. Format the database list columns as follows: hold down Ctrl and click on the L, M, and O column headings. Choose Cells from the Format menu, click on the Number tab and the Text Category, and then click OK. Then use the tools on the Formatting toolbar and apply the #,##0 format code to the N column, the #,##0.00 format code to columns P, R and S, and the 0.00% format code from the Percentage category to column Q.

7. Click on L4 and then click in the Name box of the Formula bar and type **Orders_Database**.

Again, save your work.

Preparing the Products List

Next create a list of the available products to be entered into orders with these instructions:

1. Scroll your screen so that V1 is visible at the top, make it the active cell, and widen column V to 30.

2. Enter the **Product** heading in row 1, and apply the same formatting that you used for the other list. Below the heading, enter the items that are shown in Figure 13-5 (or any other products that you want on the list).

3. Select the range of cells, starting with the first cell below the heading and going down to the last item in the list. Give the selected cells a name by choosing Insert Name Define and typing "Products" in the text box. Click the OK button.

4. Save the workbook again.

13

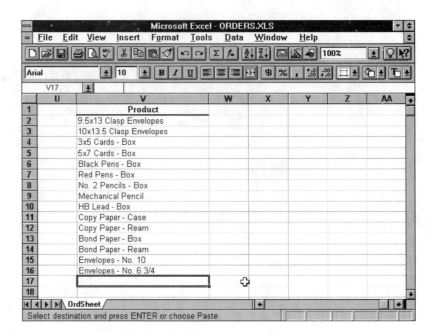

Product list
Figure 13-5.

Most of the remaining work involves creating macros that are stored on a module sheet. You will come back to the order sheet later.

Building the Macros

The next step is to automate the order sheet. This is done through a combination of recording macros and then modifying them. The macros are divided into five sections. In the first section you will build a means to prepare and control the sheet and the screen. In the next section you will build a dialog box to accept entries for the database and then build the macros to update the list with those entries. In the third section you will record the macros used to print the database list, save the workbook, and quit Excel. In the fourth section you will build macros for use with Excel's Data Form in editing the database list. In the final section you will build a custom menu and a macro that provides access to the rest of the macros. These macros provide the means for entering, editing, and printing data and saving and quitting the application. They also represent the five choices in the menu built in the final section.

While this may sound like a major undertaking, you will find it goes faster than you think. It is, however, not a trivial task. Remember that you are building a fully operable, complete application that allows a novice to do some sophisticated things with Excel. By working through this application, you should be able to build almost any application of your own.

Think of a series of interconnected macros as a logic path, a set of stepping stones along a main path that leads to other paths branching off from it. You start out on the main path and come to a branch. You make a choice, branch off, do some task, and then return to the original path. In this application you start out with a menu that provides five choices: entering, editing, printing, saving, and quitting. You choose one, do it, and then return to the menu again to make another choice. Figure 13-6 shows a simplified logic path for the order entry application.

There are two ways to build a group of macros that represent an application: using a few large macros or using many small macros. Using a few large macros—for example, one macro for each item on the menu—has the benefit of clearly delineating the program flow. Many small macros, which you would combine to perform the menu functions, have two overpowering benefits. First, it is easier to build and test the small macros because they are

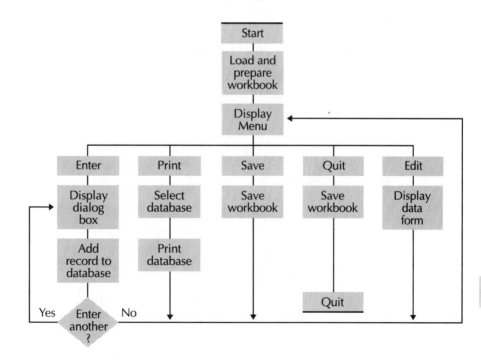

Order entry
logic path
Figure 13-6.

13

small. Second, there are several small tasks that are common subtasks in larger tasks. By building small macros that can be called by the larger tasks, you reduce repetition. Therefore, the instructions that follow have you build many small macros and then combine them to carry out the menu choices.

Preparing and Controlling the Order Sheet

Five separate macros are used to prepare and control the order sheet and the screen. The first simplifies the Excel display and positions the title graphic. The second undoes what the first did, so when you are done with the application you can return to the normal Excel environment. It is important, as you are building macros, to always have *reversing* macros so that when you test a macro you can undo its effects. You will see several reversing macros here.

The third macro maximizes the windows and calls the first macro. Here you see the first of many instances of one macro calling one or more other macros. The fourth and fifth macros position the screen on the title graphic and on a blank area of the sheet, respectively.

Preparing the Order Sheet

The first macro to be created turns off the row and column headings, gridlines, scroll bar, Formula bar, Status bar, sheet tabs, and all the toolbars. Finally, it centers the title graphic in the window.

1. Make sure that the active cell is *not* A1 (the upper-left corner of the sheet). You want to explicitly make A1 the active cell while recording the macro.

2. Choose Record Macro from the Tools menu and click on Record New Macro. Type **Prepare_Sheet**, then click on the Options button to expand the Record New Macro dialog box. Make sure that Store in This Workbook and Visual Basic are selected. Click on OK to begin recording the macro.

3. Press (Ctrl)-(Home) to position the title graphic in the center of the screen (it will probably not be in the center yet—you can fine-tune its position later).

4. Choose Options from the Tools menu and click on the View tab. Click on Formula Bar, Status Bar, Gridlines, Row & Column Headers, Horizontal Scroll Bar, Vertical Scroll Bar, and Sheet Tabs to remove the check and turn these features off. Click on OK.

5. Choose Toolbars from the View menu and uncheck the Standard and Formatting checkboxes to remove those toolbars. If other toolbars are

checked in your Toolbars dialog box uncheck them also (but don't uncheck the Stop Recording box). Click on OK.

6. Click on Stop Recorder to stop the recording, then press `Ctrl`-`Pg Dn` (since the sheet tabs are now turned off) until the macro sheet containing your new macro appears.

7. Add the line shown in Figure 13-7, just above the End Sub statement beginning "Range("F13")." This line hides the active cell behind the title graphic. This statement could not be recorded in the macro, because clicking on a graphic object selects it instead of the underlying cell.

8. Type the two comments opposite the two Toolbar statements as shown in Figure 13-7. These are the only statements in this macro that are not self-documenting.

   Your macro's Sub procedure might not look exactly the same as the one shown here if you turned off additional toolbars. Look over the statements in your macro and edit it as necessary to make it look like the one shown in Figure 13-7, unless you have additional toolbars.

9. Press `Ctrl`-`Pg Up` to get back to the order sheet (OrdSheet).

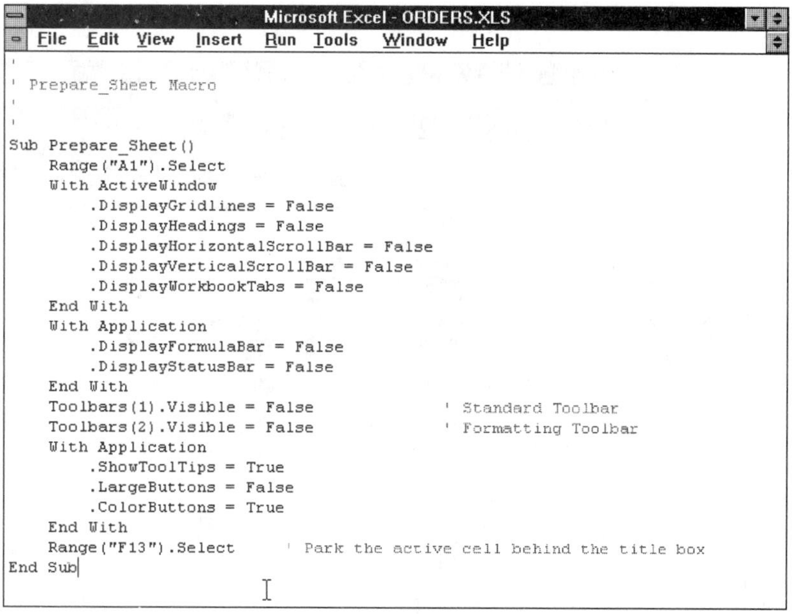

Prepare_Sheet
macro code
Figure 13-7.

```
                        Microsoft Excel - ORDERS.XLS
    File   Edit   View   Insert   Run   Tools   Window   Help

' Prepare_Sheet Macro
'
'
Sub Prepare_Sheet()
    Range("A1").Select
    With ActiveWindow
        .DisplayGridlines = False
        .DisplayHeadings = False
        .DisplayHorizontalScrollBar = False
        .DisplayVerticalScrollBar = False
        .DisplayWorkbookTabs = False
    End With
    With Application
        .DisplayFormulaBar = False
        .DisplayStatusBar = False
    End With
    Toolbars(1).Visible = False            ' Standard Toolbar
    Toolbars(2).Visible = False            ' Formatting Toolbar
    With Application
        .ShowToolTips = True
        .LargeButtons = False
        .ColorButtons = True
    End With
    Range("F13").Select        ' Park the active cell behind the title box
End Sub
```

13

Restoring the Order Sheet

Next you need a macro to restore the gridlines, headings, bars, and so forth to reverse the steps you just completed.

1. Choose Record Macro from the Tools menu and click on Record New Macro. Type **Return_Sheet** and click on OK.

2. Choose Options from the Tools menu and click on the View tab. Click on Formula Bar, Status Bar, Gridlines, Row & Column Headers, Horizontal Scroll Bar, Vertical Scroll Bar, and Sheet Tabs to turn the features back on. Click on OK.

3. Choose Toolbars from the View menu and click on the Standard and Formatting checkboxes to turn the toolbars back on. Turn on again any other toolbars that you turned off in the Prepare_Sheet macro. Click on OK.

4. Click on Stop Recorder to complete the second macro, and click on the Module1 tab to view your macro code. Compare this macro's code with that of the previous macro to make sure that everything that was turned off got turned back on.

5. Type the toolbar comments shown in Figure 13-8.

6. Switch back to OrdSheet by clicking on its tab.

7. Save your work.

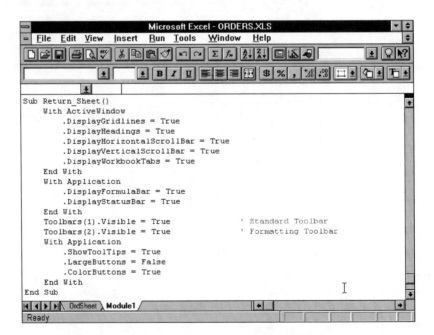

Return_Sheet
macro code
Figure 13-8.

```
Sub Return_Sheet()
    With ActiveWindow
        .DisplayGridlines = True
        .DisplayHeadings = True
        .DisplayHorizontalScrollBar = True
        .DisplayVerticalScrollBar = True
        .DisplayWorkbookTabs = True
    End With
    With Application
        .DisplayFormulaBar = True
        .DisplayStatusBar = True
    End With
    Toolbars(1).Visible = True          ' Standard Toolbar
    Toolbars(2).Visible = True          ' Formatting Toolbar
    With Application
        .ShowToolTips = True
        .LargeButtons = False
        .ColorButtons = True
    End With
End Sub
```

Maximizing Windows and Preparing the Sheet

The third macro maximizes the Excel and workbook windows and calls the Prepare_Sheet macro.

1. If your Excel application window has been maximized, click on the Restore button or choose Control Restore to reduce it to normal size (it does not matter what size it is). Do the same with the ORDERS.XLS document window.

2. Choose Record Macro from the Tools menu and click on Record New Macro. Type **Max_Prepare** and click on OK.

3. Click on the Maximize buttons for both the Excel application window and the ORDERS.XLS document window.

4. Choose Macro from the Tools menu and select Prepare_Sheet from the list of macros. Click on Run.

5. Click on Stop Recorder to complete the macro, then press [Ctrl]-[Pg Dn] until the macro sheet appears. Compare your Max_Prepare macro code with that shown here:

```
'
' Max_Prepare Macro
'
Sub Max_Prepare()
    Application.WindowState = xlMaximized
    ActiveWindow.WindowState = xlMaximized
    Application.Run Macro:="ORDERS.XLS!Prepare_Sheet"
End Sub
```

Positioning the Screen

Two macros are used to position the screen. The first positions the screen on the title graphic and the second on the blank sheet area directly below it.

1. Type the code for the first (Return_Home) macro directly into the module sheet, as shown next (it isn't as clean if you record it):

```
'
' Return_Home Macro
'
Sub Return_Home()
    Range("A1").Select       'Center the title graphic in the screen
    Range("F13").Select      'Park the active cell behind the title box
End Sub
```

13

Now you can record the second macro, as follows:

1. Press `Ctrl`-`Pg Up` to get back to OrdSheet.

2. Choose Record Macro from the Tools menu and click on Record New Macro, type **Next_Page** and click on OK.

3. Press `Ctrl`-`Home`, then press `Pg Dn`. This scrolls the title graphic up, leaving a blank screen.

4. Click on the Stop Recorder tool to complete the macro, then press `Ctrl`-`Pg Dn` until the macro sheet appears. Your macro should look like this:

```
'
' Next_Page Macro
'
Sub Next_Page()
    Range("A1").Select
    ActiveWindow.LargeScroll Down:=1
    Range("A26").Select
End Sub
```

5. Now remove the next-to-last line and add the two comments so that your macro looks like this:

```
'
' Next_Page Macro
'
Sub Next_Page()
    Range("A1").Select                  ' Center the title graphic
    ActiveWindow.LargeScroll Down:=1    ' Scroll down to blank area
End Sub
```

Removing the last Range().Select statement leaves the active cell out of sight for a cleaner background.

6. Press `Ctrl`-`Pg Up` to get back to OrdSheet, then, choosing Macro from the Tools menu, select and run the Return_Sheet macro to restore the normal Excel screen.

7. Save the workbook.

Testing and Debugging Your Macros

You now have five macros: Prepare_Sheet, Return_Sheet, Max_Prepare, Return_Home, and Next_Page. Because of the macros' small size and the use of the recorder to create them, with the illustrations in this book serving as a guide, they are probably error free. You still need to prove this by trying them out. Do so now.

1. Make sure that neither the Excel application nor the ORDERS.XLS windows are maximized. Restore them if necessary.

2. Choose Macro from the Tools menu, select Max_Prepare from the list of macros, and click on Run. This macro calls the Prepare_Sheet macro, so you actually are testing two macros in one.

You should get the title graphic displayed with nothing other than the Title bar and Menu bar at the top of your screen, as shown in Figure 13-9. You might need to center the title graphic in the center of the screen by dragging it (first make sure that you have grouped all its parts).

If you did not get the results shown in Figure 13-9, first study what you did get. Repeat the macro several times to observe what is going on. Look at any error messages. Often with macros you get an error message and are shown the line in the macro that is causing the problem. If you type in macro commands, spelling errors are frequently the cause. After looking at what happens when you execute the macro, go over to the module sheet and look carefully at the offending macro. Look at spelling, parentheses, quotation marks, and Macro function arguments. Compare what you see with the figures and illustrations shown here. These illustrations were produced by operating macros (really!).

3. After the Max_Prepare macro performs as expected, run the Next_Page macro to position the blank page on your screen. Except for the Title and Menu bars (and the mouse pointer), you should have a blank screen.

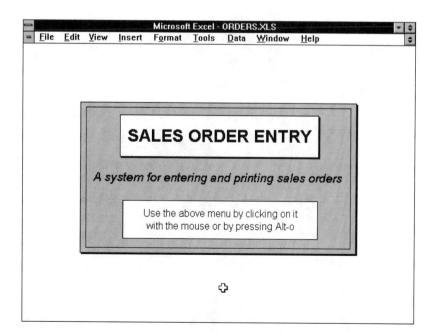

Drag the title graphic, if necessary, to center it in the screen
Figure 13-9.

13

4. Run the Return_Home macro to position the title graphic and active cell on your screen.

5. Run the Return_Sheet macro to return to normal Excel Display mode.

You should now have five proven macros. If you do not, fix them before going on and then save the workbook.

Building the Data Entry Tools

The data entry tools consist of a data entry dialog box and three macros—one that supports the dialog box controls, one that updates the database list, and one that ties the two others together.

Building a Custom Dialog Box

Building a dialog box usually involves two main tasks. The first is constructing the graphic object, and the second is writing the code necessary to make the dialog box function the way you want it to. The code creation is covered in the next section. To construct the graphic object that the user of this application will see, you start out with a skeletal dialog box on the screen and then add several text boxes, a check box, a drop-down list box, two buttons, and text. You also size and position each control, and specify properties for it. Figure 13-10 shows the completed dialog box used in this application.

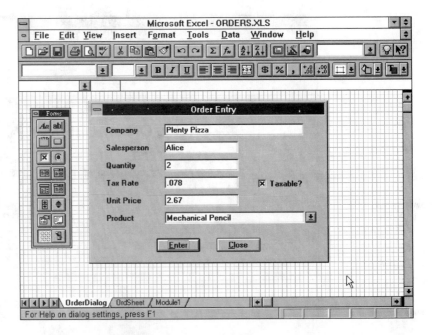

The completed dialog box with the Forms toolbar

Figure 13-10.

The Forms toolbar provides the means for you to build a dialog box graphically by positioning and sizing controls (buttons, text boxes, and so forth) on the dialog box. The techniques used to construct the graphic part of a custom dialog box are similar to those you used earlier to construct the title graphic. You choose the tool for the control you want to create, and then place and size it in the dialog box. If there is text involved, you can type the text. After you have placed a control, you can specify various format options for it. As you construct the dialog box you see exactly how the completed box will look, and you can even run it to see how it operates.

Begin the process of creating a dialog box by inserting a dialog sheet into the Orders workbook.

1. Choose Macro from the Insert menu and click on Dialog to create a new dialog sheet that looks like the one shown in Figure 13-11. Double-click on its tab and rename it OrderDialog.

2. Select the text in the Title bar and type **Order Entry** to replace it.

3. Enlarge the dialog box a bit, and drag the two buttons to the bottom to get them out of the way as you can see in Figure 13-12.

4. Click on the Label button in the upper-left corner of the Forms toolbar, then click and hold down your mouse button while dragging to create a small text box in the upper-left corner of the dialog box—don't worry

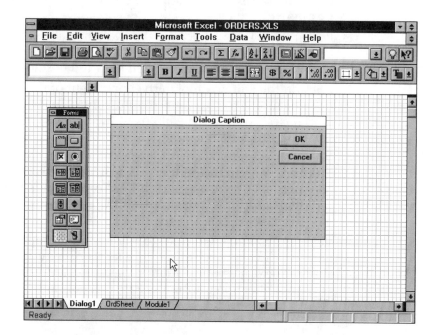

The skeletal dialog box contains two buttons and a sample caption
Figure 13-11.

13

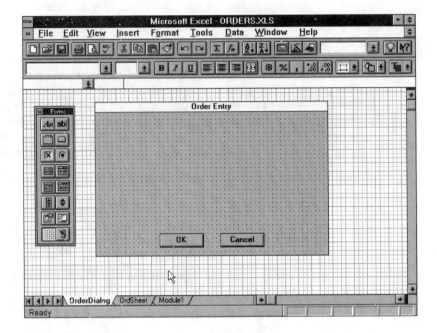

Enlarged
dialog box
with the
buttons moved
Figure 13-12.

about exact position, you will adjust it later. Refer to Figure 13-10 for approximate positioning.

5. Drag over the existing text inside the new label box and type **Company**.

6. Repeat steps 4 and 5 to create the five other labels (Salesperson, Quantity, Tax Rate, Unit Price, and Product), as shown in Figure 13-10. Don't worry too much about their sizes and positions at this point.

7. Click on the Edit Box tool in the upper-right of the Forms toolbar, then drag the mouse to create an edit box control, just as you created the label boxes. Position the edit box to the right of the Company label, using Figure 13-10 as a guide.

8. With the new edit box control selected, click on the Control Properties tool (second form the bottom on the left of the Forms toolbar). Then, click on the Control tab, and choose Text for the Edit Validation setting. This setting specifies that only text input will be accepted by the edit box. Click on OK to close the dialog box.

9. Repeat steps 7 and 8 to place edit box controls opposite the Salesperson, Quantity, Tax Rate, and Unit Price labels. Specify Text Validation for the Salesperson edit box, Integer Validation for the Quantity edit box, Number Validation for the Tax Rate edit box, and Number Validation

for the Unit Price edit box. When you are done, your screen should look like Figure 13-13.

10. Create the Product list box by clicking on the Combination Drop-Down Edit tool (fifth down on the right in the Forms toolbar). Then drag the control to size in the dialog box.

   A combination drop-down edit control allows you to enter an item not on the list by typing it into the text box.

11. Click on the Control Properties tool while the new control is selected. Click on the Control tab, then type **Product** for the Input Range. This setting identifies the list that will appear in the drop-down list. Recall that you assigned this name to the Product list when you created it. The Input Range could also be specified as V1:V16. Specify the number of Drop Down Lines as 15 and click on OK.

12. Click on the Check Box tool (third down on the right in the Forms toolbar) and drag the check box control into place opposite Tax Rate in the dialog box. Drag across the existing text and replace it with **Taxable?**. For the Control Properties of the check box, specify Checked for the Value (or specify Unchecked, if you want that to be its initial state). Then click on OK.

13. Select the text in the OK button and replace it with **Enter**. With the button still selected, click on the Control Properties tool, select the

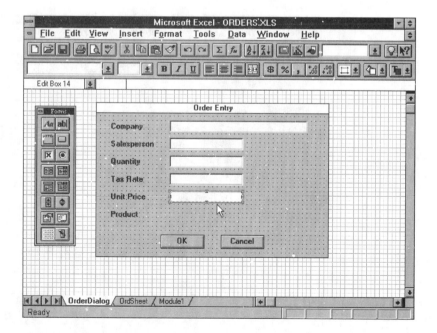

Labels and
edit boxes in
place
Figure 13-13.

13

Default and Dismiss properties, and E for the Accelerator Key, if they are not already selected.

14. Change the Cancel button text to **Close**, Cancel for its property, and C for the Accelerator Key.

15. Arrange the controls in the dialog box to your liking. It is not important to have the dialog box be an exact duplicate of the finished dialog box shown in Figure 13-14.

This completes the dialog box construction. You might want to choose Protection from the Tools menu and click on Protect Sheet to prevent accidental changes to the dialog box on the OrderDialog sheet. You will have to unprotect it before you can make changes to it.

Creating the Event Handler Procedure

Before your dialog box will work, you need to create a procedure that runs each time the Enter button is chosen. This procedure is called an *event handler* because it responds to the Enter button's click event. This procedure, which must be created manually in the module sheet, is named Button2_Click. Button2 is the button name (which appears in the Formula bar when the button is selected), and Click is the event that causes this procedure to run.

Recall that you assigned names to cells L1 through S1 in the workbook that correspond to the fields in the database list. The Button2_Click procedure

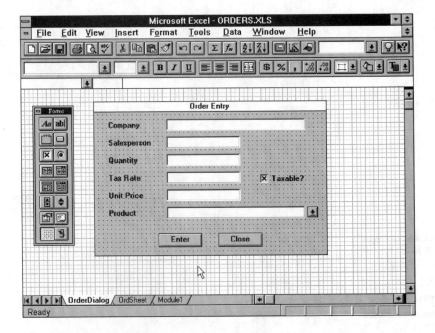

Finished
dialog box

Figure 13-14.

copies the values entered by the user in the Order Entry dialog box to those named cells. In addition, it performs some simple calculations of the tax and total.

The procedure is attached to the Enter button in the dialog box by creating a *code stub* from the dialog box and then inserting in the stub the code you want executed. The stub contains the following:

```
'
'  Button2_Click Macro
'
'
Sub Button2_Click()
End Sub
```

The stub is created by selecting the Enter button in the dialog box and then clicking on the Edit Code tool in the Forms toolbar. This writes the stub in the module sheet. Do that now (you should still have the dialog box on your screen).

1. Click on the Enter button to select it and then click on the Edit code tool (second from the bottom on the right) in the Forms toolbar. The module sheet is activated and the stub is written as shown above.

    You may have "OrderDialog_," the dialog box's name, in front of Button2. It works the same either way since you have only one dialog box.

Next you need to enter the code to be executed by this procedure. Type it carefully; for it to work, the spelling here must be the same as the range names you entered earlier. About two-thirds of the way through the code you will see the Excel constant "x1On" that is used to determine if a check box is checked. In the middle of the constant are two *letters*, a lowercase "l" and a capital "O," they are not numbers.

2. Position the insertion point on the E in End Sub, press (Enter), and then on the new line you just created, begin typing the button2_Click listing shown next. When you are done, the End Sub statement should be on a line by itself at the end.

```
Dim Quant, Unit, Rate, Tx    'Variables for computing tax and total

    'Copy company name to the order sheet
    Range("Company_Name").Value = _
        DialogSheets("OrderDialog").EditBoxes(1).Text

    'Copy salesperson name to the order sheet
```

13

```
Range("Salesperson_Name").Value = _
    DialogSheets("OrderDialog").EditBoxes(2).Text

'Copy quantity to the order sheet
Quant = Val(DialogSheets("OrderDialog").EditBoxes(3).Text)
Range("Quantity_Ordered").Value = Quant

'Copy tax rate to the order sheet
Rate = Val(DialogSheets("OrderDialog").EditBoxes(4).Text)
Range("Tax_Rate").Value = Rate

'Copy unit price to the order sheet
Unit = Val(DialogSheets("OrderDialog").EditBoxes(5).Text)
Range("Unit_Price").Value = Unit

'Check whether the taxable checkbox is checked (xlOn)
If (DialogSheets("OrderDialog").CheckBoxes(1).Value = xlOn) _
Then
    Tx = Quant * Unit * Rate
Else
    Tx = 0
End If

'Copy tax to the order sheet
Range("Tax").Value = Tx

'Calculate total and copy to the order sheet
Range("Total").Value = Quant * Unit + Tx

'Copy product description to the order sheet
Range("Product_Descrip").Value = _
    DialogSheets("OrderDialog").DropDowns(1).Text
```

3. Save your work.

   Next, try using the dialog box with the following steps and see what happens.

4. Make the Order dialog sheet the active sheet, then choose Run Dialog from the Tools menu. The dialog box should open as shown here:

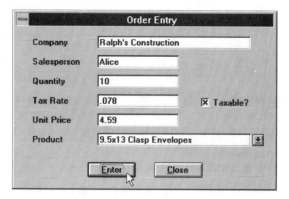

5. Enter some sample data, pressing Tab to move to each box, then choose the Enter button. If your dialog box is working correctly, it will close (leaving the model you built earlier, which was underneath the running dialog box). Now switch to the order sheet and check cells L1 through S1. They should contain the values that you entered in the dialog box.

   If something went wrong, double-check your Button2_Click procedure code for spelling errors and compare it with the listing above. Also check the properties you gave your dialog box controls, and verify that the names assigned to the cells on the order sheet match those used in the Button2_Click procedure. Keep working on it until all the values you enter in the dialog box (plus the computed tax and total) are transferred to the order sheet cells.

Updating the Database List

The next task is to build a macro that takes the data placed in L1 through S1 of the order sheet and adds it to the bottom of the database list.

1. Make OrdSheet the active sheet by clicking on its tab. Scroll the sheet until L1 is in the upper left-hand corner of the window.

2. The first row of cells (L1:S1) should contain the data that was copied from the dialog box during testing. If it doesn't, go back and complete that step, then return to step 1. Start the database list by copying this row to the first row under the database list headings. Click on L1, then press Shift-End-→ to select all the named cells.

13

3. Click on the Copy tool to copy the cells, click on the cell immediately below the Company heading (L5), and press (Shift)-(→) seven times to select the destination cells. Then choose Copied Cells from the Insert menu and verify that Shift Cells Down is specified in the dialog box. Click on OK to copy the values and create the first row of the database list. Now you are ready to record the macro.

4. Choose Record Macro from the Tools menu and click on Record New Macro. Type **Add_Record** and click on OK.

5. Again click on L1, then press (Shift)-(End)-(→) to select all the named cells (containing the dialog box values). Press (Ctrl)-(C) to copy the cells.

6. Click on the Company heading (L4). Press (Ctrl)-(↓), then (↓) again, then (Shift)-(→) seven times. You have now selected the first blank line underneath the last record in the database. Pressing (Ctrl)-(↓) is an important step because it gets you to the bottom of a database list of any length.

7. Choose Copied Cells from the Insert menu and verify that Shift Cells Down is specified in the dialog box. Click on OK.

8. Press (Esc) to clear the marquee, run the Return_Home macro, then the Next_Page macro.

9. Click on the Stop Recorder tool to complete the macro, then press (Ctrl)-(Pg Dn) until the macro sheet appears. Your Add_Record macro should look like this:

```
' Add_Record Macro
'
Sub Add_Record()
    Range("L1:S1").Select
    Selection.Copy
    ActiveWindow.SmallScroll ToRight:=-1
    Range("L4").Select
    Selection.End(xlDown).Select
    Range("L6:S6").Select
    Selection.Insert Shift:=xlDown
    Application.CutCopyMode = False
    Application.Run Macro:="ORDERS.XLS!Return_Home"
    Application.Run Macro:="ORDERS.XLS!Next_Page"
End Sub
```

10. The statement **Range("L6:S6").Select** must be changed, because it is an absolute reference to the sixth row. Since your database list will grow, this reference needs to be a relative reference. Change the line to **Selection.Offset(1, 0).Range("A1:H1").Select**. This statement specifies a relative offset (down one row) and a relative range (the first 8 cells to the right) for the selection.

11. Also, If you have a line "ActiveWindow.SmallScroll ToRight :=–1" you can delete it. This positioned your screen so you could click on L4 and

isn't needed in the code. Your revised Add_Record macro should look like this:

```
'
' Add_Record Macro
'
Sub Add_Record()
    Range("L1:S1").Select
    Selection.Copy
    Range("L4").Select
    Selection.End(xlDown).Select
    Selection.Offset(1, 0).Range("A1:H1").Select
    Selection.Insert Shift:=xlDown
    Application.CutCopyMode = False
    Application.Run Macro:="ORDERS.XLS!Return_Home"
    Application.Run Macro:="ORDERS.XLS!Next_Page"
End Sub
```

Tying Together the Data Entry Tools

Next, create a third procedure that displays the dialog box, runs the Add_Record macro, and repeats the process until the user is finished. The Orders_Dialog procedure uses a built-in message box to find out whether the user wants to enter another order. Type the following code below the Add_Record procedure in the module sheet.

```
'
' Orders_Dialog Macro
'
Sub Orders_Dialog()
Dim Continue As Integer
ShowDialog:                    'Line label for GoTo
    'Show the custom dialog box: True if user clicks the Enter button
    If DialogSheets("OrderDialog").Show Then
        Application.Run Macro:="ORDERS.XLS!Add_Record"
        'Note line-continuation characters in the following statement
        Continue = MsgBox(Prompt:="Enter another order?", _
        Buttons:=vbYesNo + vbInformation, _
        Title:="Order Entry")
        If Continue = vbYes Then
            GoTo ShowDialog
        End If
    End If
End Sub
```

Now test your data entry routines all together, by running the Orders_Dialog macro. Click on the OrdSheet tab or press Ctrl-Pg Up to return to the order sheet. Run the Max_Prepare macro first, then run the Next_Page macro, and then run the Orders_Dialog macro. You should be able to keep adding orders to the database list as long as you want. After you finish, check the list to make sure that the records are being added properly.

13

Using Data Form for Editing

With a database list in place, you now need to be able to edit and delete records. Excel has a built-in capability for this in the Data Form option. Build a macro to use this feature next.

1. Choose Record Macro from the Tools menu and click on Record New Macro. Type **Edit_It** and click on OK.

2. Open the Name box on the Formula bar and choose Orders_Database to go there. Now press Ctrl-↓ to go to the bottom of the database list.

3. Choose Form from the Data menu. Excel's data form is displayed, as shown in Figure 13-15.

   In the data form you can edit individual fields of a record, add and delete records, and find records based on criteria you enter. (Yes, you could have used this in place of the dialog box you built, but then you would not have had such an excellent opportunity to build a custom dialog box.)

4. Click on the scroll bar to go from record to record, or use the Find buttons.

5. Click on Close to leave the data form, then run the Return_Home macro.

6. Click on the Stop Recorder tool, then switch to the module sheet. The Edit_It macro is shown below, with this line added: **ActiveWindow.LargeScroll Down:=1**. This statement scrolls the screen to a blank area for an uncluttered backdrop for the data form. The active cell must remain in the list in order for the data form to recognize where the database list is.

```
'
' Edit_It Macro
'
Sub Edit_It()
    Application.Goto Reference:=Range("Orders_Database")
    Selection.End(xlDown).Select
    ActiveWindow.LargeScroll Down:=1     'Scroll down to a blank area
    ActiveSheet.ShowDataForm
    Application.Run Macro:="ORDERS.XLS!Return_Home"
End Sub
```

Printing, Saving, and Quitting

You next need to be able to print and save your workbook and leave Excel. Build macros for those purposes now.

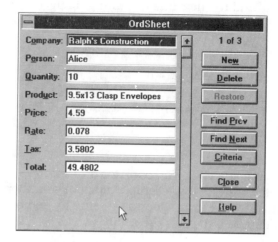

`Excel's data
form
Figure 13-15.

Building a Printing Macro

The printing macro is actually two macros: one to select the print area and the other to do the printing. Build both of these next.

1. Choose Record Macro from the Tools menu and click on Record New Macro. Type **Select_Database** and click on OK.

2. Click on the down arrow next to the Name box in the Formula bar, and choose Orders_Database. Press Ctrl-↓ to select the bottom row's first cell, then press End-→ to select the right-most bottom cell in the list. This procedure does not select the database list, but inserts code that can be manually augmented to accomplish the task.

3. Click on the Stop Recorder tool and inspect your macro code, which should look like this:

```
' Select_Database Macro
'
Sub Select_Database()
    Application.Goto Reference:=Range("Orders_Database")
    Selection.End(xlDown).Select
    Selection.End(xlToRight).Select
End Sub
```

The macro as recorded just selects the lower-right corner of the database list. An additional line can be added to select the range between the upper-left corner (Orders_Database) and the active cell (the lower-right corner).

13

4. Add the new line beginning "Range("Orders" and the comments to your code to make it look like this:

```
'
' Select_Database Macro
'
Sub Select_Database()
    Application.Goto Reference:=Range("Orders_Database")
    Selection.End(xlDown).Select        'Lower left-hand corner of the list
    Selection.End(xlToRight).Select     'Lower right-hand corner of the list
    Range("Orders_Database", ActiveCell).Select 'The entire database list
End Sub
```

To prepare your workbook for printing, you'll first make the necessary settings in the Page Setup dialog box and then record the macro. This means that if you change your page setup for some reason, you must come back and redo it to print the database.

1. Switch back to the order sheet, open the Page Setup dialog box from the File menu, and click on the Margins tab. Set the Top and Bottom margins to 1, the Left and Right margins to 0, and click on Horizontally Center on Page.

2. Click on the Header/Footer tab and the Custom Header button. Put the date in the left box, the word "ORDERS" in the center box, and "Page " and the page number in the left box. Click on OK to return to the Page Setup dialog box. Open the Footer drop-down list box and choose (none). Click on OK to close the Page Setup dialog box.

3. Choose Record Macro from the Tools menu and click on Record New Macro, type **Print_It**, and click on OK.

4. Run the Select_Database macro.

5. Choose Print from the File menu, click on Selection, then click on OK. The result is shown here:

11/14/93   ORDERS   Page 1

Company	Person	Quantity	Product	Price	Rate	Tax	Total
Ralph's Construction	Alice	10	9.5x13 Clasp Envelopes	4.59	7.80%	3.58	49.48
Jerry's Trucking	Alice	10	9.5x13 Clasp Envelopes	4.59	7.80%	3.58	49.48
Harvy's Drive-In	Sam	1	Pizza boxes - case	22.99	0.00%	0.00	22.99
Jerry's Drive-In	Alice	10	9.5x13 Clasp Envelopes	4.59	7.80%	3.58	49.48
Hal's Beanery	Alice	100	9.5x13 Clasp Envelopes	4.59	7.80%	35.80	494.80
Scott's Repair	Joe	25	Mechanical Pencil	1.14	7.80%	2.22	30.72
Hungry Pig Cafe	Alice	15	No. 2 Pencils - Box	2.15	7.80%	2.52	34.77

6. Run the Return_Home macro to return to the title screen.

7. Choose Macro Stop Recorder, then switch to the module sheet. Your code should look that shown here:

```
'
' Print_It Macro
'
Sub Print_It()
    Application.Run Macro:="ORDERS.XLS!Select_Database"
    Selection.PrintOut Copies:=1
    Application.Run Macro:="ORDERS.XLS!Return_Home"
End Sub
```

Saving and Quitting

The saving and quitting macros are trivial by comparison to what you have already done. Build them here.

1. First, save the ORDERS workbook. Now if something goes wrong, you do not lose anything.

2. Choose Record Macro from the Tools menu and click on Record New Macro. Type **Save_It** and click on OK.

3. Run the Return_Home macro to ensure you are at the title screen, then choose File Save.

4. Choose Macro Stop Recorder.

5. Choose Record Macro from the Tools menu and click on Record New Macro, type **Quit_It**, then click on OK.

6. Run the Return_Sheet macro to return to the normal Excel display, then run the Save_It macro to save the workbook.

7. Choose Macro Stop Recorder.

8. Add the **Application.Quit** statement immediately before the End Sub statement in order to actually leave Excel. The revised macro is shown here:

```
'
' Save_It Macro
'
Sub Save_It()
    Application.Run Macro:="ORDERS.XLS!Return_Home"
    ActiveWorkbook.Save
End Sub
'
' Quit_It Macro
'
Sub Quit_It()
    Application.Run Macro:="ORDERS.XLS!Return_Sheet"
    Application.Run Macro:="ORDERS.XLS!Save_It"
    Application.Quit
End Sub
```

13

Building and Using a Menu

To tie together all of the macros you have built into a system with a menu, you need one more macro and the custom menu. The menu you create is stored with the ORDERS workbook and automatically appears when the workbook is opened. The macro is used to prepare the display, run the data entry and update tasks, then redisplay the title screen. The first step is to create a macro to "package" the Orders_Dialog macro.

1. From the order sheet, choose Record Macro from the Tools menu and click on Record New Macro, type **Enter_It**, and click on OK.

2. Run the Max_Prepare macro, run the Next_Page macro, run the Orders_Dialog macro, click on Close, and run the Return_Home macro.

3. Click on the Stop Recorder tool. The Enter_It code is shown here:

```
'
' Enter_It Macro
'
Sub Enter_It()
    Application.Run Macro:="ORDERS.XLS!Max_Prepare"
    Application.Run Macro:="ORDERS.XLS!Next_Page"
    Application.Run Macro:="ORDERS.XLS!Orders_Dialog"
    Application.Run Macro:="ORDERS.XLS!Return_Home"
End Sub
```

Next, build the menu.

1. Click on the module tab to make it the active sheet, then choose Menu Editor from the Tools menu. The Menu Editor dialog box is shown in Figure 13-16.

2. Select the name of any Menu bar in the Menu Bars box. This cancels the selection of items in the other boxes. Then select the Menu bar.

3. Click on top item in the Menus list, then click on the Delete button repeatedly to delete all the Menus.

4. Click on the Insert button, type **&Ordering** in the Caption box, and click on Insert again. This creates the one menu for the custom menu system.

5. Click in the Menu Items list, click on the Insert button, and type **&Edit Database** in the Caption box. Assign a macro to this menu item by typing **Edit_It** in the Macro box. Click on Insert again.

6. Repeat the process described in step 5 to add the following menu items and associated macros to the Menu Items list: a hyphen (-) to create a divider bar (no associated macro); "&Quit Ordering" (the Quit_It macro); "&Save Database" (the Save_It macro); "&Print Database" (the

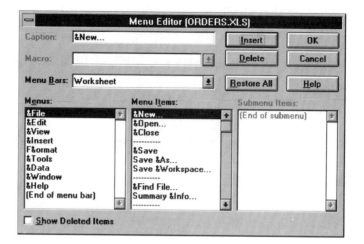

Menu Editor
dialog box
Figure 13-16.

Print_It macro); hyphen; "&Order Entry" (the Enter_It macro). The finished Menu Editor looks like this:

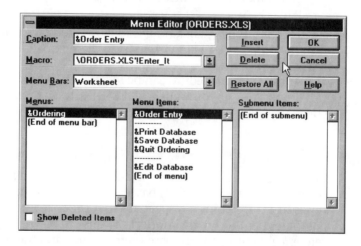

7. Click on OK. The new menu system appears whenever the ORDERS workbook is active.

Automatically Setting Up the Workbook

13

You can create a special macro named Auto_Open that Excel automatically runs when the workbook is opened. The Auto_Open macro makes OrdSheet the active sheet and prepares the display by calling the Max_Prepare macro. Also, since the above menu definition turned off the menus, you need a way to turn them back on again with a shortcut key. Enter both of these short macros next.

1. Type the Auto_Open and Reset_Menu macros shown next:

```
' Auto_Open Macro
'
Sub Auto_Open()
    Sheets("OrdSheet").Select
    Application.Run Macro:="ORDERS.XLS!Max_Prepare"
End Sub
'
' Reset_Menu Macro (Ctrl_r)
'
Sub Reset_Menu()
    Sheets("OrdSheet").Select
    ActiveMenuBar.Reset
    Application.Run Macro:="ORDERS.XLS!Return_Sheet"
End Sub
```

2. When you have entered these last two macros, choose Macro from the Tools menu to open the Macro dialog box. Click on Reset_Menu to select it and then click on Options.

3. Click on the Shortcut Key check box to turn it on, click in the key text box and type **r**, click on OK to close the Macro Options dialog box, and click on Close to close the Macro dialog box.

The Auto_Open procedure can be located anywhere in any module of the workbook. Also, if you want ORDERS.XLS to start automatically every time you start Excel, put ORDERS.XLS in the C:\EXCEL\XLSTART directory.

Testing and Correcting the Macros

The normal testing process is primarily one of trying out the macros and seeing what happens. Then, based on what you have seen, you can make the necessary corrections. To speed up that process, print out your macros and compare them to the illustrations in this chapter. Also, print out your reference names and compare them. Sometimes "desk checking" like this can eliminate the majority of errors, which are usually typographical, before you ever run the macros.

Also, if you haven't done it already, it is a good time to restore the normal menus and turn on the Status bar, Formula bar, scroll bars, and toolbars. Use these instructions to restore your screen and print out the macros and the range names:

1. Press Ctrl-R to restore the menus and screen and then click on the module sheet and choose Print from the File menu.

2. Scroll your macro sheet so Z1:AA14 is visible. Click on Z3, choose Name from the Insert menu, click on Paste, and then select Paste List.

3. Type and format the headings and adjust the column widths, as shown here:

Y	Z	AA	AB
	Name	**Reference**	
	Company_Name	=OrdSheet!$L$1	
	Orders_Database	=OrdSheet!$L$4	
	Product_Descrip	=OrdSheet!$O$1	
	Products	=OrdSheet!$V$2:$V$16	
	Quantity_Ordered	=OrdSheet!$N$1	
	Salesperson_Name	=OrdSheet!$M$1	
	Tax	=OrdSheet!$R$1	
	Tax_Rate	=OrdSheet!$Q$1	
	Total	=OrdSheet!$S$1	
	Unit_Price	=OrdSheet!$P$1	

4. Select Z2:AA13, choose Print from the File menu, click on Selection, and click on OK. The range names are printed.

5. Compare your printouts to the related illustrations and figures above.

Working Through the Application

The next step is to execute each part of the macro and see what happens. Use the following steps for that purpose.

1. Save and close the workbook. Choose Open from the File menu, select ORDERS.XLS, and click on OK. The macro begins by displaying the title screen with the single Ordering menu, as shown in Figure 13-2.

2. Select the menu, and it should open like this:

3. Choose Order Entry, and the dialog box opens in which you can enter the database information as shown in Figure 13-17.

4. Enter a record. What you put in the fields does not matter. Use Tab to go from field to field and Enter to complete the entry.

13

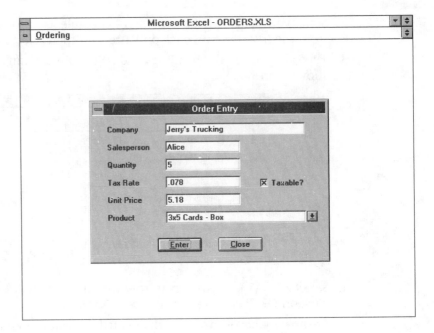

When you press Enter (or click on the Enter command button) you should see the database being updated. Then the second dialog box appears, asking if you want to enter another record, like this:

5. Click on Yes and enter another item. Follow the same procedure outlined in step 4. When you get to the "Enter another order?" message, type **n**.

6. Choose Edit Database from the menu and try out the various options on Excel's Data Form.

7. Choose Print Database. The output you get should be similar to that shown earlier in the "Building a Printing Macro" section.

8. Choose Save Database. You should see some indication that the workbook is being saved.

9. Finally, choose Quit Ordering. You should be returned to Windows.

If your macros did not execute perfectly the first time, take heart—it happens to almost everybody. Observe what is not working right. Compare your printed list of macros with the ones presented here. Within a few iterations of trying the macros and making changes, you should get them to operate properly.

Future Enhancements

A number of improvements can be made to enhance this application.

One easy enhancement is to sort the orders by Company and prepare statements from the results. Also, by sorting on the product you can look at sales by product.

Another enhancement that would usually have been in the original product is to add a date field to both the database and the data entry dialog box.

You now have an exceptionally powerful tool at your disposal. You can make of it just about whatever you wish.

13

A P P E N D I X

INSTALLING WINDOWS AND EXCEL

Windows and Excel can operate with many combinations of computers, disks, displays, and printers. Therefore, providing installation instructions would have been a complex process were it not for the Setup programs that come with both Windows and Excel. These programs do most of the work for you. You have only to determine what equipment you have and then run the Setup programs, answering the questions they ask you.

This appendix describes how to start and use both Windows and Excel Setup programs. In addition, it discusses how you prepare to store the data you create in Excel and how to start and leave the Windows and Excel programs.

The minimum requirements to run Windows 3.1 and Excel 5 are an Intel 80286 or higher processor and 4MB of memory. Of course, you will achieve much faster performance and be able to take full advantage of the multitasking abilities of Windows 3.1 with an Intel 80386 or 80486 processor and increased memory. Also, you will need at least 10MB of free hard disk space to load Windows, and an additional 24MB for a full Excel setup. Additionally, MS-DOS version 3.1 or higher is required. You also must have a 3 1/2-inch or a 5 1/4-inch floppy disk drive and a graphics display compatible with Windows 3.1 or later.

There are two options that you need to use to get the most out of Excel. A mouse is highly recommended, though technically not required. Both Excel and Windows are written with the mouse as a primary means of maneuvering through their many windows, menus, and features. Keyboard commands, in most instances, should be looked at as secondary alternatives to using the mouse. A printer is the other option not absolutely necessary for Windows and Excel to run, but you will find it very frustrating not to be able to see your work on paper. Most popular printers are supported by Windows and Excel.

This appendix is written for Windows 3.1 and Excel 5. While most of what is said here may be true for other versions of either product, you need to be on the lookout for differences.

Preparing to Store Data

When you use Excel, you are creating documents that you will want to come back to and use again at a later time. To preserve this data, you store it in files on a disk. The files are preserved when you turn the computer off. The programs that comprise Windows and Excel are also stored in files on a disk.

Computers that are based on a hard-disk system also have at least one floppy disk drive. Therefore, you can store the data on either a floppy or hard disk. From the standpoints of both speed and ease of use, it is best to store data as well as programs on your hard disk. Since hard disks end up storing so much information, they should be divided into directories, which are arbitrarily named areas that you establish for particular purposes. To prepare to store the data you create with Excel, you should create one or more directories.

Creating Directories on a Hard Disk

To store the program files on a hard disk, the Windows and Excel Setup programs automatically create directories for you or use directories you create or already have. The default name for the Windows directory is \WINDOWS and for Excel it is \EXCEL.

You *can* use existing Excel directories to hold your data files, but it is easier to locate and access your data files if you create separate directories to organize your work. If you want to create your own data directory to hold the Excel data files used in this book, use the following instructions. Your computer should be turned on and you should be at an operating system prompt, such as C> or C:\>.

1. Type **cd** and press (Enter) to make sure you are in the root directory.
2. Type **md\sheet** (short for "worksheet") and press (Enter) to create a directory named SHEET. (If you want to create a directory with a name different than SHEET, replace SHEET with the name you want to use, but this book assumes SHEET is the directory for your data files.)

Copying Your Disks

To protect the original floppy disks that contain the Windows and Excel programs, you need to make a copy or backup of these disks before installing the programs (the Microsoft licenses allow you to make one copy for this, and only this, express purpose). You will need the same number of new or reusable disks as there are disks in the original programs. (The number of disks depends on whether you are using 5 1/4-inch or 3 1/2-inch disks.) You will need to make a copy of each of the original disks, with each disk being copied to its own separate backup disk.

You can copy floppy disks in several ways. Since you need only a single floppy drive to run Windows and Excel, instructions are given for using a single floppy drive to copy the original disks. If you wish to use a different method of copying, do so.

The DISKCOPY command used here permanently removes all information on the disk. When reusing a disk with DISKCOPY, make sure you do not want any information that may be on it.

1. Count the number of disks that came with both Windows and Excel and note their type: 5 1/4-inch 360K, 5 1/4-inch 1.2MB, 3 1/2-inch 720K, or 3 1/2-inch 1.44MB—the 360K and 720K disks are labeled

DSDD (double-sided double-density) and the 1.2MB and 1.44MB are labeled DSHD (double-sided high-density). Obtain and have handy the same number and type of new or reusable disks. (Remember, if you use reusable disks you must be willing to get rid of all information currently on them.)

2. Turn on your computer. You should have already installed DOS on your hard drive and have a basic understanding of how to enter commands from your keyboard, of the size capacity of your disk drives, and of how your disk drives are labeled (A, B, C, and so on).

3. You should be at the DOS prompt (for example C> or C:\>) and in the root directory. If you have been using your computer and/or don't know which directory you are in, type **cd** to ensure that you are in the root directory.

4. Be sure your backup disks (the ones you are copying onto) are the same size as the disks that came with Windows and Excel. Insert the first Excel or Windows disk to be copied into the floppy disk drive. It is assumed for the remainder of this appendix that this is drive A. If you are using a drive other than A, use that drive letter in place of A (a, a:, or A:) in the instructions that follow.

5. At the DOS prompt, type **diskcopy a: a:** and press (Enter). You'll see the message "Insert SOURCE diskette in drive A:, Press any key when ready." The "SOURCE diskette" is the Excel or Windows disk being copied. Since it is already in the drive, press (Enter) to confirm it.

6. When you see the message "Insert TARGET diskette in drive A:," remove the Excel or Windows disk and insert the first new or reusable disk to which you wish to copy. If the disk is a new, unformatted disk, you will see a message, "Formatting while copying," telling you that the disk is also being formatted.

7. Soon you'll again see "Insert SOURCE diskette in drive A:." You must remove the first target diskette and reinsert the first Excel or Windows disk. Then you'll see "Insert TARGET diskette in Drive A:" telling you to remove the first Excel or Windows disk and reinsert the first new or reusable disk. This will be repeated a couple of times.

   Remember that "SOURCE" refers to the disk from which you are copying and is the original Excel or Windows disk, and "TARGET" refers to the disk to which you are copying and is the new or reusable disk that will hold the backup copy. The disk copying process takes several passes, so you must insert and remove each of the disks several times.

8. After several passes, you will see the message "Copy another diskette (Y/N)?" Type **y** and press (Enter).

9. Once again, you will see the message "Insert SOURCE diskette in drive A:." Remove the diskette from drive A that is now the copy of the first Excel or Windows disk, label it similarly to the original diskette, insert the second Excel or Windows original diskette in drive A, and press (Enter).

10. Repeat steps 6 through 9 until you have copied all of the disks that came with your Windows and Excel packages.

11. When you have copied all the diskettes, type **n** in response to "Copy another diskette (Y/N)?" and press (Enter). You will be returned to the DOS prompt. Remove the last copied disk from drive A and label it.

When you have completed copying all diskettes, protect the new diskettes to prevent them from being changed or infected with a virus. A 3 1/2-inch floppy disk is protected by first turning it on its back so you can see the metal hub in the center. Then, with the metal end away from you, slide the small black plastic rectangle in the lower-right corner toward you or toward the outer edge of the disk. This will leave a hole you can see through. A 5 1/4-inch disk is protected by placing an adhesive tab over the notch on the upper-right corner (if you are looking at the disk from the front). Once a disk is protected, it can't be changed until you reverse the protection process.

Place your original Windows and Excel disks in a safe location and use the copies you made for the installation process that follows. Use the original disks only to make additional copies if, for some reason, your backup copies become unusable.

Running Windows Setup

Running the Windows Setup program is very simple. As a matter of fact, you do it in only a few steps. (Your computer should be on, with the DOS prompt, C> or C:\>, onscreen.)

1. Place the Windows Setup disk in drive A or any other floppy disk drive you have and close the drive door.

2. Type **a:** and press (Enter) to make drive A current. (If you are using a different drive, type that drive letter in place of A.)

3. Type **setup** and press (Enter) to start the Setup program.

   You will have three options: 1) To learn more about Windows Setup, 2) To go ahead and set up Windows, and 3) To quit the Setup altogether.

4. Press (Enter) again to begin Setup.

5. Press (Enter) one final time to start the Express Setup.

Express Setup is a quick and easy way of installing Windows. If you are an experienced user who wants to control how Windows is installed, you can choose Custom Setup by typing **c**. Express Setup is sufficient for most users.

Windows Express Setup will begin copying files. Follow the instructions on your screen.

You can install as many printers as you have available, but the first one you choose will be the default—the one automatically used unless you instruct otherwise. When you have selected a printer (by using [↓] to move the highlight to it), click on the Install button or press [Alt]-[I]. Then click on the computer port to use (LPT1, COM1, and so on), or use [↓] to move the highlight to it, and click on Install or press [Enter] to complete installing your first printer.

Use Printers in the Main group Control Panel to install a second or third printer. On some printers—laser printers in particular—you also must set them up. To do that, choose Setup from the Printers dialog box (click on Setup or press [Alt]-[S]). Change the Printer Setup options to suit your needs.

You will be asked if you want to run a tutorial on how to use Windows and the mouse. If you are a new user of Windows, you may want to take a break in the setup to run the tutorials. If you choose to continue the setup, you can always run the tutorials later from the Program Manager Help menu. The latter assumed to be the case, complete the setup by clicking on Skip Tutorial.

Starting Windows

When you complete Setup, you are asked if you want to reboot your computer or return to DOS. Click on the Reboot icon and type **win** at the DOS prompt to load Windows.

When Windows is loaded, a screen similar to that shown in Figure A-1 appears.

The initial screen shows the Main group of Windows system applications under the Program Manager. Your next task is to run Excel Setup.

Running Excel Setup

The Excel Setup program must run under Windows—Windows must be running for Excel Setup to run. With that condition met, use these instructions to install Excel (Windows should be running from the steps performed in the last section):

1. Cancel any virus protection programs you may have. They could cause unpredictable results.

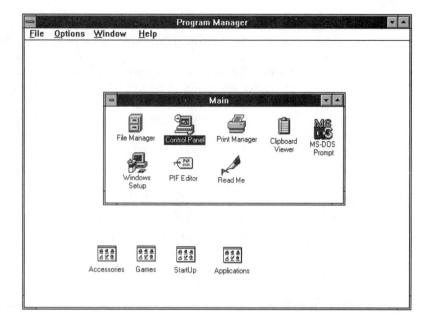

Sample of the
Main
applications
group after
Windows has
been installed
Figure A-1.

2. Place the Excel Disk 1 ("Setup") in drive A or other floppy disk drive you
   will be using and close the door.

3. Move the mouse pointer until it is on the word "File" on the left of the
   Menu bar (the second bar from the top of the screen). Press and release
   the left mouse button to "click on" and open the File menu. From the
   keyboard you can press Alt-F.

4. Move the mouse pointer to and click on the Run option of the File
   menu to choose that option, or type **r** on the keyboard.

5. Type **a:\setup** and press Enter to start the Excel Setup program (if you
   are using another disk drive, type the appropriate designation).

   You will be led through a series of screens. Respond to each as it
   presents itself. For example, if you have not recorded your serial
   number for the Excel 5 product, you will have a chance to do so when
   the Setup program displays it and reminds you to do so.

   If you have an older version of Excel installed on your disk, the Setup
   program will ask whether you want to replace it with the new one, or to
   install Exel 5 in another directory, retaining the older version. If you
   have the disk space, the latter is the preferred approach until you are
   sure you don't want the older version any longer.

6. If you have an older verion of Excel installed on your disk, click on the Change Directory button, type the name of another directory (such as **C:\EX5**) and click on OK. If it is a new directory, you will asked if you want Excel to create the directory. Click on Yes. After the directory has been changed, click on OK to "install to this directory."

If you have enough disk space, you will be given three installation options, as seen in Figure A-2. You will be asked whether you want a Typical installation, a Complete/Custom installation (which may require up to 24MB of disk space), or a Laptop (Minimum) installation. If you don't have enough disk space, you won't be shown all three options. This screen also gives you an opportunity to change your directory (your second chance if you have an older version of Excel).

Although choosing the Complete/Custom installation right now is not the recommended approach, a brief review of it might be helpful. The Complete/Custom installation is the most comprehensive and flexible installation process, allowing you to install all features or to select only those you really want on your sytem.

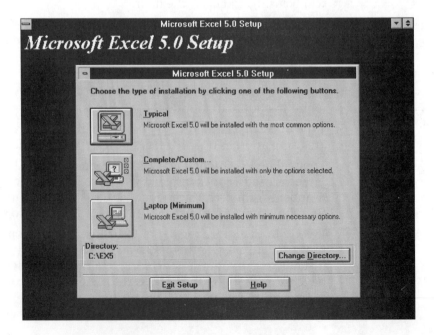

Installation
options for
Excel
Figure A-2.

If you choose the Complete/Custom installation, you will be allowed to install all or part of the following options:

Option	Content
Microsoft Excel	Excel core programs.
Online Help and Lessons	Files used to run the Excel lessons.
Data Access	Files that enable you to query and use external files.
Graphics Filters	Files for filtering graphic files, such as .BMP, .TIF, or .PCX.
Add-Ins	Supplementary applications, such as AutoSave, Solver, Report Manager, and Analysis ToolPak.
Tools	Tools such as a macro translator, converter of Multiplan or 1-2-3 spreadsheets to Excel, or the Spell Checker.

If you want to consider selecting only parts of the options listed, you could click on one of them, such as Online Help and Lessons. When an option is selected, a Change Option button becomes available. Upon clicking it, a second dialog box is displayed, listing the components of the selected option and the disk space each requires. You can select the specific parts of the option you want on your system. You select an option by placing an X in the box beside it. If no X is seen, that option will not be installed. The default is to install all of them. You have to click on an X to remove it.

After you determine which components of Excel 5 to install on your custom system, you continue with the installation in the same way as if you had selected a Typical or Laptop installation.

In this case, we are recommending a Typical installation.

7. Make sure the directory path is the one in which you want Excel installed and change it if it is not. Choose the Typical installation if it is shown as an option.

   The Setup program now asks you where you want the resulting Excel icons grouped. A Program Group named Microsoft Office is suggested. If you want to be more specific, you might type Microsoft Excel.

8. Click on the Program Group of your choice or type it in and then click on Continue.

   When Setup is complete you will get a message to that effect.

9. Click on OK or press Enter.

   A new group window will appear on the screen entitled "Microsoft Excel" (or whatever group name you chose), as shown in Figure A-3.

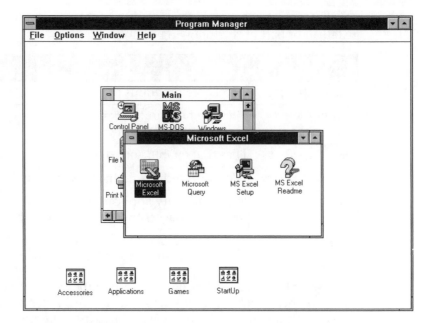

Group window after Excel installation
Figure A-3.

Starting Excel

To start Excel, simply do the following:

1. Double-click on the Microsoft Excel application icon or press ⟨Enter⟩ if it is already highlighted. Using the keyboard, press ⟨←⟩, ⟨→⟩, ⟨↑⟩, or ⟨↓⟩ to move the highlight to the Microsoft Excel application icon. Then press ⟨Enter⟩.

2. When you start Excel for the first time, you are offered four short lessons:

Getting Started	Provides the necessary steps to get you using Excel 5 quickly (takes 7 minutes).
What's New	Provides an overview of Excel 5's new features (takes 7 minutes).
Getting Information While You Work	Provides guidance on how to use Excel's extensive Help system (takes 4 minutes).
For Lotus 1-2-3 Users	Shows how to use Lotus 1-2-3 skills in Excel (takes 7 minutes).

Click on a lesson button if you want to view that lesson, or click on the Close button on the bottom left of the screen to go directly to the beginning Excel screen shown in Figure A-4.

Leaving Excel and Windows

When you wish to leave Excel and return to the DOS prompt, do so with these instructions:

1. Double-click on the bar in the upper-left corner of the Excel window (not the Sheet1 window), or press [Alt]-[Spacebar] and type **c**. You will leave Excel and return to Windows.

2. Double-click on the bar in the upper-left corner of the Program Manager window (not the Excel group window), or press [Alt]-[Spacebar] and type **c**.

3. You are asked if you want to end your Windows session. If you exit Windows now, the layout and content of the final Program Manager window will be saved. The default is to save changes. If you don't want to save changes to the Program Manager window, the default can be changed by selecting the Options menu and clicking on the Save Settings On Exit option. From this point on, any changes made to the Program Manager window will be lost, unless you change the default. Click on OK or press [Enter]. You are returned to DOS.

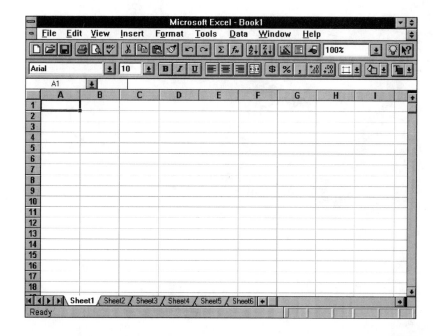

Beginning
Excel screen
Figure A-4.

APPENDIX

B

TOOLBARS

Toolbars provide a quick and easy way to access many of Excel's more frequently used features. There are a total of 13 toolbars available for your use; the Standard and Formatting toolbars are the default toolbars that are present when you first install Excel 5. You can choose to display as many toolbars as you wish, and you can customize the existing toolbars or create your own by adding and deleting individual tools.

All of the toolbars and their tools are described in the following sections. Tools are listed and described as they appear from left to right across each toolbar.

Standard Toolbar

The Standard toolbar is present when you first install Excel. You can turn it off, replace it with one of the other toolbars, or customize the tools it contains. The Standard toolbar provides a general set of tools covering file handling and editing. It has broad applicability to much that you do with Excel.

Tool	Name	Function
	New Workbook	Creates a new workbook.
	Open File	Allows you to open an existing document by displaying the Open dialog box.
	Save File	Saves the active document.
	Print	Immediately prints the active document.
	Print Preview	Displays a page onscreen as it will look when it is printed on paper.
	Spelling	Checks the spelling of text in both workbooks and charts.
	Cut	Cuts the selected cell or range and places it in the Clipboard.

B

Tool	Name	Function
	Copy	Copies the selected cell or range to the Clipboard.
	Paste	Transfers the formatting from the Clipboard to the selected cell or range.
	Format Painter	Copies only the formats from a selected cell or range.
	Undo	Undoes or reverses the last command executed, if possible.
	Repeat	Repeats the last command, if possible.
	AutoSum	Creates a SUM function in the active cell with a reference to the contiguous range of numbers either in the column above or in the row to the left.
	Function Wizard	Displays the Function Dialog box and assists with the completion of the function selected.
	Sort Ascending	Sorts the column containing an active cell from smallest to highest values.
	Sort Descending	Sorts the column containing an active cell from the highest to the smallest values.
	ChartWizard	Assists you in creating or editing charts.
	Text Box	Draws a text box that can be used to document or label items on a chart.

Tool	Name	Function
	Drawing	Displays the Drawing toolbar.
100% ⬇	Zoom Control	Allows you to change the scale of the sheet.
💡	TipWizard	Switches the TipWizard on and off to show or hide Excel suggestions on your current task.
▶?	Help	Displays a question mark for the mouse pointer. When clicked on a command or screen area, context-sensitive help is provided.

Formatting Toolbar

The Formatting toolbar, also displayed by default, provides the means to quickly apply many different types of formatting. It is very handy if you do a lot of formatting. You can customize the tools it contains, including adding customized formats you use often.

Tool	Name	Function
Arial ⬇	Font box	Displays a list of available fonts.
10 ⬇	Font Size box	Displays a list of font sizes according to the font selected in the Font box.
B	Bold	Applies or removes bold type style to selected cells.
I	Italic	Applies or removes italic type style to selected cells.

Tool	Name	Function
U	Underline	Applies or removes underlines to selected text.
(align left icon)	Align Left	Applies left-alignment to selected cells.
(center icon)	Center	Centers selected cells.
(align right icon)	Align Right	Applies right-alignment to selected cells.
+a+	Center Across Columns	Centers text horizontally from the left cell across selected columns.
$	Currency Style	Formats selected cells to a currency style, for example, $100.00.
%	Percent Style	Formats selected cells to a percent style, for example, 33%.
,	Comma Style	Formats selected cells to a comma style, for example, 1,234.00.
+.0 .00	Increase Decimal	Adds a decimal place to a number's display.
.00 +.0	Decrease Decimal	Takes away a decimal place from a number's display.
(border icon)	Border	Displays a selection of border styles to use in applying a border around selected cells.
(color icon)	Color	Allows the color of selected cells to be changed.
T	Font Color	Displays a selection of colors that may be used in text.

Query and Pivot

The Query and Pivot toolbar allows you to select among several tools for analyzing data.

Tool	Name	Function
	PivotTable Wizard	Initiates the PivotTable Wizard.
	PivotTable Field	Allows you to define and edit a field.
	Ungroup	Splits grouped pivot table items into individual parts.
	Group	Combines pivot table items into selected categories.
	Hide Detail	Hides detail rows and columns in a pivot table to show summaries only.
	Show Detail	Shows detail rows and columns in a pivot table.
	Show Pages	Shows pages of a pivot table on separate workbooks.
	Refresh Data	Updates the result of either a query or the pivot table depending on where the active cell is.

Chart Toolbar

The Chart toolbar is automatically placed onscreen when you use a chart window, either by creating a new chart or opening an existing chart. The Chart toolbar provides the means to create a quick default Column Chart, select or change the type of chart you will build, invoke the ChartWizard to lead you through the creation of a chart, or to add legends or gridlines to a chart by simply clicking on a tool.

B

Tool	Name	Function
	Chart Type	Displays a selection of chart types to apply to a selected cell range or selected or activated chart.
	Default Chart	Creates a Column Chart from a selected range of cells or a selected or activated chart.
	ChartWizard	Starts the ChartWizard, which helps you create an embedded chart or edit an active chart.
	Horizontal gridlines	Switches between adding or removing horizontal gridlines to or from a chart.
	Legend	Switches between adding or removing a legend to or from a chart.

Drawing Toolbar

The Drawing toolbar provides the tools to draw lines, arrows, rectangles, ovals, and arcs as well as to work with the objects that are drawn. When you use a drawing tool, the mouse pointer becomes a crosshair and allows you to perform the functions of the selected tool.

Tool	Name	Function
	Line	Draws a straight line.
	Rectangle	Draws a rectangle or square.
	Ellipse	Draws an unfilled oval or circle.

Tool	Name	Function
	Arc	Draws a portion of an unfilled circle or arc.
	Freeform	Draws a combination of freehand and straight lines.
	Text Box	Allows you to type text into a box you draw with a crosshair pointer.
	Arrow	Draws an arrow on a worksheet or macro sheet, or adds an arrow to a chart.
	Freehand line	Draws a freehand line.
	Filled Rectangle	Draws filled rectangles or squares.
	Filled Ellipse	Draws filled circles or ovals.
	Filled Arc	Draws filled arcs or portions of circles.
	Filled Freeform	Draws filled shapes which are a combination of freehand and straight lines.
	Create Button	Attaches a button to a macro or Visual Basic procedure.
	Drawing Selection	Selects a graphic object.
	Bring to Front	Puts the selected object in front of all others.
	Send to Back	Puts the selected object behind all others.

Tool	Name	Function
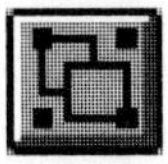	Group Objects	Combines multiple selected graphic objects into one graphic object.
	Ungroup Objects	Splits a grouped graphic object into its individual graphic objects.
	Reshape	Changes the shape of a polygon.
	Drop Shadow	Displays a shadowed right and bottom border around selected cells or object.
	Pattern	Changes the pattern and color of a selected cell, graph, object, or chart.

TipWizard Toolbar

The TipWizard toolbar, shown here, contains only two tool parts:

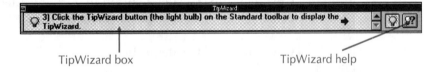

TipWizard box   TipWizard help

The TipWizard box displays the suggestion ("tip") the TipWizard is offering, and the Tip Help button displays a Help screen about the tip subject. When the subject of a tip is another tool, the referenced tool will be also displayed with an arrow pointing to it, as shown by the referenced TipWizard tool in the example.

Forms Toolbar

The Forms toolbar provides tools to use in creating forms on workbooks, charts, or dialog sheets. With it you can create custom dialog boxes or options.

Tool	Name	Function
Aa	Labels	Creates a text label.
ab|	Edit Box	Creates an edit box that allows one to type text into a text box.
xyz	Group Box	Creates a group box.
▢	Create Button	Creates a button that can be attached to a Visual Basic module or macro.
☒	Check Box	Creates a check box.
◉	Option Button	Creates an option button.
▦	List Box	Creates a list box.
▦	Drop-Down	Creates a drop-down box.
▦	Combination List-Edit	Creates a combination list and edit box.

Tool	Name	Function
	Combination Drop-Down and Edit Box	Creates a combination drop-down box and edit box.
	Scroll Bar	Creates a scroll bar.
	Spinner	Creates a spinner numeric box.
	Control Properties	Displays the Format Object dialog box, which allows you to change properties of controls.
	Edit Code	Allows you to create or edit code.
	Toggle Grid	Switches the alignment grid off and on—hides or displays it.
	Run Dialog	Executes the custom dialog box being created or edited.

Stop Recording Toolbar

The Stop Recording toolbar is automatically displayed when you begin recording a macro. It is used to stop the recording of the macro.

Visual Basic Toolbar

The Visual Basic toolbar is used when you are recording or editing a macro with Visual Basic. It is automatically displayed when you begin working with a Visual Basic module.

Tool	Name	Function
	Insert Module	Inserts a Visual Basic module in an active workbook.
	Menu Editor	Allows you to develop or edit menus with the Menu Editor dialog box.
	Object Browser	Allows you to browse through the Object Browser dialog box.
	Run Macro	Allows you to select and run a macro by displaying the Macro dialog box.
	Step Macro	Allows you to step through macro code one instruction at a time by displaying the Single Step dialog box.
	Resume Macro	Resumes execution of a macro after a pause.
	Stop Macro	Halts the running or recording of a macro.
	Record Macro	Allows you to begin recording a macro by displaying the Record Macro dialog box.
	Toggle Breakpoint	Switches between inserting or removing a breakpoint in a line of code.
	Instant Watch	Allows you to observe the changing values of expressions of a running macro by displaying the Instant Watch dialog box.
	Step Into	Runs one instruction of code at a time, including other called procedures.
	Step Over	Runs one instruction of code at a time, except for other called procedures that are run completely.

Auditing Toolbar

Use the Auditing toolbar to find errors on a workbook.

Tool	Name	Function
	Trace Precedents	Draws an arrow from an active cell containing a formula to the source of a value.
	Remove Precedents	Removes one level of trace-precedent arrows from a workbook.
	Trace Dependents	Draws arrows from the source of a value to where it is used in a formula.
	Remove Dependents	Removes one level of trace-dependent arrows from the workbook.
	Remove All Arrows	Removes all tracer arrows from the workbook.
	Trace Error	Draws an arrow connecting an active cell containing an erroneous value and cells potentially the source of the error.
	Attach Note	Allows you to attach a note to a cell by displaying the Cell Note dialog box.
	Show Info Window	Displays the Info window.

WorkGroup Toolbar

The WorkGroup toolbar is used when you are sharing files and communicating online with other users—including locating and updating files, sending or receiving mail, or working with scenarios.

Tool	Name	Function
	Find File	Helps you to find a file by displaying the Find File dialog box.
	Routing Slip	Allows you to attach a routing slip to a workbook by displaying the Routing Slip dialog box.
	Send Mail	Actually sends a workbook to another user.
	Update File	Allows you to update a read-only file.
	Toggle Read Only	Switches a file between read-only and read-write status.
	Scenario Box	Allows you to create or edit a scenario.

Microsoft Toolbar

The Microsoft toolbar is used to switch between Microsoft applications and Excel. The applications are loaded only if they are not already in memory. If they are already in memory, Excel switches you to them.

Tool	Name	Function
	Microsoft Word	Switches to Microsoft Word.
	Microsoft PowerPoint	Switches to Microsoft PowerPoint.
	Microsoft Access	Switches to Microsoft Access.
	Microsoft FoxPro	Switches to Microsoft FoxPro.
	Microsoft Project	Switches to Microsoft Project.
	Microsoft Mail	Switches to Microsoft Mail.
	Microsoft Schedule+	Switches to Microsoft Schedule+.

Full Screen Toolbar

The Full Screen button acts as a switch to make the workbook fill as much of the screen as possible and then restore the workbook window to its normal size.

Displaying the Toolbars

The toolbars can be displayed or removed from the screen in two ways. First, from the View menu you can select or deselect the Standard Bar and Formatting Bar options which display or hide those two toolbars. If there is a check mark by the option, that toolbar is selected and will be displayed onscreen. The Standard and Formatting toolbars are displayed by default. To display any of the other 11 toolbars, choose the Toolbars option on the View menu. You will be shown a list of the toolbars in the Toolbars dialog box, as shown here:

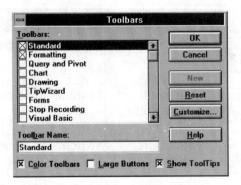

Scroll to the name of the toolbar you want and check the box next to it to display that toolbar on the screen.

A second approach to displaying the toolbars is to select the toolbar from the short menu. To use this approach, place the pointer anywhere on the toolbar and press the right mouse button. You'll see the Toolbar shortcut menu, as shown here:

Click on the toolbar you want and it will be displayed (or hidden if it is currently selected) on the screen. By selecting the Toolbars option you will be shown the Toolbars dialog box where the major toolbars are listed.

Moving and Sizing Toolbars

Toolbars may be displayed in two positions: *floating* in the application area, or *docked* above the Formula bar, below the sheet markers, and along side of the application area. When toolbars are moved from their docked location, they become standard windows that can be moved, sized, and closed.

To move from the docked toolbar area, point on any empty area of the displayed toolbar and drag the toolbar to the application area (or simply double-click on it). To move a toolbar in the application area, drag on the

Title bar as you would any window. When you are returning a toolbar to its docked location, drag it near the dock and Excel will automatically position the toolbar when you release the mouse button (again, you can simply double-click on it). An exception to the docking rule is that toolbars with drop-down lists cannot be docked.

To change the size of a toolbar in the application area, drag on the window borders of the toolbar. The toolbar window will conform to the shape to which the window has been dragged. As you drag the toolbar again near the toolbar area, it returns to its normal display.

Adding, Moving, Copying, and Deleting Tools

You can easily change the tools on the 13 toolbars to any combination you desire. The Customize dialog box, available from either the Toolbars option on the View menu or the Tool shortcut menu (click the right mouse button on the toolbar), provides a categorized listing of all the tools offered by Excel. (The Customize dialog box must be open to delete, move, or copy a tool.) Simply drag the tool you want to add to a displayed toolbar and Excel will rearrange the tools to make room for the addition.

In many cases, the last tool on the right side of the toolbar will be wrapped around to the next line, or it will go off the screen if the toolbar is docked. To delete a tool, which will then make room for any added tools, drag the tool anywhere off the displayed toolbar.

To move a tool from one toolbar to another, display both toolbars and drag the tool from one to the other. Copying tools is the same as moving, except you must press (Ctrl) while dragging.

Creating a New Toolbar

If you find the toolbars provided by Excel do not meet your needs, you can create a totally new toolbar and customize it with the tools of your choice. From the View menu, choose the Toolbars option and name the new toolbar in the Toolbar Name text box. Then choose either New or Customize. (If you don't supply a name at this point, Excel will name the toolbar for you, and only the Customize option will be available. The name will be Tool1, Tool2, and so on.) The new toolbar is displayed in the upper-left corner of the workbook. A toolbar's name cannot be changed.

The Customize dialog box is displayed as shown here:

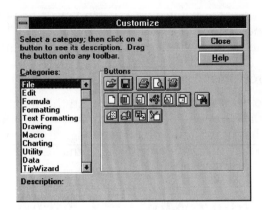

You can now move or copy tools from either the Customize dialog box by clicking on the Categories list to find the tool you want or by dragging the tool from a displayed toolbar to the new one. When you are done, choose Close and drag the new toolbar to the toolbar area. The new toolbar is added to the list of toolbars and can be displayed when needed.

Similarly, you can delete a tool from a toolbar. Display the toolbar to be changed, bring up the View menu, Toolbars option, and Customize button. The Customize dialog box will be displayed. Drag the tool off the toolbar onto the workspace. The toolbar will readjust to the reduced size. Click on Close.

Customizing Tools

You can customize individual tools in a number of ways. One of the most useful customizations allows you to create a tool and assign a macro to it. Or, you can select a tool from the list of unassigned tools in the Custom categories of tools and assign a macro to it. See Chapter 10 for more information about assigning macros to tools.

You can change the appearance of a tool in two ways: by copying the image of one tool to another, or by directly altering the image itself. As before, the Customize dialog box must be displayed in order to be able to change a tool's appearance.

To copy the image on one tool to another, display the toolbars you want to change, then display the Toolbar shortcut menu, and select Customize. Select the tool you want to copy to another (it may be on a toolbar or in the Categories list) and then choose Copy Button Image from the Tool shortcut menu (shown by clicking the right mouse button on the selected tool on the toolbar), shown here:

B

```
Copy Button Image
Paste Button Image
Reset Button Image
Edit Button Image...

Assign Macro...
```

Then select the tool you want to change from the displayed toolbar, and choose Paste Button Image from the Tool shortcut menu. The tool will immediately change its image.

To directly alter the appearance of a tool, display the toolbar containing the tool to be changed, select the tool, choose Customize from the Toolbar shortcut menu, and then choose Edit Button Image from the Tool shortcut menu (displayed by clicking the right mouse button on the selected tool on the toolbar). The Button Editor dialog box will be displayed from which you can change the image colors, pixels, or button image on the tool.

Custom tools, unlike the Excel-supplied tools, can only be displayed on their respective toolbars. If you try to drag one from a toolbar to the Customize dialog box or to another toolbar, it will be permanently deleted.

INDEX

F

G

H

Y

Z